Tatian, James Hamlyn Hill

The Earliest Life of Christ Ever Compiled from the Four Gospels

Being the Diatessaron of Tatian [circ. A. D. 160]

Tatian, James Hamlyn Hill

The Earliest Life of Christ Ever Compiled from the Four Gospels
Being the Diatessaron of Tatian [circ. A. D. 160]

ISBN/EAN: 9783744756747

Printed in Europe, USA, Canada, Australia, Japan

Cover: Foto ©ninafisch / pixelio.de

More available books at **www.hansebooks.com**

THE EARLIEST LIFE OF CHRIST

PRINTED BY MORRISON AND GIBB

FOR

T. & T. CLARK, EDINBURGH.

LONDON: SIMPKIN, MARSHALL, HAMILTON, KENT, AND CO. LIMITED.
NEW YORK: CHARLES SCRIBNER'S SONS.
TORONTO: THE WILLARD TRACT DEPOSITORY.

THE

EARLIEST LIFE OF CHRIST

EVER COMPILED FROM THE FOUR GOSPELS

BEING

The Diatessaron of Tatian

[CIRC. A.D. 160]

*Literally Translated from the Arabic Version and containing
the Four Gospels woven into One Story*

With an Historical and Critical Introduction, Notes, and Appendix

BY

The Rev. J. HAMLYN HILL, B.D.
FORMERLY SENIOR SCHOLAR OF S. CATHARINE'S COLLEGE, CAMBRIDGE
AUTHOR OF AN ENGLISH VERSION OF "MARCION'S GOSPEL"

EDINBURGH
T. & T. CLARK, 38 GEORGE STREET
1894

TO

THE REVEREND THE MOST NOBLE

THE MARQUIS OF NORMANBY

CANON RESIDENTIARY OF WINDSOR

A KIND FRIEND, A TRUE CHRISTIAN

AND AN EARNEST WORKER IN THE MASTER'S CAUSE

THIS FIRST ENGLISH VERSION

OF THE EARLIEST COMPLETE AND CONTINUOUS

LIFE OF CHRIST

EVER COMPILED FROM THE FOUR GOSPELS

IS INSCRIBED

WITH THE AFFECTIONATE RESPECT AND ESTEEM OF

THE TRANSLATOR

CONTENTS.

	PAGE
PREFATORY NOTE,	vi
ADDENDA ET CORRIGENDA,	vii
INTRODUCTION,	1
THE DIATESSARON,	39
APPENDIX I. Comparative Table of Contents,	266
„ II. Analysis of the Gospels,	281
„ III. Various Readings,	292
„ IV. Miracles in the Diatessaron,	318
„ V. Parables in the Diatessaron,	319
„ VI. Allusions to S. John the Baptist in the Diatessaron,	320
„ VII. Movements of Jesus,	321
„ VIII. Allusions to the Diatessaron in Ancient Writings,	324
„ IX. Dr. Zahn's Order,	326
„ X. The Ephraem Fragments,	333
„ XI. List of Authors,	378

PREFATORY NOTE.

The Translator desires to thank the Professors of Divinity at Cambridge for accepting the Introduction, Text, and Notes of this work as an Exercise for the degree of Bachelor of Divinity, and also for excusing him from the examination for that degree on the merits of his translation of *Marcion's Gospel* and of the first three tables of the Appendix to the present work, under the following clause of the University regulations for proceedings in Divinity :—

" 10. The Professors, if unanimous, shall have power to exempt the Candidate from this Examination, where the special merits of his dissertation or of his published works appear to them sufficient to entitle him to a degree."

At the same time he desires also to thank them for some valuable suggestions by way of additions to the notes and corrections, some of which will be found in the *Addenda et Corrigenda*.

ADDENDA ET CORRIGENDA.

Page.	Line or Note.				
6	38	*For*	-Ṭîb	*read*	-Ṭayyib
7	18				
,,	11,13,17	,,	Gûbasî	,,	Gubasî
10	32	,,	Valentinian	,,	Valentinus
11	13	,,	Βίβλιον Προβλημάτων	,,	Βιβλίον Προβλημάτων
12	38	,,	versions	,,	MSS. of it
,,	39	,,	in	,,	one being in
13	1	,,	a collated copy	,,	it
39	14	,,	The introduction led, saying,	,,	And he said as a beginning,
41	9	,,	overcame	,,	comprehended
52	note	,,	people	,,	kinsfolk
54	23	,,	one	,,	begotten
,,	30	,,	grace and truth	,,	truth and grace
,,	32	,,	only one of God	,,	only begotten, God
55	note 2	,,	alzanâdiḳa	,,	azzanâdiḳa
57	29	,,	Satan	,,	the Accuser
58	3				
,,	28	,,	temptation	,,	temptations
,,	note 3		Omit.		
60	note 1	,,	Qatîna	,,	Qaṭna
66	note 4	,,	Or,	,,	Lit.
67	note 4	,,	D A B C	,,	D a b c
70	13	,,	they put new wine	,,	new wine ought to be put
76	note 1	,,	Or . . . camels.	,,	Lit. "exactor of fines."
78	28	,,	which is	,,	*which is*
79	29	,,	rust[5] and moth	,,	moth and rust[5]
,,	32	,,	rust nor moth	,,	moth nor rust[5]
,,	note 1	,,	Lit . . . 36.	,,	The Arabic word as spelt means "power"; cf. ver. 36: but this is an error for a very similar word meaning "food."
94	9	,,	shop[2]	,,	noose[2]
,,	note 2	,,	Or . . . eating.	,,	A mistaken rendering of the Syriac for ἀσσαρίου superadded to the correct rendering.
95	17	,,	he	,,	they
,,	29	,,	for [1st]	,,	but

ADDENDA ET CORRIGENDA.

Page.	Line or Note.		
97	36	*For* 20	*read* 19ᵇ; and put 20 in the next line
113	note 2	,, Aramian	,, Aramaean
119	39	,, believe not	,, have not believed
,,	notes 2, 3	Put these readings into the text.	
123	16, 17	,, they	*read* ye; by a change of pointing in the Arabic
125	4	,, Hemesen	,, Emesa
,,	note 1	,, Cananaea	,, Canaanitish
129	15	,, Now Jesus had	,, And Jesus
135	25	,, 22	,, 12
138	13	,, the time of his coming	,, his decease
140	17	,, riseth	,, cometh
145	27	,, Let it please him, whom it may.	,, He that is able to refrain, let him refrain.
151	note 1	,, Ciasca . . . to end	,, The Arabic is literally, "seventy times seven seven": this agrees with the Peschito and the Armenian of Ephraem. Cf. Appendix X.
154	note 2	,, râmûs	,, nâmûs
161	6, 26	,, a feast	,, an entertainment
,,	9	,, you	,, you both
,,	22	,, supper or a breakfast	,, feast or an entertainment
162	8	,, mouth	,, consent
165	14, 15	,, calleth . . . saith	,, called . . . said
167	note 2	,, Tîmî	,, Tîmî
168	36	,, destitute of confidence	,, unfaithful
178	2	,, eyes.	,, eyes?
192	19	Remove the references to line 20.	
217	34	,, ministers	*read* armies
220	7	,, feet.	,, feet?
226	14	,, loved	,, had loved
,,	15	,, rejoice	,, have rejoiced
227	30	,, abide	,, abode
235	note 1	,, Perhaps	,, Lit.

THE DIATESSARON.

INTRODUCTION.

THERE is in the Vatican Library an Arabic MS. numbered XIV., which originally consisted of 125 leaves; but the 17th and the 118th are missing. From its appearance, and the handwriting, it is supposed to have been written in Egypt at some period from the twelfth to the fourteenth century, the latter date being the more probable. On the last page the copyist has written in Latin, "Here endeth, by the help of God, the sacred Gospel, which Tatian collected out of the four Gospels, and which is commonly called the *Diatessaron.*" Joseph Assemani, who brought this MS. to the Vatican about A.D. 1719, drew attention to it [1] as "Tatian's *Diatessaron*, or the four Gospels reduced into one." Stephen Assemani, Rosenmüller, and Akerblad gave short accounts of it, but differed as to the condition of the MS. and its mode of commencing. In 1881 Zahn published an elaborate attempt to reconstruct the *Diatessaron* from the quotations supposed to have been made from it by Syrian Fathers, using chiefly the Commentary of Ephraem Syrus—now only accessible through an Armenian version, of which Dr. Moesinger has published a Latin translation—and the Homilies of Aphraates. Beyond alluding to the existence of MS. XIV., and quoting the references of the above-mentioned writers to it, Zahn seems to have made no use of its contents in his work of compilation; but the publication of Zahn's remarks induced Agostino Ciasca, one of the Guild of Writers to the Vatican, to examine the MS., and to write an essay upon it, entitled "On the Arabic Version of Tatian's *Diatessaron.*" This he published [2] at Paris

[1] *Bibl. Or.* i. 619.   [2] In Pitra's *Analecta Sacra*, iv. 465.

in 1883; and in it he announced his intention to publish the MS. itself when he could spare the time. This purpose was for a while frustrated; and in 1886 Ciasca happened to show this MS., amongst others, to Antonius Morcos, Visitor-Apostolic of the Catholic Copts, who said he had seen one like it in Egypt, and could obtain it for him. In August 1886 the promised MS. arrived at Rome, as a present to the Borgian Museum from its owner, Halim Dos Gali. It is evidently a copy of the same work as MS. XIV., though it contains some important differences of detail. There is no date attached to it; but Ciasca refers it back to at least the fourteenth century. It consists of 355 leaves: each page is about 9 inches by $6\frac{1}{4}$, and has eleven lines of writing, enclosed by gold, blue, and red lines connected in the form of rectangles. The first 85 leaves are occupied by a preface, in which an anonymous author— after explaining the ornamentation and references used in the *Diatessaron* — dwells at length upon the Divine attributes, especially unity and simplicity,—pointing out how these are exhibited in the Gospels,—and upon the wisdom of God in bringing the Gentiles to Christ by means of the promulgation of a new law, whereby all nations drove out idolatry, and came to Christ. The Harmony itself begins at leaf 96, and extends to leaf 353. A note at each end plainly asserts that it is Tatian's *Diatessaron*. This work Ciasca selected as the most suitable one to be published in honour of the Jubilee of the priesthood of Pope Leo XIII., and it was accordingly published at Rome in 1888 in the original Arabic, accompanied by a Latin translation, the wording of the text being based upon a careful comparison of the two MSS. of the Vatican Library and the Borgian Museum respectively. The present volume is an attempt to lay before the English reader a literal translation of the *Diatessaron* as published by Ciasca, accompanied by such introductory explanations, historical and otherwise, and such tables of reference, as may enable him to form an idea of the nature and value of the work thus recovered, and its bearing upon modern controversies. The translation has been arrived at as follows:—In the first place, the general accuracy of Ciasca's Latin version was proved by comparing with his Arabic a number of extracts from his Latin taken at random in various parts of the *Diatessaron*.

An English version was then made from the Latin. And, lastly, this English version was compared throughout word for word with the Arabic text. For the comparison of the Latin and Arabic I am indebted to the kindness of Dr. A. Neubauer of the Bodleian Library. To the Rev. E. P. Barrow, M.A., formerly Rector of Cholderton, and sometime Classical Tutor of St. Mary's Hall, I am greatly indebted for a critical examination of a large number of points connected with the translation from Latin into English, for much valuable advice, and for enabling me, through his friend, the Rev. W. E. Daniel, Vicar of Holy Trinity, Frome, and Grinfield Lecturer on the Septuagint, to find an Arabic scholar to collate the English version with the Arabic. The Bishop of Durham had previously interested himself so far as to mention the names of two Cambridge men well qualified for this work, but neither of these gentlemen had sufficient leisure. Mr. G. Buchanan Gray, B.A. (First Class in Semitic languages), Lecturer in Hebrew and the Old Testament in Mansfield College, Oxford, Pusey and Ellerton Scholar 1889, Junior Septuagint Prizeman 1890, and Kennicott Scholar 1891, by whom this portion of the work was eventually done, was strongly recommended to Mr. Daniel for the purpose by Dr. Neubauer and Dr. Driver, both of whom had examined him for his degree. I cannot speak too highly of the care and pains which Mr. Gray has bestowed upon the work, or of the critical acumen and scholarship which he has brought to bear upon it. My obligations to Professor Robinson in regard to Appendix X. are described later on. To each and all of these gentlemen I desire to tender my sincerest thanks. I wish also at the same time to acknowledge my indebtedness to the Authors referred to in Table XI.

The MS. which reached the Borgian Museum in this singular way, has been the means of explaining the difficulties which prevented the general acceptance of the Vatican MS. as Tatian's work; for although MS. XIV. closed with a distinct statement that it contained the *Diatessaron* of Tatian, grave doubts rested upon this assertion (which it was thought might only express the opinion of the transcriber), because the contents differed in some important respects from those of the *Diatessaron* as described by some of the Fathers. In the first place, MS. XIV. contained the genealogies (S. Matt. i. 1–17 and S. Luke iii. 23ᵇ–38) so plainly declared by Theodoret[1] to be absent from the copies of the *Diatessaron* which he found in use in his diocese. The fragments quoted by Ephraem Syrus seemed to imply a similar absence in his copy. In the Borgian MS., however, these genealogies are absent from the body of the work, but are put together as an appendix, bearing the title, "The Book of the Generation of Jesus." It is not till after this appendix that a note is subjoined, saying that Ben-attib translated this work from the Syriac into Arabic; thus implying that the genealogies were inserted in the same manner in the Syriac copy from which the translation was made. It follows that the Borgian MS. represents an older and more faithful copy of a work which originally did not contain the genealogies at all, but to which they were attached in course of time, first of all in an appendix as an acknowledged addition to the original, and then eventually as a part of the text itself. Thus the presence of the genealogies in the Vatican MS. is fully and satisfactorily accounted for; and whilst it shows that that copy has been subject to corrupting influences, which may have affected it also in other respects, it in no way contradicts the idea, that we have in these MSS. the *Diatessaron* of Tatian in two of the forms which it assumed after many centuries of use. Another circumstance which raised a doubt whether MS. XIV. could be the *Diatessaron*, was the manner in which it commenced. There was a difficulty about translating the opening words of the Arabic. Assemani and Rosenmüller understood them differently; whilst Ciasca in his Essay before alluded to disagreed with both, and thought part of the disputed words an interpolation; but all were agreed that the first words of S. Mark's Gospel occurred before the first words of S. John's Gospel, contrary to the plain statements of Dionysius Bar-Salibi,[2] writing in the latter half of the twelfth century, and of Bar-Hebraeus,[3] writing in the thirteenth century, both of whom declared that the *Diatessaron* of Tatian, on which Ephraem wrote his Commentary, began with, "In the beginning was the Word." This difficulty also is removed by an examination of the Borgian MS., in which the body of the text commences with, "In the beginning was

[1] Appendix, Table VIII., No. 5.   [2] Appendix, Table VIII., No. 8.
[3] Appendix, Table VIII., No. 9.

the Word;" but before these words, and separated from them by a space, is a kind of title, taken from the opening words of S. Mark, "The Gospel of Jesus, the Son of the living God." Thus Ciasca was right in his Essay on MS. XIV., when he suggested that the words from S. Mark were an addition prefixed to the original commencement "by another hand to supply the lack of a title, that the work might not begin abruptly."

The Arabic text is divided into fifty-five chapters, which appear to have been intended for use upon the fifty-two sundays and the three principal week-day anniversaries of each year. With the exception of the last, which is shorter, these chapters are very uniform in length; and it may be for the sake of this uniformity that a chapter is sometimes made to end inconveniently before the close of some episode referred to in it. Thus the fourth chapter contains an account of the Temptation as far as the proposal to fall down and worship; but the reply of Jesus commences the fifth chapter. In the present work the fifty-five chapters are subdivided into verses for convenience of reference, the verse divisions being arranged as far as possible as they occur in the Authorised Version of the Gospels; and these chapters and verses are shown in the margin to the *left* of the text.

In the prologue of the Borgian MS., a promise was given that the Gospel from which each passage was taken should be shown throughout the *Diatessaron* by means of certain signs there mentioned; but this purpose was only carried out in a few instances. In the Vatican MS. XIV., however, there is a complete system of references, giving the Gospel, chapter, and verse corresponding to each part of the text. These Ciasca has inserted in his Latin version, with some corrections of obvious errors, and with an important change, viz. that where only a part of a verse was in the text he added a letter a, b, c, . . . to indicate the first, second, third . . . part of that verse (thus Matt. xxi. 24[b]). These references I have carefully revised and shown in the margin to the *right* of the text. As our present system of verses was not invented until the sixteenth century, they are, of course, not the work of Tatian or of the translator from Syriac into Arabic, or even of the transcriber of the copy in which they occur,—if we accept the supposed date of MS. XIV. given above,—but must have been added later; so that no authority attaches to them, and we are free to use our own judgment in cases where a different reference seems more applicable. It is desirable also to bear in mind that short phrases are often introduced into verses from elsewhere; and, in a few instances, a verse assumes such a composite character that no single reference can adequately express its source.

Whoever it was that inserted the references, he evidently did so from the divisions in the Vulgate, which, in a few instances, differ from our own. In these cases, for the convenience of English readers, I have changed the reference to suit our Authorised Version, adding a footnote to that effect. In some instances it seems as if a different reference—to the parallel passage in another Gospel—would have been preferable, especially where the reference given in the Arabic unnecessarily destroys the continuity of the passage as an extract from one and the same Gospel. In such cases I have retained the reference as in the original, but have added in a note the reference which seemed more desirable. Our own Authorised Version was greatly influenced by the Vulgate—an influence not present to the same degree in the Revised Version. Now, although in a few instances, chiefly omissions, the Arabic agrees with the Revised Version where it differs from the Authorised, yet, in the great majority of instances, the contrary is the case—so much so, as to form quite a noticeable feature in the work of translation. My observations in this respect entirely agree with the statement of Mr. Rendel Harris,[1] that "there is some unknown nexus between the text of the Western authorities for the New Testament and the text of the Harmony."

Akerblad pointed out that MS. XIV. was evidently a translation from Syriac, as the Arabic of it was full of Syriac idioms. The Borgian MS., on the other hand, is expressly stated, in a notice prefixed to the text, and also in another notice at the conclusion of it, to have been translated from Syriac into Arabic by Abû-l-Faraj Abdullah Ibn-aṯ-Ṭib. Ciasca, in his Preface, has collected several allusions to this

[1] *Diatessaron of Tatian*, p. 37.

Abdulla Ben-attib, as he is called, from which it appears that he was a celebrated Nestorian monk, born in Assyria, and was the author of several books. He died A.D. 1043, so that we may conclude that he translated the *Diatessaron* from Syriac into Arabic early in the eleventh century. The use of the Arabic language was made compulsory in Syria: it is not surprising, therefore, that the two MSS., which now survive, of a Syriac work once used by the Syrian Churches, should both be in Arabic. The closing notice above referred to adds that Ben-attib made his translation from a Syriac copy in the handwriting of Gûbasî ibn Alî Al-mutayyib, a disciple of Ḥunain ibn Isḥak. Ciasca has succeeded in identifying both these persons. Gûbasî wrote two books on medicine; and his instructor, Hunain, Honain, or Hanain, a physician of Bagdad, was born at Hira, and died A.D. 873. Thus we may conclude that the Syriac original of the Borgian MS. was written by Gûbasî in the latter half of the ninth century; that its Arabic original was written by Abdullah Ibn-aṭ-Tib early in the eleventh century; and that the Borgian MS. itself is a copy of the latter work made not later than the fourteenth century.

Now the *Diatessaron* used at Edessa[1] must have been in Syriac; the copy, upon which Ephraem Syrus commented, was in Syriac, the language which he spoke and wrote; and the copies which Theodoret[2] found in his diocese in Syria, which were being regularly used in the churches, must also have been in Syriac. Thus, wherever we meet with it in early times we find it in that language, which was Tatian's own native language; and we find no suggestion that it had been translated into that language from any other. It does not, of course, *necessarily* follow that it was not first written in Greek and afterwards translated into Syriac; and this view has been adopted by Professor Harnack and others chiefly for the following reasons:—(1) The *Address to Greeks*, the only other extant work of Tatian, and the only one extant in its original language, is in Greek. This proves nothing, for the subject required that language; it would be absurd to write in Syriac an Address to Greeks; and even a man who habitually wrote in Syriac, would not use that language for such a purpose. (2) Its title is Greek, and would be unfamiliar to

[1] Appendix, Table VIII., No. 1.   [2] Appendix, Table VIII., No. 5.

Syrian readers. Baethgen has shown, however, that some Syriac works of early Christians had Greek titles. (3) Greek fragments of the original are thought to have survived centuries later, and formed the basis of the Latin work of Luscinius.[1] This, however, is very doubtful. (4) It is assumed that the *Codex Fuldensis* of Victor[2] came from a Greek original. There is no definite evidence of this; and it is known that there was much intercourse between the Church of Rome and the Syrian Churches for some time previous to its discovery. (5) A supposed allusion to the *Diatessaron* is pointed out in the Canon of Muratori, but the reading is doubtful. (6) It is asserted that there was no recognised Syriac version of the four Gospels, out of which Tatian could have made his Harmony, such version not having been made until about half a century after his death. The controversy as to the dates of the Peschito and the Curetonian fragments is too complicated and obscure for present reference. It may suffice to say, that the history of the *Diatessaron*, as far as at present known, points to the Curetonian as the older version, and as bearing a close resemblance to the earliest form of Tatian's text. Baethgen, indeed, maintains that Tatian's Syriac is older than the Curetonian, which he thinks was based upon it. At all events, it seems incredible that the Gospels were not translated into Syriac in the first century; and though at first there may have been more than one independent private version, before the time of Tatian these must have given place to one which was more or less generally recognised. In his retirement in Syria Tatian may have had access to this before publishing the *Diatessaron*, though, in the opinion of Zahn, he also made use of a Greek version. In our opinion the supposed heretical tendency of the work, together with its omissions and insertions, is not sufficient to account for the entire disappearance of all reference to a Harmony so interesting and so unique in the writings of the Western Church until the sixth century; but all difficulties of this kind are completely and satisfactorily explained by the hypothesis, that it was written in Syriac, and thereby rendered inaccessible to Greek and Latin Churches at a time when Syrian Churches were using it

[1] See below, p. 20.   [2] See below, p. 17.

extensively, in some cases even to the exclusion of the separate Gospels.

Of the personal history of Tatian, the compiler of the *Diatessaron*, very little is known, and this little is chiefly derived from his extant work, called *An Address to Greeks*. He there says: "I was born in the land of the Assyrians, and have been first instructed in your [*i.e.* Greek] doctrines, and afterwards in those which I now undertake to proclaim."[1] Zahn thinks he was born about A.D. 110. He seems to have been a man of birth and fortune, and of exceptional literary powers, and occupied for a time the position of a Sophist. Animated by a keen desire to arrive at the truth respecting God and religion, he visited many countries, studying closely the worship of each. In Greece he obtained admission to the sacred mysteries; and subsequently he visited Rome, arriving there about the middle of the second century. The effect of his intimate study of the heathen religions was a conviction amounting to actual certainty that there was no truth in them, and that they exercised a corrupting and debasing influence on the soul. This was accompanied by a longing to ascertain the truth, and to be able to worship God in a way acceptable to Him. At Rome Tatian made the acquaintance of Justin; and it was probably he who drew his attention to "certain barbaric[2] writings, too old to be compared with the opinions of the Greeks, and too divine to be compared with their errors,"[3]—in other words, the Old Testament Scriptures. Satisfied that he had found the truth at last, Tatian received instruction in the Christian faith, and became a member of the Church at Rome. Here he continued for many years, writing in defence of the faith, exposing vigorously the falseness and licentiousness of the pagan forms of worship, and instructing converts; here, too, he probably commenced his *Diatessaron*, with the knowledge and approval of Justin. One of his pupils was Rhodon, mentioned by Eusebius, who has preserved some fragments of Rhodon's writings; and in all probability Clement of Alexandria was also his pupil, since

---

[1] *Address to Greeks*, ch. xlii. English readers will find this work translated in Clark's *Ante-Nicene Library*.

[2] *I.e.* not Greek.   [3] *Address to Greeks*, ch. xxix.

Clement speaks[1] of one of his instructors being an Assyrian. Justin and Tatian worked in complete harmony until the martyrdom of the former,[2] which was brought about by the influence of Crescens, who at a much earlier period, Tatian says, had "endeavoured to inflict on Justin, and indeed on me, the punishment of death."[3] It appears to have been after the death of Justin that Tatian, who seems to have been his successor, began to express views which gave offence to the Christians at Rome, and led to his being excommunicated as a heretic about A.D. 172. Shortly afterwards he left Rome for the East, and seems to have resided chiefly in Syria, not far from Antioch; but he is thought to have died at Edessa about A.D. 180. During his stay at Syria he placed himself at the head of a sect called Encratites—a term signifying The Continent, or Self-controlled; but it is uncertain to what extent, if at all, he was regarded as a heretic in the Churches of that country. The obscurity in which the career of Tatian is involved is largely due to his being branded as a heretic, which led the writers of the Church to concern themselves more with combating his errors than describing his life. The references to Tatian in the writings of the early Fathers are as follows: Irenæus, *Adv. Haer.* i. 28. 1, and iii. 23. 8. Clement of Alexandria, *Strom.* iii. 12, and *Ex. Theod.* 38, besides the supposed allusion in *Strom.* i. 1, given above. Eusebius, *Eccles. Hist.* iv. 16. 28 and 29; and (respecting Rhodon) v. 13. Epiphanius, *Haer.* xlvi. 1. Jerome, *De Viris Illust.* 29; *Adversus Jovin.* i. 3; and *Commentary on the Epistle to Titus*, Preface. Theodoret, *Haer. Fab.* i. 20; and his own allusions, *Address to Greeks*, chs. xix., xxix., xxxv., and xlii.

The peculiar views of Tatian may be briefly stated as follows:—(1) He held in some degree the Gnostic theory of Valentinian, that there were certain Aeons, or emanations from the Supreme Deity, the Logos or Word being the chief; (2) Like Marcion, he considered the God of this world, or God of the Old Testament, or Demiurge, as distinct from, and inferior to, the God of the New Testament. Origen tells us that he understood the words, "Let there be light," as the

---

[1] *Strom.* i. 1.
[2] Which Dr. Hort places as early as A.D. 148, but Prof. Harnack in A.D. 166.
[3] *Address to Greeks*, ch. xix.

prayer of the God of this world to His superior, which was granted; (3) Tatian believed in the non-salvability of Adam; (4) He advocated and observed celibacy, condemning marriage as no better than whoredom, believing it to be the work of the inferior God; (5) He advocated abstinence from animal food and also from wine. In this respect he introduced a modification into the celebration of the Lord's Supper, so that water might be used instead of wine.

Tatian wrote many works, of which the names of the following have come down to us:—

1. *An Address to Greeks* [Λόγος πρὸς Ἕλληνας].
2. The *Diatessaron* [Διατεσσάρων].
3. *A Book of Problems* [Βίβλιον Προβληματῶν], explaining what seemed obscure in the Old Testament.
4. *Of Perfection according to the Saviour* [Περὶ τοῦ κατὰ τὸν Σωτῆρα καταρτισμοῦ].
5. *On Animals* [Περὶ ζώων].
6. *A Collection of the Epistles of S. Paul.*

Lightfoot places his literary activity between A.D. 155 and A.D. 170, but says it may have extended a few years beyond this period either way. Westcott places it between A.D. 150 and A.D. 175. Harnack places the *Address to Greeks* as early as A.D. 152–3. The exact time at which he wrote the *Diatessaron* is uncertain.

In 1869 Professor W. Wright published in the original Syriac a series of Homilies. The MSS. containing them stated that they were the work of Aphraates, the Persian sage, and that the first ten were composed A.D. 337, the remaining twelve (according to the letters of the alphabet) A.D. 344, and an additional one A.D. 345. Some uncertainty exists about the author's history, as the name Aphraates was a common one; Professor Fuller thinks he was Bishop and Abbot of the Convent of S. Matthew, near Mosul. A very similar set of Homilies was ascribed to Jacob, Bishop of Nisibis; but Dr. Wright satisfied himself that Jacob died A.D. 338, and therefore could not be the author of these. The Homilies contain numerous and extensive quotations from the Gospel history; but Dr. Wright noticed that passages from more than one Gospel seemed mixed together in a strange way. He says in his Preface: "I must say, however, that, like most of the other ancient Fathers, Aphraates seems to me to quote the Peschitta merely from memory, sometimes mistaking the book in which the passage occurs, and at other times mixing up the words of two or more passages of Scripture. In a few cases I have not been able to discover the text at which he aims." The explanation of this is a simple one, the quotations of Aphraates were taken from the *Diatessaron*, which we know was almost exclusively used in Syria in his day. Indeed, his own statement, Homily I., implies it: "And Christ is also the Word and the Speech of the Lord as it is written in the beginning of the Gospel of our Saviour, *In the beginning was the Word*." It could not be S. John's Gospel only that is here meant, since he speaks of one book of the Gospel, and yet repeatedly cites the words of the other evangelists; but besides S. John's Gospel we know of no other that began in that way except the *Diatessaron*. Zahn has carefully examined these passages, and found undoubted evidence in the longer quotations that they changed from one Gospel to another in the same way that the *Diatessaron* does. For some interesting evidence on this point the English reader is referred to Mr. Rendel Harris's *Diatessaron of Tatian*, pp. 19-22. Taking this as established, the passages quoted by Aphraates are the only portions of the *Diatessaron* of any considerable length that have come down to us in the original tongue; and though changes may have been made in the text between the times of Tatian and Aphraates, yet the latter has retained many explanatory remarks, such as an harmonist might introduce, and these are probably the very words of Tatian.

Dionysius Bar-Salibi states that Mar Ephraem wrote a Commentary upon the *Diatessaron* of Tatian.[1] This Ephraem, the Deacon of Edessa, was the most famous of the native Syrian Fathers, and died A.D. 373. He is supposed to have written this Commentary during the last ten years of his life. Many of his works have been preserved in their original language, but this has not. It was supposed to be entirely lost; but two distinct Armenian versions, both bearing the date A.D. 1195, were discovered in the Mechitarist Monastery of S. Lazzaro near

[1] Cf. Appendix, Table VIII., No. 8.

Venice, where a collated copy was published in the Armenian language in 1836. Aucher, one of the monks, proceeded to make a Latin version, but did not publish it; and it was not rendered generally accessible until 1876, when Dr. Moesinger published a revision of Aucher's work with notes. Tatian is not alluded to personally in this Commentary, nor does Ephraem mention any one of the evangelists by name; but he is evidently taking a few words of the Gospel narrative, sometimes out of one Gospel and sometimes out of another, and commenting upon them; whilst not unfrequently the passage he deals with is of a composite character, evidently not derived from one only of our Gospels. Now, there can be little doubt that the passages which Ephraem selected for the subjects of his remarks, were taken by him in the order which they occupied in the work upon which he was commenting; and the order of the Gospel narrative in that work may, to a large extent, be inferred from them. To do this, however, it is necessary to distinguish these passages from the very large number of texts, both from the Old and New Testaments, which Ephraem has woven into his Commentary by way of argument or illustration. This Dr. Moesinger has endeavoured to do by printing the latter in inverted commas, and the former in spaced type. In doing this he had to consider certain passages that were written in red ink in the MSS.; and these he has generally included in his spaced type, as they seemed to belong to that class of quotations. But in each MS. the use of red ink is very irregular, often skipping several pages; and the red passages of Codex A are not always identical with those of Codex B. Moreover, one such passage is from the prophecies of Ezekiel; several are not quotations at all, but words of Ephraem's remarks, that indicate a fresh subject of comment; and one is a kind of heading, as follows: "The Order and Solemnity of the Apostles of the Lord," which suggests the idea that there may have been a time when the *Diatessaron* was divided into sections with appropriate headings. It is more probable, however, that before he published the Commentary Ephraem had used the substance of it as a course of addresses to students or candidates for Holy Orders, and that this was the title of one such address, since it comes *after* the extract from the *Diates-*

saron relating the first calling of disciples, but before Ephraem's comments upon the nature and importance of their office.

Now, owing to the character of Ephraem's remarks, and his mode of passing from one subject to another, it is not easy in all cases to tell when he is changing the ground of his comments, and when he is only adding further illustrations to what he has been saying already. Hence the spaced type of Moesinger, when it does not simply mean red ink in the MS., must be understood to mean quotations, which *in his opinion* Ephraem is taking as his text, on which to found his discourse. It must, however, be taken only as expressing his personal opinion, which, under the circumstances, is entitled to great weight, and not as possessing any authority beyond. In the great majority of cases no doubt his judgment is correct, but there is no reason why it should not be set aside on sufficient evidence; and a number of instances could be pointed out where such evidence exists.

Zahn made a careful examination of these passages; and, assuming that Ephraem commented upon them *in the same order* in which they occurred in the Gospel narrative from which he took them, he made out a Table of Contents of that Gospel, which he thought must be the *Diatessaron*, and published it in 1881, seven years before the issue of Ciasca's Arabic *Diatessaron*. That Table of Contents is found to agree [1] almost entirely with the order in Ciasca's work, and that notwithstanding some very singular arrangements and displacements; so that no reasonable doubt can remain (1) that the Commentary recovered from the Armenian versions was really based upon Tatian's *Diatessaron;* and (2) that in the Arabic of Ciasca, although the *text* seems to have been considerably modified since the time of Ephraem, we have the *same order* of harmonisation as existed in the copy of the *Diatessaron* which Ephraem used in the fourth century.

At the same time, the exact text of Ephraem's copy cannot with certainty be arrived at; for his quotations are not always in perfect agreement with the source from which they are taken, seeing that he several times cites the same passage differently in two or more places. Nor is it safe to infer, because he omits a clause in his quotation, that that clause was

[1] See Appendix, Table IX.

not present in his copy; for instances occur of such omissions, which are supplied another time, when the passage is again referred to. In fact, he only quotes so much, whether continuous or not, as he requires for his immediate purpose, and even that at times imperfectly, as if he trusted to his memory, and, like many other early writers, did not verify his quotations.

In Appendix X. a translation is given of all the quotations from the Gospels that are to be found in Ephraem's Commentary, whether printed by Moesinger in spaced type or not. This Appendix is the only complete English version of these fragments. It has been made at the suggestion of the Rev. J. Armitage Robinson, Norrisian Professor of Divinity in the University of Cambridge, who has spent considerable time in correcting, by means of the Armenian text, my translation of Moesinger's somewhat inaccurate Latin version. The greater part of the notes to this Appendix are also due to Professor Robinson's investigations. A much closer approximation is thus given to the *Diatessaron*, as Ephraem had it, than we have hitherto possessed, as in every instance where the reading here given differs from that of Moesinger, it may be taken to be nearer to the actual words of Ephraem. An important advance has also been made, inasmuch as the Armenian words of Ephraem's citations have been for the most part compared with the corresponding words of the Armenian Vulgate, to see whether the various readings could be due to the Armenian translator, who might have introduced the readings of his own Vulgate. Professor Robinson has visited the Monastery of S. Lazzaro for the purpose of examining and collating the two Armenian MSS. May we hope that ere long we may have a complete English version of the entire Commentary of Ephraem based upon his more careful examination and comparison of the two MSS.?

In the case of passages quoted by Ephraem merely by way of illustration,—such as are shown in the Latin in inverted commas, and not in spaced type,—there is often nothing to show what place they occupied in the Gospel narrative on which he was commenting. That place can be found, however, by reference to the Arabic *Diatessaron*, which cannot materially differ *in order* from the *Diatessaron* used by Ephraem. Accordingly the Ephraem fragments are arranged in Appendix X. in the order of the Arabic version, and with the same divisions of chapters and verses, so that the reader can at once compare Ephraem's reading of any passage with the corresponding reading found in the Arabic. At the same time, the page of Moesinger's work at which the citation is found, is shown in the margin to the right.

It is interesting to find Ephraem drawing attention to various readings. He sometimes describes his quotation as "Scripture" and sometimes as "Gospel," in all which cases Zahn thinks that he is quoting from the *Diatessaron*, and that his copy agreed closely in its wording with the Curetonian Syriac. At other times he describes his quotation as a "Reading," or refers to the "Greek." In these cases the extracts he gives are found to bear a closer resemblance to the Peschito, which was probably gaining ground in Syria at the time, and, having been more recently translated from the Greek, may not improbably have been known in contradistinction to the older Syriac version as Jaunâjâ or the "Greek." From the importance which Ephraem attaches to it, he must have looked upon its text as more reliable than the older one. It seems probable that, as time went on, the Syriac of the Peschito was substituted for the older form in the *Diatessaron*. Whilst some, like Theodoret, sought to banish the *Diatessaron* from the Churches of Syria, because of its omissions, its insertions of harmonistic comments, and its inaccuracies of translation; others sought to improve and retain it by supplying its deficiencies, eliminating most of the passing remarks due to Tatian, and inserting the more trustworthy text of the Peschito. Thus, whilst Aphraates and Ephraem quote from the older form, both the Arabic versions used by Ciasca present the work without the omissions which Theodoret mentions, without a great many of the "Tatianisms" found in those writers, and with a text closely allied to the Peschito.[1] In the Notes to the Text and to Appendix X., attention has been drawn to a number of explanatory remarks, said to have been in the *Diatessaron* once, but which are not found in the Arabic, and were not, therefore, in the Syriac copy from which it was translated; and it is easy to see how a person who substituted the words of the Peschito for the older wording, would be likely to omit Tatian's comments because he did

[1] See Appendix, Table III.

not find them in the Peschito. There is thus a special value attaching to the citations of Aphraates and Ephraem, because they are taken from such early copies of the *Diatessaron*, whereas we cannot gauge the full extent to which the text of the Arabic versions may have departed from the original wording of Tatian.[1] Yet at the same time there is little doubt that even Ephraem's copy differed considerably from Tatian's, the work of collation with the distinct Gospels having already begun.

Victor, Bishop of Capua, who died A.D. 554, met with an anonymous Harmony of the four Gospels, which interested him very much. The idea of thus blending the four Gospels into one continuous narrative seemed to him a good one; and he had never seen anything of the kind before. The work of compilation was evidently a very elaborate one, and Victor was anxious to discover its author. He searched the writings of the Fathers for mention of any such work; and he found in a letter of Eusebius to Carpian that Ammonius of Alexandria had compiled one Gospel out of the four by placing at the side of S. Matthew's Gospel corresponding extracts from the other three;[2] and that the same Ammonius had composed certain lists called Canons, showing the portions of the four Gospels, which each contained independently of the rest or in common with one or more of them. Victor also found from the *Ecclesiastical History* of Eusebius that Tatian had combined selections from the four narratives into one Gospel, which he called *Diapente*. This name *Diapente* ("through five") is evidently a mistake for *Diatessaron* ("through four"), for Victor is quoting Eusebius, and we know from other sources that Eusebius really wrote *Diatessaron*. It almost seems as if the mistake could not be due to Victor, but to the copyist; since Victor had just quoted from Eusebius, that Tatian made his Gospel "out of four" ("ex quatuor"). If the Acts of the Apostles were added in the same MS., Victor may have regarded it as a continuation of the Gospel story, which thus came "through five."

[1] For a fuller discussion of the question, how far the actual text of Tatian may be considered to be modified in the Arabic versions, the reader is referred to Dr. Sellin's Essay in the fourth volume of Zahn's *Forschungen*.

[2] Cf. Lightfoot, *Supernatural Religion*, pp. 280, 281.

Not hearing of any other Harmony of the Gospels, Victor next considered whether the one he had found was Ammonius's or Tatian's; and although the order of S. Matthew was to a large extent followed, yet the presence of so much of the early part of S. Luke's Gospel led him to decide that it must be Tatian's. This decision was in modern times set aside for a variety of reasons, chiefly because Victor's Harmony (1) began with S. Luke i. 1–4; (2) contained the genealogies of our Lord; and (3) was called *Diapente* in the above passage. Victor himself was much exercised in his mind by the fact that Tatian, after the death of his leader Justin, had adopted heretical views. Had the contents been Tatian's own composition, he would have cast the book aside at once; but recognising the words of his Lord, he felt that he was safe in using them; and so he consoled himself with the reflection that very likely Tatian had compiled it before Justin's death. Victor therefore published it with a Preface giving the above information, and with the addition of the Canons of Ammonius. To judge from this Preface we might suppose that Victor had not meddled with the text itself; but an examination of the work as published by Ranke, and entitled *Codex Fuldensis*, shows that he must have done so to a considerable extent. It was a Latin version, and Victor has left us the Table of Contents of the 182 chapters or sections in very barbarous Latin, in all probability just as he found it. But the contents themselves are given in excellent Latin, evidently copied from the Vulgate, and forming, so far as they go, one of the earliest and most reliable versions of it. A comparison of the contents with Ciasca's work shows beyond question that it was a version of Tatian's Harmony which Victor had. The insertion of S. Luke i. 1–4 and the genealogies was probably the work of Victor, since they are not mentioned in his older Table of Contents, where the numbering of the chapters also differs slightly. In all probability it was he who substituted the elegant Latin of S. Jerome for the ruder phraseology of the Harmony; and in doing so he seems to have expunged the little explanatory phrases with which undoubtedly Tatian freely sprinkled the original work, and many of which, in all probability, still survived in the copy which Victor discovered.

The following instance may serve to illustrate the relative

value of the *Codex Fuldensis*, the Arabic *Diatessaron*, and Ephraem's Commentary, and the kind of information obtained by comparing them together. Dr. Wace[1] observed in ch. xvi. of the Commentary the following order :—(1) The Cursing of the Fig-tree ; (2) the Visit of Nicodemus ; (3) the parable of the Unjust Judge. As (1) and (3) both relate to the importance of prayer, it seemed strange that they should be divided from one another by the visit of Nicodemus. On referring to the *Codex Fuldensis* he found the more natural order—Nicodemus, Fig-tree, Unjust Judge. He concluded, therefore, that the *Codex* gave the true order of the *Diatessaron*, from which Ephraem, for some unknown reason, had departed. But when we turn to the present work, which had not then been published, we find that the subject of the Fig-tree is very properly divided into two parts—(*a*) the Cursing of the Fig-tree, and (*b*) the discovery by the disciples *on another occasion* that it had withered. The visit of Nicodemus is represented as taking place during the interval of time which must necessarily have occurred between these two events. Thus Ephraem did not depart from Tatian's order (as represented in the Arabic), since the subject of the Fig-tree *begins* before that of Nicodemus ; yet the lesson on faith and prayer, which Jesus drew from the case of the Fig-tree, coming as a conclusion after the discovery by the disciples, is put later than the visit of Nicodemus, and is appropriately followed at once by the parable of the Unjust Judge.

As the *Codex Fuldensis* is divided into 182 chapters, intended for reading one at a time, we can see the object of Victor or some one before him in bringing the two parts of the story of the Fig-tree together into a chapter by themselves, to be read as a separate whole,—an object which may account for other changes observable in Victor's order. Thus we find in this case no reason to believe that Ephraem departed from the exact order of the *Diatessaron*, or that his Commentary was based on any other work ; and we find also, that at all events in this instance the *Codex* of the sixth century does not represent so truly as this present work the *Diatessaron* of Tatian in the form in which Ephraem had it in the fourth century ; for it is the Arabic which explains both the others, and is the key to the situation.

[1] *Expositor* for 1881, ii. 134.

The *Codex* is said to have been brought to Fulda in the eighth century by Boniface, the Apostle of Germany, and to have been translated into the Eastern Frankish dialect in the ninth century, about the time of Charlemagne, who finally imposed Christianity upon the Saxons. His son, Louis the Pious, caused a poetical version to be made of it for the purpose of supplanting the popular ballads relating to Woden and Thor. This celebrated epic poem is now known as *Héliand*. It was published at Munich in A.D. 1830 from a comparison of the two known MSS., one of which is in the British Museum and the other at Munich. The poem is alliterative, and gives a life of Jesus harmonised from the four Gospels. It is written in the Old Saxon dialect; and the unknown author has allowed his imagination some freedom in the treatment of his subject, adopting the popular conceptions of the day.

A portion of the prose translation of the *Codex* made in the ninth century was published at Zurich in 1706, and again at Ulm in 1726 in the second volume of Schilter's *Thesaurus Antiquitatum Teutonicarum*, under the title *Tatiani Syri Harmonia Evangelica e Latinâ Victoris Capuani versione translata in linguam Theotiscam antiquissimam.*[1]

Ottmar Nachtigall, who called himself Luscinius, published at Augsburg in 1523 a work, entitled *Evangelicae Historiae ex quatuor Evangelistis perpetuo tenore continuata narratio*, etc., which purported to be a translation from the Greek of some fragments of the Harmony of Ammonius of Alexandria. Some have thought this work was really based upon the *Codex;* but the balance of evidence is against this view. There can be little doubt, however, that the fragments referred to formed a part of some edition of Tatian's *Diatessaron.*[2] Indeed, Ottmar himself seems to have come to this conclusion; for in the following year he published a German version, in which he attributed it to Tatian.

A remarkable controversy has been carried on with regard to the meaning of the title *Diatessaron*, which was certainly given to this work by Tatian himself. Familiar as we now

---

[1] For other supposed derivatives of the *Codex*, see Hemphill, pp. 70-73.
[2] Cf. Zahn, pp. 313-328; Hemphill, pp. 63-69.

are with the idea of four Gospels, canonical and authoritative, and taking into account that Tatian's work was beyond question a Gospel compiled from more than one source, the meaning naturally suggested itself: The Gospel compiled through the four Gospels.

This idea was supported by the testimony of Eusebius, who spoke of it as "A combination and collection of the Gospels,"[1] and by Theodoret, who says, "He also composed the Gospel called *Diatessaron*, cutting out the genealogies, and whatever other passages show that the Lord was born of the seed of David according to the flesh;"[2] the inference being that these things were cut out from the canonical Gospels, the other portions of those Gospels being made use of. Such was the view very generally entertained by the Church; but there have been some who, on other grounds, did not believe that the fourth Gospel was written at so early a date, or that the three synoptic Gospels were yet collected and used in common, each being, according to their view, more or less limited in its circulation to a particular country. Holding these opinions, they could not accept the idea that Tatian was in possession of all the four Gospels, and still less that the present canonical Gospels were so well known and accepted in the Churches of Syria, that Tatian felt it sufficient to briefly designate them as the "four." They admitted that the *Diatessaron* was a kind of Gospel, and compiled from more than one source, but said it need not be literally from "four" sources, for Diatessaron was a musical term signifying "a composition based on the four principal notes."[3] It therefore only meant a Harmony, without fixing the number of things harmonised into one; and they contended that oral tradition might have been among the sources from which Tatian compiled his Harmony.

The supporters of this view criticised the wording of Eusebius, contending that he only wrote from hearsay, and had no personal knowledge of the work; and they pointed out that Epiphanius, whilst agreeing with Eusebius, from whom

---

[1] Appendix, Table VIII., No. 2.   [2] Appendix, Table VIII., No. 5.

[3] A similar term to Diapason. Its use in music was rather, according to Bishop Westcott, to signify the "concord of the fourth." In medicine it was used to signify a mixture containing four ingredients. Cf. Dr. Salmon's *Introduction to the Study of the New Testament*, p. 74, note.

they thought he borrowed the information, added, "which some call [the Gospel] according to Hebrews." They also contended that Theodoret would not have removed it from use in the churches of his diocese, if it had been composed of the four canonical Gospels.

If, as there seems no reason to doubt, the work published by Ciasca is substantially the *Diatessaron* of Tatian, subject only to such alterations as would naturally be made in it in the course of centuries, to make it conform more in details to the accepted forms of the canonical Gospels, then this controversy is decisively closed in favour of the orthodox view; for beyond all question the book in its present form is a Harmony of our four Gospels and of no others.

And with this is also set at rest in favour of the same side the further controversy, upon which so much time and labour have been spent, as to whether any or all of our four Gospels, in anything like their present form, were known to Justin Martyr, and alluded to by him in his writings. For Tatian avowedly [1] learnt his Christianity from Justin, and his knowledge of the sacred books used by the Christians of that day came to him through Justin. Not only is it highly probable that Tatian wrote the *Diatessaron*, in part at least, during the lifetime of Justin, and during the period of their intimate intercourse at Rome; but even if it be supposed that Tatian wrote it after Justin's death, and even if it be assumed that he had access to documents which were not at the disposal of Justin, is it conceivable that Tatian, who must have been "catechised" from the "Memoirs," would be imposed upon by later forgeries to such an extent as not merely to include these latter in his Gospel narrative, but absolutely to exclude the former? for no other document but our four Gospels is to be found woven into his *Diatessaron*. We may conclude, therefore, that no reasonable doubt remains that the "Memoirs (ἀπομνημονεύματα) of the Apostles," so often referred to by Justin, were in reality our four Gospels.

Now one of the objects sought to be established by those who contended that Justin was ignorant of our present Gospels was this, that the miracles of healing ascribed to Jesus were

---

[1] There can be no doubt that Justin was his "teacher" referred to by Irenaeus, *Adv. Haer.* i. 28.

a later invention, never heard of in the first century, and even unknown in the time of Justin, but created in the latter part of the second century in order to assist in the deification of the Saviour. I have already pointed out in my English version of *Marcion's Gospel*[1] that that Gospel, in which are contained all the miracles of healing found in S. Luke's Gospel except the one performed upon Malchus, was brought by him to Rome about A.D. 140. This fact sufficiently refutes the idea that they were inventions of such a late period as has been alleged. And now we find it established that Justin Martyr, who, even if we assign to him the later date, must have been a Christian from about A.D. 140 to 166, was fully acquainted with and accepted all the four Gospels. We could ourselves infer from this, that the four Gospels, being written in different countries by different persons and at different times, must have been a long time in existence before they were thus collected together at one place, and used in combination as a complete and authoritative record of the events related in them. But we are not left to draw our own inferences; for Marcion professed to trace back his Gospel to S. Paul, alleging that the apostle left copies of it with the Churches that he founded; and Justin described his records as "Memoirs of the Apostles," stating that they contained "all things concerning our Saviour Jesus Christ,"[2] and that in his day they "were still read, together with the writings of the prophets, in their weekly services."[3] In what sense Justin understood them to be memoirs of the apostles is made evident when he says: "In the Memoirs which I say were composed by the apostles and those who followed with them."[4] . . . It may, of course, be contended that Justin only stated his own belief, and was not in a position to trace back these Memoirs with certainty to their real origin, though he must have known all that was known about them by the Church in Rome. Still, even so, the fact remains that in Justin's time they were old writings, and believed to be the work of apostles and their immediate companions, and to contain the witness borne by the apostles to their Master. It is well also to observe the alternative to which the

[1] Parker & Co., Oxford and London.   [2] *Apol.* i. 33.
[3] *Apol.* i. 67.   [4] *Dial.* ch. 103.

opponents of the antiquity of our Gospels are reduced, now that it can be proved that they are the Memoirs of which Justin wrote. For if he was wrong in regard to their authorship, does not that suggest that, when he first became acquainted with them (say A.D. 140), they were already so old, and so long in use in the Church, that their true origin was lost in obscurity. This would throw back these narratives of the miraculous far into the first century, and well within the lifetime of S. John, if not of the other apostles. The recovery of Tatian's *Diatessaron* may be said, therefore, to have disproved the theory of the late invention of the miracles ascribed to our Lord in the four Gospels, if indeed any further disproof were necessary than that already given by Bishop Westcott in his work on *The Canon of the New Testament*.

The light which this discovery throws on these points is of more consequence than the value of the *Diatessaron*, either as a Harmony or for its various readings.

Again, the concluding portions of the Gospels, on the authenticity of which much doubt has been expressed, are all found in the *Diatessaron*, and woven into the narrative like the rest, leaving no room to doubt that they were placed there by Tatian himself, and thus establishing, not indeed their authenticity, but their very high antiquity, and a very early date at which they were generally recognised as parts of the Gospels, since Tatian would not have admitted them into his Harmony unless he had believed them to be portions of the Gospels. Mr. Rendel Harris produces evidence to show that Tatian employed a yet earlier Harmony of the Passion Gospels, which he calls pre-Tatian, and also that it contained some of the disputed part of S. Mark xvi. He thinks that Justin before the compilation of the *Diatessaron* quoted from pre-Tatian. The earlier we carry back the date of the first Harmony, the earlier we make the Gospels; since the Harmony would not be made until the Gospels had all been some time in use, and had been brought together and generally recognised.

When we come to examine the *Diatessaron* with a view to arriving at an estimate of its intrinsic value, as distinct from its influence upon modern controversies, we are met at the outset by certain questions, upon the answers to which the view we take of its merits must largely depend. The first question naturally relates to the degree of fidelity shown in it to the actual text of the four evangelists. It may be put in this form:

(1.) What portions of the four Gospels were omitted by Tatian, either as duplicate matter or otherwise? and what explanatory or other remarks of his own did he introduce into his Harmony?

It is essential always to bear in mind that we do not possess this work as it left the hands of Tatian himself, but only in the form it assumed after centuries of use. We are not, therefore, in a position to give a definite answer to this question.

In Table II. of the Appendix, I have given a detailed analysis of the four Gospels, showing what passages are in the *Diatessaron now*, and where to find them in it; and what passages are omitted, and whether they represent duplicate matter, the *substance* of which is not omitted, but supplied from another Gospel. From this table it appears that the only parts of the Gospels of any considerable length *now* missing from the Harmony are the two genealogies, the pericope of the woman taken in adultery, and the first four verses of S. Luke. We may conclude that Tatian himself left these out. We are expressly told so in the case of the genealogies; the story of the woman was not generally accepted in early times *as a part of S. John's Gospel*, and is not in the Peschito; and the preface of S. Luke, dealing with his private reasons for writing a Gospel, was scarcely suitable for Tatian's work. But Theodoret,[1] who had copies before him, states that Tatian left out, besides the genealogies, " all things that show our Lord to have been born of the seed of David according to the flesh." We cannot doubt that there were such omissions; but pious hands must ere long have inserted the missing passages, as they are no longer absent. It is by no means certain that Tatian left out the genealogies *because* they militated against his idea that David and others were agents of the Demiurge, for we are not certain that he had adopted that view when he made the omission. The internal difficulties they present, and the difficulty of reconciling one with the other, would be sufficient to account for

[1] Appendix, Table VIII., No. 5.

their omission. Or they may have been left out because they had been abused by some who sought to prove from them that Jesus was a mere man.

The researches of Zahn among the writings of the Syriac Fathers have resulted in the collection of a number of short additions to the Gospel narratives in the nature of explanatory or connective remarks, such as a harmonist might add for the purpose of cementing together the pieces of different Gospels, and making the combined narrative more continuous and intelligible. Upon the hypothesis that these Fathers must have quoted from the *Diatessaron*, he attributes these to Tatian; but very few of them are contained in the present Arabic version, and it may be assumed that, as time went on and they were observed to be interpolations into the text of the original or "distinct" Gospels, the majority of them were discarded. Such as remain will be found marked with an asterisk in Table III. of the Appendix, which contains a list of some of the various readings. Attention is drawn to others in the notes at the places where they are supposed to have been.

In contrasting two Greek MSS. of the same part of the New Testament, a comparison can be instituted word for word throughout; but it is otherwise in contrasting an Arabic with a Greek version, since verbal differences are often due to idiomatic differences in the way of expressing the same thought; and it is not always easy to decide whether the difference of wording represents a real various reading or not. This difficulty is increased in a work, like the present, intended for English readers, where such differences have to be expressed, not by the actual words of the Arabic and the Greek, but by the corresponding words of the English versions derived from them. I have not attempted, therefore, to include in Table III. anything like an exhaustive list of various readings, but have simply given some of the principal ones, not rigidly excluding all that may be due to idioms, and marking thus, (P) or (C), those which agree more or less closely with the Peschito or the Curetonian Syriac.

Our next question is:

(2.) What plan did Tatian adopt in arranging the contents of the *Diatessaron* in their order?

Zahn in his attempt at reconstruction arrived at substantially the same order for the contents of the *Diatessaron* as we now find them possessing; and he examined the order with a view to discovering Tatian's method of procedure. In general, he concluded that Tatian had given a decided preference to the first and fourth Gospels over the other two in fixing the order of events mentioned by more than one evangelist, and this for the obvious reason that, being of the number of the Twelve, and actively concerned in the events they were recording, they would be more likely to be correct in their description of them. Where a choice had to be made between the first and fourth, he gave the preference to S. John's order, probably because that evangelist wrote later, and with a knowledge of what S. Matthew had already written. Tatian does not seem to have regarded the evangelists as infallible in regard to the chronological order of events, and has not hesitated in some cases to change their order for one which appeared to him more suitable, his own idea being to take the Passovers as the key to the chronology. Zahn[1] divides the Harmony into 100 sections, and suggests the following plan as Tatian's basis of arrangement :—

		Sections
I.	The Logos, incarnation and childhood,	1–7
II.	The first manifestations of Jesus,	8–12
III.	The beginning of His ministerial work,	13
IV.	Jesus in Galilee,	14–37
V.	Journey through Samaria,	38–40
VI.	Sojourn in Galilee,	41–51
VII.	At the feast of Tabernacles,	52
VIII.	Through (Peraea or) Galilee and back,	53–58
IX.	The feast of the Dedication of the Temple,	59–71
X.	The raising of Lazarus, retirement to Ephraem, return to Bethany,	72, 73
XI.	From the Triumphal Entry to the institution of the Lord's Supper,	74–89
XII.	Gethsemane, Trials, Crucifixion, Resurrection,	90–100

On the whole this seems a fair description of Tatian's design as shown in the Vatican and Borgian MSS.

[1] Pp. 257-260. For a comparison of Zahn's sections with the contents of the Arabic *Diatessaron*, cf. Appendix, Table I.

(3.) We now come to the important questions—What is the value of the *Diatessaron* as a Harmony? How does it bear comparison with modern Harmonies? and, Where it differs from them, are there any indications within it that Tatian was guided by traditional information, enabling him to decide with certainty points which have appeared doubtful in modern times?

To understand all the reasons for and against a particular order of harmonisation is the work of a lifetime, and those who have arrived at that knowledge are unable to agree as to the result; the present writer, therefore, does not presume to answer these questions definitely for the reader. His object is rather to give a short outline of the state of things which he has found in the *Diatessaron*, and thus enable the reader to form his own judgment. In doing this he will be greatly assisted by a reference to the columns attached to Table I., which show, opposite to the contents of the *Diatessaron*, the order in which they are placed by some modern harmonists.

Dr. Lightfoot[1] contrasts Tatian's work with that of Ammonius (who inserted continuously the whole of S. Matthew's Gospel in its own order, merely placing at the side the passages of other Gospels, and only those, which seemed to correspond with any part of it), and says that its principle was *amalgamation*, not *comparison*. Professor Hemphill,[2] who quotes this, says himself: "It was not a Harmony in the modern sense of the word, but a kind of patchwork Gospel." In our opinion this fact puts it far above the others; because it not only brings into juxtaposition the different accounts of the same transaction, but with great elaboration weaves them into one single narrative, containing, not only the main outline, but every little detail to be found in any one account.

We have to consider Tatian's treatment of any particular subject that is related in more than one Gospel, *e.g.* the parable of the Sower, from two points of view—(1) the *internal* harmonisation of the several accounts with each other; and (2) the *external* harmonisation of the result, or the place assigned to it in the general narrative. Now, in regard to internal harmonisation, the *Diatessaron* leaves little to be

---

[1] *Supernatural Religion*, p. 281.
[2] *Diatessaron of Tatian*, Introd. p. x., note; cf. also the same, p. xxx.

desired. It has been carried out in the fullest detail; and the greatest care has been taken not to omit the slightest comment of any one evangelist, unless it was substantially preserved in the words of another. Indeed, a few instances are pointed out in the notes, where Tatian's anxiety on this point has led him into undue repetition, by placing one after the other passages of different evangelists that vary but little from one another. It is only when we consider the internal arrangements of more extended passages, such as the denunciation of the scribes etc., the eschatological discourses, and the scenes before the Sanhedrin and Pilate, which involve the *external* harmonisation of smaller passages, that we observe any considerable departures from modern ideas. A footnote is appended at such places, calling attention to the point in question, and in some instances suggesting an explanation.

The subject of the external harmonisation of passages in the *Diatessaron* is a very wide and difficult one, but full of interest. There are cases where two evangelists record each an event which is not mentioned in the other; and it is impossible, from the setting in which each event is found, to determine with certainty the relative chronological order of the two events. This is especially the case where one of the two evangelists is S. John. With such instances it is not proposed now to deal; the reader will observe them for himself, and in the more remarkable cases his attention will be drawn to them. But the cases in which two passages occurring in the *same* Gospel in one order are found in the *Diatessaron* occupying the reverse order, deserve fuller attention. It is not always possible in making a Harmony to avoid reversing at times the order of some evangelist. It sometimes happens that a group of events is related by one evangelist in such a way as to imply distinctly that they occurred in a certain order; and the same events are related by another evangelist with about equal distinctness as occurring in a different order. Here, whatever a harmonist may do, he must depart from the order of, at least, one evangelist; and if in such cases Tatian has chosen to follow—perhaps in some instances because his narrative was that of an eye-witness—a different evangelist from the one preferred by modern harmonists, who are not always unanimous on such points, we should not on that account be justified in condemning the *Diatessaron* as merely a "patchwork Gospel." And even where there is not this direct conflict between two records of the same events, a variety of circumstances may occur to render it necessary to depart from the order of a particular Gospel when its contents are interwoven with those of other Gospels. Wherever it can be shown that modern harmonists have felt obliged to take this step, Tatian may be excused for having done so too.

By means of Table II., which takes the contents of the four Gospels in their order, and shows where they are to be found in the *Diatessaron*, if present there at all, the reader can easily ascertain what passages of each Gospel are displaced from their original order. Take, for example, the first case in the table: we find that out of S. Matt. i. to iv. 11, portions are to be found in chs. ii., iii., iv., and v. of the *Diatessaron*, but in the same relative order as in the Gospel; but as we proceed with S. Matthew we find that Tatian has put iv. 12–16 in his *sixth* chapter, whilst iv. 17–22 is in the *fifth*. Here, then, is the first reversal of this evangelist's order; and in searching for Tatian's motive in making it, we may look into verses 12–16, their parallels and the various settings in which these occur, for reasons why that passage should be put *later* in the combined narrative; or we may treat verses 17–22 in like manner, to find out why these should be put *earlier*; for otherwise it is uncertain which is really the displaced portion. This uncertainty becomes greater where several small displacements occur near one another. The effect in the above instance is to place the calling of His disciples and a part of the preaching of Christ before the imprisonment of S. John the Baptist. That Jesus did commence His ministry before that imprisonment is clear from the fourth Gospel; and when that Gospel had to be blended with the first, Tatian reconciled the two accounts by means of this change of order, and so gave greater consistency to the combined narrative.

By analysing the entire *Diatessaron* in this way, there appear to be twenty-one such displacements in the Gospel of S. Matthew and twenty in S. Mark; in S. Luke, chs. i. to ix. 50, there are eight, and in chs. xx. to xxiv. there are six; but in the intermediate section there are so many that it has been found impossible to decide which parts are displaced and which are not; in S. John there are ten. Of S. Matthew's twenty-one, six appear again as displacements of S. Mark; two of the first portion of S. Luke, and one of S. John; whilst eight are associated with the doubtful part of S. Luke. Of the twenty in S. Mark, besides the six like S. Matthew's, three correspond to displacements of the early part of S. Luke, four to the doubtful part, one to the end, and two to S. John, whilst one is probably an interpolation. In the first and last parts of S. Luke there are no displacements corresponding to S. John's, and those connected with the other Gospels have already been stated. In S. John's there are two corresponding to the doubtful part of S. Luke; other correspondences are already given.

From this statement a very few displacements shown by Table II. are omitted, because they only *appear* to be displacements *through wrong references* being attached to them in the Arabic.

Most of these displacements may be attributed to one or more of the following causes:—(1) Tatian preferred the order of the event as given by another evangelist; (2) in relating two events which occurred *simultaneously*, Tatian considered himself free to put either first, as they seemed best to fit with his narrative, since in changing the evangelist's order he was not chronologically wrong; (3) in the case of short comments of the evangelist himself, Tatian inserted them anywhere where they would fit in conveniently; (4) he permitted himself to make slight internal transpositions to improve the order of his narrative; (5) where two discourses of a similar nature occur in different Gospels, Tatian has sometimes blended them together, in spite of the fact that from their respective settings they appear to have been spoken at different dates or places; (6) in one or two instances Tatian has grouped together discourses on kindred subjects— or different aspects of the same subject—as though they had been spoken in immediate succession, which does not appear to have been the case; (7) having identified portions of two Gospels, he has inferred that the parts which respectively follow them must have also happened at the same time and place, and has interwoven them accordingly. Of these, (5) and

(6) seem the only ones open to grave objection; at the same time, they throw a light upon the purpose of Tatian in compiling this work, and the use which he intended should be made of it. His method in these respects implies that he intended the *Diatessaron* as a companion to the four Gospels, and not to supersede them. He intended to present to its readers the entire teaching of Christ once only; and so he gave the Lord's Prayer only once, although he well knew that our Lord gave it on two different occasions; for he was satisfied that they would know this from the distinct Gospels. In like manner he took many passages out of their setting in S. Luke, and interwove them with similar passages in the Sermon on the Mount. He also harmonised together the parable of the Marriage of the King's Son (Matt. xxii. 1-14), and the similar parable in Luke xiv. 16-24; but not the parables of the Talents and the Pounds, nor the two anointings of the Saviour, though these latter are combined in the *Codex Fuldensis*. In one instance Tatian does great violence to the Gospel narrative in order to present continuously our Lord's teaching on the subject of riches. He identifies[1] the parable of the Lost Sheep (Luke xv. 1-7) with the similar parable, Matt. xviii. 12-14; this necessitates his continuing with the rest of Luke xv., and xvi. to ver. 12; here he branches off to other things, and Jesus actually goes up to the feast of Tabernacles before the parable of Dives and Lazarus with some introductory verses is inserted,[2] following after the parable of the Rich Fool and the incident of the Rich Young Ruler, to the latter of which S. Luke's words (xvi. 14), "And the Pharisees also, who were covetous, heard all these things," are made to apply, instead of referring to the parable of the Unjust Steward. But this interruption of S. Luke's order enabled him to resume S. Matthew's narrative, to follow up the parable of the *Unjust* Servant by that of the *Unmerciful* Servant, continuing naturally with the subject of a Brother's Offences, and afterwards to contrast with Dives the rich employer of labour, who considered he had a right to do what he liked with his own. It must be borne in mind also that Tatian looked upon S. Matthew's Gospel as the more authoritative one, and there he found the parable of the Lost Sheep

---

[1] *Diat.* xxvi. 1.   [2] *Diat.* xxix. 12.

followed immediately by that of the Unmerciful Servant and remarks on a Brother's Offences; and these he would naturally wish to bring into the narrative as closely as possible after it. His position here furnishes a good example of the seventh cause of displacement above referred to. Having decided to treat the parable of the Lost Sheep as the same in S. Matthew and S. Luke, and spoken on the same occasion, Tatian found himself confronted with a series of utterances of Jesus stated by S. Matthew to have been spoken on that occasion, and in immediate connection with the parable, and also with a totally different series of discourses stated by S. Luke to have followed immediately upon the same parable; and the blending of the two series of discourses, thus regarded as spoken on the same occasion, involved him in such difficulties that he decided to displace the parable of Dives from its setting and place it with other remarks upon riches. Modern harmonists get over the difficulty *by assuming, because of the different discourses which follow it in the two Gospels,* that the parable of the Lost Sheep *must* have been spoken twice. The grave objection to the course pursued by Tatian in the present instance is that he has made Jesus go up to Jerusalem between the utterance of the parables of the Unjust Steward and Dives, which parables, in the only Gospel that contains them, are distinctly represented as being spoken to the same audience on the same occasion. This was not necessary as a result of cause (7), and can only be ascribed to a deliberate purpose to group together the teaching of the Saviour in regard to the rich; and this purpose may be held to excuse it, provided the work was only intended for the use of persons familiar with the separate Gospels.

A few peculiarities of external harmonisation call for separate notice. Tatian gives only one Cleansing of the Temple, identifying that mentioned by S. John immediately after the Marriage at Cana with that given by the Synoptists, and inserting it at the later period of Christ's ministry. The visit of Nicodemus, which follows it in S. John, Tatian removes with it. Modern harmonists are pretty generally agreed in recognising two Cleansings, though Tischendorf admits that it is a great question.[1] Whether the strong

[1] *Synopsis Evangelica*, Introductory note to § 22.

probability now afforded, that Justin believed in only one, may induce them to modify their opinion, remains to be seen. Certainly the visit of Nicodemus seems more natural[1] at the later period. The cleansing of one leper is put much later[2] than in any of the Gospels, perhaps as a continuation of the subject of Clean and Unclean things, begun in ch. xx.; whilst the visit of Jesus to the home of Martha and Mary is placed[3] much earlier than S. Luke has it, and apparently in Galilee. S. Luke's arrangement implies that it was in Galilee, and Greswell took that view; but Lightfoot, Farrar, and others conclude that it must have been at Bethany, and that S. Luke designedly related it out of its chronological order. The warning given by some Pharisees, "Herod seeketh to kill Thee," is inserted[4] most strangely between the Transfiguration and the cure of the boy demoniac, the introductory words of S. Luke, "The same day," being retained notwithstanding. Tatian treats the cure of *two* blind men, Matt. xx., as a mistaken account of the cure of blind Bartimaeus, Mark x., on *leaving* Jericho; and this again he identifies with the cure of a blind man on *entering* Jericho, Luke xviii. 35–43. The combined narrative he places[5] after Jesus has left the house of Zacchaeus, thus causing a displacement of S. Luke's order. Some minor displacements occur also in consequence of his putting the institution of the Lord's Supper after Judas had gone out. Some further noticeable displacements seem to arise from Tatian's mode of dealing with that remarkable portion of S. Luke's Gospel already referred to, viz. ix. 51 to xix. 48. This has been called the *crux* of commentators and harmonists. It begins with a statement that, "when the time was come that He should be received up, He steadfastly set His face to go to Jerusalem." But some thought it inconceivable that the whole of this passage could refer to so short and so late a portion of our Lord's ministry. The result of modern investigation, however, is to establish in the main that such is the case, but that the arrangements for leaving Galilee were of a protracted kind, and involved a final circuit of Galilee. Moreover, S. John represents Jesus as

---

[1] See note *in loco*. [2] *Diat.* xxii. 1–6.
[3] *Diat.* xiii. 31–35; cf. *Codex Fuldensis*, cap. 64.
[4] *Diat.* xxiv. 27–29; cf. *Codex*, cap. 93. [5] *Diat.* xxxi. 25–35.

making a prolonged stay at Jerusalem after His arrival from Galilee, and then retiring to Ephraem, from which place He made His final journey to Jerusalem. Of this last journey S. Luke makes no distinct mention, and it is thought that he has included some of the incidents of it with those of the journey from Galilee. So much being premised, we may now consider how this portion of the third Gospel has been treated by Tatian. He could not help observing, as others have done since, the fewness and vagueness of the notices of time, place, and continuity contained in this passage; he knew also that S. Luke was not an eye-witness of the events he recorded; and so he completely subordinated the order and arrangement of this part of the Gospel to those of S. Matthew and S. Mark. In a few instances he identified the actual occasion, as in the parable of the Lost Sheep already referred to; in by far the greater part, however, he was contented to amalgamate or interweave extracts from S. Luke wherever passages of a similar tenor occurred in the other Gospels, and to place them in the order so suggested. In a few instances, where such parallels could not be found, he used his own judgment in selecting a position for them to occupy. The following peculiar arrangements are worthy of notice in addition to those already mentioned. The rejection by a Samaritan village, ix. 51–56, is put[1] as Jesus is setting out *from Ephraem* for Jerusalem, apparently because "the days of His going up (or 'ascension') were fulfilled," ver. 51; and Tatian inferred that this must belong to the last visit. The question of the lawyer with the consequent parable of the Good Samaritan, x. 26–37, is identified with the question of a scribe, which in the other Synoptists follows upon Christ's answer to the Sadducees about marriage in the resurrection, and is placed[2] accordingly. The parable of the Pharisee and Publican, xviii. 9–14, is inserted[3] when Jesus is in the temple,—a position very appropriate to its contents, but at variance with S. Luke, who places it before the arrival at Jericho. The Triumphal Entry into Jerusalem, xix. 28–44, seems rightly assigned[4] to the last visit, that from Ephraem; whilst the Cleansing of the Temple, briefly mentioned after

[1] *Diat.* xxxviii. 42–47.   [2] *Diat.* xxxiv. 24–45.
[3] *Diat.* xxxii. 16–21.   [4] *Diat.* xxxix. 18–41.

the Triumphal Entry, verses 45, 46, is inserted from the fuller accounts of others immediately after the arrival from Galilee.[1] This, too, seems right; for Jesus would scarcely permit the traffic to go on there whilst He was teaching daily in the temple, and after He had commenced a definite Judaean ministry, which many think lasted a considerable time. Having decided upon this course, it is not surprising that Tatian should have introduced[2] the remarks about daily teaching, xix. 47, 48, in connection with the first visit to Jerusalem after leaving Galilee, the more so as the same evangelist has similar remarks later on, xxi. 37, 38, which Tatian applied[3] to the last visit. Considering the positions occupied in the several Gospels by the request of the sons of Zebedee, Tatian could not well have done otherwise than place it where he has,[4] before the arrival at Jericho on the journey from Galilee.

Taking a general review of the external harmonisation throughout the *Diatessaron*, there seems no reason to doubt that Tatian carefully arranged all the *events* and the *movements* of our Lord in what he believed to be their chronological order, but did not consider it necessary in all cases to record parables and other *discourses* in their strictly historical places, preferring in some instances to insert these where they would best serve to illustrate the narrative, or to bring out points of comparison or contrast in the teaching of Christ. In some instances, however, he has departed so widely from the conclusions that have resulted from modern researches, that it seems incredible that he can have been guided in so doing by any reliable oral tradition. And, indeed, the more closely we study his arrangements, the more evident it becomes that such was not the case; for where we are at first inclined, in the absence of any other apparent motive, to ask whether some singular displacement could have been due to such tradition, we are sure upon closer inspection to find out another explanation of the phenomenon, which we cannot doubt is the true one, because it agrees so well with Tatian's methods as observed elsewhere. It is worthy of notice, too, that even the traces of oral tradition found in Justin's writings

---

[1] *Diat.* xxxii. 1–11.
[2] *Diat.* xxxiv. 46, 47.
[3] *Diat.* xl. 24, 25.
[4] *Diat.* xxx. 46–xxxi. 5.

are absent from the *Diatessaron* in its present form. The story of the birth of Jesus in a cave, and that of the fire kindled in Jordan at His baptism, do not appear in it; nor are they proved to have had a place in the copy used by Ephraem.[1] It is, of course, possible that Tatian did insert them, and that they were removed from the Syriac copies at a very early date. However this may be, we may safely conclude that oral tradition did not influence Tatian in regard to the majority of his displacements, though it may, for instance, have induced him to insert only one Cleansing of the Temple; for there can be little doubt that we now have Tatian's *order* practically unchanged in its main outline. At the same time, it is much to be wished that a Syriac copy of an early date could be found; and the great revival of interest in Tatian's work may perhaps lead to such a discovery. The reader of this English version will notice occasional instances of undue repetition, where a statement from one Gospel has been immediately followed by a nearly identical statement from another, showing an anxiety that no part of the Gospel narrative should lose its full expression. It may be that in some cases this is due to insertions of a later date; but the plan adopted throughout has been inclusive, not exclusive; thus, for example, if our Lord's words on a particular occasion were differently reported in different Gospels, Tatian did not attempt a choice between them, but inserted all that Jesus was reported to have said. The freedom with which he removed passages from their setting, and brought them into connection with others, is somewhat startling to us; but all the early Fathers appear to have exercised much latitude in dealing with the New Testament writings; and, if we conclude that he had no intention to supplant the separate Gospels, but intended the *Diatessaron* to be used along with them, we remove the most serious objection that would arise therefrom. Indeed, there seems no reason to doubt that, as a rule, Tatian clearly grasped the situation; for, though many passages may be pointed out in which his arrangement is chronologically incorrect, a careful study of them tends to show that these misplacements are not

---

[1] Though he alludes in his own remarks (Moes. p. 43) to a light on the waters.

blunders, but deliberate deviations in accordance with a set purpose, and carried out in furtherance of a plan, which can be inferred from them, and, when inferred, becomes the key to much which would otherwise be unintelligible. An analysis of this book brings out more and more clearly the fact that its author was a man of a powerful intellect, who saw what was a real need in the Church of his day, and set himself with singular ability to supply that need, devoting to this purpose much time and care. The heretical views which he adopted in his later years, caused the outcome of his labour to be looked upon with suspicion, which, so far as we can judge, it does not appear to have deserved; but in spite of this, its intrinsic merit and the need of such a work made it a great success for centuries in its own country, and led to its use at a later period in a modified form in other countries and in other languages, so that even in this country our Anglo-Saxon forefathers derived their conceptions of Jesus and His life on earth to a large extent from their poetical version of it. It is no small privilege to be permitted to be the first to present to English readers a full and literal translation of this great work, which has been a subject of interest to Christians of every age since it was first written, around which so many controversies have revolved, which has been in its entirety so singularly recovered in our own day, which throws so much light upon the information possessed by Christians of the second century, and which, at the same time, possesses a national interest.

Westbury-on-Trym, *July* 1893.

Note.—Besides the tables already referred to, the reader will find in the Appendix tables showing—(1) the Miracles of Jesus; (2) the Parables; (3) the references to S. John the Baptist; and (4) the Movements of Jesus during His public ministry, as these occur in the *Diatessaron*, with references. There is also in Table IX. an Analysis of the passages, which occupy a different order in the Arabic from that which Zahn obtained from the Syriac Fathers.

INTRODUCTORY NOTE IN THE BORGIAN MS.

In the name of the one God, the Father, the Son, and the Holy Spirit, to whom be glory for ever.

With the assistance of the Most High God, we begin to transcribe the Holy Gospel and most beautiful garden, entitled *Diatessaron*, the interpretation of which expression is, That which is composed of four, and which Tatian, a Greek, compiled out of the four evangelists, Matthew the chosen, whose sign is M; Mark the selected, whose sign is R; Luke the lovable, whose sign is K̤; and John the beloved, whose sign is H.

The excellent *and* learned presbyter Abû-l-Faraj Abdullah Ibn-at-Ṯabib,[1] with whom God be pleased, translated it from the Syriac into the Arabic tongue.

The introduction led, saying,

  The Gospel of Jesus the Son of the living God.

---

[1] Ciasca observes that this name is given differently in the notice at the conclusion, and says the latter is the more correct form.

ENGLISH VERSION OF THE ARABIC DIATESSARON.

1 1   In the beginning was the Word, and the   Jn.[1]   1   1
    Word was with God, and the Word itself is[2]
  2 God. The same was in the beginning with   „   2
  3 God. All things were made by him; and   „   3
    without him not even one existing thing
  4 hath been made. In him was life; and the   „   4
  5 life is the light of men. And the light   „   5
    shineth in the darkness; and the darkness
    overcame[3] it not.
  6   There was in the days of Herod the king   Lu.   1   5
    a certain priest named Zacharias, of the
    family of Abijah: and his wife was of the
    daughters of Aaron, and her name was Eliza-
  7 beth. And they were both righteous before   „   6
    God, walking in all the commandments and
  8 ordinances of God blameless. And they had   „   7
    no child, because that Elizabeth was barren,
    and they both were advanced in age.
  9   Now while he executed the priest's office   „   8

---

[1] Throughout this margin the four Gospels are briefly referred to as Mt., Mk., Lu., and Jn. respectively.

[2] Ephraem has "was God," which was probably the original reading. The reader will do well not to assume that all slight departures from the wording of our Authorised Version are due to Tatian. Some arise from the idioms of the different languages into which the work has been translated, and some from the insertions which have been made in it from the Peschito. The principal Various Readings are tabulated in Appendix III. Such as are not mentioned there may be disregarded. A full translation of Ephraem's quotations is given in Appendix X. Proper names, except when they present some marked peculiarity, are given here as in the Revised Version.

[3] Lit. "took hold of."

before God in the order of his ministration,
1 10 according to the custom of the priest's office, Lu. 1 9
his lot was to burn incense, and he entered
11 into the temple of the Lord. And the whole „ 10
multitude of the people were praying with-
12 out at the hour of incense. And there „ 11
appeared unto Zacharias an angel of the
Lord, standing on the right side of the altar
13 of incense. When Zacharias saw him, he „ 12
14 was troubled, and fear fell upon him. But „ 13
the angel saith unto him, Fear not, Zacharias,
because thy supplication is heard, and thy
wife Elizabeth shall bear thee a son, and
15 thou shalt call his name John. And thou „ 14
shalt have joy and gladness; and many shall
16 rejoice at his birth. For he shall be great „ 15
in the sight of the Lord, and he shall drink
no wine nor strong drink; and he shall be
filled with the Holy Spirit while he is yet
17 in his mother's womb. And many of the „ 16
children of Israel shall he turn unto the
18 Lord their God. And he shall go before „ 17
him in the spirit and power of Elijah the
prophet, to turn the heart of the fathers to
the children, and the disobedient to the
knowledge of the just; to make ready for
19 the Lord a perfect people. But Zacharias „ 18
said unto the angel, Whereby shall I know
this? for I am an old man, and my wife
20 advanced in age. The angel answered and „ 19
said unto him, I am Gabriel, that stand in
the presence of God; and I was sent to
speak unto thee, and to announce this unto
21 thee *as good tidings*. From henceforth thou „ 20
shalt be silent and not able to speak, until
the day wherein this shall come to pass,
because thou believedst not this my word,
22 which shall be fulfilled in its season. But „ 21
the people were standing waiting for
Zacharias, and they marvelled because he

1 23 tarried in the sanctuary. And when Zacharias came out, he could not speak unto them: and they perceived that he had seen a vision in the sanctuary: and he was making signs unto them, and remained	Lu. **1** 22
24 dumb. And when the days of his ministration were fulfilled, he departed unto his house.	„ 23
25 And after these days Elizabeth his wife conceived; and she hid herself five months,	„ 24
26 and said, This hath the Lord done unto me in the days wherein he looked upon me, to take away my reproach among men.	„ 25
27 Now in the sixth month the angel Gabriel was sent from God into Galilee,[1] unto a city	„ 26
28 named Nazareth, to a virgin betrothed to a man whose name was Joseph, of the house of David; and the virgin's name was Mary.	„ 27
29 And the angel came in unto her, and said unto her, Hail, *thou that art* full of favour, our Lord is with thee, O *thou* blessed among	„ 28
30 women. And when she beheld him, she was troubled at his saying, and was con-	„ 29
31 sidering what this salutation might be. And the angel saith unto her, Fear not, Mary;	„ 30
32 for thou hast found favour with God. Thou shalt now conceive, and bring forth a son,	„ 31
33 and shalt call his name JESUS. He shall be great, and shall be called the Son of the Most High: and the Lord God shall give unto him the throne of his father David:	„ 32
34 and he shall reign over the house of Jacob for ever; and of his kingdom there shall be	„ 33
35 no end. Mary said unto the angel, How shall this be done unto me since no man	„ 34
36 hath known me? The angel answered and said unto her, The Holy Spirit shall come, and the power of the Most High shall descend upon thee: wherefore also that	„ 35

---

[1] The Borgian MS. omits "into Galilee." The Vatican MS. above ver. 27 inserts, "The 2nd chapter" (or division) "from the Gospel of Luke."

1 37	which shall be born of thee, shall be holy, and shall be called the Son of God. And behold, Elizabeth thy kinswoman, she also hath conceived a son in her old age: and this is the sixth month with her that is	Lu.	1 36
38	called barren. For nothing shall be difficult	„	37
39	to God. Mary said, Behold, I am the handmaid of the Lord; be it done unto me according to thy word. And the angel departed from her.	„	38
40	Then Mary arose in those days, and went into the hill country with haste, unto a city	„	39
41	of Judah; and entered into the house of	„	40
42	Zacharias, and saluted Elizabeth. And when Elizabeth heard the salutation of Mary, the babe rejoiced in her womb; and Elizabeth was filled with the Holy Spirit;	„	41
43	and she cried out with a loud voice, and said unto Mary, Blessed *art* thou among women, and blessed *is* the fruit that is in	„	42
44	thy womb. Whence is this to me, that the mother of my Lord cometh unto me?	„	43
45	When the voice of thy salutation came to mine ears, the babe leaped in my womb in	„	44
46	great joy. And blessed *is* she that believed; for that shall be performed, which was spoken	„	45
47	from the Lord. And Mary saith: My soul doth magnify the Lord,	„	46
48	And my spirit hath rejoiced in God my Saviour,	„	47
49	Who hath looked upon the low estate of his handmaiden: Behold, from henceforth all generations shall call me blessed.	„	48
50	For he that is mighty hath done to me great things; And holy is his name;	„	49
51	And his mercy from a generation to generations Embraceth them that fear him.	„	50

1 52	He hath wrought victory by his arm, And he hath scattered the proud in their opinions.	Lu.	1 51
53	He hath put down the haughty from the thrones, And hath exalted the humble.	,,	52
54	The hungry he hath filled with good things; And the rich he hath left without anything.	,,	53
55	He hath holpen Israel his servant, And remembered his mercy	,,	54
56	(As he spake unto our fathers) Unto Abraham and unto his seed for ever.	,,	55
57	And Mary abode with Elizabeth about three months, and returned unto her house.	,,	56
58	Now Elizabeth's time of bringing forth was *come*; and she brought forth a son.	,,	57
59	And her neighbours and kinsfolk heard that God had multiplied his mercy towards her;	,,	58
60	and they rejoiced with her. And on the eighth day they came to circumcise the child; and they called him Zacharias, after the	,,	59
61	name of his father. And his mother answered and said unto them, Not so; but	,,	60
62	he shall be called John. And they said unto her, There is no one among thy kindred	,,	61
63	that is called by this name. And they made signs to his father, How do you wish to call	,,	62
64	him? And he asked for a writing tablet, and wrote, saying, His name is John. And	,,	63
65	they all marvelled. And his mouth was opened immediately, and his tongue *loosed*,	,,	64
66	and he spake, and praised God. And fear fell on all their neighbours: and this was noised abroad over all the hill country of	,,	65
67	Judaea. And all that heard *it*, thought in their heart saying, What shall this child be? For the hand of the Lord was with him.	,,	66
68	And his father Zacharias was filled with the Holy Spirit, and prophesied, and said,	,,	67

1	69	Blessed *be* the Lord, the God of Israel, Who hath regarded his people, and wrought salvation for them,	Lu.	1 68
	70	And hath raised up a horn of salvation for us In the house of his servant David,	,,	69
	71	As he spake from eternity by the mouth of his holy prophets,	,,	70
	72	That he would save us from our enemies, And from the hand of all that hate us.	,,	71
	73	And he showed mercy towards our fathers, And remembered his holy covenant,	,,	72
	74	And the oath which he sware unto Abraham our father,	,,	73
	75	That he would grant unto us salvation from the hand of our enemies That we may serve before him without fear	,,	74
	76	In justice and righteousness all our days.	,,	75
	77	And thou, child, shalt be called the prophet of the Most High; Thou shalt go before the face of the Lord to make ready his way,	,,	76
	78	To give knowledge of life unto his people Unto the remission of their sins	,,	77
	79	Through the tender mercy of our God, Whereby he visits[1] us, rising from on high	,,	78
	80	To shine upon them that sit in darkness, and under the shadow of death,	,,	79
		And to establish our feet in the way of peace.	,,	80
	81	And the child grew, and waxed strong in spirit, and was waiting in the desert till the day of his showing unto the children of Israel.		
2	1	Now the birth of Jesus Christ was on this wise: When his mother had been betrothed to Joseph, before they came together	Mt.	1 18

[1] Or, "shall visit."

she was found with child of the Holy Spirit.

2 2 And Joseph her husband was a righteous man, and unwilling to make her a public example, and thought to put her away 3 privily. But while he was thinking of this, an angel of the Lord appeared unto him in a dream, saying, Joseph, son of David, fear not to take unto thee Mary thy wife: for that which is begotten in her is of 4 the Holy Spirit. She shall bring forth a son; and thou shalt call his name JESUS; for he shall save his people from their sins. 5 Now all this is come to pass, that it might be fulfilled which was spoken by the Lord through the prophet,
6   Behold, the virgin shall conceive, and shall bring forth a son,
And they shall call his name Emmanuel; which is, being interpreted, Our God is 7 with us. And when Joseph arose from his sleep, he did as the angel of the Lord commanded him, and took unto him his wife; 8 and knew her not till she brought forth her firstborn son.
9   Now in those days there went out a decree from Caesar Augustus, that all the people of his dominion should be enrolled. 10 This was the first enrolment made in the 11 governorship of Quirinius in Syria. And all were going into their own city to be 12 enrolled. And Joseph also went up from Nazareth, a city of Galilee, into Judaea, to the city of David, which is called Bethlehem, because he was of the house and family of 13 David, with Mary his betrothed, who was great with child, that he might be enrolled 14 there. And while they were there, the days were fulfilled that she should bring 15 forth. And she brought forth her firstborn son; and she wrapped him in swaddling

Mt.	1	19
„		20
„		21
„		22
„		23
„		24
„		25^a
Lu.	2	1
„		2
„		3
„		4
„		5
„		6
„		7

clothes, and laid him in a manger, because there was no room for them, where they were staying.

2 16 And there were shepherds staying in that country, who were guarding their flock in Lu. 2 8
17 the watch of the night. And behold, an „ 9 angel of God came near unto them; and the glory of the Lord shone round about them; and they were afraid with a great
18 fear. And the angel said unto them, Be „ 10 not afraid; for I bring you as good tidings a great joy that shall be to the whole world:
19 there is born to you this day in the city of „ 11 David a Saviour, which is the Lord the
20 Messiah. And this *is* the sign unto you: „ 12 Ye shall find a babe wrapped in swaddling
21 clothes, and laid in a manger. And suddenly „ 13 there appeared with the angels an abundant heavenly host praising God, and saying,
22 Glory to God in the highest, „ 14
And on earth peace, and good hope to men.
23 And when the angels went away from them „ 15 into heaven, the shepherds spake one to another, saying, Let us go to Bethlehem, and see this saying that is come to pass,
24 even as the Lord hath showed us. And „ 16 they came with haste and found Mary and Joseph, and the babe laid in the manger.
25 And when they had seen it, they related the „ 17 saying which had been spoken to them about
26 the child. And all that heard it wondered „ 18 at the description, which the shepherds had
27 described to them. But Mary was keeping „ 19 all these sayings, and comparing them in
28 her heart. And those shepherds returned, „ 20 glorifying and praising God for all the things that they had seen and heard, even as it was described unto them.
29 And after eight days were fulfilled, that „ 21

the child should be circumcised, his name was called JESUS; and this is what he was called by the angel, before he was conceived in the womb.

2 30 And when the days of their purification according to the law of Moses were fulfilled, they brought him to Jerusalem to present   Lu. 2 22

31 him before the Lord, as it is written in the law of the Lord, Every male that openeth the   „ 23

32 womb shall be called holy to the Lord, and to offer a sacrifice according to that which is said in the law of the Lord, A pair of turtle   „ 24

33 doves, or two young pigeons. And there was a man in Jerusalem, whose name was Simeon; and this man was righteous, devout, and looking for the consolation of Israel: and the Holy Spirit was upon him.   „ 25

34 And it had been said unto him by the Holy Spirit, that he was not going to see death, until he set his eyes upon the Lord's   „ 26

35 Christ. And he came in the Spirit into the temple: and when his parents brought in the child Jesus, that they might offer a sacrifice for him, as it is written in the law,   „ 27

36 he took him up into his arms, and praised God, and said,   „ 28

37   Now wilt thou loose the bonds of thy servant, O Lord,
    According to thy word, in peace.   „ 29

38   For already mine eyes have witnessed thy mercy,   „ 30

39   Which thou hast prepared on account of the whole world,   „ 31

40   A light for the unveiling of the Gentiles,
    And a glory for thy people Israel.   „ 32

41 And Joseph and his mother were marvelling at these things which were spoken concerning him;   „ 33

42 and Simeon blessed them, and said unto Mary his mother, Behold he is set for the falling and for the rising again of many   „ 34

2 43	in Israel; and for a sign of contradiction; and a sword shall pierce through thine own soul, that the thoughts of many hearts may	Lu. 2 35
44	be revealed. And Anna, a prophetess, the daughter of Phanuel, of the tribe of Asher, she also was advanced in age, and had lived with her husband for seven years from her	,, 36
45	virginity; and she remained a widow about fourscore and four years, and departed not from the temple worshipping with fastings and	,, 37
46	supplications night and day. And she also stood up at that hour, and gave thanks unto the Lord, and spake of him to all that were looking for the deliverance of Jerusalem.	,, 38
47	And when they had accomplished all things according to what is in the law of the Lord, they returned into Galilee, to their own city Nazareth.	,, 39
3 1	After these things wise men[1] from the	Mt. 2 1ᵇ
2	east came to Jerusalem, saying, Where is the king of the Jews, who has been born? We have seen his star in the east, and are come	,, 2
3	to worship him. And when Herod the king heard it, he was troubled, and all Jerusalem	,, 3
4	with him. And gathering together all the chief priests and scribes of the people, he inquired of them, where the Messiah should	,, 4
5	be born. And they said, In Bethlehem of Judah: thus it is written in the prophet,	,, 5
6	And thou, Bethlehem of Judah, Art in no wise least among the kings of Judah; For out of thee shall come forth a king, And he shall rule my people Israel.	,, 6
7	Then Herod, when he had privily called the wise men, inquired of them the time	,, 7

---

[1] Arabic, "al majûs." By removing the opening words of S. Matthew, "Now when Jesus was born in Bethlehem of Judaea, in the days of Herod the king," and substituting more vaguely, "After these things," Tatian avoids the difficulty felt by harmonists in assigning a place to Luke ii. 39.

at which the star appeared unto them.
3 8 And he sent them to Bethlehem, and said Mt. 2 8
unto them, Go, and inquire carefully concerning the child; and when ye have found him, come and bring me word, that I also
9 may come and worship him. And when   „   9
they had heard the king they went their way; and lo, the star, which they had seen in the east, went before them, till it came and stood over the place, where the child
10 was. And when they saw the star, they   „   10
11 rejoiced with exceeding great joy. And   „   11
they came into the house, and saw the child with Mary his mother; and they fell down and worshipped him; and opening their cases, they offered unto him offerings, gold,
12 myrrh, and frankincense. And they saw in   „   12
sleep that they should not return to Herod; and they departed by another way to go into their own country.
13 And when they had departed, behold, an   „   13
angel of the Lord appeared to Joseph in a dream, and said unto him, Arise, and take the child and his mother, and flee into Egypt, and be thou there until I tell thee: for Herod sets about to seek the child to
14 destroy him. And Joseph arose, and took   „   14
the child and his mother by night, and fled
15 into Egypt, and remained there until the   „   15
death of Herod: that it might be fulfilled, which was spoken by the Lord through the prophet, saying, Out of Egypt did I call my
16 son. Then Herod, when he saw that he   „   16
was mocked by the wise men, was exceeding wroth, and sent forth, and slew all the male children that were in Bethlehem, and in all the borders thereof, from two years old and under, according to the time which he had carefully inquired of the
17 wise men. Then was fulfilled that which   „   17

was spoken through Jeremiah the prophet, saying,

3 18	A voice was heard in Ramah, Weeping and great mourning: Rachel weepeth for her children, And is unwilling to be consoled for the loss of them.	Mt.	2 18
19	But when king Herod was dead, the angel of the Lord appeared in a dream to Joseph	,,	19
20	in Egypt, and said unto him, Arise and take the child and his mother, and go into the land of Israel: for they are dead that sought	,,	20
21	the child's life. Joseph arose, and took the child and his mother, and came into the land	,,	21
22	of Israel. But when he heard that Archelaus was become king in Judaea instead of his father Herod, he was afraid to go thither; but he saw in a dream that he should go	,,	22
23	into the land of Galilee, and that he should dwell in a city that is called Nazareth: that it might be fulfilled which was spoken through the prophet, He shall be called a Nazarene.	,,	23
24	And the child grew, and waxed strong in spirit, filled with wisdom: and the grace of God was upon him.	Lu.	2 40
25	And his parents[1] went every year to	,,	41
26	Jerusalem at the feast of the passover. And when he was twelve years old, they went up	,,	42
27	after their custom to the feast; and when the days were fulfilled, they returned; but the boy Jesus tarried behind in Jerusalem; and Joseph and his mother knew it not,	,,	43
28	supposing him to be with the children of their company. And when they had made a day's journey, they sought for him among	,,	44
29	their kinsfolk and acquaintance: and when they found him not, they returned to Jeru-	,,	45
30	salem, seeking for him again. And after	,,	46

[1] Arabic, "people."

	three days they found him in the temple, sitting in the midst of the doctors, hearing			
3 31	them, and asking them questions: and all that heard him were amazed at his wisdom	Lu.	2	47
32	and sayings. And when they saw him, they were astonished: and his mother said unto him, My son, why hast thou thus dealt with us? Behold, I and thy father were seeking	„		48
33	thee with great anxiety. And he saith unto them, How is it that ye sought me? did ye not know that I must be in my Father's	„		49
34	house? And they understood not the say-	„		50
35	ing, which he spake unto them. And he went down with them, and came to Nazareth; and he was subject unto them: and his mother kept all *these* sayings in her heart.	„		51
36	And Jesus advanced in stature and wisdom, and in favour with God and men.	„		52
37	Now in the fifteenth year of the reign of Tiberius Caesar, Pontius Pilate being governor of Judaea, and Herod being tetrarch of Galilee, and his brother Philip tetrarch of the region of Ituraea and Trachonitis, and Lysanias	„	3	1
38	tetrarch of Abilene, under the high priests Annas and Caiaphas, the word of God went forth unto John, the son of Zacharias, in the	„		2
39	wilderness. And he came into all the region round about Jordan, preaching the baptism	„		3
40	of repentance with remission of sins; and he	Mt.	3	1[b]
41	preached in the wilderness of Judaea, and said, Repent ye, the kingdom of the heavens	„		2
42	is at hand. This is he that was spoken of through Isaiah the prophet, The[1] voice which crieth in the wilderness,	„		3[a]
43	Make ye ready the way of the Lord, And establish in the plain a way for our God.	Lu.	3	4[b]
44	All the valleys shall be filled;	„		5

[1] Omitting Mark i. 2; cf. xiii. 47.

And every mountain and hill shall be
   brought low;
And the crooked shall become straight;
And the difficult place easy;
3 45 And all flesh shall see the salvation[1] of   Lu. 3 6
God.
46 The same came for a witness, that he might   Jn. 1 7
bear witness of the light, that all might
47 believe through him. He was not the light,   „   8
but *came* that he might bear witness of the
48 light, which is the true light, lighting every   „   9
49 man, coming into the world. He was in the   „   10
world, and the world was made through him,
50 and the world knew him not. He came unto   „   11
51 his own, and his own received him not. But   „   12
as many as received him, to them gave he
the power to become children of God, *even* to
52 them that believe on his name: which were   „   13
born, not of blood, nor of the will of the
flesh, nor of the will of man, but of God.
53 And the Word became flesh, and dwelt   „   14
among us (and we saw his glory, as it were
the glory of the only one from the Father),
54 full of grace and truth. John bare witness   „   15
of him, and preached, saying, This is he of
whom I said, He that is about to come after
me is preferred before me: for he was before
55 me. And of his fulness we all received, grace   „   16
56 for grace. For the law was given through   „   17
Moses; grace and truth came through Jesus
4 1 Christ. No man hath seen God at any   „   18
time; the only one of God, who is in the
bosom of the Father, he hath declared *him*.
2 And this is the witness of John, when the   „   19
Jews sent unto him from Jerusalem priests
and Levites to ask him, Who art thou?
3 And he confessed, and denied not; and he   „   20
acknowledged that he was not the Messiah.
4 And again they asked him, What then? Art   „   21

[1] Or, "life."

4	5	thou Elijah? And he said, I am not. Art thou a prophet? He answered, No. They said unto him, Who art thou? that we may give an answer to them that sent us. What	Jn. 1 22
	6	sayest thou of thyself? He saith, I am the voice of one crying in the wilderness, Set in order the way of the Lord, as said Isaiah	„ 23
	7	the prophet. And they that had been sent	„ 24
	8	were of the Pharisees.¹ And they asked him, and said unto him, Why then baptizest thou, since thou art not the Messiah, nor	„ 25
	9	Elijah, nor a prophet? John answered and said unto them, I baptize in ² water: in the midst of you standeth one whom ye know	„ 26
	10	not. This is he, of whom I said, that he cometh after me, and he was before me, of whom I am not worthy to unloose the latchet	„ 27
	11	of his shoes. These things were done in Bethany beyond Jordan, where John was baptizing.	„ 28
	12	Moreover John had his raiment of camel's hair, and a leathern girdle;³ and his food	Mt. 3 4
	13	was locusts and wild honey. Then went out unto him the people of Jerusalem, and all Judaea, and all the region round about Jordan;	„ 5
	14	and they were baptized by him in the river	„ 6
	15	Jordan, confessing their sins. But when he saw many of the Pharisees and Sadducees⁴ coming to be baptized, he said unto them, Ye offspring of vipers, who warned⁵ you to	„ 7
	16	flee from the wrath to come? Bring forth	„ 8
	17	therefore fruits worthy of repentance: and do not think, and say within yourselves, We have Abraham as our father; for I say unto you, that God is able of these stones to	„ 9
	18	raise up children unto Abraham. Behold, the axe is laid unto the root of the tree:	„ 10

---

¹ Arabic, "almu 'tazila."   ² Or, "with."
³ Omitting "about his loins."   ⁴ Arabic, "alzanâdika.'
⁵ Lit. "guided."

	every tree therefore that bringeth not forth good fruit shall be taken away, and cast into	
4 19	the fire. And the multitudes asked him,	Lu. 3 10
20	saying, What shall we do? He answered, and said unto them, He that hath two coats, let him give to him that hath none; and he	„ 11
21	that hath food, let him do likewise. And there came also publicans to be baptized, and they said unto him, Master, what shall	„ 12
22	we do? He saith unto them, Ask nothing more than that which you are commanded	„ 13
23	to ask. And soldiers asked him, saying, What shall we also do? He saith unto them, Do violence to no man, neither act unjustly towards him; and be content with your wages.	„ 14
24	And as the people were considering, and all men were reasoning in their hearts concerning John, whether haply he were the	„ 15
25	Christ; John answered, and said unto them, I baptize you with water; there will come after me he that is mightier than I, of whom I am not worthy to unloose the latchets of his shoes: he shall baptize you	„ 16
26	in the Holy Spirit and in fire: who, grasping a fan in his hand to cleanse his threshing floor, will gather the wheat into his garners; but the chaff he will burn up with unquenchable fire.	„ 17
27	And other things he taught, and preached good tidings unto the people.	„ 18
28	Then cometh Jesus from Galilee to the Jordan unto John, to be baptized of him.	Mt. 3 13
29	And Jesus was about thirty years of age, and was supposed to be the son of Joseph.	Lu. 3 23ª
30	Now John saw Jesus coming unto him, and saith, This is the Lamb of God, which taketh	Jn. 1 29
31	away the sin of the world. This is he of whom I said, After me shall come a man, which is preferred before me, for he is	„ 30

4 32 before me. And I knew him not; but that	Jn.	1 31
he may be made manifest to Israel, for this		
33 cause am I come baptizing in¹ water. Now	Mt.	3 14
John was forbidding him, saying, I have		
need to be baptized of thee, and comest		
34 thou to me? Jesus answered him, and said,	„	15
Suffer *it* now: thus it becometh us to fulfil		
all righteousness. Then he suffered him.		
35 And when all the people were baptized,	Lu.	3 21ᵃ
36 Jesus also was baptized;² and he went up	Mt.	3 16ᵇ
straightway from the water: and the heaven		
37 was opened unto him. And the Holy Spirit	Lu.	3 22ᵃ
descended upon him in the form of a dove's		
38 body: and lo, a voice from heaven, saying,	Mt.	3 17
This is my beloved Son, in whom I am well		
39 pleased. And John bare witness, saying,	Jn.	1 32
Furthermore I saw the Spirit descending as		
a dove out of heaven; and it abode upon		
40 him. And I knew him not; but he that	„	33
sent me to baptize in³ water, he said unto		
me, Upon whomsoever thou shalt see the		
Spirit descending and abiding, this is he		
41 that baptizeth in⁴ the Holy Spirit. And I	„	34
have seen, and have borne witness, that this		
is the Son of God.		
42 And Jesus, full of the Holy Spirit, re-	Lu.	4 1ᵃ
43 turned from the Jordan, and straightway	Mk.	1 12
the Spirit drove⁵ him forth into the wilder-		
ness, that he might be tempted of Satan;	„	13ᵇ
44 and he was with the wild beasts; and he	Mt.	4 2ᵃ
fasted forty days and forty nights;⁶ and	Lu.	4 2ᵇ
tasted nothing in those days: and he after-	Mt.	4 2ᵇ
45 ward hungered. And the tempter came,	„	3
and said unto him, If thou art the Son of		
God, command that these stones become bread.		
46 He answered and said, It is written, Man	„	4

¹ Or, "with."   ² Omitting "and praying."   ³ Or, "with."
⁴ Or, "with."   ⁵ Or, "led."
⁶ Both Ephraem and the Curetonian Syriac omit "and forty nights," which therefore may not have been originally in the *Diatessaron*.

	liveth not by bread alone, but by every word that proceedeth out of the mouth of God.		
4 47	Then Satan brought him into the holy city, and set him on the pinnacle of the temple,	Mt.	4 5
48	and said unto him, If thou art the Son of God, cast thyself down; for it is written,	„	6
	He giveth his angels charge concerning thee;[1]		
	And in their arms they shall receive thee up,		
	Lest haply thou dash thy foot against a stone.		
49	Jesus saith unto him, Again it is written, Thou shalt not tempt the Lord thy God.	„	7
50	And the devil took him up into a high mountain, and showed him all the kingdoms of the world and the glory of them in a	Lu.[2]	4 5
51	moment of time. And the devil saith unto him, To thee will I give all this authority, and the glory of it, which have been delivered unto me, that I may give them	„	6
52	to whomsoever I will. If therefore thou wilt worship before me, all shall be thine.	„	7
5 1	Jesus answered and said unto him, Get thee hence, Satan: for it is written, Thou shalt worship the Lord thy God, and him only	Mt.	4 10
2	shalt thou serve. And when the devil had completed all his temptation, he departed	Lu.	4 13
3	from him until the season; and behold, angels came and ministered unto him.	Mt.	4 11[b]
4	On the next day John was standing, and	Jn.	1 35
5	two of his disciples; and he looked upon Jesus, as he walked, and said, Behold the	„	36
6	Lamb of God! And his two disciples heard him speaking; and they followed Jesus.	„	37
7	And Jesus turned, and saw them following, and said unto them, What seek ye? They said unto him, Master,[3] where dwellest thou?	„	38

[1] Omitting Luke iv. 10, "to keep thee." [2] Or, Matt. iv. 8.
[3] Arabic, "Our great one."

5 8 He said unto them, Come, and see. And they came, and saw the place of his abode; and they remained with him that day: and	Jn.	1 39
9 it was about the tenth hour. One of the two, that had heard from John, and had followed Jesus, was Andrew, Simon's brother.	,,	40
10 He first saw his own brother Simon, and said	,,	41
11 unto him, We have found the Messiah.¹ And he brought him unto Jesus. And Jesus looked upon him, and said, Thou art Simon, the son of Jonah: thou shalt be called The rock.	,,	42
12 On the morrow Jesus wished to go forth into Galilee; and he found Philip, and said	,,	43
13 unto him, Follow me. Now Philip was from Bethsaida, the city of Andrew and Simon.	,,	44
14 And Philip found Nathanael, and said unto him, We have found him, of whom Moses in the law, and the prophets, did write, to be Jesus, the son of Joseph, from Nazareth.	,,	45
15 Nathanael said unto him, Can any good thing be found from Nazareth? Philip said	,,	46
16 unto him, Come, and see. And Jesus saw Nathanael coming to him, and said of him, This is indeed a son of Israel, in whom is no	,,	47
17 guile! Nathanael said unto him, Whence knowest thou me? Jesus said unto him, Before Philip called thee, when thou wast	,,	48
18 under the fig-tree, I saw thee. Nathanael answered, and saith unto him, Master, thou art the Son of God; thou art king of Israel.	,,	49
19 Jesus said unto him, Because I said unto thee, I saw thee under the fig-tree, thou believedst: thou shalt see what is greater	,,	50
20 than this. And he said unto him, Verily, verily, I say unto you, Henceforth ye shall see the heavens opened, and the angels of God ascending and descending upon the Son of man.²	,,	51

[1] The clause interpreting "Messiah" is absent.
[2] Lit. "flesh." After commenting on the call of Nathanael Ephraem has

5 21	And Jesus returned in the power of the Spirit into Galilee.	Lu.	4 14ᵃ
22	And the third day there was a feast in Cana,¹ a city of Galilee; and the mother of	Jn.	2 1
23	Jesus was there: and Jesus also was bidden,	,,	2
24	and his disciples, to the feast. And when the wine failed, his mother said unto Jesus,	,,	3
25	They have no wine. And Jesus said unto her, Woman, what have I to do with thee?	,,	4
26	hath not my hour come? But his mother said unto the servants, Whatsoever he saith	,,	5
27	unto you, do it. There were six waterpots of stone set there for the purification of the Jews, containing two or three firkins apiece.	,,	6
28	And Jesus said unto them, Fill the waterpots with water. And they filled them up	,,	7
29	to the brim. He said unto them, Draw out now, and bear unto the ruler of the feast.	,,	8
30	And they did *so*. And when the ruler of the feast tasted the water, which was become wine, and knew not whence it was (but the servants knew, because they had drawn the water), the ruler of the feast	,,	9
31	called the bridegroom, and said unto him, Every man setteth on first the good wine; and when *men* have drunk freely,² he brings that which is worse: but thou hast kept	,,	10
32	the good wine until now. This was the first sign, *namely, that* which Jesus did in Cana of Galilee, and manifested his glory; and	,,	11
33	his disciples believed on him. And his fame	Lu.³	4 14ᵇ

a heading, "*Ordo et solemnitas Apostolorum Domini*," followed by remarks upon the class of men chosen for the twelve disciples. Dr. Wace thought this an introduction to the calling of disciples; see later, ver. 44 *et seq*. But is it not rather retrospective, dealing with the call of the first four just related? This heading is only found in one of the two Armenian versions, and there it is in red ink, as if it were a quotation from the *Diatessaron*, which may originally have been divided into sections suitable for instruction. Cf. p. 13.

¹ Arabic, "Qatîna." The *Codex Fuldensis* puts this "beginning of miracles" after the miraculous draught of fishes, Luke v. 1–11!

² Lit. "at the time of drunkenness."   ³ Cf. vii. 8.

5	34	was published in all the neighbouring region. And he taught in their synagogues, and was glorified by all men.	Lu.	4 15
	35	And he came to Nazareth, where he had been brought up: and he entered, according to his custom, into the synagogue on the	„	16
	36	sabbath day, and stood up to read. And there was delivered unto him the book of the prophet Isaiah. And Jesus opened the book, and found the place where it was written,	„	17
	37	The Spirit of the Lord is upon me, Because he anointed me to preach good tidings unto the poor; And sent me to heal the bruised in heart; To[1] proclaim forgiveness to the wicked[2] and sight to the blind; To bring the broken into forgiveness,	„	18
	38	And to proclaim the year acceptable to the Lord.	„	19
	39	And he closed the book and gave it back to the attendant; and went away, and sat down: and the eyes of all, that were standing in the synagogue, were turning upon him.	„	20
	40	And he began to say unto them, To-day hath this scripture been fulfilled, which ye	„	21
	41	have heard with your ears. And all bare him witness, and wondered at the words of grace, which proceeded out of his mouth.	„[3]	22ᵃ
	42	From that time began Jesus to preach the gospel of the kingdom of God, and to say,	Mt.	4 17ᵃ
	43	Repent ye, and believe in the gospel. The time is fulfilled,[5] and the kingdom of the heavens is at hand.	Mk.[4]	1 15

---

[1] The Vulgate and Ciasca's Latin commence Luke iv. 19 here.

[2] Mr. Rendel Harris thinks the Arabic translator misread the Syriac word for "captives."

[3] For the continuation of this part of S. Luke see xvii. 42, and note thereon.

[4] The internal order of this verse is altered.

[5] Or, "has arrived."

5 44 And walking by the sea of Galilee, he saw two brethren, Simon, who is called Cephas, and Andrew his brother, casting their nets	Mt.	4 18
45 into the sea; for they were fishers. And Jesus saith unto them, Follow me, and I will	„	19
46 make you fishers of men. And they immediately left the nets there, and followed	„	20
47 him. And going on from thence he saw other two brethren, James the son of Zebedee, and John his brother, in the boat with Zebedee their father, mending their nets;	„	21
48 and Jesus called them. And they straightway left the boat and their father Zebedee, and followed him.	„	22
49 And when the multitudes were come together unto him, to hear the word of God, and he was standing by the lake of Gen-	Lu.	5 1
50 nesaret, he saw two boats standing by the lake: but the fishermen, who had come up	„	2
51 therefrom, were washing their nets. And one of them was Simon Cephas's; and into it Jesus went up, and sat down in it, and commanded them to put out a little from the land into the water. And sitting down he taught the multitudes out of the boat.	„	3
52 And when he ceased to speak, he said unto Simon, Put out into the deep, and let out[1]	„	4
53 your nets for a draught. Simon answered, and said unto him, Master, we toiled all night, and took nothing: but at thy word	„	5
54 I will let out[1] the nets. And when they had done this, they inclosed an abundant multitude of fishes; for their net was nigh	„	6
55 to be broken; and they beckoned unto their partners that were in the other boat, that they should come and help them. And when they were come, they filled both the	„	7
6 1 boats, so that they were almost sunk. But when Simon Cephas saw it, he fell down at	„	8

[1] Or "cast."

Jesus' feet, and said unto him, Lord, I
beseech of thee, that thou depart from me,
6 2 for I am a sinful man. For amazement¹ Lu. 5 9
had taken possession of him, and all that
were with him, at the draught of the fishes,
3 which they had taken; so also it had seized „ 10
James and John, the sons of Zebedee, which
were Simon's partners. And Jesus saith
unto Simon, Fear not; from henceforth thou
4 shalt be catching men unto life. And when „ 11
they had brought their boats to land, they
left all, and followed him.
5 After these things came Jesus and his Jn. 3 22
disciples into the land of Judah; and there
he went about with them, and baptized.
6 John also was baptizing in Aennon near to „ 23
Salim, because there was much water there:
and they were coming, and were being
7 baptized. For John had not yet come into „ 24
8 prison. Now there arose a questioning „ 25
between a disciple of John and a Jew about
9 purification. And they came unto John, „ 26
and said unto him, Master, he that was
with thee beyond Jordan, to whom thou
barest witness, behold, he also baptizeth,
10 and many come to him. John answered „ 27
and said unto them, A man can receive
nothing of himself, except it have been
11 given him from heaven. Ye yourselves bear „ 28
me witness, that I said, I am not the
12 Messiah, but one sent² before him. He „ 29
that hath the bride is the bridegroom: and
the friend of the bridegroom is he, which
standeth and heareth him attentively, and
rejoiceth with great joy at the bridegroom's

---

¹ Tatian seems right in putting this incident before Luke iv. 38, 39, as S. Peter would scarcely have felt such "amazement," if he had previously witnessed the miraculous cure of his own mother-in-law. S. Matthew put the latter after the Sermon on the Mount, which position Tatian considered too late.

² Lit. "an apostle."

voice: behold, now my joy is already fulfilled.

6 13 He must increase, but I must decrease.   Jn.   3 30

14   He that cometh from above is above all: „   31
he that is from the earth is from the earth,
and from the earth he speaketh: he that
hath come down from heaven is above all.

15 And what he hath seen and heard, of this he   „   32
beareth witness; and no man receiveth his

16 witness. He that hath received his witness,   „   33
hath set his seal to this, that he is truly

17 God. For he whom God hath sent, speaketh   „   34
the word of God: God giveth not the Spirit

18 by measure. The Father loveth the Son,   „   35

19 and hath put all things in his hands. He   „   36
that believeth on the Son hath eternal life;
but he that is disobedient to the Son shall
not see life, but the wrath of God abideth
on him.

20   And Jesus knew that the Pharisees had   „   4 1
heard, that he had admitted, and that he

21 baptized more disciples than John (not that   „   2
Jesus himself was baptizing, but his dis-

22 ciples); and he left Judaea.[1]   „   3[a]

23   Now Herod the governor, when he was   Lu.   3 19
reproved by John concerning Herodias his
brother Philip's wife, and concerning all the

24 evil things which he was doing, added this   „ [2]   20
also above all, that he shut up John in
prison.

25   Now when Jesus heard that John had   Mt.[2]   4 12
been delivered up, he withdrew into Galilee;

26 and he entered again into Cana, where he   Jn.   4 46
made the water wine. And there was at
Capernaum a certain officer of the king,

27 whose son was sick.[3] When he heard, that   „   47

---

[1] See note to xxi. 8.

[2] These passages are displaced from their original order, so as to represent Jesus as calling His disciples before the imprisonment of S. John the Baptist.

[3] This narrative is inserted earlier than S. John's setting of it would imply because Tatian places it during the visit to Galilee mentioned in Matt. iv. 12.

		Jesus was come out of Judaea into Galilee, he went unto him, and besought *him*, that he would come down, and heal his son; for	Jn.	4 48
6	28	he was very near to death. Jesus said unto him, Except ye see signs and wonders, ye		
	29	do not believe. The officer of the king said unto him, Sir, come down, lest my child die.	„	49
	30	Jesus said unto him, Go thy way; thy son liveth. The man believed the saying, that Jesus spake unto him, and he went his way.	„	50
	31	And when he went down, his servants met him, and announced to him,[1] saying, Thy son	„	51
	32	liveth. And he inquired of them in what hour he got better. They said unto him, Yesterday at the seventh hour the fever left	„	52
	33	him. And his father knew, that this had happened at that hour, in which Jesus said unto him, Thy son liveth: and himself believed, and the whole family of his house.	„	53
	34	And this is the second sign, that Jesus did, when he returned out of Judaea into Galilee.	„	54
	35	And he was preaching in the synagogues	Lu.	4 44
	36	of Galilee: and leaving Nazareth he came and dwelt in Capernaum, in the seaside parts, in the borders of Zebulun and Naphtali:	Mt.	4 13
	37	that it might be fulfilled, which was spoken through Isaiah the prophet, saying,	„	14
	38	The land of Zebulun, the land of Naphtali, The way of the sea beyond Jordan, Galilee of the peoples,	„	15
	39	The people which sat in darkness Saw a great light; And to them which sat in the region and in the shadow of death, To them did light spring up.	„	16
	40	And he was teaching them on the sabbaths:	Lu.	4 31[b]
		and they were astonished at his teaching,	„	32
		for his speech was as if it had authority.		
	41	And in the synagogue there was a man,	„	33

[1] Or, "gave him the good news."

6 42 which had an unclean devil;[1] and he cried out with a loud voice, saying, Let me alone, what have I to do with thee, Jesus of Nazareth? thou art come to destroy us. I know thee who thou art, the Holy One of God. Lu. 4 34

43 And Jesus rebuked him, saying, Shut up thy mouth, and go out of him. And the devil threw him down into the midst, and went out of him, when he had done him no hurt. „ 35

44 And great wonder took hold of all, and they spake one with another, saying, What is this word, which in authority and power commandeth the unclean spirits, and they go „ 36

45 out. And a rumour concerning him was published into all the neighbouring region. „ 37

46 And Jesus going out of the synagogue, saw a man sitting among the publicans, Matthew[2] by name; and he saith unto him, Come after me. And he arose, and followed him. „ 38[a]
Mt. 9 9[b]

47 And Jesus came[3] into the house of Simon Mk. 1 29[b]
48 and Andrew, with James and John. And Simon's wife's mother was holden[4] with a great fever; and they besought him for her. Lu. 4 38[c]

49 And he stood over her, and commanded her fever; and it left her; and immediately she „ 39

50 rose up, and ministered unto them. And when even was come, they brought unto him many possessed with devils: and he cast out Mt. 8 16

51 their devils with a word. And all that had any sick with grievous and divers diseases, brought them unto him; and laying his hand Lu. 4 40[b]

52 on each, he healed them; that it might be fulfilled which was spoken, through Isaiah the prophet, saying, Himself shall take our Mt. 8 17

53 infirmities, and bear our diseases. And all the city was gathered together unto the door Mk. 1 33

---

[1] Lit. "demon," and so in all cases *after this* except xx. 10, xxxv. 55, and xliii. 53.

[2] Cf. note to vii. 9.   [3] See note to vi. 2.   [4] Or, "weakened."

6 54 of Jesus; and again he cast out devils from   Lu.   4 41
many, because they cried out, and said, Thou
art the Son of God. And he rebuked them,
and suffered not the devils to speak, because
they knew that he was Christ the Lord.

7 1 And very early in the morning of that day,   Mk.   1 35
he went out, and departed into a desert
2 place, and was there praying. And Simon   „   36
and they that were with him sought him;
3 and when they had found him, they said unto   „   37
4 him, All are seeking thee. He saith unto   „   38
them, Let us go into the next villages and
cities, that I may preach there also; for to
5 this end am I come. And the multitudes   Lu.   4 42^b
sought after him, and came until they over-
took him; and they laid hold of him, that
6 he should not depart from them. And Jesus   „   43
said unto them, I must preach as a gospel
the kingdom of God to the other cities also,
because for the sake of this gospel was I
7 sent. And Jesus was going about all the   Mt.[1]   9 35
cities and the villages, and taught in their
synagogues, and preached the gospel of the
kingdom, and healed all diseases and all
8 infirmities, and cast out devils; and his fame { Mk.   1 39^b
                                                  Lu.[2] 4 14^b
was published abroad, for[3] he taught in   „   15
9 every place, and was magnified by all. And   Mk.   2 14
as he passed by, he saw Levi,[4] the son of

---

[1] Repeated almost identically at xii. 40. Tatian may have meant this for Matt. iv. 23, varied; see ver. 10. This is fuller than Luke iv. 44, for which see vi. 35.

[2] Repeated from v. 33; cf. Mark i. 28 and Luke iv. 37.   [3] Or, "that."

[4] Cf. vi. 46 and vii. 25. Tatian seems to have considered that Levi and Matthew were different persons. For a *resumé* of the reasons for and against this view see Alford's *Greek Testament* under Matt. ix. 9. Alford thought the preponderance of testimony was in favour of the distinctness of the persons. It is interesting to find him quoting Clement of Alexandria, who is supposed to have been a pupil of Tatian, as a supporter of the view here taken by Tatian. Ver. 9, 10 are not in the *Codex Fuldensis*. Ephraem, Moes. p. 58, commenting on the disciples baptizing, says, "He chose James the publican," etc., from which some have inferred that his copy had "*James* the son of Alphaeus" here, as D A B C and Origen.

Alphaeus, sitting at the place of toll, and he saith unto him, Follow me. And he arose, 7 10 and followed him. And the report of him was heard in the whole region of Syria: and they brought unto him all that were sick with the more serious and divers diseases, and that were enduring torments, and demoniacs and lunatics and paralytics; and he healed them.   Mt. 4 24

11   And Jesus entered again into Capernaum   Mk. 2 1
12 after *some* days, and when it was heard, that he was in the house, many came together, so that it would not hold them, not even at the door; and he announced the word   „   2
13 of God unto them. And there were there certain of the Pharisees and doctors of the law sitting, which were come out of every village of Galilee and Judaea and Jerusalem: and the power of the Lord was present[1] unto   Lu. 5 17[b]
14 healing them. And there came some[2] with a couch, whereon there was a man that was paralytic: and they sought to bring him in,   „   18
15 and to lay him before him. And not finding a way by which they might bring him in because of the multitude, they went up to the roof, and let him down through the tiles with the couch into the midst before Jesus.   „   19
16 And when Jesus saw their faith, he said unto the paralytic, My son, thy sins are forgiven   „   20
17 thee. And the scribes and the Pharisees began to reason in their heart, Why doth this man speak blasphemies? who can for-   „   21
18 give sins but God alone? And Jesus perceived in his spirit that they reasoned these things within themselves, and said unto them, Why reason ye these things in your heart?   Mk. 2 8
19 Which is easier, to say to the paralytic, Thy   „   9

---

[1] Lit. "found."
[2] Tatian omits Mark ii. 3, "which was borne of *four*." See also Mark ii. 4. S. Matthew puts this miracle after the Sermon on the Mount.

	sins are forgiven thee; or to say unto him,		
7 20	Arise, and take up thy bed, and walk? That ye may know, that the Son of man hath authority on earth to forgive sins (he saith	Mk.	2 10
21	to the paralytic), I say unto thee, Arise, take up thy bed, and depart unto thy house.	„	11
22	And he arose straightway, and took his bed,	„	12^a
	and went forth in the sight of all, and de-	Lu.	5 25^b
23	parted to his house, magnifying God. And	Mt.	9 8^a
	when the multitudes saw it, they were afraid; for amazement took hold on them, and they	{ Lu. { Mt.	5 26^a 9 8^b
	glorified God, which gave such authority		
24	unto man, saying, Truly we have already	Lu.	5 26^b
	seen wonderful things to-day, the like whereof	Mk.	2 12^b
	we never saw.		
25	And after these things Jesus went forth and saw a publican, named Levi,¹ sitting among the publicans, and saith unto him,	Lu.	5 27
26	Follow me. And he forsook all, and rose	„	28
27	up, and followed him. And Levi made him a great feast in his house; and there was a great multitude of publicans and of others,	„	29
28	that were reclining *at meat* with him. And the scribes and Pharisees murmured, saying unto his disciples, Why do ye eat and drink	„	30
29	with the publicans and sinners? Jesus answered, and said unto them, A physician doth not seek the whole, but those that are	„	31
30	afflicted with evils. I am not come to call	„	32
31	the righteous but sinners to repentance. But ² they said unto him, Why do the disciples of John fast continually, and make supplications; likewise also the Pharisees; but thy	„	33
32	disciples eat and drink? He said unto	„	34

¹ See note to ver. 9. Tatian follows S. Luke in putting this before the Sermon on the Mount.

² Omitting Mark ii. 18: "And the disciples of John, and of the Pharisees used to fast; and they come." S. Matthew attributes the question, which follows, to the disciples of John only. Tatian, following S. Luke, attributes it to the scribes and Pharisees.

	them, It is not given to you to make the sons of the bridegroom fast, while the bride-		
7 33	groom is with them.¹ The days will come, when the bridegroom shall have been taken away from them, then will they fast in those	Lu.	5 35
34	days. And he spake a parable unto them:	„	36ᵃ
	No man putteth on a new patch, and seweth it on an old garment; lest the new addition take from the old, and a great rent be made.	Mk.	2 21
35	And no man putteth new wine into old wine-skins; lest the wine burst the skins, and the skins perish,² and the wine be poured out: but they put new wine into new wine-skins, and both are preserved.	„ Lu.	22 5 38ᵇ
36	And no man drinking old wine straightway asketh for new; for he saith, The old is better.	„	39
37	When³ Jesus was walking through the cornfields on the sabbath day, his disciples were hungry; and rubbing the ears of corn	Mt.	12 1
38	with their hands they were eating. But some of the Pharisees, when they saw them, said unto him, See, why do thy disciples⁴ on the sabbath day that which is not lawful?	„ Mk.	2ᵃ 2 24ᵇ
39	And Jesus saith unto them, Have ye not heretofore read what David did,⁵ when he had need, and was hungry, he, and they that	„	25
40	were with him? How he entered into the house of God, when Abiathar was high priest, and did eat the bread of the Lord's table, which it was not lawful to eat save for the priests, and gave also to them that were	„	26
41	with him? And he said unto them, The sabbath was created for man, and man was	„	27

---

¹ Omitting Mark ii. 19: "As long as they have the bridegroom with them, they cannot fast."

² Slight change of order.

³ Tatian follows S. Luke in putting this before the Sermon on the Mount, of which he appears to have considered Luke vi. 17–49 as a part.

⁴ Or, "what thy disciples do."

⁵ "What of old David did" does not agree so well with the Arabic.

7	42	not created for the sabbath. Or have ye not read in the law, how that the priests in the temple break the sabbath, and are guilt-	Mt. 12	5
	43	less? But I say unto you, that a greater	„	6
	44	than the temple is here. If[1] ye knew that I love mercy not sacrifice, surely ye would	„	7
	45	not have condemned the innocent. The Son	„	8
	46	of man is lord of the sabbath. And his *kindred* heard it, and they went out to lay hold on him: for they said, Truly he is beside himself.	Mk.[2]	3 21
	47[3]	And on another sabbath he entered into the synagogue and taught: and there was a man there, whose right hand was withered.	Lu.	6 6
	48	And the scribes and the Pharisees watched him, whether he would heal on the sabbath; that they might find a way to blame him.	„	7
	49	He knew their thoughts; and he saith to the man, whose hand was withered, Rise up, and come into the midst of the synagogue. And	„	8
	50	when he had come and stood forth, Jesus saith unto them, I ask you, What is lawful to do on the sabbath day, good or evil? to save lives, or to destroy them? But they	„	9
	51	held their peace. Looking round about them with anger, and being grieved at the hardness of their heart, he said unto the man, Stretch forth thy hand. And he stretched it forth: and his hand was made like *the*	Mk. „	3 4[b] 5
	52	*other*. Then he said unto them, What man shall there be of you that shall have one	Mt. 12	11

---

[1] A similar statement in Matt. ix. 13 is omitted at vii. 30.

[2] It is strange how Tatian removes this verse from the further account, Mark iii. 31, etc., and attributes it to Christ's claim to be lord of the sabbath. It is thus dissociated from the two statements of S. Mark, by which it might be explained, viz.: His neglecting to take food (Mark iii. 20); and the report that he had an unclean spirit (Mark iii. 22 and 30), for which see xiv. 15 and 30; also cf. xvi. 13.

[3] The first leaf missing from the Vatican MS. seems to have extended from this verse to viii. 17 inclusive, this passage being obtained from the Borgian MS. only.

		sheep, and if it fall into a well on the sabbath day, he will not lay hold on it, and			
7	53	lift it out? But how much rather is a man better than a sheep! Therefore it is lawful	Mt.	12	12
8	1	to do good on the sabbath days. But the Pharisees went out,[1] and took counsel against	"		14
	2	him, that they might destroy him. But Jesus perceiving *it* withdrew from thence: and great multitudes followed him; and he	"		15
	3	healed them all, and restrained them, that	"		16
	4	they should not make him known: that it might be fulfilled which was spoken through Isaiah the prophet, saying,	"		17
	5	Behold, my child in whom I am well pleased, My beloved in whom my soul hath rested: I have put my Spirit upon him; And he shall declare judgment to the nations.	"		18
	6	He shall not strive, nor cry aloud; Neither shall any one hear his voice in the streets.	"		19
	7	A bruised reed shall he not break; And a smoking lamp[2] shall he not put out, Till he bring forth judgment unto victory.	"		20
	8	And in his own name shall he preach good tidings unto the nations.	"		21
	9	In those days Jesus went out into the mountain to pray; and he was there in the	Lu.	6	12
	10	morning *engaged* in prayer to God. And when it had become day, he called the	"		13[a]
		disciples, and withdrew to the sea: and much people from Galilee followed him to	Mk.	3	7[b]
	11	pray; and from Judaea, and from Jerusalem, and from Idumaea and beyond Jordan, and from Tyre and Sidon, and from Decapolis: and a great multitude, hearing what things	"		8
	12	he did, came unto him. And he spake to	"		9

[1] S. Mark adds: "straightway ... with the Herodians." [2] Or, "wick."

8 13	his disciples, that they should bring unto him a boat, because of the crowd, lest they should press upon him: and he healed many; so that as many as had plagues were nigh to throng him on account of their eagerness to	Mk.	3 10
14	touch him. And the unclean spirits, when they saw him, fell down, and cried, saying,	„	11
15	Thou art the Son of God. And he urgently threatened them, that they should not make	„	12
16	him known. And they that were troubled	Lu.	6 18
17	with unclean spirits were cured. And all the multitude sought to touch him; for power went out from him, and healed *them* all.	„	19
18	And Jesus, seeing the multitudes, went	Mt.	5 1ᵃ
19	up into the mountain: and he called his disciples, and chose from them twelve, whom	Lu.	6 13ᵇ
20	he named apostles: Simon, whom he named Cephas, and Andrew his brother, James and	„	14
21	John, Philip and Bartholomew, Matthew and Thoma, James the son of Alphaeus, and	„	15
22	Simon, which is called the Zealot, and Judas the son of James, and Judas Iscariot, and	„	16
23	this is he that betrayed him. And Jesus came down with them, and stood on a level place, and a crowd of his disciples, and an	„	17
24	abundant multitude of the people. And he selected these twelve, that they might be with him, and that he might send them	Mk.	3 14
25	forth to preach, and that they might have the power of curing diseases, and casting out devils.	„	15
26	Then he lifted up his eyes on them, and opened his mouth, and taught them, saying,	{Lu. {Mt.	6 20ᵃ 5 2
27	Blessed are the poor in spirit: for theirs is the kingdom of the heavens.	Mt.	5 3
28	Blessed are the mournful: for they shall be comforted.	„	4
29	Blessed are the meek: for they shall possess the earth.¹	„	5

¹ Aphraates gives, "the land of life."

8	30	Blessed are they that hunger and thirst after righteousness: for they shall be filled.	Mt.	5 6
	31	Blessed are the merciful: for they shall obtain mercy.	„	7
	32	Blessed are the pure in heart: for they shall see God.	„	8
	33	Blessed are the peacemakers: for they shall be called sons of God.	„	9
	34	Blessed are they that are cast out for righteousness' sake: for theirs is the kingdom of the heavens.	„	10
	35	Blessed shall ye be, when men shall hate you, and when they shall separate you, and cast you out, and reproach you, and say every evil word against you, speaking falsely,	Lu. Mt.	6 22^a 5 11^b
	36	for my sake. Then rejoice, and be exceeding glad; for your reward is abundant in the heavens: for so cast they out the prophets, *that were* before you.	„	12
	37	But woe unto you that are rich! for ye have received your consolation.	Lu.	6 24
	38	Woe unto you that are full! ye shall hunger. Woe unto you that laugh now! ye shall mourn and weep.	„	25
	39	Woe unto you, when men shall praise you! for so did their fathers to the false prophets.	„	26
	40	I say unto you which hear, Ye are the salt of the earth: but if the salt lose its savour, wherewith shall it be salted? it is good for nothing; but it shall be cast out,	{Lu. Mt.	6 27^a 5 13
	41	and trodden down by men. Ye are the light of the world. A city built upon a	Mt.	5 14
	42	mountain cannot be hid. Neither do *men* light a lamp, and put it under the bushel, but on the lamp-stand, that it may shine	„	15
	43	upon all that are in the house. So let your light shine before men, that they may see your good works, and glorify your Father,	„	16
	44	which is in the heavens. For there is	Mk.	4 22

8 45	nothing secret, except it shall be also manifested; nor hidden, except it shall be also known. He that hath ears to hear, let him hear.	Mk. 4 23
46	Think not that I came to destroy the law or the prophets: I came not to destroy, but	Mt. 5 17
47	to fulfil. Verily I say unto you, Till heaven and earth pass away, one point or one letter shall not pass away from the law, till all of	„ 18
48	it be accomplished. Whosoever therefore shall break one of these least commandments, and shall teach men so, shall be called least in the kingdom of the heavens: whosoever shall do and teach them, he shall be called	„ 19
49	great in the kingdom of the heavens. For I say unto you, Except your righteousness shall exceed *the righteousness* of the scribes and Pharisees, ye shall not enter into the kingdom of the heavens.	„ 20
50	Ye have heard that it was said to them of old time, Thou shalt not kill; for whosoever shall kill shall be accountable to the	„ 21
51	judgment:[1] but I say unto you, that every one who is angry with his brother without a cause shall be accountable to the judgment;[1] and whosoever shall say to his brother, O! horrid one,[2] shall be accountable to the council; but whosoever shall say to him, Thou fool, shall be accounted worthy of the	„ 22
52	Gehenna of fire. If therefore thou shalt be offering thy gift upon the altar, and there shalt remember, that thy brother hath con-	„ 23
53	ceived any hatred against thee, leave thy gift upon the altar, and go thy way first, and be reconciled to thy brother, and then	„ 24
54	return, and offer thy gift. Agree with thine adversary quickly: whilst thou art still with him in the way, give a ransom and be	„ 25^a Lu. 12 58^b

[1] Or, "deserve sentence."
[2] The word "Raca" is not retained in the Arabic.

8	55	freed from him; lest haply the adversary deliver thee to the judge, and the judge deliver thee to the officer,[1] and thou be cast	Mt.	5	25ᶜ
	56	into prison. Verily I say unto thee, Thou shalt not go out thence, till thou payest the last mite.[2]	„		26
	57	Ye have heard that it was said, Thou	„		27
	58	shalt not commit adultery: but I say unto you, that whosoever looketh on a woman, lusting after her, hath committed adultery	„		28
	59	with her there already in his heart. If thy right eye injureth thee, pluck it out, and cast it from thee: for it is expedient for thee that one of thy members should perish, rather than that thy whole body should go into	„		29
	60	Gehenna. And if thy right hand injureth thee, cut it off, and cast it from thee: for it is better for thee that one of thy members should perish, than that thy whole body	„		30
	61	should fall into Gehenna. It was said, Whosoever shall put away his wife, let him	„		31
	62	give her a certificate of divorcement: but I say unto you, Whosoever shall put away his wife, without the cause of fornication, maketh her already commit adultery; and whosoever shall marry one who is put away, committeth adultery.	„		32
9	1	Again, ye have heard that it was said to them of old time, Thou shalt not forswear thyself; but call thou upon God in thy	„		33
	2	faith: but I say unto you, Swear not at all; not by the heaven, for it is the throne	„		34
	3	of God; nor by the earth, for it is the footstool under his feet; nor even by Jerusalem,	„		35
	4	for it is the city of the great king. Neither swear by thy head, for thou canst not make	„		36
	5	one hair black or white. But let your	„		37

[1] Or, "attendant;" technically the word means a collector of water for camels.

[2] Arabic fals, i.e. $\frac{1}{48}$ of a dirhem = half a farthing.

speech be either, Yes, or No; but what is more abundant than this, is of the evil *one*.

9	6	Ye have heard that it was said, An eye for an eye, and a tooth for a tooth: but I say unto you, Resist not an evil *man:* but whosoever smiteth thee on thy right cheek, offer him the other also. And to him that wisheth to strive at law with thee, and take away thy coat, to him give up thy cloke also.	Mt. 5 38
	7		,, 39
	8		,, 40
	9	And whosoever shall impress thee to go a mile, go with him two. Give to him that asketh of thee, and from him that wisheth to borrow of thee withhold it not: and do not restrain[1] him that taketh away the things that are thine. And as ye wish that men should do to you, do ye also to them likewise.	,, 41
	10		,, 42
			Lu. 6 30^b
	11		,, 31
	12	Ye have heard that it was said, Love thy neighbour, and hate thine enemy: but I say unto you, Love your enemies, bless them that curse you, do good to them that hate you, and pray for them that receive[2] you harshly and drive you out; that ye may be sons of your heavenly Father, who maketh his sun to rise on the good and the evil, and sendeth his rain on the just and the unjust. If ye love them that love you, what reward shall ye have? for publicans and sinners likewise love those that love them. And if ye do good to them that do good to you, where is your superiority? since even sinners do so. And if ye give a loan to him, of whom ye expect repayment, where is your superiority? for even sinners lend to sinners, expecting as much from them. But love your enemies, and do them good, and give a loan, and cut off no man's hope, that your reward may be great, and that ye may be sons of the Most High:	Mt. 5 43
	13		,, 44
	14		,, 45
	15		,, 46^a
			Lu. 6 32^b
	16		,, 33
	17		,, 34
	18		,, 35

[1] Or, "punish."   [2] Or, "seize."

		for he is kind toward the evil and the un-		
9	19	thankful. Be ye merciful, even as your	Lu.	6 36
		Father also is merciful.		
	20	And if ye salute your brethren only, what	Mt.	5 47
		do ye more *than others?* do not even the		
	21	publicans the same? Be ye therefore per-	,,	48
		fect, as your heavenly Father also is perfect.		
	22	Take heed that ye do not your alms	,,	6 1
		before men, to be seen of them: otherwise		
		ye shall have no reward with your Father,		
	23	which is in the heavens. When therefore	,,	2
		thou doest alms, sound not a trumpet before		
		thee, as the hypocrites do in the synagogues		
		and in the streets, that they may be praised		
		of men. Verily I say unto you, They have		
	24	received their reward. But when thou	,,	3
		doest alms, let not thy left hand know		
	25	what thy right hand doeth: that thine alms	,,	4
		may be secret; and thy Father which seeth		
		in secret shall recompense thee openly.		
	26	And when thou prayest, be not as the	,,	5
		hypocrites, who love to stand and pray in		
		the synagogues and in the corners of the		
		streets, that they may be seen of men.		
		Verily I say unto you, They have received		
	27	their reward. But thou, when thou prayest,	,,	6
		enter into thy bedchamber, and having shut		
		the door, pray to thy Father which is in		
		secret, and thy Father which seeth in secret		
	28	shall recompense thee openly. And in pray-	,,	7
		ing speak not much, as the heathen *do:*		
		for they think that they shall be heard in		
	29	much speaking. Be not therefore likened	,,	8
		unto them, for your Father knoweth your		
	30	petition, before ye ask him. One[1] of his	Lu. 11	1[b]
		disciples said unto him, Lord, teach us to		
		pray, even as John taught his disciples.		
	31	Jesus saith unto them, After this manner	,,	2[a]
	32	then pray ye: Our Father which art in the	Mt.	6 9[b]

[1] This interruption during the Sermon on the Mount is noticeable.

9 33 heavens, hallowed be thy name. Thy kingdom come. Thy will be done, as in heaven	Mt.	6 10
34 so on earth. Give us the sustenance[1] of to-	,,	11
35 day. And forgive us our faults, as we also forgive those who commit faults against us.	,,	12
36 And bring us not into temptation, but deliver us from the evil *one*. For thine is the kingdom, and the power, and the glory,	,,	13
37 unto the ages of ages. If ye forgive men their trespasses,[2] your Father which is in the	,,	14
38 heavens will forgive you. But if ye forgive not men, neither will your Father forgive you your trespasses.	,,	15
39 When ye fast, become not, as the hypocrites, mournful: for they disfigure their faces, that they may appear unto men as fasting. Verily, I say unto you, They have	,,	16
40 received their reward. But thou, when thou fastest, wash thy face, and anoint thy	,,	17
41 head, that thou appear not unto men as fasting, but unto thy Father which is in secret: and thy Father, which seeth in secret, shall recompense thee.	,,	18
42 Fear not, little flock, for it hath pleased your Father well to give you the kingdom.	Lu.	12 32
43 Sell what ye possess, and give alms; make for yourselves purses which wax not old.	,,	33ᵃ
44 Lay not up[3] for yourselves treasure upon[4] the earth, where rust[5] and moth doth corrupt, and where thieves dig through and	Mt.	6 19
45 steal: but lay up for yourselves treasure in heaven, where neither rust nor moth doth corrupt; and thieves do not dig through, nor	,,	20
46 steal: for where thy treasure is, there is	,,	21
47 thy heart also. The lamp of the body is the eye: for if thine eye be unimpaired, thy	,,	22

---

[1] Lit. "power;" cf. ver. 36.
[2] Or rather, "folly," and so in ver. 38.
[3] Lit., "Treasure not," and so in ver. 45.
[4] Or, "in."   [5] Or, "woodworm."

9 48 whole body shall be full of light. But if   Mt. 6 23
thine eye be worthless, thy whole body shall
be full of darkness. If therefore the light
that is in thee be darkness, how great will
49 thy darkness be! Beware, lest the light   Lu. 11 35
50 that is in thee be darkness. For if thy   „   36
whole body be full of light, not having any
part dark, it shall be wholly full of light,
as a lamp lightens thee with its bright
shining.

10 1   No man can serve two masters: for he is   Mt. 6 24
obliged to hate one of them, and love the
other; and to honour one, and despise the
other. Ye cannot serve God and riches.
2 Therefore I say unto you, Be not anxious for   „   25
your lives, what ye shall eat, and what ye
shall drink; nor for your bodies, what ye
shall put on   Is not the life more than the
food, and the body more than the raiment?
3 Consider attentively the birds of the   „   26
heaven, which sow not, nor reap, nor gather
into barns; and your Father, which is in the
heavens, feedeth them. Are not ye of more
4 value than they? And which of you, when   „   27
he tries, shall be able to add one cubit unto
5 his stature? If then ye are not able *to do*   Lu. 12 26
even that which is least, why are ye anxious
6 concerning the rest? Consider the lilies of   Mt. 6 28[b]
the field, how they grow, though they toil
7 not, nor spin. And I say unto you, that   „   29
even Solomon in the magnificence of his glory
was not arrayed even as one of these.
8 But if God doth so clothe the grass of the   „   30
field, which to-day is, and to-morrow is cast
into the oven, how much rather shall it be
9 done to you, O ye of little faith. Be not   „   31
therefore anxious, saying, What shall we
eat? or, What shall we drink? or, Where-
withal shall we be clothed? nor let your   Lu. 12 29[b]
10 mind be troubled because of this. All   Mt. 6 32

	these things do the nations of the world seek after; and your Father, which is in the heavens, knoweth that ye have need of	
10 11	all these things. Seek ye first the kingdom of God, and his righteousness; and all these	Mt. 6 33
12	things shall be added unto you. Be not anxious for the morrow: for the morrow will be anxious for what is its own.¹ Its own evil is sufficient for the day.	,, 34
13	Judge not, that ye be not judged: condemn not, that ye be not condemned:	{Mt.² 7 1 {Lu. 6 37ᵇ
14	forgive, and ye shall be forgiven: release,³ and ye shall be released: give, and it shall be given unto you; good measure, pressed together and full, shall they thrust into your bosom. With the same measure wherewithsoever ye measure, it shall be measured	Lu. 6 38
15	to you. Take heed what ye hear: with whatever measure⁴ ye measure, it shall be measured to you again, and it shall be added to you. I say unto these, which hear,	Mk. 4 24ᵇ
16	He that hath,⁵ to him shall be given: and he that hath not, even that which he can have, shall be taken away from him.	,, 25
17	And he spake a parable unto them: Can a blind man guide a blind man? do they	Lu. 6 39
18	not both fall into a pit? The disciple is not superior to his master: but every per-	,, 40
19	fect man shall be as his master. Why lookest thou at the mote⁶ that is in thy brother's eye, but considerest not the beam	,, 41
20	that is in thine own eye? Or how canst thou say to thy brother, Brother, let me cast out the mote from thine eye, when thou thyself beholdest not the beam in thine own eye? Thou hypocrite, cast out first the beam	,, 42

---

¹ Or, "peculiar to it." ² Or, Luke vi. 37ᵃ.
³ This clause appears to be an addition. ⁴ Unnecessary repetition.
⁵ Repeated from Matt. xiii. 12 at xvi. 33.
⁶ Or, perhaps, "stalk," a bit of wood like the "beam," but extremely small.

from thine own eye, and then shalt thou see
to draw out the mote from thy brother's eye.

10 21 Give not that which is holy unto the   Mt. 7 6
dogs, neither cast your pearls before swine,
lest haply they trample them with their feet,
and turn and rend you.

22 And he saith unto them, Which of you   Lu. 11 5
shall have a friend, and shall go unto him
at midnight, and say to him, Friend, lend

23 me three loaves; for a friend is come to me   „   6
from a journey, and I have nothing to offer

24 him; and the friend from within shall   „   7
answer and say unto him, Trouble me not:
the door is now shut, and my children are
with me in bed; I cannot rise and give unto

25 thee? Verily I say unto you, Though he   „   8
will not give [1] unto him because of friend-
ship, yet because of his importunity he will
arise and give unto him what he asked of

26 him. And I say unto you, Ask, it shall   „   9
be given you; seek, ye shall find; knock,

27 it shall be opened unto you. Every one   „   10
that asketh receiveth; and he that seeketh
findeth; and to him that knocketh it shall

28 be opened. What father among you, whose   „   11
son asketh of him a loaf, do you think, will
give him a stone? and if he ask of him a fish,
will he, do you think, for a fish give him a

29 serpent? and if he ask of him an egg, will he,   „   12

30 think you, hold out to him a scorpion? If   „   13
ye then, whilst ye are evil, know good gifts,
and give them unto your sons, how much more
shall your Father, which is in the heavens,
give the Holy Spirit to them that ask him!

31 All things whatsoever ye wish that men   Mt. 7 12
should do unto you, do ye also unto them:
this is the law and the prophets.

32 Strive earnestly [2] at the narrow gate: for   „   13

---

[1] Omitting "rise and."

[2] The root is the same as in ver. 25, "importunity."

10	33	a wide gate, and a broad way leadeth to destruction; and they are many that go therein. How narrow is the gate,¹ and confined the way, that leadeth unto life! and they are few that find it.	Mt.	7	14
	34	Beware of false prophets, which come to you in lambs' clothing, whilst inwardly they are ravening wolves: but by their fruits ye	„		15
			„		16ª
	35	shall know them. For each tree is known by its own fruit. For not of thorns do they gather figs, nor of a bramble-bush do	Lu.	6	44
	36	they gather grapes. Even so every good tree bringeth forth good fruit; but an evil tree	Mt.	7	17
	37	produceth evil fruit. A good tree cannot bring forth evil fruit, nor an evil tree pro-	„		18
	38	duce good fruit. The good man out of the good treasure, which is in his heart, bringeth forth good things; and the evil man out of the evil treasure, which is in his heart, bringeth forth evil things: for out of the abundance of the heart the lips	Lu.	6	45
	39	speak. Every tree that produceth not good fruit shall be hewn down, and cast into	Mt.	7	19
	40	the fire. Therefore by their fruits ye shall	„		20
	41	know them. Not every one that saith unto me, Lord, Lord, shall enter into the kingdom of the heavens; but he that doeth the will of my Father, which is in the heavens.	„		21
	42	Many will say unto me in that day, Lord, Lord, did we not prophesy in thy name, and in thy name cast out devils, and in thy name	„		22
	43	do many mighty works? Then will I say unto them, I never knew you: depart from	„		23
	44	me, ye servants of iniquity. Every one that cometh unto me, and heareth my words, and doeth them, I will show you to what he is	Lu.	6	47

---

¹ In Addai, though absent from some of the Greek MSS. Addai, however, does not give it as an exact quotation, but in his speech he says: "Because that the gate of life is straight, and the way of truth is narrow therefore few are the believers of truth," etc.

10	45	like. He is like a wise man, that built a house, and digged, and went deep, and laid	Lu.	6	48ᵃ
	46	the foundations upon the rock: and the rain descended, and the floods overflowed, and the winds blew, and shook that house; and it fell not: for its foundations had been	Mt.	7	25
	47	laid upon the rock. And every one that heareth these words of mine, and doeth them not, shall be like a foolish man, which built his house upon the sand without a founda-	„		26
	48	tion: and the rain descended, and the floods overflowed, and the winds blew, and burst into that house; and it fell: and great was the fall thereof.	„		27
11	1	And when Jesus had ended these words, the multitudes were astonished at his teaching:	„		28
	2	for he taught them as *one* having authority, not as their scribes and the Pharisees.	„		29
	3	And when he was come down from the mountain, great multitudes followed him.	„	8	1
	4	And when Jesus had entered into Caper- naum, the servant of a certain distinguished officer, *who was* dear unto him, was sick, and	„ Lu.	7	5ᵃ 2
	5	was already very near to death. And he heard concerning Jesus, and came¹ unto him	„		3ᵃ
	6	with the elders of the Jews, and besought him, and said, Lord, my boy lieth in the house paralytic,² and he is grievously tormented.	Mt. „	8	5ᵇ 6
	7	And the elders besought him earnestly, saying, He is worthy that this should be	Lu.	7	4ᵇ
	8	done for him: for he loveth our nation, and	„		5
	9	he built us even the synagogue. Jesus saith unto him, I will come and heal him. The	Mt.	8	7
	10	officer answered, and saith, Lord, I am not worthy that my roof should overshadow thee:³	„		8

¹ According to S. Matthew, he came himself; but according to S. Luke, he *sent* the elders. Ephraem has "elders of the people."

² Or, "crippled."

³ Omitting Luke vii. 7, "Wherefore neither thought I myself worthy to come unto thee." Cf. note to ver. 5.

	but it is enough that thou speak the word,		
11	11 and my boy shall be healed. For I also	Lu.	7 8
	am a man under obedience to authority, having under me soldiers: and I say to this one, Go, and he goeth; and to another, Come, and he cometh; and to my servant, that he should do this, and he doeth it.		
	12 And when Jesus heard this, he marvelled,	,,	9ª
	and turned, and said unto the multitude that were coming with him, Verily I say unto	Mt.	8 10ᵇ
	you, I have not found such faith in Israel.		
	13 I say unto you, that many shall come from	,,	11
	the east and the west and shall lie down with Abraham, and Isaac, and Jacob, in the		
	14 kingdom of the heavens: but the sons of	,,	12
	the kingdom shall be cast forth into the outer darkness: there shall be the weeping		
	15 and gnashing of teeth. And Jesus said	,,	13
	unto the officer, Go thy way; and as thou hast believed, *so* be it done unto thee. And		
	16 the boy was healed in that hour. And the	Lu.	7 10
	officer returned home, and found that sick servant already whole.		
	17 And the day after he went to a city,	,,	11
	which is called Nain, and with him his		
	18 disciples and an abundant multitude. Now	,,	12
	when he drew near to the gate of the city, he saw people that were attending one that was dead, the only son of his mother, and his mother was a widow: and a great multitude		
	19 of the city was with her. And when Jesus	,,	13
	saw her, he was moved with compassion on her,		
	20 and said unto her, Weep not. And he went,	,,	14
	and came near to the bier: and they that were bearing him, stood still. And he saith,		
	21 Young¹ man, I say unto thee, Arise. And	,,	15

¹ Aphraates has "Young man" twice, and in Mark v. 41 also he has "Maid, maid." Cf. "Martha, Martha," Luke x. 41; "Simon, Simon" (not in the Arabic), Luke xxii. 31; also "Saul, Saul," Acts ix. 4. These passages suggest a tendency to reduplication in Christ's words.

		he that was dead sat up, and began to speak.		
11	22	And he gave him to his mother. And fear took hold on all: and they magnified God, saying, A great prophet is arisen among us:	Lu.	7 16
	23	and, God hath visited his people. And this report was spread abroad into the whole of Judaea concerning him, and into all the region round about.	„	17
	24	Now when Jesus saw great multitudes about him, he gave commandment to go	Mt.	8 18
	25	across. And¹ as they were departing in the way, one scribe came near, and saith unto him, Master, I will follow thee whither-	Lu. Mt.	9 57ᵇ 8 19
	26	soever thou goest. Jesus said unto him, The foxes have holes, and the birds of the heaven *have* nests; but the Son of man hath not a place, where he may lay his	„	20
	27	head. And he saith unto another, Follow me. But he said, Lord, suffer me first to go	Lu.	9 59
	28	and bury my father. Jesus said unto him, Leave the dead to bury their own dead; but follow thou me, and announce the kingdom	„	60
	29	of God. And another saith unto him, I will follow thee, Lord; but suffer me first to go and bid farewell to my household, and I	„	61
	30	will come. Jesus said unto him, No man,² putting forth his hand to the plough, and looking back, is fit for the kingdom of God.	„	62
	31	And³ on that day, when it was become late, he saith unto them, Let us cross over the lake.	Mk. Lu.	4 35ᵃ 8 22ᶜ
	32	And sending away the multitudes, Jesus went up into a boat, and sat down, himself	{Mk. {Lu.	4 36ᵃ 8 22ᵇ

---

¹ If the two accounts are to be identified, S. Luke's seems a better setting, when Jesus was about to leave Galilee finally, and it was a question, who would leave Galilee for his sake, and accompany Him. So Schleiermacher and Tischendorf.

² Addai remarks, "A husbandman, who puts his hand to the ploughshare, if he looks behind, the furrows before him cannot be straight."

³ Continuing S. Matthew's order.

11 33 and his disciples. And other boats were	Mk.	4 36^b
with them. And a great tumult was stirred	Mt.	8 24^a
up in the sea by^1 a whirlwind and a wind;		
and the boat was nigh to be sunk through	Lu.	8 23
34 the abundance of the waves. But Jesus was	Mk.	4 38^a
in the stern, asleep on the cushion: and his	Mt.	8 25
disciples came to him, and awoke him, say-		
35 ing, Lord, save us, behold, we perish. But	Lu.	8 24^b
he arose, and rebuked the wind and the		
waves of the water, and said unto the sea,	Mk.	4 39^b
Be still, for thou art rebuked. And the		
wind was silent; and a great calm took		
36 place. And he saith unto them, Why are	,,	40
ye so fearful? and why have ye not faith?	{Mk.^{2}	4 41^a
37 And they feared with a great fear; and they	{Lu.	8 25^b
marvelled, saying one to another, Who, think		
you, is this, that commandeth even the wind		
and waves and sea, and they obey him?		
38 And they departed, and came to the	Lu.	8 26
country of the Gadarenes,^{3} which is beyond		
the sea over against the land of Galilee.		
39 And when he was come forth from the ship	,,	27^a
to the land, there met him out of the tombs	Mk.	5 2^b
a man^4 that had a devil now for a long time,	Lu.	8 27^c
and was wearing no garment, and abode not		
40 in a house but in the tombs. And no man	Mk.	5 3^b
could bind him with chains; for as often as	,,	4^a
he was confined with chains and fetters, he		
rent asunder the chains, and brake in pieces		
41 the fetters: and he was driven by the devil	Lu.	8 29^b
into the desert: and no man was able to	Mk.	5 4^b
42 tame him. And always day and night he	,,	5^a
was in the tombs and in the mountains, so	Mt.	8 28^b
that no man could pass by that way; and	Mk.	5 5^b
he was crying out, and cutting himself with		

---

^{1} Or, "owing to."

^{2} Included with ver. 40 in the Arabic, which follows the numbering of the Vulgate, in which there is no ver. 41.

^{3} Arabic, "Hadarenes" throughout.

^{4} One only, as at Mark v. 2; not two, as at Matt. viii. 28.

11 43	stones. And when he saw Jesus from afar,	Mk.	5 6
44	he ran and worshipped him; and crying out with a loud voice, he said, What have we to do with thee, Jesus, thou Son of the Most High God?[2] I adjure thee by God, torment	„ Lu.[1] Mk.	7[a] 8 28[b] 5 7[c]
45	me not. And Jesus commanded the unclean spirit to go out from the man: for for a long	Lu.	8 29[a]
46	time he was in captivity to it. And Jesus asked him, What is thy name? He said unto him, Legion: for many devils had	„	30
47	entered into him. And they intreated him that he would not command them to go into	„	31
48	the abyss. Now there was there a herd of many swine feeding on the mountain: and those demons intreated him that he would give them leave to enter into the swine. And he	„	32
49	gave them leave. The devils therefore went out of the man, and entered into the swine: and the herd ran to the summit, and fell into	„ Mk.	33[a] 5 13[b]
50	the middle of the sea, about two thousand; and they were choked in the water. And when the herdsmen saw what had happened, they fled, and told it to them that were in	Lu.	8 34
51	the cities and in the villages. And some went out to see what was come to pass; and they came to Jesus, and found the man, from whom the devils were gone out, sitting, clothed and ashamed,[3] at the feet of Jesus:	„	35
52	and they were afraid. And they related what they had seen, and how that man, in whom there had been a devil, had been made whole, and also concerning the swine.	„ Mk.	36 5 16[b]
12 1	And all the multitude of the Gadarenes besought him to depart from them; for they were holden with great fear.	Lu.	8 37[a]
2	And Jesus went up into a boat, and	Mt.	9 1

[1] Or, Mark v. 7[b] nearly.

[2] Omitting Matt. viii. 29, "Art thou come hither to torment us before the time?"

[3] Probably derived from σωφρονοῦντα.

		crossed over, and came into his own city.			
12	3	And the man, from whom the devils were gone out, besought him that he might remain with him: but Jesus sent him away, and	Lu.	8	38
	4	said unto him, Return to thy house, and declare what things God hath done for thee.	„		39^a
	5	And he went his way, and began to publish in Decapolis how great things Jesus had done for him: and all men did marvel.	Mk.	5	20
	6	And when Jesus had passed over in the boat across the sea, a great multitude welcomed him; for they were all waiting for	„ Lu.		21^a 8 40^b
	7	him. And a certain man, whose name was Jaïrus, a ruler of the synagogue, fell down at	„		41^a
	8	Jesus' feet, and prayed him much, saying, I have one daughter, and she is already very near death: but come, lay thy hand upon	Mk. Mt.	5 9	23^a 18^b
	9	her, and she shall live. And Jesus arose,	„		19
	10	and his disciples, and followed him. And a great multitude came to him; and they were pressing upon him.	Mk.	5	24^b
	11	And a woman, in whom there was an	„		25
	12	issue of blood for twelve years, and who had suffered many things of many physicians, and had spent all her *means*, and had made no	„		26
	13	progress, but even grew worse;[1] when she had heard concerning Jesus, came in the press of the crowd behind, and touched his	„		27
	14	garment. For she said secretly within herself, If I touch his garment, I shall live.	„		28
	15	And straightway the fountain of her blood was dried up; and she felt in her body that	„		29
	16	she had been healed of her plague. And straightway Jesus perceived in himself, that power had gone out from him, and he turned round to the crowd, and said, Who touched	„		30
	17	my garments? And when all denied, Simon Cephas and they that were with him, said unto him, Teacher, the multitudes press thee	Lu.	8	45^b

[1] Lit. "her injury even increased."

12		and crush thee, and sayest thou, Who touched		
	18	me? But he said, Some one did touch me:	Lu.	8 46
		for I perceived that power had gone out[1]		
	19	from me. And[2] when the woman saw that	,,	47ª
		she was not hid from him, fearing and	Mk.	5 33ª
		trembling, because she knew what had been		
	20	done in her, she came, and falling down, she	Lu.	8 47ᵇ
		worshipped him, and declared in the presence		
		of all the people for what cause she touched		
		him, and how she was healed immediately.		
	21	And Jesus said unto her, Daughter, be	,,	48
		of good cheer, thy faith hath made thee		
		whole; go in peace, and be whole from thy	Mk.	5 34ᵇ
		plague.[3]		
	22	While he yet spake, there came one from	Lu.	8 49
		the ruler of the synagogue's house, and said		
		unto him, Thy daughter is dead: trouble not		
	23	the Teacher. But Jesus hearing it, said	,,	50
		unto the father of the maid, Fear not: but		
	24	believe only, and she shall be saved. And	Mk.	5 37
		he suffered no man to go with him, save		
		Simon Cephas, and James, and John the		
	25	brother of James. And they came into the	,,	38
		house of the ruler of the synagogue; and		
		he saw them excited,[4] weeping and wailing.		
	26	And when he had entered in, he saith unto	,,	39
		them, Why are ye excited,[4] lamenting? the		
	27	maid is not dead, but sleepeth. And they	Lu.	8 53
		laughed at him, knowing that she was dead.		
	28	But he, having put them all forth, took the	Mk.	5 40ᵇ
		father and the mother of the maid, and		
		Simon, and James, and John, and went into		
	29	the room, where the maid was lying.[5] And	,,	41
		taking the hand of the maid, he saith unto		

---

[1] Or, "went forth."

[2] Omitting Mark v. 32, "And he looked round about to see her, that had done this thing;" but cf. ver. 16.

[3] Omitting Matt. ix. 22, "and the woman was made whole from that very hour;" but cf. ver. 15.

[4] Or, "terrified."   [5] Or, "laid."

THE DIATESSARON. 91

	her, Maid,¹ arise. And her spirit returned;	Lu.	8	55ᵃ
12 30	and she rose up immediately, and walked: she	Mk.	5	42ᵇ
	was about twelve years *old*. And he com-	Lu.	8	55ᵇ
	manded that something should be given her			
31	to eat. And her father was amazed with	„		56
	great amazement; and he charged them to			
32	tell no man what had been done. And this	Mt.	9	26
	report went forth into all that land.			
33	And as Jesus passed by from thence, two	„		27
	blind men followed him, crying out, and			
	saying, Have mercy on us, thou son of David.			
34	And when he was come home, the two blind	„		28
	men came to him: and Jesus said unto them,			
	Believe ye that I am able to do this? They			
35	said unto him, Yea, Lord. Then touched	„		29
	he their eyes, and said, Even as ye have			
36	believed, be it done unto you. And im-	„		30
	mediately their eyes were opened. And			
	Jesus warned them, saying, See that no man			
37	know it. But they went forth, and published	„		31
	abroad the news in all that land.			
38	And when Jesus had gone forth, they	„		32
	brought to him a dumb man that had a devil.			
39	And when the devil was cast out, the dumb	„		33
	man spake: and the multitudes marvelled,			
	saying, It was never so seen in Israel.			
40	And Jesus went about all the cities and	„²		35
	villages, teaching in their synagogues, and			
	preaching the gospel of the kingdom, and			
	healing every sickness and disease. And			
41	many followed him. And when Jesus saw the	„		36
	multitudes, he was moved with compassion			
	for them, because they were wearied out and			
	forsaken, as sheep not having a shepherd.			
42	And he called his twelve disciples,³ and	Mt.	10	1ᵃ
	gave them power and great authority over	Lu.	9	1ᵇ

¹ Aphraates had "Maid, maid;" cf. note on xi. 20. The original words, "Talitha cumi," being Syriac, needed no interpreting clause in a *Diatessaron* for Syrian readers; hence the absence of such a clause in our text.

² Cf. vii. 7.   ³ Cf. note to xv. 16.

12 43 all devils and sickness. And he sent them — Lu. 9 2
two and two to preach the kingdom of God,
44 and to heal the sick. And he charged them, — Mt. 10 5[b]
saying, Into the way of the heathen depart
not, and into the cities of the Samaritans
45 enter not: attend chiefly to the sheep, that — ,, 6
have perished, of the children of Israel.
46 And as ye go, preach, saying, The kingdom — ,, 7
47 of the heavens is at hand. Heal the sick, — ,,[1] 8
cleanse the lepers, cast out devils: freely ye
48 received, freely give. Possess no gold, nor — ,, 9
49 silver, nor brass in your girdles;[2] nor carry — ,, 10[a]
anything on the way, save a wand[3] only; — Mk. 6 8[b]
no wallet, nor bread, neither have two coats, — Lu. 9 3[b]
50 nor shoes, nor staff; but be shod with { Mt. 10 10[b]
{ Mk. 6 9[a]
sandals: for the labourer is worthy of his — Mt. 10 10[c]
51 food. And into whatsoever city or village — Mt. 10 11
ye shall enter, inquire who in it is worthy;
52 and there abide till ye go forth. And as ye — ,, 12
53 enter into the house, salute it. And if the — ,, 13
house be worthy, your peace shall come upon
it: but if it be not worthy, your peace shall
54 return to you. And whosoever shall not — ,, 14[a]
receive you, nor hear your words, as ye go
forth out of that house, or out of that city,
shake off the dust that is under your feet — Mk. 6 11[b]
55 upon them for a testimony. Verily I say — Mt. 10 15
unto you, There shall be rest for the land of

---

[1] Omitting "raise the dead." [2] Or, "purses."

[3] The distinction which Tatian here draws between "wand" and "staff," receives no support from the Greek, where we find the same word for what was allowed according to S. Mark, and for what was forbidden according to the other synoptists. The actual Greek phrases are: Matt. μηδὲ ῥάβδον; Mark, εἰ μὴ ῥάβδον μόνον; Luke, μήτε ῥάβδον.

Ephraem has this distinction; but it is not in the *Codex Fuldensis*, where the "wand" alone is mentioned, and is forbidden. According to the Armenian the word "staff" seems more applicable to what was allowed; whilst what was forbidden was a rough stick. The Peschito has the same word throughout. The Curetonian (Luke only) has also that word. The Jerusalem Syriac (Luke only) has a different word, which occurs in the Peschito of Mark xiv. 43. There can be little doubt that Tatian first drew the distinction in his Syriac.

Sodom and Gomorrah in the day of judgment in preference to that city.

13 1   I send you forth as lambs in the midst of wolves: be ye therefore wise as serpents,   Mt. 10 16
2 and spotless¹ as doves. Beware of men,² „   17
who will deliver you up to councils, and
3 scourge you in their synagogues; and before „   18
governors and before kings shall they bring you for my sake, for a testimony to them
4 and to the Gentiles. But when they „   19
deliver you up, do not premeditate and consider what ye speak: but it shall be given you in that hour what ye must speak.
5 For it is not ye that speak; but the Spirit „   20
6 of your Father speaketh in you. A brother „   21
shall deliver up his brother unto death, and a father *his* son; and sons shall rise up against their parents, and put them to death.
7 And ye shall be hated of all men for my „   22
name's sake: but whosoever endureth to the
8 end, the same shall live. When they shall cast „   23
you out of this city, flee into another. Verily I say unto you, Ye shall not complete all the cities of the people of Israel, till the Son of man come.
9   A disciple is not superior to his master, „   24
10 nor a servant to his lord. For it is enough „   25
for the disciple that he be as his master, and for the servant *that he be* as his lord. If they have called the master of the house Beelzebub,³ how much more *shall*
11 *they call* them of his household! Fear them „   26
not therefore: for there is nothing covered, that shall not be revealed; nor hidden, that shall not be shown forth, and made known.
12 What I tell you in the darkness, speak ye in „   27ᵃ
the light: and what ye have spoken secretly   Lu.⁴ 12 3ᵇ

¹ Or, "peaceable."   ² Cf. xli. 43, etc.   ³ Lit. "Beelzebul."
⁴ Tatian probably meant this as a continuation of Matt. x. 27; as he brings this in later at xli. 20ᵇ.

13	13	in the ears in the bedchambers, shall be proclaimed upon the housetop. I say unto you, my friends, be not afraid of them, which kill the body, but are not able to kill the	Lu. Mt.	12 10	4ᵃ 28ᵇ
	14	soul. I will show you whom ye shall fear: him, who is able to destroy both soul and body into Gehenna: yea, I say unto you,	Lu. Mt. Lu.	12 10 12	5ᵃ 28ᶜ 5ᶜ
	15	Fear him especially. Are not two sparrows sold for a mite¹ in a shop,² and not one of them falleth to the ground without your	Mt.	10	29
	16	Father: but in what relates to you, even	,,		30
	17	the hairs of your head are numbered. Fear not therefore: ye are better than many	,,		31
	18	sparrows. Every one therefore, who shall confess me before men, him will I also confess before my Father, which is in the	,,		32
	19	heavens. But whosoever shall deny me before men, him will I also deny before my Father, which is in the heavens.	,,		33
	20	Think ye that I am come to send peace unto the earth? I am not come to send	Lu.	12	51
	21	peace but division: there shall be from henceforth five in one house; three of them shall be divided against two, and two against	,,		52
	22	three. They shall be divided, the father against his son, and the son against his father; the mother against the daughter, and the daughter against her mother; the mother-in-law against her daughter-in-law, and the daughter-in-law against her mother-	,,		53
	23	in-law: and a man's foes shall be they of his	Mt.	10	36
	24	own household. He that loveth father or mother more than me, is not worthy of me: and he that loveth son or daughter with a deeper love than me, is not worthy of me.	,,		37
	25	And every one that doth not take his cross,	,,		38
	26	and follow me, is not worthy of me. He that findeth his life, shall lose it; and who-	,,		39

¹ Arabic, "fals;" cf. viii. 56.
² Or, "tavern," showing that they were sold for eating.

	soever loseth his life for my sake, shall find it.	
13 27	He that receiveth you, receiveth me; and he that receiveth me, receiveth him that sent	Mt. 10 40
28	me. And he that receiveth a prophet in the name of a prophet, shall receive a prophet's reward: and he that receiveth a righteous man in the name of a righteous man, shall	„ 41
29	receive a righteous man's reward. And whosoever shall give as a drink unto one of these very little ones a cup of water only, in the name of a disciple, verily I say unto you, He shall not lose his reward.	„ 42[a] Mk.[1] 9 41[b]
30	And when Jesus had ended his commands to his twelve disciples, he passed over from thence to teach and preach in their cities.	Mt. 11 1
31	And as they went on their way, he entered into a certain village: and a woman named	Lu.[2] 10 38
32	Martha entertained him in her house. And she had a sister named Mary, who came[3] and sat at the Lord's feet, and listened to his	„ 39
33	word. But Martha was distracted about much serving; and she came, and saith unto him, Lord, dost thou not care that my sister hath left me to serve alone? bid her that	„ 40
34	she help me. Jesus answered, and said unto her, Martha, Martha, thou art anxious and	„ 41
35	troubled about many things: and that which is needed is one: for Mary hath chosen for herself a good part, which shall not be taken away from her.	„ 42
36	And the apostles went out, and preached	Mk. 6 12
37	unto men, that they should repent. And	„ 13

---

[1] Or conclusion of Matt. x. 42.

[2] A singular displacement from S. Luke's order. It may have been put here to illustrate ver. 27-29 above. Tatian makes the sisters reside apparently in Galilee, not at Bethany. This is the natural impression conveyed by S. Luke, and it was adopted by Greswell; but the idea prevails that S. Luke has intentionally placed it *too early.*

[3] So Ephraem, the Curetonian, and the Peschito.

	they cast out many devils, and anointed with oil many sick *men*, and healed them.	
13 38	And the disciples of John told him of	Lu. 7 18
39	all these things. And John, when he had heard in the prison the works of the Christ,	Mt. 11 2ᵃ
	called two of his disciples, and sent them to Jesus, saying, Art thou he that cometh,	Lu. 7 19
40	or look we for another? And they came unto Jesus, and said, John the Baptist hath sent us unto thee, and said, Art thou he	„ 20
41	that cometh, or look we for another? Now in that hour he cured many of diseases, and of plagues of an evil spirit; and on	„ 21
42	many blind *men* he bestowed sight. Jesus answered, and said unto them, Go, and relate to John all things which ye have seen and heard; the blind receive their sight, the lame walk, the lepers are cleansed, the deaf hear, the dead rise again, the poor have	„ 22
43	good tidings preached to them: and blessed is he whosoever shall not be made to stumble in me.	„ 23
44	And when the disciples of John were departed, Jesus began to say unto the multitudes concerning John, What went ye out into the wilderness to see? a reed	„ 24
45	shaken with the wind? Otherwise, what went ye out to see? a man clothed in soft raiment? Behold, they which are in a costly robe and luxuries, are in king's	„ 25
46	houses. Otherwise, what went ye out to see? a prophet? Yea, I say unto you, and	„ 26
47	more than a prophet. This is he of whom it is written,	„ 27
	Behold I send my messenger before thy face,	
	To prepare a way before thee.	
14 1	Verily I say unto you, Among them that are born of women there hath not arisen a greater than John the Baptist: yet he that	Mt. 11 11

14 1 is less in the kingdom of the heavens, is   Lu. 7 29
2 greater than he. And all the people that
were listening, and the publicans, justified
God, for they had been baptized with the
3 baptism of John. But the Pharisees and   „ 30
the scribes treated unjustly the counsel of
God among themselves, for they had not
4 been baptized by him. But[1] from the days   Mt. 11 12ᵃ
of John the Baptist until now the kingdom
5 of the heavens is seized with violence. The   Lu. 16 16
law and the prophets *were* until John: from
thenceforth the kingdom of God is announced
as good tidings, and all men push themselves forward, that they may enter; and   Mt. 11 12ᵇ
those who strive hard, take it by force.
6 All the prophets and the law prophesied   „ 13
7 until John. And if ye are willing, receive   „ 14
it that he is Elijah, which is about to come.
8 He that hath ears to hear let him hear.   „ 15
9 It is easier for heaven and earth to perish,   Lu. 16 17
than for one point to fall[2] from the law.
10 Unto whom then shall I liken the men of   „ 7 31ᵇ
this generation, and to whom are they like?
11 They are like unto children sitting in the   „ 32
market place, which summon their companions, and say, We chaunted unto you,
and ye did not dance; we mourned unto
12 you, and ye did not weep. John the Baptist   „ 33
came eating no bread nor drinking wine;
13 and ye said, He hath a devil. But the Son   „ 34
of man came eating and drinking; and ye
said, Behold, a gluttonous man, and a wine-
bibber, and a friend of publicans and sinners!
14 And wisdom was justified by all her children.   „ 35
15 And when he had said this, they came   Mk. 3 20
into the house. And the multitudes came
together unto him again, so that they

---

[1] The discourse of Jesus is resumed here without remark, ver. 2, 3 being explanatory on the part of some person recording what took place.

[2] Or, "cease."

14

16 could not even eat bread. And he was Lu. 11 14
casting out a devil, which was dumb.¹ And
when he had cast out that devil, the dumb
man spake, and the multitudes marvelled.

17 But when the Pharisees heard it, they said, Mt. 12 24
This man doth not cast out devils, except in
Beelzebub,² the prince of the devils, who is

18 in him. And others, tempting him,³ sought Lu. 11 16

19 of him a sign from heaven. But Jesus, Mt. 12 25
knowing their thoughts, said unto them in
parables, Every kingdom divided against
itself will be brought to desolation: and
every house or city divided against itself

20 will not stand: and if Satan casteth out   „   26ª
Satan, he is divided against himself, and Mk. 3 26ᵇ
will not be able to stand, but his end will

21 be. How then shall his kingdom stand? Mt. 12 26ᵇ
because ye say that I cast out devils in Lu. 11 18ᵇ

22 Beelzebub.² And if I in Beelzebub² cast Mt. 12 27
out devils, by what do your sons cast them
out? therefore shall they be your judges.

23 But if I in the Spirit of God cast out devils,   „   28
then is the kingdom of God come near unto

24 you. Or how can any one enter into the   „   29
house of a strong *man*, and rob his goods,⁴
except he first render himself safe from the
strong man? and then he will spoil his

25 house. When the strong *man* armed Lu. 11 21
guardeth his own court, those things which

26 he possesseth are in peace: but if a stronger   „   22
than he come upon him, he will overcome
him, and will take from him his whole
armour wherein he trusteth, and divide his

27 spoils. He that is not with me is against   „   23
me; and he that gathereth not with me

---

¹ Tatian does not identify with this miracle the cure of a demoniac "*blind and dumb*," prefixed (Matt. xii. 22) to the same discourse, but puts the latter afterwards. Tischendorf identifies the former with Matt. ix. 32-34.

² Lit. "Beelzebul."   ³ Or, "that he might be put to the test."

⁴ Lit. "garments."

14 28	surely scattereth. Therefore I say unto you,	Mk.	3 28
	All sins shall be forgiven unto men, and the blasphemies, wherewithsoever they shall		
29	blaspheme; but whosoever shall blaspheme against the Holy Spirit shall never have forgiveness, but shall be accounted worthy	,,	29
30	of eternal punishment. Because[1] they said, that there was in him an unclean spirit,	,,	30
31	he said again, Whosoever shall speak a word against the Son of man, it shall be forgiven him; but whosoever shall speak against the Holy Spirit, it shall not be forgiven him, neither in this world[2] nor in the world[2] to	Mt.	12 32
32	come. Either ye make the tree good, and its fruit good; or ye make the tree evil, and its fruit evil: since the tree is known by its	,,	33
33	fruit. Ye offspring of vipers, how can ye, since ye are evil, speak good things? out of the abundance of the heart the mouth	,,	34
34	speaketh. The good man out of the good treasure, which is in his heart, bringeth forth good things; and the evil man out of the evil treasure, which is in his heart, bringeth	Lu.[3]	6 45[a]
35	forth evil things. I say unto you, that every idle word that men shall speak, there shall be exacted from them an account of it in	Mt.	12 36
36	the day of judgment. For out of thy words thou shalt be justified; and out of thy words	,,	37
37	thou shalt be condemned. And he said to the multitudes, When ye see a[4] cloud rising	Lu.	12 54

[1] This clause is made to begin the new sentence instead of closing the old.

[2] Or, "age."

[3] Apparently meant by Tatian for Matt. xii. 35, making the passage continuous. Luke vi. 45 he has before identified with the Sermon on the Mount; cf. x. 38.

[4] Or, "the." It is very remarkable that, whereas both S. Matthew (xii. 38) and S. Luke (xi. 29) continue the preceding discourse with the demand for a sign from heaven, Tatian postpones that until xvi. 1, and inserts instead the signs of coming weather. Many commentators think the former ought to be postponed and the visit of Christ's brethren inserted here, followed by the series of parables, as in Mark iii. 31, etc.

14	38	from the west, straightway ye say, The rain cometh; and so it cometh to pass. And when it bloweth a south wind, ye say, There will be a scorching heat; and it cometh to	Lu.	12 55
	39	pass. And when it is evening, ye say, It	Mt.[1]	16 2[b]
	40	will be fair, for the heavens are dull. And in the morning ye say, To-day there will be a storm: for the redness of the heavens is dull. Ye hypocrites, ye know how to judge the face of the heaven and the earth; but ye know not how to discern the signs of this time.	„	3
	41	Then[2] was brought unto him one that had a devil, dumb and blind; and he healed him, so that the dumb and blind man spake and	Mt.	12 22
	42	saw. And all the multitudes were amazed, and said, Is this, think you, the son of David?	„	23
	43	And the apostles returned[3] unto Jesus, and recounted unto him all things, which	Mk.	6 30
	44	they had done, and wrought. And he saith unto them, Come, let us go apart into a desert place,[4] and rest a little. For there were many going and returning; and they had no leisure even to eat bread.	„	31
	45	After these things came a certain man of the Pharisees, and asked him to eat bread with him. And he entered into the Phari-	Lu.	7 36
	46	see's house, and reclined *to meat*. And there was in that city a woman, a sinner; and when she knew that he had reclined *to meat* in the Pharisee's house, she took a flask of	„	37
	47	ointment, and standing behind at his feet, weeping, she began to wet his feet with tears, and wiped them with the hair of her head, and kissed his feet, and anointed them	„	38

---

[1] Cf. xxiii. 13, where Matt. xvi. 1ᵃ is made to introduce Mark viii. 11ᵇ, followed by Matt. xvi. 4ᵇ, etc.

[2] Cf. note to ver. 16.

[3] Put before Mark vi. 14-29 (death of S. John), because S. Matthew, who does not mention this return, puts that death at a later period of the history.

[4] Tatian omits Luke ix. 10, "belonging to the city called Bethsaida."

14	48	with the ointment. Now when the Pharisee, which had bidden him, saw it, he thought within himself, saying, This man, if he were a prophet, would certainly know who she is, and of what sort her character is, since the woman, that touched him, was a sinner.	Lu.	7 39
15	1	Jesus answered, and said unto him, Simon, I have somewhat to say unto thee. Then	„	40
	2	he saith, Master, say on. Jesus said unto him, A certain creditor had two debtors: the one owed five hundred pence, and the	„	41
	3	other owed fifty pence. When they had not from whence to pay, he forgave them both. Which ought to love him the more?	„	42
	4	Simon answered, and said, He, I suppose, to whom he forgave the more. Jesus said unto	„	43
	5	him, Thou hast rightly judged. And, turning to the woman, he said unto Simon, See this woman. I entered into thine house; and water for washing my feet thou gavest not: but she hath wetted my feet with	„	44
	6	tears, and wiped them with her hair. A kiss thou gavest me not: but she, since the time she came in, hath not ceased to kiss	„	45
	7	my feet. My head with oil thou didst not anoint: but she hath anointed my feet with	„	46
	8	ointment. On account of which I say unto thee, Many sins are forgiven her; for she loved much: but to whom little is forgiven,	„	47
	9	*the same* loveth little. And he said unto the woman, Thy sins are forgiven thee.	„	48
	10	And they that were bidden began to say within themselves, Who is this that even	„	49
	11	forgiveth sins? And Jesus said unto the woman, Thy faith hath saved thee; go in peace.	„	50
	12	And many believed on him, beholding	Jn.[1]	2 23[b]

[1] Tatian having removed these remarks of the evangelist from their setting, has found it necessary to omit the first part of this verse, which applied them to a particular occasion.

15	13	the signs which he did. But Jesus did not trust himself with them, for that he knew	Jn.	2 24
	14	all men, and he had no need that any one should bear witness unto him concerning a man; for he himself knew what was in the man.	,,	25
	15	Now¹ after these things Jesus appointed out of his disciples seventy² others, and sent them two and two before his face³ into every country and city, whither he himself	Lu.	10 1
	16	was about to come. And he said unto them, The⁴ harvest is plenteous, but the labourers are few; pray ye therefore the Lord of the harvest, that he may send forth labourers	,,	2
	17	into his harvest. Go your ways: behold, I send you forth as lambs in the midst of	,,	3
	18	wolves. Take with you no purses,⁵ nor wallet, nor shoes: and salute no man on the	,,	4
	19	way. Into whatsoever house ye enter, first	,,	5
	20	salute that house. And if a son of peace be there, your peace shall rest upon him: and if he be not *there*, your peace shall turn to	,,	6
	21	you again. And in the same house remain, eating and drinking of their substance: for the labourer is worthy of his hire. And	,,	7
	22	cross not from house to house. And into whatsoever city ye enter, and they receive	,,	8

¹ See note to ver. 27.

² The *Codex Fuldensis* and the *Doctrine of Addai* have "seventy-two." Ephraem implies the same in two places (Moesinger, pp. 59 and 160). Cf. Appendix X., text and note at xv. 15.

³ Ephraem has, "after his own likeness," instead of "before his face." Cf. xii. 43 in Appendix X., where an insertion has been made from this passage.

⁴ The *Codex Fuldensis*, cap. 68, goes on here with ver. 32, "He that heareth," etc.; and Ephraem omits all comment on the instructions to the Seventy as such, but seems to refer to them in connection with the Mission of the Twelve (xii. 42 to xiii. 29). It seems likely that Tatian *harmonised* the two sets of instruction at the earlier place, and these verses have been inserted here since.

⁵ Addai, who is represented as one of the seventy-two, says, "That which was ours we have forsaken, as we were commanded by our Lord to be without purses and without scrips, and carrying crosses upon our shoulders we were commanded to preach His gospel to the whole creation."

15	23	you, eat the things which are set before you: and heal the sick that are therein, and	Lu.	10	9
	24	say unto them, The kingdom of God is come nigh unto you. But into whatsoever city ye	,,		10
	25	enter, and they receive you not, go out into the street, and say, Even the dust from your city, that clave to our feet, we do wipe off against you: howbeit know this, that the	,,		11
	26	kingdom of God is come nigh unto you. I say unto you, There shall be ease for Sodom in the day of judgment but not for that city.	,,		12
	27	Then began Jesus to upbraid[1] the cities, wherein many mighty works had been done,	Mt.	11	20
	28	and they had not repented. And he said, Woe unto thee, Chorazin! woe unto thee, Bethsaida! if the signs had been done in Tyre and Sidon, which were done in thee, they would peradventure have repented in	,,		21
	29	sackcloth and ashes. Howbeit I say unto you, There shall be rest for Tyre and Sidon in the day of judgment, rather than for you.	,,		22
	30	And thou, Capernaum, which art exalted even unto heaven, thou shalt sink down into the abyss: for if the gifts had been made to Sodom, which were made to thee, it would surely have remained even until this day.	,,		23
	31	And now I say unto thee, that there shall be ease for the land of Sodom in the day of judgment, rather than for you.	,,		24
	32	He said again to the apostles, He that heareth you, heareth me; and he that heareth me, heareth him that sent me; and he that rejecteth you, rejecteth me; and he that rejecteth me, rejecteth him that sent me.	Lu.	10	16

[1] Tatian has identified this passage with Luke x. 13-15; this appears to be his reason for placing Luke x. 1-12, which cannot well be dissociated from the latter, so much earlier than S. Luke did; for the evangelist clearly intended it to belong to the final departure from Galilee; and surely no time could be more appropriate for this upbraiding, than when Jesus was about to quit the country of these ungrateful cities.

15 33 And those seventy returned with great Lu. 10 17
joy, and said unto him, Lord, even the devils
34 are made subject unto us in thy name. He „   18
saith unto them, I saw Satan as lightning,
35 falling from heaven. Behold I have given „   19
you authority to tread upon serpents and
scorpions, and over every kind of enemies,
36 and nothing shall hurt you. Howbeit ye „   20
need not to rejoice, that the spirits are
subject unto you; but rejoice, because your
names are written in heaven.
37[1] And in the same hour Jesus rejoiced in „   21
the Holy Spirit, and said, I acknowledge
thee, O Father, Lord of heaven and earth,
that thou didst hide these things from the
wise and understanding, and didst reveal them
unto children: yea, Father, so was thy will.
38 And he turned unto his disciples,[2] and said „   22
unto them, All things have been delivered
unto me of my Father: and no one knoweth
who the Son is, save the Father; and who
the Father is, save the Son, and he to whom-
39 soever the Son willeth to reveal *him*. Come Mt. 11 28
unto me, all ye that are wearied and heavy
40 laden, and I will give you rest. Carry my „   29
yoke upon you, and learn of me; for[3] I am
meek and lowly in my heart: and ye shall
41 find rest for your souls. For my yoke is „   30
pleasant, and my burden light.
42 And when great multitudes were going Lu. 14 25
forth with him, he turned, and said unto
43 them,[4] He that cometh unto me, and hateth „   26
not his father, and his mother, and brethren,
and sisters, and wife, and children, yea, and
his own life also, cannot be my disciple.

---

[1] Cf. note on this passage in Appendix X.
[2] This additional clause is found in several MSS.
[3] Or, "that."
[4] Similarity of subject with the preceding seems to be the cause of the insertion of this passage here.

15 44 And he that doth not bear his own cross, Lu. 14 27
and follow me, cannot be my disciple.
45 Which of you, desiring to build a palace, „ 28
doth not first sit down and count his
expenses, and whether he have *wherewith*
46 to complete it? Lest after he lays the „ 29
foundations, and is not able to finish, all
47 that see him say, This man began to build, „ 30
48 and was not able to finish. Or what king, „ 31
about to go to commit war against another
king, doth not first consider, whether he is
able with ten thousand to meet him that
cometh against him with twenty thousand?
49 And if he is not equal to it, while he is yet „ 32
a great way off, he sendeth an embassy unto
50 him, and asketh for peace. So let every one of „ 33
you, that wisheth to be my disciple, consider:
for if he renounce not all that he possesseth,
he cannot be my disciple.

16 1 Then[1] certain of the scribes and Phari- Mt. 12 38
sees answered *him*, that they might tempt
him, saying, Master, we wish to see a sign
2 from thee. And he answering saith, This „ 39
evil and adulterous generation seeketh after
a sign; and there shall no sign be given to
3 it but the sign of Jonah the prophet: for Lu. 11 30
even as Jonah was a sign unto the Nine-
vites, so shall also the Son of man be to
4 this generation. And even as Jonah was Mt. 12 40
three days and three nights in the belly of
the whale, so shall the Son of man be three
days and three nights in the heart of the
5 earth. The queen of the south shall rise Lu. 11 31
up in the judgment against the men of this
generation, and shall condemn them: for
she came from the ends of the earth to
hear the wisdom of Solomon; and a better
6 than Solomon is here. The men of Nineveh Mt. 12 41
shall rise up in the judgment against this

[1] Cf. xxiii. 13-15. See note to xiv. 37.

16	7	generation, and shall condemn it: for they repented at the preaching of Jonah, and a greater than Jonah is here. When the unclean spirit goeth out of the man, it walketh and goeth about through waterless places to find rest for itself; and when it findeth it not, it saith, I will turn back	Lu. 11	24
	8	unto my house, whence I went out. And if it come, and find it adorned and arranged,	„	25
	9	then it goeth, and taketh with itself seven other spirits more evil than itself; and they enter in and dwell therein: and the last state of that man becometh worse than the former.	„	26
	10	So shall it be unto this evil generation.	Mt. 12	45[b]
	11	And as he said these things, a certain woman out of the multitude lifted up her voice, and said unto him, Blessed is the womb that bare thee, and the breasts which	Lu. 11	27
	12	gave thee milk. But he said unto her, Blessed is he that heareth the word of God, and keepeth it.	„	28
	13	While he was yet speaking to the multitudes, there came to him his mother and	Mt. 12 46[a] Lu. 8 19[a]
	14	brethren; and they sought to speak to him, and they could not for the crowd; and standing without, they sent to call him to	Mt. 12 46[b] {Lu. 8 19[b] {Mk. 3 31[b]
	15	them. A certain man said unto him, Behold, thy mother and thy brethren stand	Mt. 12	47
	16	without, and seek to speak to thee. He answered him that told him, Who is my	„	48
	17	mother? and who are my brethren? And motioning with his hand outstretched towards his disciples, he said, Behold, my	„	49
	18	mother, and behold, my brethren! For whosoever shall do the will of my Father, which is in the heavens, he is my brother, and sister, and mother.	„	50
	19	And after these things Jesus went round the cities and villages, preaching and announcing as good tidings the kingdom of	Lu. 8	1

16 20 God, and with him the twelve, and the | Lu. | 8 | 2
women which had been healed of infirmities
and of evil spirits, Mary that is called
Magdalene, from whom he had cast out
21 seven devils, and Joanna the wife of Chusa, | „ | | 3
Herod's steward, and Susanna, and many
others, which ministered unto them of their
substance.
22 And after these things Jesus went out | Mt. | 13 | 1
of the house, and sat on the seashore.
23 And there were gathered unto him great | „ | | 2
multitudes; and when the press of men
around him was great, he went up, and
sat in a boat; and all the multitude were
24 standing on the seashore. And he spake | „ | | 3
unto them many things in parables, saying,
25 He that soweth went forth to sow; and | „ | | 4^a
when he sowed, some[1] fell by the wayside,
and were trodden under foot, and the birds | Lu. | 8 | 5^b
26 devoured them: and others fell upon a | Mt. | 13 | 5
rock: and others,[2] where they had not much
earth: and straightway they sprang up, because they had no deepness in the earth:
27 and when the sun was risen, they were | „ | | 6
scorched; and because they had no root,
28 they withered away. And some fell among | Lu. | 8 | 7
the thorns; and the thorns sprang up at the
same time, and choked them; and they | Mk. | 4 | 7^b
29 yielded no fruit. And others fell into | Lu. | 8 | 8^a
ground good and beautiful, and came up, | Mk. | 4 | 8^b
and grew, and brought forth fruit, some
thirty, some sixty, and others a hundred.
30 When he had said these things, he cried, | Lu. | 8 | 8^c
He that hath ears to hear, let him hear.
31 And when they were alone, his disciples | Mk. | 4 | 10
came near, and asked him, and said unto him,
What is this parable? and why dost thou

---

[1] In the Arabic idiom "some" and "others" and the words dependent on them are given in the singular form throughout this parable.

[2] "And others" added.

16 32 speak unto them in parables? He answer- Mk. 4 11
ing saith unto them, Unto you is given the
knowledge of the secrets of the kingdom of
God: but it is not given unto them that
33 are without. He that hath, to him shall be Mt. 13 12
given, and he shall have increase: but he
that hath not, from him shall be taken
34 away even that which he hath. Therefore „ 13
speak I to them in parables; because seeing
they see not, and hearing they hear not,
35 nor understand. And in them is fulfilled „ 14
the prophecy of Isaiah, saying,
By hearing they shall hear,[1] and shall not
understand;
And seeing they shall see, and shall not
learn thoroughly:
36 For the heart of this people is waxed „ 15
gross,
And in their ears their hearing hath
become dull,
And their eyes they have closed;
Lest they should see with their eyes,
And hear with their ears,
And understand with their heart,
And should turn again,
And I should heal them.
37 But ye, blessed are your eyes, which see; „ 16
38 and your ears, which hear. Blessed are the Lu. 10 23[b]
eyes, which see the things which ye see.
39 Verily I say unto you, Many prophets and Mt. 13 17
righteous men desired to see the things
which ye see, and saw them not; and to
hear the things which ye hear, and heard
40 them not. If ye know not this parable, Mk. 4 13[b]
41 how shall ye know all the parables? Hear Mt. 13 18
42 ye the parable of the sower. The sower, Mk. 4 14
that soweth, soweth the word of God.
43 Every one that heareth the word of the Mt. 13 19
kingdom, and understandeth it not, the evil

[1] *I.e.* "They shall surely hear."

		one cometh, and snatcheth away the word sown in his heart. This is he[1] that was		
16	44	sown by the wayside. And he[1] that was	Mt. 13	20
		sown upon a rock, this is he that heareth the word, and straightway with joy receiveth		
	45	it; yet, since he hath no root in himself,	Mt. 13	21a
	46	but his faith in it is for a time, when	{ Lu. 8 13b / Mt. 13 21b	
		tribulation or persecution ariseth because of the word, straightway he is made to stumble.		
	47	And he[1] that was sown in the thorns, this	Mt. 13	22a
		is he that heareth the word; and the care of this world, and the deceitfulness of riches,		
		and the remaining lusts enter in, and choke	Mk. 4	19b
		the word, and it is rendered unfruitful.		
	48	And that which was sown into the good	Lu. 8	15
		ground, he it is that in a pure and excellent heart heareth my word, and understandeth, and holdeth it fast, and bringeth forth fruit		
		in patience, and produceth either a hundred-	Mt. 13	23b
		fold, or sixtyfold, or thirtyfold.		
	49	And he said, So is the kingdom of God	Mk. 4	26
		even as a man that should cast seed into		
	50	the earth, and should sleep and rise night	„	27
		and day; and the seed should sprout and		
	51	grow while he knoweth not. For the earth	„	28
		bringeth it through into fruit; first there will be the blade, afterwards the ear, and at		
	52	length the full corn in the ear. And when	„	29
		the fruit ripeneth,[2] straightway he bringeth the sickle, because the harvest is here.		
17	1	Another parable set he before them, saying,	Mt. 13	24
		The kingdom of heaven is likened unto a		
	2	man that sowed good seed in his field: but	„	25
		while men slept, his enemy came and sowed tares amidst the wheat, and went away.		
	3	But when the blade had sprung up, and	„	26
		brought forth fruit, then appeared the tares		
	4	also. And the servants of the householder	„	27
		came, and said unto him, Sir, didst thou not		

[1] Or, "that which," as ver. 48.   [2] Lit. "fatteneth."

17	5	sow good seed in thy field? whence are the tares in it? He saith unto them, An enemy hath done this? The servants said unto him, Wilt thou that we go, and pick them	Mt. 13	28
	6	out? He saith unto them, Would you not perchance, when you picked out the tares,	„	29
	7	root up also the wheat with them? Let both grow together until the harvest, and at the time of the harvest I will say to the reapers, Pick out first the tares, and bind them into bundles for burning with fire: but gather the wheat into my barns.	„	30
	8	And another parable set he before them,	„	31^a
	9	saying, Unto what is the kingdom of God like? and whereunto shall I liken it? and	Lu. 13 Mk. 4	18^b 30^b
	10	with what parable shall I compare it? It is like unto a grain of mustard seed, which	Lu. 13 Mt. 13	19^a 31^c
	11	a man took, and sowed in his field: and which of all things that are sown in the earth, is less than all the things that are	Mk. 4	31^b
	12	sown, that are upon the earth; but when it hath sprung up, it is greater than all the herbs, and maketh great branches; so that the birds of the heaven build nests in its branches.	Mt. 13 Mk. 4	32^b 32^b
	13	And another parable set he before them.	Mt. 13	33^a
	14	Whereunto shall I liken the kingdom of God?	Lu. 13	20^b
	15	It is like unto leaven, which a woman took, and kneaded in three measures of meal, till the whole was leavened.	Mt. 13	33^b
	16	All these things spake Jesus in parables unto the multitudes, as they were able to hear *them*: and without parables spake he	„ Mk. 4 Mt. 13	34^a 33^b 34^b
	17	not unto them: that it might be fulfilled, which was spoken by the Lord through the prophet, saying, I will open my mouth in parables, And I will utter things hidden before the foundation of the world.	„	35
	18	But privately to his disciples he expounded all things.	Mk. 4	34^b

17 19	Then Jesus sent the multitudes away, and came into the house: and his disciples came near unto him, and said unto him, Explain unto us the parable of the tares and the	Mt. 13	36
20	field. He answered and saith unto them, He that sowed the good seed is the Son of	,,	37
21	man; and the field is the world; the good seed are the sons of the kingdom; and the	,,	38
22	tares are the sons of the evil *one;* and the enemy that sowed them is Satan: but the harvest is the end of the world; and the	,,	39
23	reapers are angels. And even as the tares are picked out, and burned with fire; so	,,	40
24	shall it be in the end of this world. The Son of man shall send forth his angels, and they shall pick out of his kingdom all things that cause stumbling,[1] and all the workers	,,	41
25	of iniquity, and shall cast them into the furnace of fire: there shall be the weeping	,,	42
26	and gnashing of teeth. Then shall the righteous shine forth as the sun in the kingdom of their Father. He that hath ears to hear, let him hear.	,,	43
27	Again, the kingdom of heaven is like unto a treasure hidden in the field; which the man that findeth, hideth; and for joy thereof goeth and selleth all that he hath, and buyeth that field.	,,	44
28	Again, the kingdom of heaven is like unto a merchant-man seeking pearls of great	,,	45
29	price: and having found one pearl of great price, he went and sold all that he had, and bought it.	,,	46
30	Again, the kingdom of heaven is like unto a net cast into the sea, and gathering of	,,	47
31	every kind: which, when it was filled, they drew up on the seashore; and sat down to pick them out, and they cast the good into vessels, but the bad they threw away out-	,,	48

[1] Or, "injure."

17 32 side. So shall it be in the end of the world: Mt. 13 49
the angels shall go forth, and sever the
wicked from the midst of the righteous,
33 and shall cast them into the furnace of fire: „   50
there shall be the weeping and gnashing of
teeth.
34 Jesus saith unto them, Have ye understood „ 51
all these things? They said unto him, Yea,
35 Lord. He saith unto them, Therefore every „ 52
scribe, *that is* a disciple of the kingdom of
the heavens, is like unto a man that is a
householder, which bringeth forth out of his
treasure things new and old.
36 And when Jesus had finished all these „ 53
37 parables, he passed over from thence, and „ 54ᵃ
came into his own city, and taught them in
their synagogues, insomuch that they were
38 astonished. And when the sabbath was Mk. 6 2
come, Jesus began to teach in the synagogue:
and many of those that heard him were
astonished, and said, Whence are these things
39 done unto this man?[1] And many envied
him, and did not apply their mind to him,
but said, What is this wisdom that is given
unto this man, so that such mighty works
40 are wrought by his hands? Is not this the Mt. 13 55
carpenter, the son of the carpenter? is not
his mother called Mary? and his brethren,
James, and Joses, and Simon, and Judas?
41 And his sisters, are they not all with us? „ 56
Whence hath this man all these things?
42 And they were suspicious of him. But { Mt. 13 57ᵃ / Lu.[2] 4 23 }
Jesus, knowing their thoughts, saith unto

---

[1] Or, "hath this man these things?"

[2] It is noticeable how Tatian has cut off part of a continuous account of a visit to Nazareth, beginning at Luke iv. 16, in order to harmonise it with parallel passages in S. Matthew and S. Mark belonging to a later portion of Christ's ministry. The reason for this may have been the mention of a previous visit to Capernaum not recorded earlier in S. Luke, and which had not been placed in the *Diatessaron*, when the first portion of this narrative was inserted at v. 35.

		them, Peradventure ye will say unto me this parable, Physician, heal thyself first: all things that we have heard that thou hast done in Capernaum, do also here in			
17	43	thine own city. And he saith, Verily I say unto you, No prophet is accepted in his own	Lu.	4	24
	44	country, nor among his own brethren: for a prophet is not without[1] honour save in his own country, and among his own kin, and in	Mk.	6	4[b]
	45	his own house. Verily I say unto you, There were many widows among the children of Israel in the days of Elijah the prophet, when the heaven was shut up three years and six months, and a great famine was in	Lu.	4	25
	46	all the land; and unto none of them was Elijah sent, but only to Sarepta of Sidon,	,,		26
	47	unto a widow woman. And there were many lepers among the children of Israel in the days of Elisha the prophet; and no one of them was cleansed, but only Naaman the	,,		27
	48	Nabathaean.[2] And he could not do many mighty works there, because of their unbelief, save that he laid his hands upon a few sick	Mk.	6	5
	49	folk, and healed them. And he marvelled	,,		6[a]
	50	at their lack of faith. And when they that were in the synagogue had heard, they were	Lu.	4	28
	51	all filled with wrath; and they rose up and brought him forth out of the city, and led him unto the brow of the hill whereon their city was built, that they might cast him	,,		29
	52	from its summit. But he, passing through the midst of them, went away.	,,		30
	53	And he went about the villages around Nazareth, and taught in their synagogues.	Mk.	6	6[b]
18	1	At that time Herod the tetrarch heard the fame of Jesus, and all things that were done by his hand: and he marvelled, for	Mt. Lu. Mk.	14 9 6	1 7[b] 14[b]
	2	his fame had firmly stood. And some said,	Lu.	9	7[c]

[1] Or, "despised."
[2] Or, "of Nebaioth." The Peschito has "Aramian."

8

		John the Baptist is risen from the dead;	Lu.	9	8a
18	3	but others said, Elijah hath appeared; but	Mt.[1]	16	14b
		others, Jeremiah; and others, A prophet out	Lu.	9	8b
	4	of the ancient prophets is risen; and others	Mk.	6	15b
		said, He is a prophet, just as one of the			
	5	prophets. Herod said unto his servants,	,,		16
		This is John the Baptist, whose head I cut			
		off: he is risen from the dead, therefore	Mt.	14	2b
	6	mighty works are wrought by him. For	Mk.	6	17
		Herod had sent forth, and laid hold upon John, and cast him into prison for the sake of Herodias, his brother Philip's wife, whom			
	7	he had married. For John said unto Herod, Thou hast no right to have thy brother's	,,		18
	8	wife. And Herodias avoided him, and desired	,,		19
	9	to kill him; and she could not; for Herod feared John, knowing that he was a righteous man, and a holy; and he used to keep him safe, and hear him much, and do, and obey	,,		20
	10	him gladly. And when he wished to put him to death, he feared the people, because	Mt.	14	5
	11	they counted him as a prophet. And there occurred a festival; for Herod on his birthday made a feast to his great men and to the officers and the chief men of Galilee;	Mk.	6	21
	12	and the daughter of Herodias came in and danced in the midst of the assembly, and fascinated Herod and them that reclined *at meat* with him; and the king said unto the damsel, Ask of me what thou wilt, and I	,,		22
	13	will give it thee. And he sware unto her, Whatsoever thou shalt ask of me, I will	,,		23
	14	give it, unto the half of my kingdom. And she went out, and said unto her mother, What shall I ask of him? She said unto	,,		24
	15	her, The head of John the Baptist. And she came in straightway with haste unto the	,,		25

[1] Tatian seems to have added the words, "but others Jeremiah," to the opinions which Herod heard about Jesus, copying them from the opinions which the disciples had heard about Him. Cf. xxiii. 33.

18 16	king, and said unto him, I will that in this hour thou give me in a dish the head of John the Baptist. And the king was exceed-	Mk.	6 26
17	ing sorry; but for the sake of the oath, and of the guests, he would not deny her. But straightway the king sent forth an execu-	„	27
	tioner, and commanded that the head of John should be brought: and he went and		
18	cut off the head of John in the prison, and brought it upon a dish, and handed it to the damsel; and the damsel gave it to her	„	28
19	mother. And when his disciples heard thereof, they came and took up his body, and	„	29
	buried it: and they came to tell Jesus what	Mt.	14 12^b
20	had happened. For this cause Herod had said, John I beheaded: who is this, about whom I hear these things? and he wished	Lu.	9 9
21	to see him. Now Jesus when he had heard	Mt.	14 13^a
	it, withdrew from thence in a boat to a desert place apart,[1] to the other side of the sea of Galilee of Tiberius.	Jn.	6 1^b
22	And many saw them going, and recognised	Mk.	6 33
	them; and hurrying on foot from all the cities went thither before them; because they saw	Jn.	6 2^b
23	the signs which he did on the sick. Jesus	„	3
	therefore went up into the mountain, and		
24	there he sat with his disciples. Now the feast	„	4
	of the passover of the Jews was very near.		
25	And Jesus lifted up his eyes, and saw a	„	5^a
	great multitude coming unto him; and he	Mk.	6 34^b
	had compassion on them, because they were		
26	as sheep not having a shepherd: and he	Lu.[2]	9 11^b
	welcomed them, and spake to them of the kingdom, and them that had need of healing,		
27	he healed. And when even was come, the	Mt.	14 15^a
	disciples came to him, saying, The place is		
28	desert, and the time is already past; send	Mk.	6 36
	away the multitudes of men, that they may		

[1] Or, "by himself;" cf. ver. 46.
[2] Cf. xxxii. 23. This seems the right place for the extract.

	go into the surrounding farms¹ and villages, and buy themselves bread, for they have		
18 29	nothing to eat. But he said unto them,	Mt. 14	16
30	They have no need to go away; give ye them to eat. They said unto him, We have none here. He said unto Philip, Whence may we buy bread, that these may eat?	„ Jn. 6	17ª 5ᵇ
31	And this he said proving him: for he him-	„	6
32	self knew what he was about to do. Philip said unto him, Two hundred pennyworth of bread is not sufficient for them, that every	„	7
33	one may take a little. One of his disciples, to wit Andrew, the brother of Simon Cephas,	„	8
34	said unto him, There is a lad here, which hath five barley loaves, and two fishes: but	„	9
35	this amount, what is it for all these? but wilt thou that we go and buy for all the people what they may eat? for we have no more than these five loaves and two fishes.	Lu. 9	13ᵇ
36	Now there was much grass in that place. Jesus said unto them, Arrange them all, so that they may sit upon the grass by companies of fifty each. And the disciples did	Jn.² 6	10
37	so. And they all reclined by companies, a	Mk. 6	40
38	hundred each, and fifty each. Then Jesus saith unto them, Bring hither those five	Mt. 14	18
39	loaves and the two fishes. And when they had brought them, Jesus took the loaves and the fishes, and looking up to heaven, he blessed, and brake, and gave to his disciples	Mk. 6	41
40	to set before them; and the disciples set before the multitudes the bread and the fish. And they did all eat and were filled.	Mt. 14 „	19ᵇ 20ª
41	And when they were filled, he said to his disciples, Gather up the broken pieces which	Jn. 6	12
42	remain over, that nothing be lost. And they gathered them up, and filled twelve baskets with the broken pieces, which remained over from them that had eaten out	„	13

¹ Or, "towns." ² And parallel passages.

of the five barley loaves and the two fishes.

18 43 And they that had eaten were five thousand   Mt. 14 21
men, besides the women and children.

44   And straightway he constrained his dis-   Mk. 6 45
ciples to go up into the boat, and to go
before him across the sea to Bethsaida, while

45 he himself sent the multitudes away. Now   Jn. 6 14
those men that had seen the sign which
Jesus had done, said, This is of a truth a
prophet that hath come into the world.

46 And Jesus, knowing of their intention to   ,,   15
come to take him by force, and make him
king, left them, and went up into the mountain, himself alone, to pray.

47   And when it was become late, his dis-   ,,   16

48 ciples went down unto the sea, and sitting   ,,   17
in a boat they came across the sea unto
Capernaum. And darkness prevailed, and

49 Jesus had not come to them. Now the sea   ,,   18
was swelling against them on account of a

50 violent wind blowing: and the boat was   Mt. 14 24
many furlongs[1] distant from the land, and
they were much tossed about[2] by the waves;

19 1 *for* they had a contrary wind. And in the   ,,   25
fourth watch of the night Jesus came unto

2 them, walking upon the water. After they   Jn. 6 19[a]
had with difficulty made way about five and
twenty or thirty furlongs, and when he had

3 come nigh unto their boat, his disciples saw   Mt. 14 26
him walking on the water; and they were
troubled, thinking that it was an apparition;[3]

4 and they cried out for fear. And straight-   ,,   27
way Jesus spake unto them, saying, Be of

5 good cheer; it is I; be not afraid. And   ,,   28
Cephas answered, and said unto him, Lord, if
it be thou, bid me come unto thee upon the

---

[1] So in some versions, including the Curetonian and Peschito; but cf. John vi. 19, from which Tatian may have taken it. Cf. also the margin of the Revised Version.

[2] Or, "damaged."   [3] Lit. "delusive appearance."

19 6 waters. And Jesus said unto him, Come. And Cephas went down from the boat, and walked upon the water, to come to Jesus.	Mt.	14 29
7 But when he saw the wind was strong, he was afraid; and when he was near to sink, he lifted up his voice, and said, Lord, save	„	30
8 me. And immediately the Lord stretched forth his hand, and took hold of him, and said unto him, O thou of little faith, where-	„	31
9 fore didst thou doubt? And when Jesus had come near, he went up into the boat, himself and Simon, and immediately the	„	32
10 wind ceased. And they that were in the boat came, and worshipped him, saying, Of	„	33
11 a truth thou art the Son of God. And straightway the boat arrived at the land,[1] to	Jn.	6 21^b
12 which they were going. And when they were come out of the boat unto the land, they marvelled greatly one with another, and	Mk.	6 54^a
	„	51^b
13 were amazed among themselves; for they had not understood concerning that bread, because their heart was hard.	„	52
14 And when the people of that country perceived the arrival of Jesus, they ran about that whole land, and began to bring on their beds those that were sick, where	„	54^b
	„	55
15 they heard that he was. And whithersoever he entered into villages and into cities, they laid the sick in the streets, and besought him that they might touch even the fringe of his garment: and as many as touched him were made sound and whole.	„	56
16 On the next day the multitude that stood on the other side of the sea, beheld, and there was no other boat there save that, into which the disciples had gone up; and *they beheld* that Jesus had not gone up with	Jn.	6 22

---

[1] Tatian seems to have omitted the mention of Gennesareth (Mark vi. 53 and Matt. xiv. 34) as superfluous after the mention of Bethsaida in xviii. 44. He slightly transposes S. Mark for better order of the combined narrative.

THE DIATESSARON.

19 17 his disciples into the boat; but there were   Jn.   6   23
18 other boats from Tiberias nigh unto the place, where they had eaten the bread, when Jesus blessed *it*. When the multitude there-   „   24
19 fore saw that Jesus was not there, nor his disciples, they went up into those boats, and came to Capernaum, and sought Jesus. And   „   25
20 when they had found him on the other side of the sea, they said unto him, Master, when camest thou hither? Jesus answered, and   „   26
21 said unto them, Verily, verily, I say unto you, Ye have not sought me, because ye saw the signs, but because ye ate of the bread, and were filled. Work not for the food   „   27
22 which perisheth, but for the food which abideth unto[1] eternal life, which the Son of man shall give unto you: him God the Father hath sealed. They said unto him,   „   28
23 What shall we do, that we may work the work of God? Jesus answered, and said   „   29
24 unto them, This is the work of God, that ye believe in him whom he hath sent. They   „   30
25 said unto him, What sign hast thou done, that we might see and believe in thee? what hast thou wrought? Our fathers ate the   „   31
26 manna in the wilderness, as it is written, He gave them bread out of heaven to eat. Jesus said unto them, Verily, verily, I say   „   32
27 unto you, Moses gave you not the bread out of heaven; but my Father giveth[2] you the true bread out of heaven. The bread of   „   33
God is that which cometh[3] down out of heaven, and giveth life unto the world.
28 They said unto him, Lord, give us this bread   „   34
29 always. Jesus said unto them, I am the   „   35
bread of life: he that cometh to me shall not hunger, and he that believeth in me
30 shall never thirst. But I said unto you,   „   36
31 Ye have seen me, and believe not. Every-   „   37

[1] Or, "in."   [2] Or, "gave."   [3] Or, "came."

	thing which my Father hath given me shall come unto me; and him that cometh to me		
19 32	I will not cast out. For I am come down from heaven not to do mine own will, but to	Jn.	6 38
33	do the will of him that sent me. And this is the will of him that sent me, that I should lose nothing of what he hath given me, but	,,	39
34	should raise it up in the last day. This is the will of my Father, that every one that seeth the Son, and believeth in him, should have eternal life; and I will raise him up in the last day.	,,	40
35	The Jews therefore murmured concerning him, because he had said, I am the bread	,,	41
36	which came down out of heaven. And they said, Is not this Jesus, the son of Joseph, whose father and mother we know? how then doth this man say, Surely I am come	,,	42
37	down out of heaven? Jesus answered, and said unto them, Murmur not with one	,,	43
38	another. No man can come to me, unless the Father which sent me draw him: and I	,,	44
39	will raise him up in the last day. It is written in the prophet, They shall all be taught of God. Everyone that listeneth to the Father, and learneth from him, cometh	,,	45
40	unto me. Not that any man seeth the Father, save he which is from God: he it is	,,	46
41	that seeth the Father. Verily, verily, I say unto you, He that believeth in me hath	,,	47
42	eternal life. I am the bread of life.	,,	48
43	Your fathers did eat the manna in the	,,	49
44	wilderness, and they died. This is the bread which cometh down out of heaven, that a man may eat thereof and not die.	,,	50
45	I am the bread of life which came down out of heaven: and[1] if any man eat of this bread, he shall live for ever: and the bread	,,	51

---

[1] This is made the commencement of John vi. 52 (as in the Vulgate), and the numbers of the remaining verses of John vi. are increased by one.

which I will give, is my body, which I will deliver up for the life of the world.

19 46 The Jews therefore strove[1] one with another, saying, How can he give us his 47 body to eat? Jesus said unto them, Verily, verily, I say unto you, Except ye eat the body of the Son of man, and drink his blood, ye 48 shall not have life in yourselves. He that eateth of my body, and drinketh of my blood, hath eternal life; and I will raise 49 him up in the last day. My body is food[2] indeed, and my blood is drink[3] indeed. 50 He that eateth my body, and drinketh my 51 blood, abideth in me, and I in him. Even as the living Father sent me, and I live because of the Father, he that eateth me, 52 he also shall live because of me. This is the bread which came down from heaven: but not in that way wherein your fathers did eat manna, and died: he that eateth of 53 this bread shall live for ever. This said he in the synagogue, as he taught in Capernaum.

54 And many of his disciples, when they heard *this*, said, Surely this saying is hard; **20** 1 who can hear it? But Jesus, knowing in himself that his disciples murmured about this, said unto them, Doth this cause you to 2 stumble? *What* then if ye see the Son of man ascending to the place, where he was 3 before? It is the spirit that quickeneth; but the body profiteth nothing: the saying that I speak unto you is spirit and life. 4 But some of you do not believe. For Jesus knew beforehand who they were that believeth not, and who would betray him. 5 And he saith unto them, For this cause have I said unto you, No man can come

Jn. 6 52
„ 53
„ 54
„ 55
„ 56
„ 57
„ 58
„ 59
„ 60
„ 61
„ 62
„ 63
„ 64
„ 65

[1] Or, "questioned." [2] Lit. "what is eaten."
[3] Lit. "what is drunk."

	unto me, except this be given unto him of the Father.		
20 6	And because of this word many of the disciples turned back, and walked not with	Jn.	6 66
7	him. Jesus said therefore unto the twelve,	,,	67
8	Do ye also wish to go away? Simon Cephas answered, and saith, Lord, to whom shall we go? thou hast¹ the words of eternal life.	,,	68
9	And we have believed, and know that thou art the Christ, the Son of the living God.	,,	69
10	Jesus said unto them, Did not I choose you,	,,	70
11	the twelve, and one of you is a devil? He said this because of Judas, the son of Simon Iscariot, who, being one of the twelve, was going to betray him.	,,	71
12	And as he spake, a certain Pharisee came, and asked him to eat with him: and he	Lu.	11 37
13	went in and lay down *to meat*. And the Pharisee, when he saw him, marvelled that he had not first purified himself, before he	,,	38
14	ate.² Jesus saith unto him, Now do ye Pharisees cleanse the outside of the cup and of the platter, and think that ye are clean; but the inside of yourselves is full of un-	,,	39
15	righteousness and wickedness. Ye foolish ones, did not he that made that which is outside, make that which is inside also?	,,	40
16	Now give your substance as alms, and all things are clean unto you.	,,	41
17	And there came up to him Pharisees and	Mk.	7 1
18	scribes from Jerusalem; and when they had seen that some of his disciples ate their bread without having washed their hands,	,,	2
19	they found fault with them. For all the Jews and Pharisees, unless they wash their hands thoroughly, eat not, because they hold	,,	3
20	to the tradition of the elders: and that which is bought from the market, except they wash *it*, they eat not: and many other	,,	4

¹ Or, "with thee are." ² Lit. "before his eating."

	things they keep of those which they have received in the way of washings of cups, and measures, and brazen vessels, and couches.		
20	21 And the scribes and Pharisees asked him, Why walk not thy disciples according to the traditions of the elders, but eat bread with-	Mk. 7	5
	22 out having washed their hands? Jesus answered, and said unto them, Why do ye also transgress the commandment of God	Mt. 15	3
	23 because of your tradition? God said, Honour thy father and mother: and, Whosoever shall speak evil of his father and his	„ Mk. 7	4ª 10ᵇ
	24 mother, let him die the death: but ye say, If a man shall say concerning¹ his father or mother, Whatsoever he receiveth² from me	„	11
	25 is Corban,³ they do not allow him to do	„	12
	26 anything for his father and mother. They also make void and reject the word of God, because of the tradition, which ye have delivered and commanded about the washing of cups and measures: and many such like	„⁴	13
	27 things ye do. For leaving the commandment of God, ye hold fast the tradition of	„	8ª
	28 men. Do ye well, when ye transgress against the commandment of God, that ye	„	9
	29 may keep your tradition? Ye hypocrites, well did Isaiah the prophet prophesy of you, saying,	Mt. 15	7
	30 This people honoureth me with their lips; But their heart is very far from me.	„	8
	31 But in vain do they reverence me, Teaching the commandments of men.	„	9
	32 And Jesus called unto him the whole multitude, and said unto them, Hear me all of	Mk. 7	14

¹ Or "to."   ² Or, "thou receivest."   ³ Or, "an offering."

⁴ With Mark vii. 8ᵇ inserted in it. This 8ᵇ is rejected in the Revised Version without comment as an undoubted gloss. If we suppose it inserted here after Tatian's time, much of the difficulty of translation would be removed. The Arabic in its present form reads as if the fifth commandment was broken by observing the tradition about the washing of cups!

20 33	you, and understand: there is nothing outside the man that, going into him then, can defile him: but that which proceedeth out	Mk. 7 15
34	of him, that is what defileth the man. If any man hath ears to hear, let him hear.	,, 16
35	Then his disciples came near, and said unto him, Knowest thou that the Pharisees that heard this saying, were filled with indigna-	Mt. 15 12
36	tion? He answered, and said unto them, Every planting which my Father, which is in the heavens, planted not, shall be rooted up.	,, 13
37	Let them alone: for they, whilst they are blind, lead the blind. And if a blind man guide a blind man, both fall into a pit.	,, 14
38	And when Jesus had entered into the house from the multitude, Simon Cephas asked him, saying unto him, Lord, explain	Mk. 7 17ª Mt. 15 15
39	unto us this parable. He saith unto them, Do ye also so comprehend not? Understand ye not that everything entering the man from without cannot render him un-	Mk. 7 18
40	clean; because it entereth not into his heart; it goeth into his stomach only, and from thence is cast out in purgation, which	,, 19
41	maketh all meats clean? That which proceedeth out of a man's mouth, cometh forth out of the heart; and this is what	Mt. 15 18
42	defileth the man. From within, out of the heart of men, evil thoughts proceed,	Mk. 7 21
43	adulteries, fornications, thefts, false witness, murders, injustice, wickedness, deceit, folly, an evil glance, railing, pride, foolish-	,, 22
44	ness: all these evil things proceed from within out of the heart; and these are what	,, 23
45	defile the man. But if any one eat without having washed *his* hands, he is not defiled.	Mt. 15 20ᵇ
46	And Jesus went out thence, and came into the borders of Tyre and Sidon. And he entered into a house, and was unwilling that any one should know about him: and he could not	{ Mt. 15 21ª Mk. 7 24ᵇ

20 47	be hid. For straightway a woman of Canaan [1]	Mk.	7 25
	heard of him, whose daughter had an unclean		
48	spirit. And the woman was a Gentile from	„	26ᵃ
49	Hemesen [2] of Syria. And she came out,	Mt. 15	22ᵇ
	and cried after him, saying, Have mercy		
	on me, O Lord, thou son of David; my		
	daughter is very grievously vexed with a		
50	devil. And he answered her not a word.	„	23
	And his disciples came near, and besought		
	him, saying, Send her away, for she crieth		
51	after us. He answered, and said unto them,	„	24
	I was not sent but unto the sheep that		
	have wandered from the house of Israel.		
52	But she came and worshipped him, saying,	„	25
53	Lord, help me, have mercy on me. Jesus	„	26
	said unto her, It [3] is not good that the		
	children's bread should be taken, and cast		
54	to the dogs. But she said, Yea, Lord: even	„	27
	the dogs eat of the crumbs which fall from		
55	their masters' table, and live. Then Jesus	„	28ᵃ
	saith unto her, O woman, great is thy faith:		
56	be it done unto thee even as thou wilt. Go,	Mk.	7 29ᵇ
	and for this saying the devil is gone out of		
57	thy daughter. And her daughter was healed	Mt. 15	28ᵇ
58	in that hour. And the woman went away	Mk.	7 30
	unto her house, and found her daughter laid		
	upon the bed, and that the devil was gone		
	out of her.		
21 1	And again Jesus went out from the	„	31
	borders of Tyre and Sidon, and came unto		
	the sea of Galilee, towards the borders of		
2	Decapolis. And they brought unto him a	„	32
	deaf and dumb *man;* and sought from him		

---

[1] Lit. "a Cananaea woman."

[2] Mr. Rendel Harris thinks this may have arisen from a corrupt reading of the Greek for Syrophœnician. The name Justa is given to this woman in the Clementine *Homilies;* and as the quotations from the gospel narrative in that work appear to have been taken from the *Diatessaron,* the name Justa may have been put there by Tatian.

[3] Omitting Mark vii. 27, "Let the children first be filled."

21		that he would lay his hand upon him, and		
	3	heal him. And leading him out from the	Mk.	7 33
		multitude, he went away by himself, and spitting on his own fingers,[1] put them into		
	4	his ears, and touched his tongue; and looking up into heaven, he sighed, and saith	,,	34
	5	unto him, Be opened. And in that hour his ears were opened, and the bond of his tongue was loosed, and he spake readily.	,,	35
	6	And Jesus charged them much, that they should tell this to no man: and all things, which he forbade them, they published the	,,	36
	7	more. And they were much astonished, saying, He doeth all things well: he hath made even the deaf to hear, and the dumb to speak.	,,	37
	8	And as he was passing through the land	Jn.	4 4
	9	of Samaria,[2] he came to a city of the Samaritans, that is called Sychar, near to the parcel of ground that Jacob gave to his	,,	5
	10	son Joseph: and Jacob's spring of water was there. And Jesus, being wearied with the toil of his journey, sat by the spring.	,,	6
	11	The time was about the sixth hour. And there came a woman of Samaria to draw water: Jesus said unto her, Give me water,[3]	,,	7
	12	that I may drink. Now his disciples were gone into the city to buy themselves food.	,,	8
	13	The Samaritan woman therefore said unto him, How dost thou, since thou art a Jew, ask of me, which am a Samaritan woman, to give thee to drink? (For Jews have no	,,	9

[1] MS. W^d has a similar reading.

[2] Tatian seems to make this happen on the way from Galilee to Judaea, if we connect it with the opening of this chapter—this is the reverse of S. John's order (John iv. 3). Yet at the close of this visit (xxi. 47) Jesus departs from Sychar to Galilee, as in S. John's Gospel. Perhaps we should rather understand an interval between ver. 7 and 8, during which Jesus has gone to Judaea, so that he is now on his return journey.

[3] So Ephraem. Added by Tatian for explanation, not to support Encratite views.

21	14	dealings with Samaritans.) Jesus answered, and said unto her, If thou knewest the gift of God, and who it is that said to thee, Give me to drink; thou wouldest have asked of him, and he would have given thee	Jn. 4 10
	15	the water of life. The woman said unto him, Sir, thou hast no bucket, and the well is deep: from whence hast thou the water	,, 11
	16	of life? Art thou greater than our father Jacob, who gave us this well, and drank thereof himself, and his children, and his	,, 12
	17	cattle? Jesus answered, and said unto her, Every one that drinketh of this water shall	,, 13
	18	thirst again: but whosoever drinketh of the water, that I shall give him, shall never thirst; but[1] the water that I shall give him, shall become in him a spring of water	,, 14
	19	springing up unto eternal life. The woman said unto him, Sir, give me of this water, that I thirst not again, nor come to draw	,, 15
	20	from hence. Jesus said unto her, Go, and	,, 16
	21	call thy husband, and come hither. She said unto him, I have no husband. Jesus said unto her, Thou saidst well, I have no	,, 17
	22	husband: thou hast had five husbands; and he whom thou now hast is not thy husband:	,, 18
	23	and in this thou spakest truly. The woman said unto him, Sir, I see that thou art a prophet.	,, 19
	24	Our fathers worshipped in this mountain; and ye say, that at Jerusalem is the place	,, 20
	25	where *men* ought to worship. Jesus said unto her, O woman, believe me, the hour cometh, when neither in this mountain, nor in Jerusalem, shall ye worship the Father.	,, 21
	26	Ye worship that which ye know not: but we worship that which we know: for salva-	,, 22
	27	tion is from the Jews. But the hour shall come, and now is, when the true worshippers shall worship the Father in spirit and truth:	,, 23

[1] John iv. 14 is made to begin here as in the Vulgate.

for the Father also seeketh such worshippers.

21 28 For God is a Spirit: and they that worship him, must worship him in spirit and truth.   Jn. 4 24
29 The woman said unto him, I know that the Messiah will come: when therefore he is „ 25
30 come, he will teach us all things. Jesus said unto her, I that speak with thee, am „ 26
31 *he.* And while he was speaking, his disciples came, and marvelled how he was speaking with a woman: yet no one of them said unto him, What seekest thou? or, Why „ 27
32 speakest thou with her? And the woman left her waterpot, and went away into the „ 28
33 city, and said to the men, Come, and see a man which told me all things that I have „ 29
34 done. Perhaps he is the Messiah? And some went out of the city, and came to him. „ 30
35 In the meanwhile his disciples besought „ 31
36 him, saying unto him, Master, eat. But he said unto them, I have food to eat, that ye „ 32
37 know not. The disciples therefore said one to another, Hath any man brought him „ 33
38 what he could eat? Jesus said unto them, My food is to do the will of him that sent „ 34
39 me, and to accomplish his work. Say not ye, that there are yet four months, and the harvest will come? behold, I say unto you, lift up your eyes, and see the countries, that they are white; for the harvest is come „ 35
40 before the time. And he that reapeth receiveth his hire, and gathereth the fruit of life eternal; and he that soweth, and he „ 36
41 that reapeth, rejoice together. For herein is the saying true,[1] There is one that soweth, „ 37
42 and there is another that reapeth. I sent you to reap that whereon ye have not laboured: others have laboured, and ye have entered into their labours. „ 38
43 And from that city many of the Samari- „ 39

[1] Lit. "herein is the saying of truth found."

tans believed on him because of the word of the woman, who bare witness and said, He told me all things that I have done.

21 44 And when the Samaritans were come unto him, they besought him to abide with them: Jn. 4 40
45 and he abode with them two days. And many believed on him because of his speech;   „ 41
46 and they said to the woman, Now we believe on him, not because of thy saying: for we ourselves have heard, and know that this is indeed the Messiah, the Saviour of the world.   „ 42
47 And after the two days Jesus went forth from thence, and departed into Galilee.   „ 43
48 Now[1] Jesus had testified that a prophet   „ 44
49 hath no honour in his own country. When therefore he was come unto Galilee, the Galilaeans received him.   „ 45^a

22 1 And when Jesus was come to a certain village, there came near unto him a man full of leprosy:[2] and falling down at his feet, he besought him, saying, If thou wilt, thou   Lu. 5 12
2 canst make me clean. And Jesus had compassion on him, and stretched forth his hand, and touched him, and said, I will that thou   Mk. 1 41
3 be made clean. And straightway the leprosy departed from him, and he was made clean.   „ 42
4 And he strictly charged him, and sent him   „ 43
5 out, and said unto him, See thou tell no man: but go thy way, show thyself to the priests, and offer for thy cleansing an offering, even as Moses commanded, for their   „ 44
6 testimony. But he went out, and began to publish it much, and to spread abroad the   „ 45^a

---

[1] Instead of "For."

[2] Professor Fuller, in his article on Tatian in Smith's *Dictionary of Christian Biography*, suggests that this miracle may have been put so late as a continuation of the subject of cleansing begun at xx. 13, and which he thinks has been going on in different forms ever since. The *Codex Fuldensis* has it earlier.

news, insomuch that Jesus could not openly
enter into any of the cities, because his fame
was spread abroad exceedingly, but he was
22 7 without in a desert place: and much people Lu. 5 15b
came to him from many places to hear his
word, and to be healed of their infirmities.
8 And he withdrew himself from them into „ 16
the desert, and prayed.
9 After that there was a feast of the Jews, Jn.[1] 5 1
and Jesus went up to Jerusalem.
10 Now there was at Jerusalem a place pre- „ 2
pared for bathing, which is called in Hebrew
11 Baitharrahmat,[2] having five porches. In „ 3
these lay a great multitude of *them that were*
sick, blind, lame, and withered, waiting for
12 the moving of the water. For the angel „ 4
went down at fixed seasons[3] into the place
of bathing, and moved the water. And the
first who should go down after the move-
ment of the water, all the infirmities that
13 were in him were cured. And a certain „ 5
man was there, that was already suffering
from a disease for thirty and eight years.
14 When Jesus saw him lying, and had learnt „ 6
that he had *it* a long time,[4] he said unto
him, Wishest thou to be made whole?
15 The sick man answered, and said, Yea, Lord, „ 7
I have no man, when the water is moved,
to put me into the bath: but while I am
coming, another passeth before me, and goeth
16 down. Jesus said unto him, Arise, take up „ 8
17 thy bed, and walk. And straightway the „ 9
man was made whole, and arose, and took
up his bed, and walked. Now that day was

[1] Repeated xxx. 31.

[2] *I.e.* "house of mercy"—the Arabic equivalent of the Syriac Bethesda, which the translator should have left unchanged, especially after saying "in Hebrew."

[3] Or, "season after season;" lit. "in the season after the season."

[4] Lit. "had a long time."

22	18	the sabbath. And when the Jews saw him	Jn.	5	10
		that had been healed, they said unto him,			
		It is the sabbath day: thou hast no right			
	19	to take up thy bed. He answered, and said	,,		11
		unto them, He that made me whole,[1] the			
		same said unto me, Take up thy bed, and			
	20	walk. They asked him therefore, Who is	,,		12
		the man that said unto thee, Take up thy bed,			
	21	and walk? But he that had been made whole,	,,		13
		knew not who it was: for Jesus turned			
		aside from that place into another because			
		of the press of the multitude, which was			
	22	there. And after two days Jesus met him	,,		14
		in the temple, and said unto him, Behold,			
		thou art whole, sin no more, lest something			
	23	worse befall thee. And the man went away	,,		15
		and told the Jews, that it was Jesus, who			
	24	made him whole. For these things did the	,,		16
		Jews persecute[2] Jesus, and sought to kill			
		him, because he did these things on the			
	25	sabbath. But Jesus said unto them, My	,,		17
		Father worketh until now, and I also work.			
	26	And for this especially the Jews sought to	,,		18
		kill him, not only because he brake the			
		sabbath, but also because he said God was			
		his Father, and made himself equal with			
	27	God. Jesus answered, and said unto them,	,,		19
		Verily, verily, I say unto you, The Son can			
		do nothing of himself, but whatsoever he			
		seeth the Father doing: whatsoever the			
		Father doeth, this the Son also doeth in			
	28	like manner. The Father loveth his Son,	,,		20
		and sheweth him all things that himself			
		doeth: and greater works than these will			
	29	he shew him, that ye may marvel. For	,,		21
		even as the Father raiseth the dead, and			
		quickeneth them, so the Son also quickeneth			
	30	whom he will. For neither doth the Father	,,		22
		judge any man, but he hath given all judg-			

[1] Lit. "exempt."   [2] Or, "cast out."

22 31 ment unto the Son; that all may honour the   Jn.   5 23
Son, even as they honour the Father. And
he that honoureth not the Son honoureth
32 not the Father which sent him. Verily,   „   24
verily, I say unto you, He that heareth my
word, and believeth him that sent me, hath
eternal life, and shall not come into judgment, but shall pass from death unto life.
33 Verily, verily, I say unto you, The hour   „   25
shall come, and now is, when the dead shall
hear the voice of the Son of God; and who-
34 soever hear shall live. For even as the   „   26
Father hath life in himself, so gave he to
35 the Son also to have life in himself: and   „   27
also authority to execute judgment, because
36 he is the Son of man. Marvel not at this: „   28
namely the arrival of the hour, in which all
that are in the tombs shall hear his voice,
37 and shall come forth; they that have done   „   29
good, unto the resurrection of life; but they
that have done evil, unto the resurrection of
judgment.
38   I can of myself do nothing: but even   „   30
as I hear, I judge: and my judgment is
righteous. I seek not mine own will, but
39 the will of him that sent me. If I bear   „   31
witness of myself, my witness is not true.
40 It is another that beareth witness of me;   „   32
and I know that the witness which he
41 beareth of me is true. Ye have sent unto   „   33
John, and he hath borne witness unto the
42 truth. But I seek not witness from man: „   34
howbeit I say this, that ye may be saved.
43 He was the lamp that burneth and shineth: „   35
and for the while ye were willing to boast
44 in his light. But I have witness greater   „   36
than that of John: the works which the
Father hath given me to accomplish them,
the very works that I do, bear witness of
45 me, that the Father hath sent me. And   „   37

22 46	the Father which sent me, himself hath borne witness of me. Ye have neither heard his voice at any time, nor seen his form. And his word is not confirmed in you: for whom he sent, him ye believe not.	Jn. 5	38
47	Seek ye the scriptures, in which ye boast that ye have eternal life; and they are they	,,	39
48	which bear witness of me; and ye are unwilling to come to me, that ye may have	,,	40
49	eternal life. I seek not glory from men.	,,	41
50	But I know you, that the love of God is	,,	42
51	not in you. I am come in my Father's name, and ye received me not: but if another come in his own name, him ye will receive.	,,	43
52	How can ye believe, which¹ receive glory one of another, and seek not glory from	,,	44
53	the only God? Think ye that I am going to accuse you to the Father? there is one that accuseth you, *even* Moses, in whom ye	,,	45
54	boast. If ye had believed Moses, ye would have believed me also; of me Moses wrote.	,,	46
55	But if ye believe not his writings, how shall ye believe my words?	,,	47
23 1	And Jesus departed thence, and came nigh unto the sea of Galilee; and he went up	Mt. 15	29
2	into the mountain, and sat there. And there came unto him great multitudes, having with them the lame, blind, dumb, withered, and many others, and they cast them down	,,	30ᵃ
3	at the feet of Jesus: for they had seen all the signs that he did at Jerusalem, when they were assembled on the feast day: and	Jn.² 4	45ᵇ
		Mt. 15	30ᵇ
4	he healed them all: and the multitudes wondered, when they saw the dumb speaking, the withered healed, the lame walking, and the blind seeing: and they magnified the God of Israel.	,,	31

¹ Or, "seeing that ye."
² A passing remark of the evangelist, which Tatian displaced to improve the order.

23	5	And Jesus called his disciples together, and said unto them, I have compassion on this multitude, because they are continuing with me three days, and have nothing to eat: and I am unwilling to send them away fasting, lest they faint in the way, for some of	Mt. 15	32
			Mk. 8	3[b]
	6	them are come from far. His disciples said unto him, Whence should we have in the desert the bread, wherewith we may fill all	Mt. 15	33
	7	this multitude? Jesus saith unto them, How many loaves have ye? They said unto	„	34
	8	him, Seven, and a few small fishes. And he commanded the multitudes to lie down	„	35
	9	on the ground; and he took the seven loaves and the fishes; and he blessed, and brake, and gave to his disciples to set before them; and the disciples set *them* before the multi-	„	36
	10	tudes. And they did all eat, and were filled: and they took up seven baskets full, which remained over of the broken pieces.	„	37
	11	And they that did eat, were four thousand	„	38
	12	men, besides women and children. And when the multitudes were gone away, he went up into the boat, and came into the borders of Magheda.	„	39
	13[1]	And the Pharisees and Sadducees came unto him, and began to question with him, seeking of him, that he would show them	„ 16	1[a]
			Mk. 8	11[b]
	14	a sign from heaven, tempting him. And Jesus sighed in himself, and said, What sign seeketh this evil and adulterous genera-	„	12[a]
		tion? it seeketh after a sign; and there shall no sign be given unto it, but the sign	Mt.[2] 16	4[b]
	15	of Jonah the prophet. Verily I say unto you, There shall no sign be given unto this	Mk. 8	12[b]
	16	generation. And he sent them away, and went up into the boat; and they departed across the sea.	„	13

[1] With ver. 13-15 cf. xvi. 1-4; see also notes to xiv. 37 and 39.
[2] This is blended with Mark viii. 12.

23 17 And his disciples forgot to take bread; Mk. 8 14
for they had not even one loaf in the boat
18 with them. And Jesus charged them, say- „ 15
ing, Take heed, and beware of the leaven of
the Pharisees and Sadducees, and of the
19 leaven of Herod. But they reasoned among Mt. 16 7
themselves, because they had taken no bread
20 with them. And Jesus perceiving it said „ 8ᵃ
unto them, O ye of little faith, why reason
ye within yourselves, and are anxious because Mk. 8 17ᵇ
ye have no bread? do ye not yet perceive,
nor understand? is your heart still hard?
21 Having eyes, see ye not? and having ears, „ 18
hear ye not? and do ye not remember,
22 when I brake the five loaves unto the five „ 19
thousand, how many baskets¹ full of broken
pieces ye took up? They said, Twelve.
23 He said unto them, And again the seven „ 20
unto the four thousand: how many baskets²
full of broken pieces took ye up? They
24 said, Seven. He said unto them, How do ye ⎰ Mk. 8 21ᵃ
not perceive, that I spake not to you con- ⎱ Mt. 16 11
cerning bread, but that ye should beware of
the leaven of the Pharisees and Sadducees?
25 Then understood they how that he said not, Mt. 16 22
that they should beware of the leaven of
bread, but of the teaching of the Pharisees
and Sadducees, which he called leaven.³
26 After these things he came unto Beth- Mk. 8 22
saida; and they brought to him a certain
blind man, and besought him to touch him.
27 And he took hold of the blind man's hand, „ 23
and brought him outside the village. And
when he had spit on his eyes, and applied
his own hand, he asked him, What seest
28 thou? And the blind man looked up,⁴ and „ 24
said unto him, I see men as trees walking.

¹ Arabic, "sinn." ² Arabic, "zumbil," a basket of palm leaves.
³ No MSS. support this reading, which is evidently due to Tatian.
⁴ Or, "considered."

23	29	And again he laid his hand upon his eyes,	Mk.	8 25
	30	and they were restored, and he saw all things clearly. And he sent him away to his home, saying, Do not either enter into the village, or tell anyone in the same.	,,	26
	31	And Jesus went forth and his disciples into the villages of Caesarea Philippi: and as he was walking in the way, himself and	,,	27[a]
	32	his disciples apart, he asked his disciples, saying, What[1] do men say concerning me,	Mt. 16	13[b]
	33	that I, the Son of man, am? They said unto him, Some say John the Baptist; and some, Elijah; but others, Jeremiah,[2] or one	,,	14
	34	of the prophets. He said unto them, But	,,	15
	35	ye, who say ye that I am? Simon Cephas answered, and said, Thou art the Messiah,	,,	16
	36	the Son of the living God. Jesus answered, and said unto him, Blessed art thou Simon son of Jonah: flesh and blood hath not revealed it unto thee, but my Father which	,,	17
	37	is in the heavens. And I say unto thee, that thou art the rock, and upon this rock I will build my church; and the gates of the	,,	18
	38	lower world shall not subdue it. I will give unto thee the keys of the kingdom of the heavens, and whatsoever thou shalt bind on earth shall be bound in heaven: and whatsoever thou shalt loose on earth shall be	,,	19
	39	loosed in heaven. And he charged his disciples, and warned them, that they should tell no man concerning him, that he was the Messiah.	,,	20
	40	And from that time Jesus began to show unto his disciples, how that he must go unto	,,	21[a]
	41	Jerusalem, and suffer many things, and be	Mk.	8 31[b]

[1] S. Luke supposes this question put shortly after the return of the twelve, who may very naturally have heard opinions expressed during their journey. Tatian, however, preferred S. Matthew's order, which is supported by S. Mark.

[2] Cf. note to xviii. 3.

23 42	rejected by the elders, and by the chief priests, and by the scribes, and be killed, and on the third day rise again. And he spake clearly. And Simon Cephas, as if sympathising¹ with him, said, Be this far from thee,	Mk. Mt.	8 32ᵃ 16 22
43 44	Lord: and he, turning about, and looking at his disciples, rebuked Simon, saying, Get thee behind me, Satan: thou art a stumbling block unto me: for thou thinkest not those things which belong to God, but those which belong to men.	Mk. Mt.	8 33ᵃ 16 23ᵇ
45	And he called unto him the multitudes with his disciples, and said unto them, He that wisheth to come after me, let him deny himself, and take up his cross daily, and	Mk. Lu.	8 34ᵃ 9 23ᵇ
46 47	follow me. And whosoever wisheth to save his life shall lose it; but whosoever loseth his life for my sake, and for the sake of my gospel, shall save it. What doth a man	Mk. Lu.	8 35 9 25
48 49	profit, if he gain the whole world, and lose his own soul, or damage it? or what shall a man give in exchange for his soul? Whosoever shall deny me and my words in this sinful adulterous generation, the Son of man also shall deny him, when he cometh in the glory of his Father with the holy angels.	Mk. „	8 37 38
50	For the Son of man is about to come in the glory of his Father with his holy angels; and then shall he render unto every man according to his works.	Mt.	16 27
24 1	And he said unto them, Verily I say unto you, there are indeed some standing here, which shall not taste of death, till they see the kingdom of God coming in power, and the Son of man coming in his kingdom.	Mk.² Mt.	9 1 16 28ᵇ

¹ Or, "vexed."

² Called viii. 39 as in the Vulgate, and all the verses from Mark ix. are numbered one less than in our Authorised Version; the numbers of the Authorised Version are given here.

24	2	And after six days Jesus took with him Simon Cephas, and James, and John his brother, and brought them unto a high	Mt.	17	1
	3	mountain, the three of them apart. And as they were praying,[1] Jesus was transfigured, and made into the form of another	Lu.	9	29[a]
	4	person, and his face did shine as the sun,	Mt.	17	2[b]
		and his raiment became exceeding white as	Lu.	9	29[b]
		snow, and even as the brightness of lightning, so that nothing on earth can become	Mk.	9	3[b]
	5	so white. And there appeared unto him[2]	„		4
	6	Moses and Elijah talking with Jesus. And they thought that the time of his coming, destined to be accomplished at Jerusalem,	Lu.	9	31[b]
	7	was already come. Now Simon and they that were with him were oppressed with the drowsiness of sleep, and they were scarcely awakened,[3] and they saw his glory,	„		32
	8	and the two men that stood with him. And when these had begun to depart from him, Simon saith unto Jesus, Master, it is a good	„		33[a]
	9	thing that we are here: if thou wilt, let us	Mt.	17	4[b]
		make here three tabernacles; one for thee,	Lu.	9	33[c]
		and one for Moses, and one for Elijah, not knowing what he said, because of the fear	Mk.	9	6[b]
	10	which had seized them. While he was yet	Mt.	17	5[a]
		saying this, thereupon a bright cloud over-			
	11	shadowed them: and when they had seen	Lu.	9	34[b]
		Moses and Elijah[4] entering into the cloud,			
	12	they feared again. And a voice was heard	Mt.	17	5[b]
		out of the cloud, saying, This is my beloved Son, whom I have chosen;[5] hear ye him.			

[1] The Ferrar group of MSS. has this reading in Mark ix. 3, showing that those MSS. are influenced by the *Diatessaron*. Tatian used considerable freedom of harmonisation throughout this passage.

[2] "Him" is apparently an error of the Arabic for "them;" there is no such reading in any other MS.

[3] Or, "by an effort they wakened themselves."

[4] The Peschito has "Moses and Elijah;" and the Curetonian Syriac implies that they were the ones that entered the cloud.

[5] Cf. Revised Version, Luke ix. 35, "my chosen."

24 13 And when this voice was heard, Jesus was Lu. 9 36ᵃ
14 found alone. And when the disciples heard Mt. 17 6
the voice, they fell on their face for the fear
15 which had seized them. And Jesus came, „   7
and touched them, and said, Arise, be not
16 afraid. And lifting up their eyes they saw „   8
Jesus even as he was.¹
17 And as they were coming down from the „   9
mountain, Jesus commanded them, and said
unto them, Tell no man what ye have seen,
until the Son of man riseth again from the
18 dead. And they kept the saying among Mk. 9 10ᵃ
themselves, and told no man in those days Lu. 9 36ᵇ
19 that which they had seen. And they Mk. 9 10ᵇ
reasoned among themselves, What is this
word which he said unto us: When I shall
20 have risen from the dead? And his disciples „² 11ᵃ
asked him, saying, What is it then that the Mt. 17 10ᵇ
scribes say, that Elijah must first come?
21 He saith unto them, Elijah will come first to Mk. 9 12
restore³ all things; and how it was written
of the Son of man that he should suffer
22 many things and be rejected. But I say „ 13
unto you, Elijah is come, and they knew
him not, and did unto him whatsoever they
23 wished, even as it is written of him. Even Mt. 17 12ᵇ
so the Son of man is going to suffer from
24 them. Then understood the disciples, that „ 13
he had spoken unto them of John the
Baptist.
25 And on the day whereon they came Mk. 9 14
down from the mountain, there met him a
multitude of many men, standing with his
disciples; and the scribes were discussing
26 with them. And when the men saw Jesus, „ 15

¹ Perhaps an allusion to "as he is" (1 John iii. 2). As these words are evidently due to Tatian, this would imply that the first epistle of S. John was known to him.

² Or, Matt. xvii. 10ᵃ.

³ Or, "put in order."

	they drew near, and hastening for joy,[1] saluted him.[2]		
24 27	In that very day there came certain of the Pharisees, saying to him, Get thee out, and go hence: for Herod seeketh to	Lu. 13	31
28	kill thee.[3] Jesus saith unto them, Go, and say to that fox, Behold, I cast out devils and perform cures to-day and to-morrow, and the third day I shall be perfected.	,,	32
29	Howbeit I must be careful to-day and to-morrow, and depart the day following: for a prophet cannot perish outside Jerusalem.	,,	33
30	And after that a man from the multitude came to him, and falling on his knees, said unto him, I beseech thee, O Lord, look upon	,, Mt. 17 Lu. 9	9 38[a] 14[b] 38[b]
31	my son; he is my only one: for a spirit riseth unexpectedly upon him, and he be-	,, Mt. 17	39[a] 15[b]
32	cometh lunatic, and feeleth ill.[4] And wheresoever it falleth in with him, it dasheth him down: and he foameth, and grindeth with	Mk. 9	18
33	his teeth, and trembleth.[5] And oft-times it casteth him into the water and into the fire to destroy him: and it hardly departeth	Mt. 17 Lu. 9	15[c] 39[c]
34	from him after it hath torn him. And I brought him to thy disciples, and they could	Mt. 17	16
35	not cure him. Jesus answered, and said, O faithless and perverse generation, how long shall I be with you? and how long shall I	,,	17
36	bear with you? bring thy son hither. And he brought him unto him: and when he saw him, straightway the spirit struck him; and falling on the ground, he raged and	Mk. 9	20
37	foamed. And Jesus asked his father, How long time is it during which he *hath been*	,,	21

[1] Possibly due to a misreading of the Greek.
[2] Omitting Mark ix. 16, "And he asked the scribes, What question ye with them?"
[3] No reason is apparent for the insertion of this incident between the Transfiguration and the cure of the demoniac boy.
[4] Lit. "meeteth evil." [5] Or, "crieth out."

	so? And he said, From youth even until		
24	38 now: but wherein thou canst, Lord, help me,	Mk.	9 22^b
	39 and have compassion on me. Jesus saith unto him, If thou canst believe: then all things are possible to him that believeth.	,,	23
	40 And straightway, weeping, the father of the child cried out, saying, I believe, Lord; help	,,	24
	41 thou my lack of faith. And when Jesus saw a running together of men, and their assembling together at the cry, he rebuked the unclean spirit, saying unto him, Thou deaf spirit which speakest not, I command thee, come out of him, and enter no more	,,	25
	42 into him. And the spirit the devil,¹ crying out much, and rending him, went out: and the child fell as dead; and many thought	,,	26
	43 that he was dead. But Jesus took him by	,,	27^a
	the hand, and raised him up, and gave him	Lu.	9 42^b
	44 to his father: and the boy was cured from	Mt.	17 18^b
	that hour. And they were all astonished at the greatness of God.	Lu.	9 43^a
	45 And when Jesus had entered into the house, his disciples came near,² and questioning him between themselves and him, they said unto him, Why could not we cure him?	Mk.	9 28
	46 Jesus said unto them, Because of your lack of faith: verily I say unto you, If ye have faith as a grain of mustard seed, ye shall say unto this mountain, Remove hence; and it shall remove; and nothing shall with-	Mt.	17 20
	47 stand you: for this kind can be cast out by nothing, save by fasting and prayer.	Mk.	9 29
	48 And when he had gone forth from thence, they passed through Galilee; and he was unwilling that any man should know about	,,	30
	49 him. And³ he taught his disciples, and said	,,	31^a
	unto them, Keep ye these sayings in your	Lu.	9 44^a

¹ Lit. "the Satan."   ² Cf. Matt. xvii. 19.
³ Omitting Luke ix. 43^b, "But while they wondered every one at all things that Jesus did."

24	50	ears and hearts. For the Son of man shall be delivered up into the hands of men, and they shall kill him; and when he is killed,	Mk.	9	31[b]
	51	he shall rise again on the third day. But they knew not the word, which he said unto them, for it was hidden from them, that they should not understand it: and they were afraid to ask him about this matter.	Lu.	9	45
	52	And they were exceeding sorry.	Mt.	17	23[b]
25	1	In that day this questioning arose among the disciples, for they said, Who of them	Lu.	9	46

— using list form instead:

24 50 ears and hearts. For the Son of man shall be delivered up into the hands of men, and they shall kill him; and when he is killed,   Mk. 9 31[b]

51 he shall rise again on the third day. But they knew not the word, which he said unto them, for it was hidden from them, that they should not understand it: and they were afraid to ask him about this matter.   Lu. 9 45

52 And they were exceeding sorry.   Mt. 17 23[b]

25 1 In that day this questioning arose among the disciples, for they said, Who of them   Lu. 9 46

2 was the greater? And when they were come to Capernaum, and had entered into the house, Jesus saith unto them, What were ye reasoning among yourselves in the   Mk. 9 33

3 way? But they held their peace, since they had reasoned about this.   „ 34[a]

4 And when Simon was gone outside, they that received the didrachma[1] of the tribute, came to Cephas, and said unto him, Doth   Mt. 17 24[b]

5 not your master pay the didrachma?[1] He saith unto them, Certainly. And when Cephas had entered into the house, Jesus anticipated him, saying unto him, What thinkest thou, Simon? the kings of the earth, from whom do they receive toll and tribute? from their sons, or from strangers?   „ 25

6 Simon said unto him, From strangers. Jesus said unto him, Therefore the sons are free. Simon saith unto him, Yea. Jesus said unto him, Give thou also unto them as if a   „ 26

7 stranger.[2] And lest it should distress them, go thou to the sea, and cast a hook; and when thou hast opened the mouth of the fish that first cometh up, thou shalt find a stater: that take, and give *it* for me and thee.   „ 27

8 In that hour came the disciples unto Jesus, and said unto him, Who, think you,   „ 18 1

---

[1] Lit. "two dirhems."   [2] Found in *Codex Algerinae Peckover.*

25	9	is the greater in the kingdom of the heavens? But Jesus, knowing the reasonings of their heart, called a child, and set him in the midst: and taking him into his	Lu. Mk.	9 47ª 9 36
	10	arms, he said unto them, Verily I say unto you, Except ye turn, and become as little children, ye shall not enter into the kingdom	Mt.	18 3
	11	of the heavens. Whosoever receiveth one like this child in my name, receiveth me: and whosoever receiveth me, receiveth not	Lu. Mk.	9 48ª 9 37ᵇ
	12	me, but him that sent me: for he that is less among you all, the same is greater.	Lu.	9 48ᶜ
	13	But whosoever causeth one of these little ones which believe in me, to stumble, it were better for him if a great millstone should be hanged about his neck, and he should be sunk into the depth of the sea.	Mt.	18 6
	14	John answered, and said, Teacher, we saw some one casting out devils in thy name; and we forbade him, because he followeth	Lu.	9 49
	15	thee not with us. Jesus saith unto them, Forbid him not: for there is no man that doeth mighty works in my name, and is able	Mk.	9 39
	16	quickly to speak evil of me. Everyone that	Lu.	9 50ᵇ
	17	is not against you is with you. Woe unto the world because of strifes![1] but woe to that man through whom the strife cometh!	Mt.	18 7
	18	If thy hand or thy foot causeth thee to stumble, cut it off, and cast it from thee: for it is better for thee to enter into life lame or maimed, than having two hands or two feet to be cast into the fire kindled	„	8
	19	for ever, where their worm dieth not, and	Mk.	9 44
	20	their fire is not quenched. And if thine eye	Mt.	18 9ª

---

[1] Omitting "for it must needs be that offences come." Aphraates here inserts before the missing part, "It must needs be that good come, and blessed be he by whom it cometh." It seems probable that some one struck out this latter, and in doing so erased too much. That it was originally in the *Diatessaron* is the more probable, as it occurs in the Clementine *Homilies*, xii. 29.

	incite thee to strife, pluck it out, and cast it		
25 21	from thee: for it is better for thee to enter	Mk.	9 47[b]
	into the kingdom of God with one eye, than		
	having two eyes to fall into the fire of		
22	Gehenna, where their worm dieth not, and	„	48
23	their fire is not quenched. Everyone shall	„	49
	be salted with fire; and every sacrifice shall		
24	be salted with salt. How good is salt!	„	50[a]
	but if even the salt have lost its savour,	Lu. 14	34[b]
25	wherein shall it be salted? It is fit neither	„	35
	for the land nor for the dung; but it is cast		
	out. He that hath ears to hear, let him		
26	hear. Let there be salt in yourselves, and	Mk.	9 50[c]
	be ye at peace one with another.		
27	And he arose[1] from thence, and came into	„	10 1
	the borders of Judaea beyond Jordan: and		
	great multitudes came unto him thither, and		
	he healed them; and, as he had been wont,		
28	he taught them again. And there came	„	2
	unto him Pharisees, to tempt him, and say		
	unto him, Is it lawful for a man to put		
29	away his wife?[2] He said, What did Moses	„	3
30	command you? They said, Moses gave us	„	4
	permission that, if any man wished, he might		
	write a certificate of divorcement, and put		
31	away his wife. Jesus answered, and said	„	5[a]
	unto them, Have ye not read this, He which	Mt. 19	4[b]
	made *them* from the beginning, made them		
32	male and female, and said, For this cause	„	5
	shall a man leave his father and mother, and		
	shall cleave to his wife; and they both shall		
33	be one body? So that now they are not	„	6
	two, but one body. What therefore God		
	hath joined together, let not man put		
34	asunder. The Pharisees said unto him, Why	„	7
	did Moses consent that a certificate of		

---

[1] S. Mark's order is here preferred to S. Matthew's. The journey referred to at xxviii. 9 is the same, according to the evangelists; yet between the two statements of it Jesus is represented as walking in Galilee (xxvii. 30).

[2] Omitting Matt. xix. 3, "for every cause."

25 35	divorcement should be given, and she should be put away? Jesus saith unto them, Moses	Mt. 19	8
36	for the hardness of your heart gave you permission to put away your wives: but in the beginning it was not so. I say unto	„	9ᵃ
37	you, Whosoever shall put away his wife without fornication, and shall marry another, exposeth her to adultery. And when he had	Mk. 10	10
38	entered into the house, his disciples asked him also about the same thing. And he	„	11
39	saith unto them, Whosoever shall put away his wife, and marry another, exposeth her to adultery: and if a woman shall put away	„	12
	her husband, and marry another, she committeth adultery: and whosoever marrieth her when she is put away, committeth adultery.	Mt. 19	9ᵇ
40	His disciples said unto him, If between a husband and a wife there is such blame, it is not expedient for a man to marry a wife.	„	10
41	He said unto them, All men do not endure this saying, but he to whom it was given.	„	11
42	There are eunuchs, which were so born from their mother's womb: and there are eunuchs, which were made *so* by men: and there are eunuchs, which made themselves eunuchs for the sake of the kingdom of the heavens. Let it please¹ him, whom it may.	„	12
43	Then were there brought unto him little children, that he should lay his hand on them, and pray: and the disciples rebuked	„	13ᵃ
44	those that were bringing them. When Jesus	Mk. 10	13ᵇ
	saw it, it grieved him, and he saith unto them, Suffer the little children to come unto me, and forbid them not: for of such is the	„	14
45	kingdom of God. Verily I say unto you, Whosoever shall not receive the kingdom of God as this little child, he shall not enter	„	15
46	into it. And he took them up into his arms, and blessed them, laying his hand upon them.	„	16

¹ Or, "content."

26 1 And the publicans and sinners drew near Lu.[1] 15 1
2 unto him, to hear his word. And the scribes „ 2
and Pharisees murmured, saying, This man
receiveth sinners, and eateth with them.
3 And Jesus, when he had perceived their „ 3
murmuring, said unto them this parable,
4 What man of you that hath a hundred sheep, „ 4
if one of them wander, doth not leave the
ninety and nine in the wilderness, and go
and seek the straying *one*, until he find it?
5 Verily I say unto you, When he findeth it, Mt. 18 13[b]
he rejoiceth over it more than over the ninety
6 and nine which did not go astray. And he Lu. 15 5[b]
layeth it on his shoulders, and bringing it „ 6
home, he calleth together his friends and
neighbours, saying unto them, Rejoice with
me, for I have found my straying sheep.
7 Even so your Father, which is in the heavens, Mt. 18 14
willeth not that one of these little ones
should perish, whom after erring he calleth
8 to repentance. I say unto you, that even so Lu. 15 7
there shall be joy in heaven over one sinner
that repenteth, more than over ninety and nine
righteous persons, which need no repentance.
9 And what woman having ten drachmas, „ 8
and losing one of them, doth not light a
lamp, and sweep the house, and seek it dili-
10 gently until she find it? And when she „ 9
findeth it, she calleth together her friends
and neighbours, saying unto them, Rejoice
with me, for I have found my drachma,
11 which was lost. I say unto you, that even „ 10
so there shall be joy in the presence of the
angels of God over one sinner that repenteth,
more[2] than over ninety and nine righteous
persons, which need no repentance.

---

[1] Identified with Matt. xviii. 12-14, and put with it into a position due to the preference of S. Mark's order noticed at xxv. 27.

[2] This clause has evidently been copied from Luke xv. 7, where alone this allusion to ninety-nine is appropriate.

26 12   And again Jesus saith unto them another   Lu. 15 11
13 parable, A certain man had two sons: and   „   12
   the younger said unto him, Father, give me
   my portion of thy property that falleth to me.
   And he divided unto them his substance.
14 And after a few days the younger son   „   13
   gathered all together that belonged to him,
   and took his journey into a far country: and
   there he squandered his substance in living
15 extravagantly. And when he had spent all, „   14
   there arose a mighty famine in that country,
16 and he was reduced to want, and went and   „   15
   joined himself unto one of the citizens of
   that country; and he sent him into a field
17 to feed swine. And he longed to fill his   „   16
   belly with the pods that those swine were
18 eating: and no man gave unto him. But   „   17
   when he came to himself, he said, How many
   now of hired servants in my father's house
   abound in bread, and I am perishing with
19 hunger! I will arise and go to my father's „   18
   house, and will say unto him, My father, I
   have sinned against heaven, and in thy sight:
20 I am not worthy now to be called thy son: „   19
21 make me as one of thy hired servants. And he „   20
   arose, and came to his father. But while he
   was yet afar off, his father saw him, and had
   compassion on him, and made haste, and fell
22 on his neck, and kissed him. And his son   „   21
   said unto him, My father, I have sinned
   against heaven, and in thy sight: and I am
23 not worthy to be called thy son. His father „   22
   said to his servants, Bring forth the best
   robe, and put it on him; and put a ring on
   his hand, and with shoes clothe his feet:
24 and bring the fatted calf, and kill it, that we „   23
25 may eat, and make merry: for this my son   „   24
   was dead, and is alive; he was lost, and is
26 found. And they began to feast. Now his   „   25
   elder son was in the field: and as he came,

26	27	and drew nigh to the house, he heard the sound of the singing of many. And he called one of the lads, and asked him, What	Lu. 15 26
	28	is this? He said unto him, Thy brother hath arrived; and thy father hath killed the fatted calf, because he hath found him well.	„ 27
	29	And he was angry, and would not go in: and his father came out, and intreated him	„ 28
	30	to enter. But he said to his father, So many years do I serve thee as a slave; and I never transgressed thy commandment: and *yet* thou never gavest me a kid, that I might feast	„ 29
	31	with my friends: and after this thy son came, having squandered thy substance with harlots, thou killedst for him the fatted	„ 30
	32	calf. His father said unto him, My son, thou art ever with me, and all mine is	„ 31
	33	thine. But it was meet to rejoice and to feast, since this thy brother, *that* was dead, is now alive: and *that* was lost, hath been found.	„ 32
	34	And he spake a parable unto his disciples, There was a certain rich man, and he had a steward, and he was denounced unto him,	„ 16 1
	35	that he had wasted his substance. His lord therefore called him, and saith unto him, What is this that I hear of thee? give me the account of thy stewardship; for now thou	„ 2
	36	wilt[1] not be able to be my steward. The steward saith within himself, What shall I do, seeing that my lord taketh away the stewardship from me? I cannot dig; and	„ 3
	37	to beg I am ashamed. I know what I will do, that when I am put out of the stewardship, they may receive me into their houses.	„ 4
	38	Therefore calling unto him each one of his lord's debtors, he said unto the first, How	„ 5
	39	much owest thou unto my lord? He said unto him, A hundred jars[2] of oil. He said	„ 6

[1] Or, "canst not be my steward."
[2] Or, "vessels."

			Lu.	16	
26	40	unto him, Take thy bond,¹ sit down, and write quickly fifty jars. And he said to the next, but how much owest thou unto my lord? He said unto him, A hundred cors² of wheat. He said unto him, Take thy account, sit down and write fourscore cors.	Lu.	16	7
	41	And his lord commended the steward of unrighteousness, because he had done a wise deed: for the sons of this world are in their own generation wiser than the sons of	„		8
	42	light. And I say unto you, Make to yourselves friends from the money of this unrighteousness; that, when it shall fail, they may receive you into the eternal tabernacles.	„		9
	43	He that is faithful over a little is faithful also in much: and he that is unrighteous over a little is unrighteous also in much.	„		10
	44	If therefore ye have not been faithful in the unrighteous money, who will commit to your	„		11
	45	trust the true? If therefore ye have not been found faithful in that which is not your own,³ who will give you what is your own?³	„		12
27⁴	1	Therefore have I likened the kingdom of the heavens unto a certain king, that wished to make a reckoning with his servants.	Mt.	18	23
	2	And when he had begun to make it, one was brought unto him, which owed him ten	„		24
	3	talents.⁵ But as he had not wherewith to pay, his lord commanded him to be sold, and his wife, and children, and all that he had,	„		25
	4	and payment to be made. And the servant, falling down and worshipping, said unto him, Lord, have patience with me, and I will pay	„		26
	5	thee all. And the lord of that servant had	„		27

---

¹ Or, "bill:" lit. "writing."
² A "cor" contained about 87 gallons.   ³ Or, "peculiar to you."
⁴ In ver. 1-29 of this chapter Tatian has dealt very freely with the internal arrangement of passages relating to offences.
⁵ Arabic "badra:" valued by some at 10,000 drachmas each.

27	6	mercy, and released him, and forgave him his debt. But that servant went out and found one of his fellowservants, which owed him a hundred pence: and he laid hold on him, and treated him with hardness, saying,	Mt.	18	28
	7	Give me what thou owest. And the fellowservant fell down at his feet, and besought him, saying, Grant me delay, and I will	„		29
	8	satisfy thee. And he would not: but went and cast him into prison, till he should pay	„		30
	9	the debt. And when the fellowservants of both saw what had happened, they were very displeased, and came and told unto their	„		31
	10	lord all that had been done. Then his lord called him unto him, and saith to him, Thou wicked servant, I forgave thee all that debt	„		32
	11	because thou besoughtest me: shouldest not thou also have had mercy on thy fellow-	„		33
	12	servant, even as I had mercy on thee? And his lord was wroth, and delivered him to the tormentors, till he should pay everything	„		34
	13	that he owed. So shall also my Father which is in heaven do unto you, if a man forgive not his brother from his heart his trespasses.	„		35
	14	Take heed to yourselves: if thy brother sin, rebuke him; and if he repent, forgive him.	Lu.	17	3
	15	And if he sin against thee seven times in the day, and seven times in the day turn again to	„		4
	16	thee, saying, I repent, forgive him. And if thy brother sin against thee, go and reprove him between thee and him alone: if he hear thee,	Mt.	18	15
	17	thou hast gained thy brother. But if he hear thee not, take with thee one or two; for in the mouth of two or three every word	„		16
	18	standeth.[1] And if he hear not even them, tell it unto the church: and if he hear not the church also, let him be unto thee as a	„		17
	19	publican and a heathen. Verily I say unto	„		18

[1] Or, "is confirmed."

27	20	you, What things soever ye shall bind on earth shall be bound in heaven: and whatsoever ye loose on earth shall be loosed in heaven. Again I say unto you, If two of	Mt. 18	19
	21	you shall agree on earth to ask anything, it shall be done for them by my Father which is in heaven. For where two or three are	„	20
	22	gathered together in my name, there am I in the midst of them. Then Cephas came	„	21
		near, and said unto him, Lord, how often, if my brother sin against me, shall I forgive		
	23	him? until seven times? Jesus said unto him, I say not unto thee, Until seven times;	„	22
	24	but, Until seventy times seven times.[1] For	Lu. 12	47
		the servant, which knew his Lord's will, and prepared not for him according to his will,		
	25	shall be punished much; but he that knew	„	48
		not, and did something worthy of punishment, shall be punished little. And every one, to whom much is given, of him shall much be required: and *every one*, to whom much is committed, at his hand much will be sought.		
	26	I came to cast fire upon the earth; and I could wish that it were already kindled.	„	49
	27	And I have a baptism to be baptized with; and I am much straitened till it be accomplished.	„	50
	28	See that ye despise not one of these	Mt. 18	10
		little ones, which believe in me; verily I say unto you, Their angels [2] always see the face		
	29	of my father which is in heaven. The Son of man came to save that which was lost.	„	11
	30	And after these things Jesus walked in Galilee: for he would not walk in Judaea, because the Jews sought to kill him.	Jn. 7	1

[1] Ciasca adds another "seven times." The Peschito adds "and seven times." Ephraem has "seventy times seven seven times."

[2] Addai alludes to this, saying, "Let your solicitude for the young lambs be great, for their angels behold the face of the invisible Father."

27	31	Now there came some which told him of the Galilaeans, whose blood Pilate mingled	Lu.[1] 13	1
	32	with their sacrifices. Jesus answered, and said unto them, Think ye that these Galilaeans were sinners more than all the Galilaeans, so	„	2
	33	that this happened unto them? Nay: verily I say unto you, Except ye also all repent,	„	3
	34	ye shall in like manner perish. Or those eighteen, upon whom the tower in Siloam fell, and killed *them*, think ye that they were guilty more than all the men that dwell in	„	4
	35	Jerusalem? Nay: verily I say unto you, Except ye all repent, ye also shall perish even as they.	„	5
	36	And he spake this parable unto them, A certain man had a fig-tree planted in his vineyard; and he came seeking fruit thereon,	„	6
	37	and found none. And he said unto the husbandman, Behold, for three years I come seeking fruit on this fig-tree, and find none: cut it down; why doth it leave the ground	„	7
	38	unoccupied? The husbandman said unto him, Sir, let it alone this year also, that I	„	8
	39	may dig about it, and dung it: and if indeed it bear fruit, *well*: but if not, next year cut it down.	„	9
	40	And when Jesus was teaching on the	„	10
	41	sabbath day in a certain synagogue, there was a woman there, which had a spirit of infirmity eighteen years; and she was bowed together,	„	11
	42	and could not raise herself up. And when Jesus saw her, he called her, and saith unto her, O woman, be set free from thine in-	„	12
	43	firmity. And he laid his hand upon her: and immediately she was raised up, and glorified	„	13
	44	God. The ruler of the synagogue, being moved with indignation because Jesus had healed on the sabbath, answered and said to	„	14

[1] This passage seems correctly put before leaving Galilee for the Feast of Tabernacles. See note to Appendix X. here.

		the multitudes, There are six days in which men ought to work: in them therefore come and be healed, and not on the day of the			
27	45	sabbath. But Jesus answering saith unto him, Ye hypocrites, doth not each one of you on the sabbath day loose his ox or his ass from the stall, and go away to give him	Lu.	13	15
	46	water? Ought not this woman, that is a daughter of Abraham, and whom Satan hath bound for eighteen years, to have been loosed from this bond on the day of the sabbath?	„		16
	47	And as he said this, all his adversaries standing by were put to shame: and all the people rejoiced in all the marvellous things that were done by him.	„		17
28	1	At that time the Jews' feast of Taber-	Jn.	7	2
	2	nacles was at hand. And the brethren of Jesus said unto him, Depart hence, and go into Judaea, that thy disciples may see the	„		3
	3	works which thou doest. Surely no man doeth anything in secret, and wisheth to be known openly. If thou doest this, manifest	„		4
	4	thyself to the world. For until this time even the brethren of Jesus did not believe in him.	„		5
	5	Jesus said unto them, My time is not yet	„		6
	6	come; but your time is always ready. The world cannot hate you; but me it hateth, because I bear witness of it, that its works	„		7
	7	are evil. Go ye up unto this feast: but I go not up now unto this feast, because my	„		8
	8	time is not yet accomplished. He said this, and remained in Galilee.	„		9
	9	But when his brethren were gone up unto	„		10^a
		the feast, he removed from Galilee, and came into the borders of Judaea beyond Jordan;[1]	Mt.	19	1^b
	10	and great multitudes followed him; and he	„		2
	11	healed them all there. And he departed, and went to the feast, not openly, but like	Jn.	7	10^b
	12	one who conceals himself. Now the Jews	„		11

[1] Cf. note to xxv. 27.

28	13	sought him at the feast, and said, Where is he? And much murmuring took place there concerning him in the great multitude, which had come to the feast: for some said, He is good; and others said, Nay, but he leadeth	Jn. 7 12
	14	the people astray. Howbeit no man spake an open word concerning him for fear of the Jews.	„ 13
	15	But when the days of the feast of Tabernacles were now dividing in half, Jesus went	„ 14
	16	up into the temple and taught. And the Jews marvelled, saying, How knoweth this man letters, since he hath not learned?	„ 15
	17	Jesus answered, and said, My teaching is not	„ 16
	18	mine, but his that sent me. Whosoever desireth to do his will, he shall know my teaching, whether it be of God, or *whether*	„ 17
	19	I speak from myself. He that speaketh from himself, seeketh glory for himself: but he that seeketh glory for him that sent him, is true, and unrighteousness is not found in	„ 18
	20	his heart. Did not Moses give you the law,[1] and no one of you keepeth the law?	„ 19
	21	Why do ye seek to kill me? The multitude answered, and said unto him, Thou hast a	„ 20
	22	devil: who seeketh to kill thee? Jesus answered, and said unto them, I did one work, and ye all marvel because of this.	„ 21
	23	Moses hath given you circumcision (not that it is of Moses but of the fathers); and	„ 22
	24	on the sabbath ye circumcise a man. And if a man is circumcised on the day of the sabbath, so that the law[2] of Moses may not be broken; are ye wroth with me because I made an entire man whole on the day of the	„ 23
	25	sabbath? Judge not according to appearance, but give a righteous decision.	„ 24
	26	And some out of Jerusalem said, Is not	„ 25

[1] Arabic, "sunna."
[2] Arabic, "rāmūs," *i.e.* νόμος.

28	27	this he whom they seek to kill? And lo, he speaketh openly to them, and they say nothing unto him. Think you, that our elders know that this man is really the	Jn.	7 26
	28	Messiah? But this man is known whence he is: now when the Messiah cometh, no	„	27
	29	man will know whence he is. But Jesus lifting up his voice, while he was teaching in the temple, said, Ye both know me, and know whence I am; and I am not come of myself, but he that sent me is true, whom	„	28
	30	ye know not. But I know him; because I	„	29
	31	am from him, and he sent me. And they sought to take him: and no man laid his hand on him, because his hour was not	„	30
	32	yet come. But of the multitude many believed in him; and they said, Will the Messiah when he cometh, do more signs than those which this man doeth?	„[1]	31
	33	And a certain man[2] out of that multitude said unto the Lord, Teacher, tell my brother to divide the inheritance with me.	Lu. 12	13
	34	Jesus said unto him, Man, who appointed	„	14
	35	me a judge and a divider over you? And he said unto his disciples, Beware of every evil: for life consisteth not in the abund-	„	15
	36	ance of possessions. And he set this parable before them, The ground of a certain rich	„	16
	37	man brought forth abundant fruits: and he reasoned within himself, saying, What shall I do, because I have not a place where I can	„	17
	38	collect my fruits? And he said, This will I do: I will pull down the buildings of my barns, and build again, and make greater ones; and there will I collect all my corn	„	18
	39	and my goods. And I will say to my soul,	„	19

[1] Repeated xxxiv. 48.
[2] This passage seems to have been asserted here on account of its similarity of subject with what follows at ver. 42, etc. It is thus made to appear as if the incident happened at the Feast of Tabernacles.

28	40	Soul, thou hast many goods laid up for many years; take thine ease; eat, drink, enjoy thyself. God said unto him, O destitute of understanding, this night thy soul shall be taken away from thee; and the things which thou hast prepared, whose shall they be?	Lu. 12	20
	41	So is he that layeth up treasures for himself, and is not rich toward God.	„	21
	42	And when Jesus had walked on his way, there came near[2] to him a young man of the rulers, and fell upon his knees, and asked him, saying, Good Teacher, what shall I do	Mk.[1] 10	17
	43	that I may have eternal life? Jesus said unto him, Why callest thou me good? whereas there is none good save one, *even*	„	18
	44	God. Thou knowest the commandments:[3] if thou desirest to enter into life, keep the	„ Mt. 19	19[a] 17[b]
	45	commandments.[4] The young man said unto him, Which commandments?[3] Jesus said	„	18[a]
	46	unto him, Do not commit adultery, Do not steal, Do not kill, Do not speak false witness, Do not defraud, Honour thy father and thy mother, and, Love thy neighbour as	Mk. 10 Mt. 19	19[b] 19[b]
	47	thyself. The young man said unto him, All these things have I guarded from my youth:	„	20
	48	what is *there* then that I lack? And Jesus looking upon him loved him, and said unto	Mk. 10	21[a]
	49	him, If thou desirest to be perfect, one thing thou lackest, go away, sell all that thou hast, and give to the poor, and thou shalt have treasure in heaven: and take up	Mt. 19	21[b]
	50	thy cross, and follow me. At this word the young man frowned, and he went away	„	22

---

[1] Tatian here resumes the thread of the common order of S. Matthew and S. Mark, which he dropped at the close of xxv., but whether Jesus has meanwhile returned to the place, where they represent this as happening, viz. "the borders of Judaea beyond Jordan," is not made clear.

[2] Omitting "running."   [3] Arabic, "awâmir."

[4] Arabic, "waṣ-âyâ," primarily meaning a commission from one dying, but used also of the "ten commandments."

28 51	sad; for he was very rich. And Jesus seeing his sadness, looked towards his disciples, and saith unto them, How difficult it is for them that have riches to enter into the kingdom of God!	Lu. 18 23^b " 24^a Mk. 10 23
29 1	Verily I say unto you, It is difficult for a rich man to enter into the kingdom of	Mt. 19 23^b
2	heaven. And again I say unto you, It is easier for a camel to press through the eye of a needle, than for a rich man to enter	" 24
3	into the kingdom of God. And the disciples were amazed at these words. But Jesus answered again, and said unto them, My children, how difficult it is for them that trust in their possessions to enter into	Mk. 10 24
4	the kingdom of God. And they that heard were the more astonished, saying among themselves, being now afraid, Who, think	" 26
5	you, can be saved? And Jesus looking upon them, said unto them, With men this is not possible, but with God. God can do	" 27
6	all things. Simon Cephas saith unto him, Lo, we have left all, and followed thee:	Lu. 18 28
7	what then shall we have? Jesus saith unto them, Verily I say unto you, Ye which have followed me, in the new world when the Son of man shall sit on the throne of his glory, ye also shall sit upon twelve thrones, and shall judge the twelve tribes	Mt. 19 27^b " 28
8	of Israel. Verily I say unto you, There is no man that leaveth houses, or brethren, or sisters, or father, or mother, or wife, or children, or kindred, or lands, for the kingdom of God's sake, or for my sake, and for	Mk. 10 29^b
9	my gospel's sake, and that doth not receive twice as many in this time and in the world	Lu. 18 30
10	to come inherit eternal life: now in this time, houses, and brethren, and sisters, and mothers, and children, and lands, with persecution; and in the world to come ever-	Mk. 10 30^b

29	11	lasting life. Many *that are* first shall be last; and the last first.	Mk. 10 31
	12	And when the Pharisees had heard all these things, because they loved riches, they	Lu.[1] 16 14
	13	scoffed at him. But Jesus knowing what was in their hearts, said unto them, Ye are they that justify yourselves in the sight of men; but God knoweth your hearts: for that which is exalted among men, is small in the sight of God.	„ 15
	14	And he began to say, A certain man was rich, and was clothed in silk and purple, and	„ 19
	15	enjoyed himself surpassingly every day: and there was a certain beggar named Lazarus, who lay at the rich man's gate afflicted with	„ 20
	16	sores, and longed to fill his belly out of the crumbs that fell from the rich man's table;[2] so that the dogs came and licked his sores.	„ 21
	17	And it happened that the beggar died, and the angels carried him into Abraham's bosom: and the rich man also died, and was	„ 22
	18	buried. And while he was tormented in the lower world, he lifted up his eyes from afar off, and saw Abraham, and Lazarus in his	„ 23
	19	bosom. And he cried with a loud voice, and said, Father Abraham, have mercy on me, and send Lazarus, that he may wet the tip of his finger with water, and moisten my tongue; for behold, I am scorched in	„ 24
	20	this flame. Abraham said unto him, My son, remember that thou receivedst good things in thy lifetime, and Lazarus his calamities: but now behold, he resteth here,	„ 25
	21	but thou art tormented. Add to all these things, that between us and you a great	„ 26

---

[1] This passage appears to have been removed to this position for the purpose of comparing its teaching about the use of riches with that of the passages which here precede and follow it. The words "all these things" are thus applied differently. Cf. pp. 32, 33.

[2] Aphraates adds "and no man gave unto him;" cf. Luke xv. 16.

	abyss hath been placed,¹ so that they that wish to cross from hence to you may not be able, nor to cross over from thence to us.		
29 22	He said unto him, I beseech thee therefore, my father, to send him unto my father's	Lu. 16	27
23	house: for I have five brethren; that he may go, lest they also sin,² and come into	,,	28
24	this place of torments. Abraham saith unto him, They have Moses and the	,,	29
25	prophets; let them hear them. He said unto him, Nay, my father Abraham: but if one of the dead go to them, they will re-	,,	30
26	pent. Abraham saith unto him, If they hear not Moses and the prophets, not even if one of the dead rise again, will they believe him.	,,	31
27	The kingdom of heaven is like unto a man that is a householder, which went out early in the morning to hire labourers into his vine-	Mt. 20	1
28	yard. And when he had made an agreement with the labourers for a penny a day for each labourer, he sent them into his vine-	,,	2
29	yard. And he went out about the third hour, and seeing others standing in the	,,	3
30	marketplace idle, he said unto them, Go ye also into my vineyard, and that which is fair	,,	4
31	I will give you. And they went their way. And again he went out at the sixth and ninth hour, and did likewise, and sent them.	,,	5
32	And about the eleventh hour he went out, and finding others standing idle, he said unto	,,	6
33	them, Why stand ye all the day idle? They said unto him, Because no man hath hired us. He said unto them, Go ye also into the vineyard; and³ that which is fair ye shall	,,	7

¹ Or, "is placed."

² Mr. Rendel Harris accounts for this peculiar reading as arising from the confusing of two similar Greek words.

³ "And ... receive" is omitted in the Revised Version as deficient in MS. authority. It seems to have been added from the preceding verses to

29 34	receive. And when even was come, the lord of the vineyard said unto his overseer, Call the labourers, and pay them their hire: begin indeed from the last, and continue	Mt. 20	8
35	until the first. And the labourers of the eleventh hour came and received every man	,,	9
36	a penny. And when the first were come, they supposed that they were going to receive more; but they also received every man a	,,	10
37	penny. And when they received it, they	,,	11
38	murmured against the householder, saying, These last have laboured one hour, and thou hast made them equal unto us, which have borne the scorching heat of the day and its	,,	12
39	burden. He answered one of them, and said, Friend, I do thee no wrong: didst not thou	,,	13
40	agree with me for a penny? Take up that which is thine, and go thy way; but it is my will to give unto this last, even as I have	,,	14
41	given unto thee. Either have I not a right to do what I will about mine own business? or perchance is thine eye evil, because I am	,,	15
42	good? So the last shall be first, and the first last: many are called, and few chosen.	,,	16
43	And when Jesus entered into the house of a certain ruler of the Pharisees on a sabbath day to eat bread, they were watch-	Lu. 14	1
44	ing him to see what he would do. And there was before him a certain man which had	,,	2
45	the dropsy. Jesus answered, and said unto the lawyers and Pharisees, Is it lawful to	,,	3
46	heal on the sabbath? But they held their peace. However he took him, and healed	,,	4
47	him, and let him go. And he said unto them, Of which of you shall a son or an ox fall into a well on a sabbath day, and he will not straightway draw him up, and give	,,	5

make the eleventh hour correspond to the others mentioned. But, in fact, the eleventh was an exceptional hour, not being one of the regular quarters of the day.

29 48	him to drink? And they could not answer him a word unto these things.	Lu. 14	6
30 1	And he set a parable before those which were bidden there, because he saw them	,,	7
2	choosing out the chief couches: When any one bids thee to a feast, do not go to recline in the chief place of the assembly; lest haply a more honourable man than thou be there,	,,	8
3	and he that bade you, come and say to thee, Give this man place; and thou be put to shame in the presence of them that stand by, and another place shall receive thee.	,,	9
4	But when thou art bidden, go and lie down last; that when he that hath bidden thee cometh, he may say to thee, Friend, go up higher: and thou shalt have glory in the presence of all them that are invited with	,,	10
5	thee. For everyone that exalteth himself shall be humbled, and every one that humbleth himself shall be exalted.	,,[1]	11
6	And he said to him that had bidden him, When thou makest a supper or a breakfast, call not thy friends, nor thy brethren, nor thy kinsmen, nor rich neighbours; lest haply they also bid thee, and a recompense be	,,	12
7	made thee. But when thou makest a feast, bid the poor, the weak, the lame, and the	,,	13
8	blind: and thou shalt be blessed; because they have not from whence they may recompense thee: that thy recompense may be made in the resurrection of the righteous.	,,	14
9	When one of them that were bidden had heard these things, he said unto him, Blessed is he that shall eat bread in the kingdom of God.	,,	15
10	Jesus answering again in parables, said,	Mt.[2] 22	1

[1] Cf. xxxii. 21 taken from Luke xviii. 14, and xl. 40 taken from Matt. xxiii. 12.
[2] Tatian is at variance with most modern harmonists in combining as one the two parables of S. Matthew and S. Luke. The position he assigns to the result is not at variance with S. Luke, but is earlier than S. Matthew places it.

30 11 The kingdom of the heavens is likened unto a certain king, which made a feast for his son, and prepared a great banquet, and	Mt. 22	2
	Lu. 14	16[b]
12 invited many: and he sent forth his servants at the time of the banquet to signify to them that were bidden, Come; for all things are ready for you: and they would not come.	„	17
	Mt. 22	3[b]
13 But they all began with one mouth[1] to excuse themselves. The first saith unto them, Tell him, I have bought a farm, and I am obliged to go out to see it: I beseech	Lu. 14	18
14 thee, let me go, for I am excused. And another said, I have bought five yoke of oxen, and I go to look at them: I beseech	„	19
15 thee to let me go, for I am excused. And another said, I have married a wife, and therefore I cannot come.	„	20
16 Again the king sent forth other servants, saying, Tell them that are bidden, My feast is prepared: my oxen and my fatlings are killed, and all things are ready: come to	Mt. 22	4
17 the banquet. But they disregarded it, and went their ways, one to his farm, and an-	„	5
18 other to his merchandise: but the rest laid hold on his servants, and entreated them	„	6
19 shamefully, and killed them. And one of the servants came, and told his lord that	Lu. 14	21[a]
20 which had happened. But the king, when he heard *it*, was wroth; and he sent his armies, and they destroyed those murderers,	Mt. 22	7
21 and burned their cities. Then saith he to his servants, The banquet is ready; and they	„	8
22 that were bidden were not worthy. Go out quickly into the streets and lanes of the city, and bring in hither the poor and sick and lame and blind. And the servants did as	Lu. 14	21[b]
23 the king had commanded them; and they came, and said unto him, Lord, we have done whatsoever thou didst command, and yet	„	22

[1] Or, "saying."

30 24 there is room here. And the lord said unto	Lu. 14	23ᵃ
his servants, Go out into the highways and lanes and wider roads, and whomsoever ye	Mt. 22	9ᵇ
shall find, invite to the banquet, and constrain them to come in, that my house may	Lu. 14	23ᵇ
25 be filled. I say unto you, that no one of those men which were invited shall taste of	,,	24
26 my breakfast. And the servants went out into the highways, and gathered together all that they found, good and bad: and the banqueting house was filled with those re-	Mt. 22	10
27 clining. But when the king came in to see those reclining, he saw there a man not	,,	11
28 clothed in a wedding-garment: and he saith unto him, Friend, how camest thou in hither not having a wedding-garment? And he	,,	12
29 was speechless. Then the king said to the attendants, Bind his hands and feet, and cast him out into the outer darkness; there shall be the weeping and gnashing of teeth.	,,	13
30 Many are called, and few chosen.	,,	14
31 After these things was the Jews' feast of	Jn.¹ 5	1ᵃ
unleavened *bread;* and Jesus went forth to	Lu.² 17	11
32 go unto Jerusalem. And as he was making the journey⁴ there met him ten leprous men,	,,³	12
33 which stood afar off: and they lifted up their cry, saying, Jesus, Master, have mercy	,,	13
34 on us. And when he saw them, he said unto them, Go and shew yourselves unto the priests. And when they went, they were	,,	14
35 cleansed. And one of them, when he saw that he was cleansed, turned back, and with	,,	15
36 a loud voice praised God; and he fell upon his face before the feet of Jesus, giving him	,,	16
37 thanks: and he was a Samaritan. Jesus answered, and said, Were not they that were cleansed ten? and the nine, where are they?	,,	17

¹ Repeated from xxii. 9 with variation.   ² Part only, and varied.
³ Varied: omitting "through the midst of Samaria and Galilee."
⁴ Or, "going in the way."

30 38 Not even one of them hath turned aside to come and give glory to God, save this one,	Lu. 17	18
39 who is of an alien tribe. He saith unto him, Arise, go thy way: thy faith hath	„	19
40 made thee whole. And as they were in the way, going up to Jerusalem, Jesus was going before them: and they were amazed; and they were following him afraid. And he took his twelve disciples apart, and began to make known to them, between himself and them, the things that were going to	Mk.[1] 10	32
41 happen unto him. For he saith unto them, We are going up to Jerusalem, and all the things that are written in the prophets concerning the Son of man shall be accomplished.	Lu. 18	31[b]
42 He shall be delivered unto the chief priests and the scribes; and they shall condemn him to death, and shall deliver him unto	Mk. 10	33[b]
43 the Gentiles: and they shall mock him, and scourge him, and shall spit into his face:	„	34[a]
44 they shall condemn him: they shall crucify and kill him: and the third day he shall	Lu. 18	33
45 rise again. And they understood none of these things; but this saying was hid from them, and they knew not these things that were said.	„	34
46 Then came near to him the mother of the sons of Zebedee, herself and both her sons, and worshipped him, and asked something of him. He said unto her, What wilt	Mt. 20	20
	„	21[a]
47 thou? And there came near unto him James and John, her sons, and said unto him, Teacher, we wish that thou shouldest	Mk. 10	35
48 do for us whatsoever we shall ask. He saith unto them, What will ye that I should	„	36
49 do for you? They said unto him, Grant unto us that one may sit on thy right, and the other on thy left, in thy kingdom and	„	37
50 glory. But Jesus saith unto them, Ye	„	38

[1] Varied: resuming S. Mark's order from xxix. 11.

know not what ye ask. Are ye able to
drink the cup that I am going to drink?
and to be baptized with the baptism that I
30 51 am going to be baptized with? They said   Mk. 10 39
unto him, We are able. Jesus saith unto
them, The cup that I am going to drink ye
shall drink; and with the baptism that I
am going to be baptized with shall ye be
52 baptized: but that ye should sit on my   „   40
right and on my left is not mine to give:
but *it is for them* for whom my Father hath
31 1 prepared *it*. And when the ten had heard   „   41
it, they were moved with indignation at
2 James and John. And Jesus calleth them,   „   42
and saith unto them, Ye know that the
chiefs of the Gentiles are their lords, and
their rulers are those who have dominion
3 over them. It shall not be so among you: „   43
but whosoever shall wish to become the
greater among you, let him be your minister:
4 and whosoever shall wish to be the first of   „   44
5 you, let him be the servant of all. Even as   Mt. 20 28
the Son of man also came not to be minis-
tered unto, but to minister, and to give his
life as a ransom for many.
6   He said these things, and went round   Lu. 13 22
the villages and cities, and taught, and made
7 a journey unto Jerusalem. And a certain   „   23
man asked him, Are they few that shall be
saved? Jesus answered, and saith unto
8 them, Strive to enter in through the   „   24
narrow gate: for I say unto you, Many
shall seek to enter in, and shall not find *it*.
9 From the hour, when the master of the   „   25
house shall rise up, and shut the door, ye
shall be standing without, and shall knock
at the door, and shall begin to say, Lord,
open to us; and he shall answer and say,
I say unto you,[1] I know you not whence

---

[1] "I tell you" removed from ver. 11.

31 10 ye are; and ye shall begin to say, We did	Lu. 13	26
eat in thy presence, and drink, and thou		
11 didst teach in our streets; and he shall say	„	27
unto you, I know you not whence ye are;		
depart from me, ye servants of iniquity.¹		
12 There shall be the weeping and gnashing of	„	28
teeth, when ye shall see Abraham, and Isaac,		
and Jacob, and all the prophets, in the		
kingdom of God, but yourselves cast forth		
13 without. And they shall come from the	„	29
east and west, and from the north and south,		
and shall recline in the kingdom of God.		
14 And then the last shall become first, and	„	30
the first shall become last.		
15 And when Jesus had entered and walked	„² 19	1
16 through Jericho, a certain man Zacchaeus by	„	2
name, a rich man, and the chief of the		
17 publicans, wished to see Jesus, who he was;	„	3
and could not for the closeness of the crowd,		
because Zacchaeus was little in stature.		
18 And he made haste and went before Jesus,	„	4
and climbed up into a sycomore tree to see		
Jesus: for so he was going to pass by.		
19 And when Jesus was come to the place, he	„	5
saw him, and said unto him, Zacchaeus, make		
haste, and come down; to-day I must be in		
20 thy house. And he made haste, and came	„	6
21 down, and received him joyfully. And when	„	7
they had all seen it, they murmured, saying,		
He hath gone in to a man that is a sinner,		
22 and remained. But Zacchaeus stood *still*,	„	8
and said unto Jesus, Behold, the half of my		
goods, Lord, I give to the poor; and what		
I have taken in excess from each man I		
23 restore fourfold. Jesus saith unto him,	„	9
To-day is salvation come to this house, for-		
asmuch as he also is a son of Abraham.		
24 For the Son of man came to seek and to	„	10
save that which was lost.		

¹ Or, "lies." ² On this displacement of S. Luke's order see note to xxxi. 25.

31	25	And when Jesus went out from Jericho,	Lu.[1] 18 35[a]
		himself and his disciples, a great multitude	Mt. 20 29[b]
	26	followed him, and a blind man was sitting	Lu. 18 35[b]
		by the wayside begging: and his name was	Mk. 10 46[b]
	27	Bartimaeus,[2] the son of Timaeus. And hearing the sound of a multitude going by, he	Lu. 18 36
	28	inquired who it was. They said unto him,	„ 37
	29	Jesus of Nazareth passeth by. And when	Mk. 10 47[a]
		he had heard that it was Jesus, he cried with a loud voice, saying, Jesus, thou son of	Lu. 18 38
	30	David, have mercy on me. And they that	„ 39[a]
		were going in front of Jesus rebuked him, that he should hold his peace: but he cried	Mk.[3] 10 48[b]
		out the more, saying, Thou son of David,	
	31	have mercy on me. And Jesus stood *still*,	„ 49
		and commanded him to be called. And they called the blind man, saying unto him, Be of good cheer: rise, for behold, he calleth	
	32	thee. And the blind man, casting away	„ 50
		his garment, stood up, and came to Jesus.	
	33	Jesus said unto him, What wilt thou that	„ 51
		I should do unto thee? And the blind man said unto him, My lord and master, that thou mayest open mine eyes, and I	
	34	may see thee.[4] And Jesus had mercy on	Mt. 20 34[a]
		him, and touched his eyes, and said unto	
		him, Receive thy sight: thy faith hath	Lu. 18 42[b]
	35	made thee whole. And immediately he	„ 43
		received his sight, and followed him, praising God: and all the people that saw it, gave praise unto God.	

[1] Or Mark x. 46[a]. Placed after leaving Zacchaeus's house in accordance with S. Mark's account, from which the words "went out" are taken. See Introduction, p. 34.

[2] Arabic, "Ibn-Tîmî."

[3] Or Luke xviii. 39[b].

[4] This reading is in the Curetonian Syriac of S. Matthew and S. Luke. Ephraem and Aphraates do not quote it, but Ephraem's comment is "that He might be visible and manifest unto him," etc. And at Moes. p. 248, he says, "who could open the eyes of the blind, *that they might see Him.*" We may conclude that this reading is due to Tatian.

31 36	And he employed a parable,[1] for the reason that he was near Jerusalem, and because they supposed that the kingdom of God would be made known at that time.	Lu. 19	11[b]
37	He saith unto them, A certain man of a noble family went into a far country, to receive for himself a kingdom, and to return.	„	12
38	And when he had called his ten servants, he gave them ten minas, and saith unto them, Trade ye *herewith* until my arrival.	„	13
39	But his citizens hated him, and sent ambassadors after him, saying, We do not wish	„	14
40	this man to reign over us. And when he came back again, having received the kingdom, he commanded the servants, unto whom he gave the money, to be called to him, that he might know how much each	„	15
41	one had traded. And the first came, saying, Lord, thy mina hath acquired ten minas	„	16
42	more. The king said unto him, O thou good and faithful servant, who hast been found faithful in a very little, be thou	„	17
43	holding authority over ten districts. And another came, saying, Lord, thy mina hath	„	18
44	gained five minas. And to this man he said, Thou also shalt be holding authority	„	19
45	over five districts. And another came, saying, Lord, behold thy mina, which I kept	„	20
46	laid up in a napkin: I feared thee, because thou art an austere man: thou takest up that which thou layedst not down, thou exactest that which thou gavest not, and	„	21
47	reapest that which thou sowedst not. His lord said unto him, Out of thy mouth I judge thee, thou wicked servant, negligent[2] and destitute of confidence.[3] Thou knewest	„	22

---

[1] Tatian does not identify this parable with that of the talents (Matt. xxv. 14-30), which he inserts at xliii. 22-38.

[2] Cf. Matt. xxv. 26, "slothful."

[3] Curetonian Syriac, "that art not faithful."

		that I am an austere man, taking up that which I laid not down, and reaping that		
31	48	which I sowed not; wherefore didst thou not place my money at the bank, so that at my coming I might have exacted it with	Lu. 19	23
	49	interest? And he said unto them that stood by, Take away from him the mina, and give it unto him that hath the ten	„	24
	50	minas. They said unto him, Lord, he hath	„	25
	51	ten minas. He saith unto them, I say unto you, Unto every one that hath shall be given; but from him that hath not, even that which he hath shall be taken away	„	26
	52	from him. Howbeit those mine enemies, which did not wish me to reign over them, bring hither, and slay them before me.	„	27
32	1¹	And when Jesus had entered Jerusalem, he went up into the temple of God; and he	Mt. 21 Jn. 2	12ᵃ 14ᵃ
	2	found there oxen, sheep, and doves. And when he saw them that sold and bought, and the money changers sitting, he made for himself a scourge of cords, and cast all of them out of the temple, the sheep also, and the oxen, and the money changers, whose money he poured out, and overthrew the tables, and the seats of them that sold	Mt. 21 Jn. 2 „	12ᵇ 14ᵇ 15
	3	the doves; and he was teaching and saying unto them, Is it not written, My house is a house of prayer for all nations: but ye have	Mt. 21 „²	12ᶜ 13
	4	made it a den of robbers? And to them that sold the doves he said, Take these things hence; and make not my Father's	Jn. 2	16
	5	house a house of merchandise. And he suffered not that any man should carry	Mk. 11	16
	6	vessels through the temple. And his disciples remembered the scripture, The zeal	Jn. 2	17

---

¹ On the identification of the Cleansing of the Temple in S. John with that in the Synoptists, see Introduction, p. 33.

² Mk. xi. 17 seems to agree more closely with the text than the reference given in the Arabic.

32	7	of thine house hath eaten me up. The Jews answered and said unto him, What sign shewest thou unto us, that thou	Jn.	2 18
	8	shouldest do this? Jesus answered, and said unto them, Destroy this temple, and in	„	19
	9	three days I will raise it up. The Jews said unto him, In forty and six years was this temple built, and wilt thou raise it up	„	20
	10	in three days? But¹ he spake unto them of the temple of his body: that when they destroyed it, he would raise it up in three	„	21
	11	days. And when he rose again from the dead, his disciples remembered that he had said this; and they believed the scriptures,	„	22
	12	and the saying that Jesus spake. And Jesus sat down² over against the treasury, and observed how the multitudes cast their offerings into the treasury: and many that	Mk. 12	41
	13	were rich cast in much. And there came a poor widow, and she cast in two mites.³	„	42ᵃ
	14	And Jesus called his disciples, and said unto them, Verily I say unto you, This poor widow cast in more than *they* all into the	Lu.⁴ 21	3
	15	treasury: for all these did cast in of the superfluity of their substance into the ark⁵ of the offering of God; but she of her want did cast all that she possessed.⁶	Mk. 12	44
	16	And he set before them this parable⁷ about certain which trusted in themselves that they were righteous, and despised the	Lu. 18	9
	17	rest. Two men went up into the temple to pray; the one a Pharisee, and the other	„	10

¹ Aphraates has, "And his disciples understood that he spake of his body, in that he would, after they had broken it, raise it up in three days."

² Placed a little earlier than the evangelists have it, but during the same visit to Jerusalem.

³ Omitting Mark xii. 42ᵇ, "which make a farthing."

⁴ Or Mark xii. 43 slightly varied.   ⁵ Lit. "house."

⁶ Omitting "*even* all her living."

⁷ S. Luke puts this parable before the arrival at Jericho. Tatian seems to have thought it likely from its nature to have been spoken in the temple.

32 18 a publican. The Pharisee stood and prayed Lu. 18 11
thus with himself, Lord, I thank thee, that I
am not as the rest of men, unjust, adulterers,
19 extortioners, or even as this publican. But „ 12
I fast twice in the week, and I give tithes
20 of all my substance. And the publican, „ 13
standing afar off, would not lift up even
his eyes unto heaven, but smote his breast,
saying, Lord, be propitious to me the
21 sinner. I say unto you, This man went „ 14
down to his house justified more than the
Pharisee: Every[1] one that exalteth himself
shall be humbled; and every one that
humbleth himself shall be exalted.
22   And when evening was come, he left $\begin{cases} \text{Mk.}^2 11\ 19^{\text{a}} \\ \text{Mt.}\ 21\ 17 \end{cases}$
them all, and went forth outside the city
to Bethany, himself and the twelve, and was
23 there. And all the people, because they Lu.[3] 9 11
knew the place, came unto him; and he
received them; and he healed those that
24 had need of healing. And on the morning Mk. 11 12
after, when he returned from Bethany to
25 the city, he hungered. And he saw from „ 13
afar beside the road a fig-tree having leaves,
and he came to it, that he might find something on it: and when he was come, he
found nothing on it but leaves; for it was
26 not the season of figs. And he said unto it, „ 14
Henceforward and for ever no man shall eat
fruit from thee.[4] And his disciples heard it.
27   And they came to Jerusalem. Now $\begin{cases} \text{Mk. 11 15}^{\text{a}} \\ \text{Jn.}\ \ 3\ \ 1 \end{cases}$
there was there a man of the Pharisees,
named Nicodemus,[5] a ruler of the Jews:

---

[1] Cf xxx. 5 and xl. 40.

[2] Tatian may have meant this for Mark xi. 11ᵇ, especially as Mark xi. 12 follows in ver. 24. He gives Mark xi. 19 at xxxiii. 1.

[3] Repeated with variations from xviii. 26. Tatian exercised considerable freedom with general statements of this class.

[4] Omitting Matt. xxi. 19: "And presently the fig-tree withered away."

[5] The account of this interview is naturally moved along with S. John's

32	28	this man came to Jesus by night, and	Jn.	3 2
		said unto him, Teacher, we know that thou		
		wast sent from God as a teacher: for no		
		man can do these signs that thou doest,		
	29	except he with whom God is. Jesus answered,	,,	3
		and said unto him, Verily, verily, I say unto		
		thee, except a man be born anew, he cannot		
	30	see the kingdom of God. Nicodemus said	,,	4
		unto him, How can a man be born *when he*		
		is old? can he again enter a second time		
		into his mother's womb, and be born?		
	31	Jesus answered, and said unto him, Verily,	,,	5
		verily, I say unto thee, Except a man be		
		born of water and the Spirit, he cannot		
	32	enter into the kingdom of God. That which	,,	6
		is born of the flesh is flesh; and that which is		
	33	born of the Spirit is spirit. Marvel not that	,,	7
		I said unto thee, Ye must be born anew.		
	34	The wind bloweth where it will, and thou	,,	8
		hearest the voice thereof, but knowest not		
		whence it cometh, and whither it goeth:		
		so is every one that is born of the Spirit.		
	35	Nicodemus answered, and said unto him,	,,	9
	36	How can this be? Jesus answered, and	,,	10
		said unto him, Art thou a teacher of Israel,		
	37	and art ignorant of these things? Verily,	,,	11
		verily, I say unto thee, We speak that which		
		we know, and testify that which we have		
	38	seen; and ye receive not our witness. If I	,,	12
		told you earthly [1] things, and ye believe not,		
		how shall ye believe, if I tell you heavenly [2]		
	39	things? And no man hath ascended into	,,	13
		heaven, but he that descended out of heaven,		

version of the Cleansing of the Temple, since they clearly belong to the same visit to Jerusalem. From its nature such an interview would seem more likely, when Jesus was well known, and had come to stay at Jerusalem. Professor Fuller observes, "This position ignores John vii. 50; and has not been imitated." This is not accurate, since that allusion to Nicodemus does not occur in the *Diatessaron* until xxxv. 14.

[1] Lit. "what is in the earth."   [2] Lit. "what is in heaven."

		even the Son of man, which is in heaven.¹		
32	40	And as Moses lifted up the serpent in the wilderness, even so is the Son of man about	Jn. 3	14
	41	to be lifted up: that everyone that believeth on him may not perish, but have eternal life.	,,	15
	42	God so loved the world that he gave his only Son, that everyone that believeth in him should not perish, but have eternal life.	,,	16
	43	God sent not his Son into the world to judge the world; but that the world should	,,	17
	44	be saved through him. He that believeth in him is not judged: he that believeth not is judged already, because he believeth not	,,	18
	45	in the name of the only Son of God. This is the judgment: the light is come into the world, and men loved the darkness rather than the light; for their works were evil.	,,	19
	46	Everyone that worketh infamies hateth the light, and cometh not to the light, that his	,,	20
	47	works may not be reproved. But he that worketh truth cometh to the light, that his works may be recognised, that they have been wrought in God.²	,,	21
33	1	And when the evening was come, Jesus went forth outside the city, himself and his	Mk.³ 11	19
	2	disciples. And as they passed by in the morning, the disciples saw that fig-tree	,,	20
	3	withered away from the root. And as they went by, they said, How did the fig-tree	Mt. 21	20ᵇ
	4	wither away already? And Simon, calling to remembrance, said unto him, Teacher,⁴ behold, that fig-tree which thou cursedst, is	Mk. 11	21
	5	withered away. And Jesus answering saith	,,	22

¹ Ephraem omits "which is in heaven;" this does not prove that he had not this clause; but that is probable, as it is wanting in some of the best Greek MSS.

² The *Codex Fuldensis* inserts here John viii. 1-11 (the Woman taken in Adultery), followed by the Cursing of the Fig-tree given above, ver. 24-26. Cf. Introduction, pp. 19 and 25.

³ Part of this verse occurred at xxxii. 22ᵃ. See note there.

⁴ Or, "Master."

	unto them, Let the faith of God be in you.		
33	6 Verily I say unto you, If ye shall believe, and shall not be undecided in your hearts, and shall hold it as certain, that whatsoever ye shall say is coming to pass, whatsoever ye shall say shall come to pass unto you.	Mk.[1] 11	23
	7 Even if ye shall say unto this mountain, Remove, and fall into the sea, it shall be	Mt. 21	21[b]
	8 done. And all things, whatsoever ye shall ask of God in prayer, believing, he shall give you.	„	22
	9 And the apostles said unto the Lord, In- 10 crease our faith. He said unto them, If there be in you faith as a grain of mustard seed, ye shall say unto this fig-tree, Be thou rooted up, and be thou transplanted into the	Lu.[2] 17 „	5 6
	11 sea, and it shall obey you. Who is there of you, having a servant guiding [3] oxen or feeding sheep, to whom, when he cometh from the field, he saith straightway, Go, and lie down	„	7
	12 *to meat?* But he will say unto him, Make ready for me wherewith I may sup, and gird thy loins, and serve me, until I eat and drink; and afterward thou also shalt eat	„	8
	13 and drink? Will that servant who did the thing that he had commanded him, receive	„	9
	14 his thanks? I think not. Even so ye also, when ye shall have done all the things that are commanded you, say, We are unprofitable servants; we have done that which it was our duty to do.	„	10
	15 Therefore I say unto you, All things, whatsoever ye pray and ask for, believe that ye shall receive them, and they	Mk. 11	24
	16 shall be unto you. And when ye stand for praying, forgive that which ye have in	„	25

[1] With the first part of Matt. xxi. 21.

[2] S. Luke is not very definite as to when this occurred. Tatian has put it where it would illustrate the previous narrative.

[3] Perhaps equivalent to the Authorised Version, "plowing."

33 17	your heart against *any* man; and your Father which is in the heavens shall forgive you also your trespasses.¹ And if ye for-	Mk. 11 26
	give not men their trespasses,¹ neither will your Father forgive you also your trespasses.¹	
18	And he set forth also a parable² unto	Lu. 18 1
	them to the end that they should always	
19	pray, and not be slothful. There was in	„ 2
	a city a judge, which feared not God, and	
20	regarded not men: and there was a widow	„ 3
	in that city; and she came unto him, saying, Avenge me of mine adversary.	
21	And he would not for a long time: after-	„ 4
	wards he said within himself, Though I	
22	fear not God, nor regard men, yet because	„ 5
	of the importunity of this widow, I will avenge her, that she may not come per-	
23	petually, and bring me weariness. And	„ 6
	our Lord said, Hear what the judge of un-	
24	righteousness said. And shall not God per-	„ 7
	form still more the avenging of his elect, which cry to him day and night, and be	
25	longsuffering³ in respect to them? I say	„ 8
	unto you, He will perform the avenging of them speedily. When the Son of man cometh, think you he will find faith on the earth?	
26 27	And they came again to Jerusalem. And it came to pass, on one of the days, as Jesus was walking, and teaching the people in the temple, and announcing the good tidings, there stood near him the chief priests and the scribes with the elders;	Mk.⁴ 11 15ᵃ Lu. 20 1
28	and they said unto him, Tell us: By what authority doest thou this? and who gave	Lu. 20 2ᵃ Mk. 11 28ᵇ

¹ Or, "follies."

² Placed here because it relates to the subject of prayer now being referred to. See Introduction.

³ Or, "tarry." ⁴ A mistake for 27ᵃ. Cf. xxxii. 27ᵃ.

33 29 thee this authority to do this? And Jesus { Mk. 11 29ᵃ / Mt. 21 24ᵇ
saith unto them, I also will ask you one word; and if ye tell me, I also will tell
30 ye by what authority I do this. The baptism of John, whence was it? from heaven Mt. 21 25ᵃ
31 or from men? tell me. But they reasoned among themselves, saying, If¹ we shall say unto him, From heaven, he will say unto { Mk. 11 30ᵇ / Mt. 21 25ᵇ
32 us, Why did ye not believe him? But if Mt. 21 26ᵃ
we shall say, From men, we fear that all Lu. 20 6ᵇ
33 the people may stone us: for all held, that Mk. 11 32ᵇ
34 John was a true prophet. They answered, „ 33
and said unto him, We know not. Jesus saith unto them, Neither tell I you by what authority I do *these things*.
35 What think ye? A certain man had two Mt. 21 28
sons; and he came to the first, and said unto him, My son, go to-day, and work² in the
36 vineyard. He answereth, and saith, I will „ 29
not: but at last he repented himself, and
37 went. And he came to the other, and said „ 30
unto him likewise. And he answered and
38 said, Yea, sir: and went not. Which of „ 31
these two did the will of his father? They said unto him, The first. Jesus saith unto them, Verily I say unto you, The publicans and the harlots go before you into the king-
39 dom of God. John came unto you in the „ 32
way of righteousness, and ye believed him not: but the publicans and the harlots believed him: but ye, not even after ye had seen it, did ye at last repent, that ye might believe him.
40 Hear another parable: There was a man, „ 33ᵃ
a householder, which planted a vineyard, and set a hedge about it, and digged a winepress
41 in it, and built a tower in it, and granted it Lu. 20 9ᵇ
to husbandmen, and was abroad for a long
42 time. And when the season of the fruits Mt. 21 34

¹ Ver. 26 begins here as in the Vulgate.   ² Or, "till."

33	43	had come near, he sent his servant¹ to the husbandmen, that they might send him of the fruits of his vineyard. But these husbandmen beat him, and sent him away empty.	Mk. 12	3
	44	And again he sent unto them another servant; and they stoned and wounded him,	„	4
	45	and sent him away shamefully handled. And again he sent another; and him they killed: and many other servants sent he unto them.	„	5ᵃ
	46	²And the husbandmen took his servants, and beat one, and stoned another, and killed	Mt. 21	35
	47	another. Again, he sent other servants more than the former: and they did unto	„	36
	48	them in like manner. And the lord of the vineyard said, What shall I do? I will send my beloved son: for perchance they	Lu. 20	13
	49	will see him, and reverence him. At last he	Mk. 12	6ᵃ
	50	sent unto them his beloved son.³ But the husbandmen, when they saw the son, said	Mt. 21	38ᵃ
	51	among themselves, This is the heir; and they said, Let us kill him, and the inherit-	Lu. 20	14ᵇ
	52	ance will be ours. And they took him, and brought him forth outside the vineyard, and	Mt. 21	39
	53	killed him. When therefore the lord of the vineyard cometh, what will he do unto those	„	40
	54	husbandmen? They said unto him, He will miserably destroy the miserable men, and will let out the vineyard unto other husbandmen, who will render him the fruits in	„	41
	55	their seasons.⁴ Jesus said unto them, Did ye never read in the scripture,	„	42ᵃ
		The stone which the builders rejected, The same was made into the head of the corner:	Lu.⁵ 20	17ᵇ

¹ Arabic, "servants," but see "him" in ver. 43.
² Ver. 46, 47 appear to repeat from S. Matthew the substance of ver. 42-45.
³ Lit. "his beloved son which was his."
⁴ Omitting Luke xx. 16ᵇ: "And when they heard it, they said, God forbid."
⁵ Or continuation of Matt. xxi. 42.

33	56	This was done by God; And it is marvellous in our eyes.	Mt. 21	42ᶜ
	57	Therefore I say unto you, The kingdom of God shall be taken away from you, and shall be given to a nation bringing forth	„	43
	58	fruits. And whosoever falleth on this stone, shall be broken to pieces: but on whomsoever it shall fall, it will grind him	„	44
	59	to powder. And when the chief priests and the Pharisees had heard his parables, they	„	45
	60	perceived that he spake of them. And[1] they sought to lay hold on him; and they feared the multitudes, because they regarded him as a prophet.	„	46
34	1	Then the Pharisees went away, and took counsel how they might catch him in *his* talk, and deliver him up to the authority of the court, and to the authority of the	„ Lu. 20	22 15 20ᵇ
	2	governor. And they sent to him their disciples with the Herodians,[2] saying unto him, Teacher, we know that thou art true, and teachest the way of God in truth, and carest not for anyone: for thou regardest	Mt. 22	16
	3	not man. Tell us therefore, What thinkest thou? Is it lawful to give tribute unto Caesar, or not? Shall we give, or shall	„ Mk.[3] 12	17 15ᵃ
	4	we not give? But Jesus, knowing their craftiness, saith unto them, Why tempt ye	Mt. 22	18ᵇ
	5	me, ye hypocrites? Show me the tribute penny. And they brought unto him a	„	19
	6	penny. Jesus saith unto them, Whose is	„	20
	7	this image and inscription? They said unto him, Caesar's. He said unto them, Render unto Caesar the things that are Caesar's; and unto God the things that are God's.	„	21
	8	And they could not bring[4] it to pass that	Lu. 20	26

[1] Omitting Luke xx. 19, "the same hour."
[2] Omitting Luke xx. 20, "spies, which should feign themselves just men."
[3] Part of this is called 14ᵇ, as in the Vulgate.
[4] "Bring ... fall," or "succeed in making him slip."

he should fall in his speech before the people: and they marvelled at his saying, and restrained themselves.¹

34	9	On that day there came Sadducees, and said unto him, The dead have no life: and	Mt. 22	23
	10	they asked him, saying unto him, Master, Moses said unto us, If a man die, having no children, let his brother marry his wife, and	,,	24
	11	raise up seed unto his brother. Now there	,,	25ᵃ
		were with us seven brethren: and the first	Lu. 20	29ᵇ
		took a wife, and died without children;²		
	12	and the next took his wife, and died without	,,	30
	13	children; and the third also took her; and likewise all the seven, and they died without	,,	31
	14	leaving a child. And at the last of all of	Mt. 22	27
	15	them the woman also died. In the resurrection therefore³ whose wife shall she be of these seven? for they all took her.	,,	28
	16	Jesus answered, and saith unto them, Do ye not therefore err, because ye know not the	Mt. 22 29 / Mk. 12 24ᵇ	
	17	scriptures, nor the power of God? The sons of this age marry wives; and the women are	Lu. 20	34ᵇ
	18	delivered up to husbands: but they that shall be accounted worthy of that age, and the resurrection from the dead, shall not marry wives; nor shall the women be for	,,	35
	19	husbands: nor shall they be able to die any more: but they shall be even as the angels⁴ and the sons of God, because they have been	,,	36
	20	made sons of the resurrection. Moreover, concerning the resurrection of the dead,	Mt. 22	31ᵃ
		have ye not read in the book of Moses, how God said unto him out of the bramble bush, I am the God of Abraham, and the God of	Mk. 12	26ᵇ
	21	Isaac, and the God of Jacob? Now he is not the God of the dead, but of the living:	Lu. 20	38

¹ Omitting Matt. xxii. 22, "and left him, and went their way."
² Omitting Matt. xxii. 25, "left his wife unto his brother."
³ Omitting Mark xii. 23, "when they shall rise."
⁴ Omitting Mark xii. 25, "which are in heaven."

	for all live with him. Ye therefore do greatly err.	Mk.	12	27[b]
34	22 And when the multitudes heard it, they	Mt.	22	33
	23 were astonished at his teaching. And certain of the scribes answering said unto him,	Lu.	20	39
	24 Teacher, thou hast well said. But all the Pharisees, when they had seen that he had put the Sadducees to silence in this way, assembled themselves together against him,	Mt.	22	34
	25 to strive with him. And one of the scribes,	„		35[a]
	a doctor of the law, when he had seen the appropriateness of his answer to them,	Mk.	12	28[b]
	26 wished to tempt him, saying, What shall I	Lu.[1]	10	25[b]
	do to inherit eternal life? and which is the greater and first commandment in the law?	Mk.[1]	12	28[c]
	27 Jesus said unto him, The first commandment of all is, Hear, O Israel; The Lord our	„		29
	28 God, the Lord is one: and: Thou shalt love the Lord thy God from all thy heart, and	„		30[a]
	from all thy soul, and from all thy mind,	Mt.	22	37[b]
	29 and from all thy strength. This is the	„		38
	30 greatest and first commandment. But *there is* a second, which is like unto it, Thou shalt love thy neighbour as thyself. There is no other commandment greater than these.	Mk.	12	31
	31 From these two commandments hangeth the	Mt.	22	40
	32 law, and the prophets. The scribe saith unto him, An excellent opinion, Master! with truth thou hast said that *God* is one,	Mk.	12	32
	33 and there is none other but he: and that a man should love him from all his heart, and from all his mind, and from all his soul, and from all his strength, and that he should love his neighbour as himself, is a better thing than all the burnt offerings and sacrifices.	„		33
	34 And when Jesus saw that he had answered discreetly, he answered, and said unto him,	„		34[a]

[1] Modern harmonisers do not combine these passages, but assign to S. Luke's incident an earlier place in the narrative, and thus avoid combining the two questions. Tatian puts the result in the order of the two first evangelists.

Thou art not far from the kingdom of God.
34 35 Thou hast said the right word: this do, and   Lu. 10 28[b]
36 thou shalt live. But he, desiring to justify   „   29
himself, said unto him, And who is my
37 neighbour? Jesus said unto him, A certain   „   30
man was going down from Jerusalem to
Jericho; and robbers fell upon him, which
plundered him, and having beaten him
38 departed, leaving him half dead.[1] And it   „   31
happened that a certain priest was going
down the same way: and when he saw him,
39 he passed by. In like manner came a   „   32
Levite also, and when he reached the place,
40 and saw him, he passed on. But a certain   „   33
Samaritan, as he journeyed, when he came
to the place where he was, and saw him,
41 had compassion on him, and came near, and   „   34
bound up his wounds, pouring on *them* wine
and oil; and he set him on an ass, and
brought him to an inn, and took care of
42 him. And on the next day he took out   „   35
two pence, and gave them to the host, and
saith unto him, Take care of him; and
whatsoever thou spendest more, I, when I
43 come back again, will repay thee. Which   „   36
of these three seems to thee to have been
more a neighbour unto him that fell among
44 the robbers? He said unto him, He that   „   37
had compassion on him. Jesus saith unto
45 him, Go, and do thou likewise. And no man   Mk. 12 34[b]
ventured to ask him anything after that.
46   And he was teaching daily [2] in the temple.   Lu. 19 47
But the chief priests and the scribes and the
elders of the people sought to destroy him:
47 and they could not do anything to him; for   „   48
all the people were in suspense to hear him.
48   Now of the multitude many believed on   Jn.[3] 7 31

[1] Lit. "with only his soul left in him."
[2] On this arrangement, see Introduction, p. 35.
[3] Repeated from xxviii. 32.

him, and said, Will the Messiah, when he cometh, do more signs than those which this
34 49 man doeth? And the Pharisees heard the Jn. 7 32
multitudes saying these things concerning him; and the chief priests sent soldiers to
50 take him. And Jesus said unto them, Yet „ 33
a little while am I with you, and I shall go
51 unto him that sent me. And ye shall seek „ 34
me, and shall not find me: and where I am,
52 ye cannot come. The Jews said among „ 35
themselves, Whither is this man about to go, so that we shall not be able to go? Do you think, that he is about to go unto the countries of the Gentiles, and teach the
53 heathen? What is this word that he said, „ 36
Ye shall seek me, and shall not find me: and where I am, ye cannot come?

35 1 Now on the great day, the last of the „ 37
festival, Jesus stood, crying and saying, If any man is thirsty, let him come unto me,
2 and drink. Everyone that believeth on me, „ 38
even as the scriptures say, out of his belly
3 shall flow rivers of sweet water. This spake „ 39
he signifying the Spirit, which they that believed on him were about to receive: for the Spirit had not yet been given, because
4 Jesus had not yet been glorified. And many „ 40
of the multitude that heard his words, said, This is of a truth the prophet. And
5 some said, This is the Messiah. But others „ 41
said, Shall the Messiah come from Galilee?
6 Doth not the scripture say that the Messiah „ 42
shall come of the offspring of David, and
7 from Bethlehem the village of David? So „ 43
there arose a disagreement in the multitude
8 because of him. And some of them wished „ 44
to take him; and no man laid hand on him.
9 And the soldiers came to the chief priests „ 45
and Pharisees; and the priests said unto
10 them, Why did ye not bring him? The „ 46

soldiers said, Never man so spake, as this
35 11 man speaketh. The Pharisees said unto   Jn.   7 47
12 them, Are ye also led astray? Hath anyone   „   48
13 of the rulers or of the Pharisees believed in
him? except this multitude which knoweth   „   49
14 not the law, who are accursed? Nicodemus,   „   50
one of themselves, who came to Jesus by
15 night, said unto them, Doth our law judge a   „   51
man, except it shall before have heard from
16 himself, and known what he doeth? They   „   52
answered, and said unto him, Art thou also
of Galilee? Search, and see, for from
Galilee ariseth no prophet.
17 Now when the Pharisees were gathered   Mt. 22 41
18 together, Jesus asked them a question, saying,   „   42
What say ye of the Messiah? whose son is
he? They said unto him, The son of David.
19 He saith unto them, How then doth David   „   43
in the Holy Spirit call him Lord, for he
saith,
20 The Lord said unto my Lord,   „   44
Sit thou on my right hand,
That I may put thine enemies underneath
thy feet.
21 If David then calleth him Lord, how is he   „   45
22 his son? And no one was able to answer   „   46
him; neither did any man venture from that
day forth to ask him about any matter.
23 And again Jesus spake unto them, saying,   Jn.   8 12
I am the light of the world: he therefore
that followeth me, doth not walk in the
darkness, but shall find the light of life.
24 The Pharisees said unto him, Thou bearest   „   13
witness of thyself; thy witness is not genuine.
25 Jesus answered, and said unto them, If I bear   „   14
witness of myself, my witness is genuine;
for I know whence I came, and whither I
go; but ye know not whence I came, nor
26 whither I go. For ye judge a material   „   15
27 judgment; but I judge no man. And if I   „   16

	judge, my judgment is genuine; for I am not alone, but I and my Father that sent	
35 28	me. And in your law it is written, that the	Jn. 8 17
29	witness of two men is genuine. I am he that beareth witness of myself; and my Father that sent me beareth witness of me.	„ 18
30	They said unto him, Where is thy Father? Jesus answered, and saith unto them, Ye know me not, nor my Father: for if ye knew me, ye would know my Father.	„ 19
31	These words spake he in the treasury, as he taught in the temple: and no man took him, because his hour was not yet come.	„ 20
32	Jesus said again unto them, I go away indeed; and ye shall seek me, and shall not find me, and shall die in your sins: and	„ 21
33	whither I go ye cannot come. The Jews said, Will he kill himself, that he may say,	„ 22
34	Whither I go ye cannot come? He saith unto them, Ye are from beneath; but I am from above: ye are of this world; and I	„ 23
35	am not of this world. I said unto you, Ye shall die in your sins: if ye believe not that	„ 24
36	I am *he*,[1] ye shall die in your sins. The Jews said, And who art thou? Jesus said	„ 25
37	unto them, If I begin to speak unto you, I have many things to speak concerning you, and to judge: but he that sent me is true; and the things which I heard from him,	„ 26
38	these speak I in the world. And they understood not that he referred to the	„ 27
39	Father in this. Jesus said again unto them, When ye have lifted up the Son of man, then shall ye perceive that I am *he*,[1] and *that* I do nothing of myself, but as the	„ 28
40	Father taught me, so I speak. And he that sent me is with me; for my Father hath not left me alone; for I do always the	„ 29
41	things that are pleasing to him. As he	„ 30

[1] Lit. "I am I."

spake these things many believed on him.
35 42 And Jesus said to those Jews which Jn. 8 31
ye believed on him, If ye abide in my word,
43 ye shall be truly my disciples; and ye shall „   32
know the truth; and the truth shall make
44 you free. They said unto him, We are the „   33
offspring of Abraham, and have never served
any man as bondsmen: how then sayest
45 thou, Ye shall be free children? Jesus „   34
said unto them, Verily, verily, I say unto
you, Everyone that committeth sin is the
46 bondservant of sin. And the bondservant „   35
abideth not in the house for ever: but the
47 son abideth for ever. If therefore the Son „   36
shall make you free, ye shall be free chil-
48 dren indeed. I know that ye are the off- „   37
spring of Abraham; yet ye seek to kill me,
49 because ye are unequal to [1] my word. For „   38
I speak that which I have seen with my
Father: and ye do that which ye have seen
50 with your father. They answered, and said „   39
unto him, Our father is Abraham. Jesus
said unto them, If ye were Abraham's children, ye would do the works of Abraham.
51 Now, behold, ye seek to kill me, a man that „   40
speaketh the truth with you, which I have
heard from God: this did not Abraham.
52 But ye do the works of your father. They „   41
said unto him, We are not of fornication;
53 we have one father, which is God. Jesus „   42
said unto them, If God were your Father,
ye would certainly have loved me. I came
forth from God, and came down; nor have
54 I come of myself, but he sent me. For why „   43
do ye not perceive my word? *Even* because
55 ye cannot hear my word. Ye are of *your* „   44
father the devil, and the desire of your
father ye wish to do, who is a murderer
from the beginning, and abideth [2] not in the

[1] Or, "too weak for."   [2] Or, "standeth."

35	56	truth, because there is no truth in him: and when he speaketh a lie, he speaketh of his own: for he is a liar, and the father of lies. And I, that speak in the truth, ye	Jn.	8 45
	57	believe me not. Which of you rebuketh me of sin? And if I say the truth, ye do	„	46
	58	not believe me. He that is of God heareth the words of God: for this cause ye hear	„	47
	59	*them* not, because ye are not of God. The Jews answered, and said unto him, Said we not well that thou art a Samaritan, and	„	48
	60	hast a devil? Jesus saith unto them, I certainly have not a devil; but I honour	„	49
	61	my Father, and ye dishonour me. I seek not mine own glory: here is one who	„	50
36	1	seeketh and judgeth. Verily, verily, I say unto you, Whosoever keepeth my saying	„	51
	2	shall never see death. The Jews said unto him, Now we know that thou hast a devil. Abraham is dead, and the prophets; and thou sayest, Whosoever keepeth my saying	„	52
	3	shall never taste death. Art thou greater than our father Abraham, which is dead? and the prophets, which are dead? whom	„	53
	4	makest thou thyself? Jesus saith unto them, If I glorify myself, my glory is nothing: it is my Father that glorifieth	„	54
	5	me, of whom ye say, He is our God; and ye know him not: but I know him; and if I say, I know him not, I shall be a liar like unto you: but I know him, and keep his	„	55
	6	saying. Your father Abraham longed with burning eagerness[1] to see my day; and he	„	56
	7	saw it, and was glad. The Jews said unto him, Thou art not yet fifty years old, and	„	57
	8	hast thou seen Abraham? Jesus said unto them, Verily, verily, I say unto you, Before	„	58
	9	Abraham was, I am. And they took stones to stone him: but Jesus hid himself, and	„	59

[1] Or, "earnestly longed."

went out of the temple, and ¹ passing among them went away.

36 10   And as he passed by, he saw a man blind   Jn.   9   1
11 from his mother's womb. And his disciples   „   2
     asked him, Master, who did sin, this man or
12 his parents, that he was born blind? Jesus   „   3
     saith unto them, Neither did this man sin,
     nor his parents: but that the works of God
13 may be made manifest in him. I must work   „   4
     the works of him that sent me, while the
     day lasts: the night will come, and no man
14 will be able to work at will. As long as I   „   5
     am in the world, I am the light of the world.
15 When he had said these things, he spat on   „   6
     the ground, and made clay of the spittle, and
     rubbed it upon the eyes of the blind man,
16 and said unto him, Go, wash in the bath   „   7
     of Siloam. He went away therefore, and
17 washed, and came seeing. And his neigh-   „   8
     bours which had seen him beg aforetime,
     said, Is not this he that sat begging? Some
18 said, It is he: and others said, Not at all,   „   9
     but he is exactly like him. He said, I am
19 he. They said unto him, How then were   „   10
20 thine eyes opened? He answered, and saith   „   11
     unto them, A man whose name is Jesus
     made clay, and rubbed it upon mine eyes,
     and said unto me, Go, and wash in the water
     of Siloam; so I went away, and washed, and
21 received sight. They said unto him, Where   „   12
     is he? He saith, I know not.
22   And they brought to the Pharisees him   „   13
23 that had before been blind. Now the day   „   14
     on which Jesus made the clay, and opened
24 his eyes, was the day of the sabbath. And   „   15
     again the Pharisees asked him: How didst
     thou receive thy sight? He said unto them,
     He put clay upon mine eyes; and I washed,
25 and received sight. Some of the Pharisees   „   16

¹ The rest of this verse is called 60, and is absent from the Vulgate.

said, This man is not from God, because he keepeth not the sabbath. But others said, How can a man that is a sinner do these signs? And a division took place among
36 26 them. And again they said unto the blind man, What sayest thou of him that opened thine eyes for thee? He said unto them, I   Jn. 9 17
27 say, that he is a prophet. And the Jews did not believe concerning him, that he had been blind, and had received his sight, until they called the parents of him that had   „ 18
28 received his sight; and they asked them: Is this your son, of whom ye say, that he was born blind? how then doth he now see?   „ 19
29 His parents answered, and said, We know that this is our son, and that he was born   „ 20
30 blind: but how he now seeth, or who opened his eyes, we know not: ask him; he is already arrived at the age of manhood, and   „ 21
31 he may speak for himself. These things said his parents, because they feared the Jews: for the Jews had decided already, that if any man should confess him to be the Messiah, they would expel him from the   „ 22
32 synagogue. Therefore said his parents, He is arrived at the age of manhood; ask him.   „ 23
33 And they called a second time him that had been blind, and said unto him, Give glory to God: we know that this man is a sinner.   „ 24
34 He answered, and saith unto them, Whether he be a sinner I know not: one thing I know, that, whereas I was blind, now I see.   „ 25
35 They said again unto him, What did he to thee? how opened he thine eyes for thee?   „ 26
36 He saith unto them, I told you, and ye did not hear: wherefore do ye wish to hear it again? do ye also wish to become his dis-   „ 27
37 ciples? And they despised him, and said unto him, Thou art his disciple; but we are   „ 28
38 disciples of Moses. For we know that God   „ 29

36	39	hath spoken unto Moses: but as for this man, we know not whence he is. The man answered, and said unto them, Therefore indeed is the marvel, that ye know not whence he is, and *yet* he opened mine eyes.	Jn.	9	30
	40	And we know that God heareth not the voice of sinners: but he that feareth him,	„		31
	41	and doeth his will, him he heareth. From eternity it was never heard that anyone opened the eyes of a blind man, born in	„		32
	42	blindness. Therefore if this man were not	„		33
	43	from God, he could not do this. They answered, and said unto him, Thou wast altogether born in sins, and dost thou teach us? And they cast him out.	„		34
	44	And Jesus heard of his casting out; and finding him, he said unto him, Dost thou	„		35
	45	believe on the Son of God? He that had been made whole, answered, and said, Who is he, Lord, that I may believe on him?	„		36
	46	Jesus said unto him, Thou hast seen him,	„		37
	47	and he it is that speaketh with thee. He saith, Lord, I believe. And he fell down	„		38
37	1	worshipping him. And Jesus said, For judging the world am I come, that they which see not may see; and that they which	„		39
	2	see may become blind. And some of the Pharisees which were with him, heard this,	„		40
	3	and said unto him, Are we blind? Jesus said unto them, If ye were blind, surely ye would have no sin: but now ye say, We see: and for this cause your sin remaineth.	„		41
	4	Verily, verily, I say unto you, He that entereth not by the door into the fold of the sheep, but climbeth up some other way, the	„	10	1
	5	same is a thief and a robber. But he that entereth in by the door is the shepherd of	„		2
	6	the sheep. And to him the porter openeth the door; and the sheep hear his voice: and he calleth his own rams by name, and they	„		3

37 7 go out unto him. And when he hath sent Jn. 10 4
forth his own sheep, he goeth before them,
and his rams follow him: for they know his
8 voice. And a stranger the sheep do not „ 5
follow, but flee from him: for they hear not
9 the voice of a stranger. This proverb spake „ 6
Jesus unto them: but they understood not
what he spake unto them.
10   Jesus said unto them again, Verily, verily, „ 7
I say unto you, I am the door of the sheep.
11 For all, as many as came, are thieves and „ 8
robbers: but the sheep did not hear them.
12 I am the door: and if any man enter in „ 9
through me, he shall live, and shall go in
13 and out, and shall find pasture. Now the „ 10
thief cometh not, but that he may steal,
and kill, and destroy; I assuredly came that
they may have life, and may have what is
14 more excellent. I am the good shepherd: „ 11
now the good shepherd giveth his life for
15 his sheep. But the hireling, who is not „ 12
a shepherd, and whose the rams are not,
when he seeth the wolf coming, leaveth the
sheep, and fleeth; and the wolf cometh, and
16 snatcheth, and scattereth the sheep. Now „ 13
the hireling fleeth, because he is a hireling,
17 and hath no care for the sheep. I am the „ 14
good shepherd; and I know mine own; and
18 mine own know me. Even as my Father „ 15
knoweth me, I also know my Father; and I
19 lay down my life for my sheep. And other „ 16
sheep also I have, which are not of this
fold: them also must I call, and they shall
hear my voice; and there shall become one
20 flock and one shepherd. Therefore doth the „ 17
Father love me, because I lay down my life,
21 that I may take it again. No one shall „ 18
take it away from me; but I lay it down of
my own accord; and I have a right to lay
it down, and I have a right to take it.

		This commandment received I from my Father.		
37	22	And there arose a disagreement among the	Jn. 10	19
	23	Jews because of these sayings. And many	„	20
		of them said, He hath a devil, and suffereth from epilepsy; why are ye silent in his		
	24	presence? And others said, These are not	„	21
		the words of them that have a devil. Can a devil open the eyes of the blind?		
	25	And the feast of the dedication in Jeru-	„	22
	26	salem arrived: and it was winter; and Jesus	„	23
		was walking in the temple in Solomon's porch.		
	27	And the Jews came round about him, and	„	24
		said unto him, How long wilt thou torment our hearts? If thou art the Messiah, tell us		
	28	plainly. He answered, and said unto them,	„	25
		I told you, and ye believe not: and the works that I do in my Father's name, themselves		
	29	bear witness of me. But ye believe not,	„	26
	30	because ye are not of my rams. Even as I	„	27
		told you,[1] My rams hear my voice, and I		
	31	know them, and they follow me: and I give	„	28
		unto them eternal life; and they shall never perish; and no one shall snatch them out of		
	32	my hand. For the Father, which hath given	„	29
		them unto me, is greater than all; and no one is able to take *them* away out of my		
	33	Father's hand. I and my Father are one.	„	30
	34	And the Jews took up stones to stone	„	31
	35	him. Jesus saith unto them, Many good	„	32
		works have I showed you from my Father; for which of those works do ye stone me?		
	36	The Jews said unto him, Not for good works	„	33
		do we stone thee, but because thou blasphemest, and, being a man, makest thyself		
	37	God. Jesus said unto them, Is it not written	„	34

[1] The preceding words, "Even . . . you," which in the Greek and the Authorised Version are part of John x. 26, and belong to that sentence, are here removed to the next verse, and made to commence the new sentence. They are absent from the Revised Version.

37 38 thus in your law, I said, Ye are gods. And   Jn. 10 35
if he called them gods, because the word of
God came unto them (and nothing can be
39 broken in the scripture), tell ye him, whom   „   36
the Father sanctified and sent into the world,
that he blasphemeth; because I said unto
40 you, I am the Son of God? For if I do   „   37
not the works of my Father, believe me not.
41 But if I do *them*, even though ye believe not   „   38
me, believe the works: that ye may know
and believe that my Father is in me, and I
42 in my Father. And they sought again to   „   39
take him: and he went forth out of their
hands.
43   And he went away beyond Jordan into   „   40
the place where John was before baptizing;
44 and there he abode. And many men came   „   41
unto him; and they said, John did not even
45 one sign: but all things whatsoever John   „   42
spake of this man are true. And many
believed on him.
46   Now a certain man was sick, Lazarus by   „   11   1
name, of the village of Bethany, the brother
47 of Mary and Martha. Now Mary is she   „   2
who anointed the feet of Jesus with ointment, and wiped them with her hair, whose
48 brother was Lazarus the sick man. His   „   3
sisters therefore sent unto Jesus, saying,
Lord, behold, he whom thou lovest is sick.
49 But Jesus said, This sickness is not unto   „   4
death, but for the glory of God, that the
50 Son of God may be glorified thereby. Now   „   5
Jesus loved Martha, and Mary, and Lazarus.
51 When therefore he heard that he was sick,   „   6
he abode two days in the place where he
52 was. And after these things he said to his   „   7
53 disciples, Come, let us go into Judaea. His   „   8
disciples said unto him, Master, the Jews
now wish to stone thee; and goest thou
54 thither again? Jesus said unto them, Are   „   9

37 55	there not twelve hours in the day? If any man walk in the day, he stumbleth not, because he seeth the light of the world. But	Jn. 11	10
56	if a man walk in the night, he stumbleth, because the brightness is not in him. These things said Jesus: and afterwards he said unto them, Our friend Lazarus sleepeth;[1] but I go that I may awake him out of	„	11
57	sleep. His disciples said unto him, Lord, if	„	12
58	he is sleeping,[2] he will get well. Jesus had spoken this of his death: but they thought that he spake of taking rest in	„	13
59	sleep. Then Jesus said unto them plainly,	„	14
60	Lazarus is dead. And I am glad for your sakes that I was not there, in order that ye may believe; nevertheless let us go thither.	„	15
61	Thauma,[3] who is called Thoma,[4] said unto his fellow-disciples, Let us also go, that we may die with him.	„	16
38 1	Jesus therefore came to Bethany, and found that he had been in the tomb four days.	„	17
2	Now Bethany was nigh unto Jerusalem, and	„	18
3	was distant from it fifteen furlongs; and many of the Jews came to Mary and Martha, to console their heart concerning	„	19
4	their brother. Martha therefore, when she heard that Jesus was coming, went out to meet him: but Mary was sitting at home.	„	20
5	Martha therefore said unto Jesus, Lord, if thou hadst been here, my brother would not	„	21
6	have died. But now I know that, whatsoever thou shalt ask of God, he will give thee.	„	22
7	Jesus said unto her, Thy brother shall rise.	„	23
8	Martha said unto him, I know that he shall rise again in the resurrection at the last	„	24
9	day. Jesus said unto her, I am the resurrection, and the life; he that believeth in	„	25

[1] Or, "resteth;" cf. ver. 58, "taking rest."
[2] Or, "resting;" cf. ver. 58.   [3] Arabic, Thâwamâ.
[4] Arabic, Thâmâ; cf. liv. 17.

38 10 me, even though he die, shall live: and   Jn. 11 26
everyone that liveth and believeth in me
11 shall never die. Believest thou this? She   „   27
said unto him, Yea, Lord: I believe that thou
art the Messiah, the Son of God, who art come
12 into the world. And when she had said   „   28
this, she went away, and called Mary her
sister secretly, and said unto her, The Master
13 is come, and calleth thee. And Mary, when   „   29
she heard it, arose quickly, and came unto
14 him. For Jesus was not yet come into the   „   30
village, but was in that place where Martha
15 had met him. The Jews also which were   „   31
with her in the house to console her, when
they saw Mary rising up quickly and going
out, followed her, supposing that she was
16 about to go unto the tomb to weep. Mary   „   32
therefore, when she was come where Jesus
was, and had seen him, fell down at his feet,
and said unto him, Lord, if thou hadst been
17 here, my brother would not have died. And   „   33
Jesus came, and when he saw her weeping,
and the Jews which were with her, weeping
18 *also*, he was distressed in his soul, and sighed,   „   34
and said, Where have ye laid him? They
19 said unto him, Lord, come and see. And the   „   35
20 tears of Jesus were shed. The Jews there-   „   36
21 fore said, See how much he loved him! And   „   37
some of them said, Could not this man,
which opened the eyes of that blind man,
also have caused that this man should not die?
22 Jesus therefore, being distressed in his soul,   „   38
cometh to the tomb. Now the tomb was a
cave, and a stone was laid at the mouth of
23 it. Jesus saith, Take ye away this stone.   „   39
Martha, the sister of him that was dead,
said unto him, Lord, by this time he
stinketh: for he hath been *dead* four days.
24 Jesus said unto her, Said I not unto thee, If   „   40
thou believest, thou shalt see the glory of

38 25 God? So they moved away the stone. Jn. 11 41
And Jesus lifted up his eyes, and said, My
Father, I thank thee that thou heardest me.
26 I indeed know that thou hearest me always: „   42
but because of this multitude which standeth
by I say this to thee, that they may believe
27 that thou didst send me. When he had   „   43
said these things, he cried with a loud voice,
28 Lazarus, come forth. And the dead man   „   44
came forth, bound hand and foot with
bandages; and his face was wrapped up in
a napkin. Jesus said unto them, Loose
him, and let him go.
29 And many of the Jews, which were   „   45
come to Mary, when they saw what was
30 done by Jesus, believed in him. But some   „   46
of them went away to the Pharisees, and told
them all the things which Jesus had done.
31 And the chief priests and the Pharisees   „   47
gathered together, and they said, What do
we? for, behold, this man doeth many signs.
32 For if we let him thus alone, all men will   „   48
believe in him: and the Romans will come
and take away our country and nation.
33 But one of them, Caiaphas by name, who   „   49
was the high priest of that year, said unto
34 them, Ye know nothing at all, nor do ye   „   50
take into account that it is expedient for us
that one man should die for the people, and
35 that the whole nation perish not. Now this   „   51
he said not of himself: but as he was the
high priest of that year, he prophesied that
36 Jesus was going to die for the people; and   „   52
not only for the people, but that he might
also gather together at one time the children
37 of God that had been scattered abroad. So   „   53
from that day forth they took counsel to put
him to death.
38 Jesus therefore walked not openly among   „   54
the Jews, but departed thence into a place

		near to the wilderness, into a hermitage¹ which is called Ephraem; and there he was		
38	39	going about with his disciples. Now the passover of the Jews was near: and many went up to Jerusalem out of the villages before	Jn. 11	55
	40	the feast, to purify themselves. And they sought for Jesus, and said one to another in the temple, What think ye of his lateness²	„	56
	41	for the feast? Now the chief priests and the Pharisees had given commandment, that, if any man knew where he was, he should disclose it unto them, that they might take him.	„³	57
	42	And when the days of his going up⁴ were fulfilled, he prepared himself to go to Jeru-	Lu. 9	51
	43	salem, and sent messengers before him: and they went, and entered into a village of	„	52
	44	Samaria, to make ready for him. And they did not receive him, because he was prepared	„	53
	45	to go to Jerusalem. And when his disciples James and John saw *this*, they said unto him, Lord, wilt thou that we bid fire to come down from heaven, and uproot them, even as	„	54
	46	Elijah did? And Jesus turned, and rebuked them, saying, Ye know not what *manner of*	„	55
	47	spirit ye are of. Surely the Son of man came not to destroy lives, but to save them. And they went to another village.	„	56
39	1	Jesus therefore six days before the passover came to Bethany,⁵ where Lazarus was,	Jn. 12	1

¹ Arabic, "kirh." ² Or, "absence from."
³ Included in ver. 56, as in Vulgate.
⁴ Referred by Tatian to the last visit, six days before the crucifixion, perhaps because of the first part of this verse.
⁵ Tatian here follows S. John, who fixes the exact time of the Anointing by Mary, and puts it before the Triumphal Entry. In *internal* harmonisation, however, he displaces John xii. 9-11 for the sake of neatness in the combined account. Ephraem follows the same peculiarities of order (Moes. p. 205). The mention of Simon's house is followed by the plot to kill Lazarus before the Anointing. The *Codex Fuldensis* identifies this anointing with that in Luke vii. 36, etc.

39 2 whom Jesus raised from the dead. And a Jn. 12 2
breakfast was made for him there: and
Martha served; but Lazarus was one of them
3 that reclined *at meat* with him. And while Mk. 14 3ᵃ
Jesus was at Bethany, in the house of Simon
4 the leper, a great multitude of the Jews Jn. 12 9
heard that Jesus was there: and they came,
not for Jesus' sake only, but that they might
see Lazarus also, whom he raised from the
5 dead. But the chief priests took counsel „ 10
that they might put Lazarus also to death,
6 because by reason of him many of the Jews „ 11
went away, and believed on Jesus.
7 Now Mary took a case of ointment of the „ 3ᵃ
best nard, very costly, and opened it, and Mk. 14 3ᶜ
poured it upon the head of Jesus, as he
8 reclined *at meat*; and anointed his feet, Jn. 12 3ᵇ
and wiped them with her hair: and the
house was filled with the odour of the
9 ointment. But one of the disciples, Judas „ 4
Iscariot, who was going to betray him, said,
10 Why was not this ointment sold for three „ 5
11 hundred pence, and given to the poor? He „ 6
said this, not because of his care for the
poor; but because he was a thief, and having the bag himself carried the things that
12 were put therein. The rest of the disciples Mk. 14 4
also were vexed at this among themselves,
and said, To what purpose is this ointment
13 wasted? For it might have been sold for Mt. 26 9
much, and given to the poor. And they Mk. 14 5ᵇ
14 murmured at Mary. But Jesus perceiving Mt. 26 10ᵃ
it, saith unto them, Let her alone; why Mk. 14 6ᵇ
trouble ye her? she hath performed a good
work on me. She hath kept it for the day Jn. 12 7ᵇ
15 of my burying. For the poor are always „ 8ᵃ
with you; and when ye will ye can do Mk. 14 7ᵇ
them good: but I am not always with you.
16 On that account, when pouring this ointment Mt. 26 12
upon my body, she did it as it were for my

39 17 burial, and came beforehand to anoint my body. Verily I say unto you, Wheresoever this my gospel shall be preached in the whole world, that which this woman hath done shall be related for a memorial of her.   Mk.[1] 14 8[b]
,,   9

18 And when he had said these things,[2] Jesus went forth slowly to proceed to Jerusalem.   Lu. 19 28

19 And when he was arrived at Bethphage and Bethany, near the mount that is called the   ,,   29[a]

20 mount of Olives, Jesus sent two of his disciples, saying unto them, Go into the   Mt. 21 1[b]
,,   2[a]

21 village that is over against you, and when ye are entered into it, ye shall find an ass tied, and a colt with her, whereon no man ever yet sat:[3] loose it, and bring *them* unto   Mk. 11 2[b]
Mt. 21 2[b]
Lu. 19 30[b]
Mt. 21 2[c]

22 me. And if anyone say unto you, Why do ye loose them? say thus unto him, We seek them for the Lord; and straightway send[4]   Lu. 19 31[a]
Mt. 21 3[b]

23 them both hither. All this is come to pass, that it might be fulfilled which was spoken through the prophet, saying,   ,,   4

24 Tell ye the daughter of Sion,
Behold, thy King cometh unto thee,
Meek, and sitting upon an ass,
And upon a colt the foal of an ass.   ,,   5

25 This understood not his disciples at that time: but after Jesus was glorified, his disciples remembered that these things had been written of him, and that they did these things unto him.   Jn.[5] 12 16

26 And the disciples went, and found even as he had said unto them,[6] and they did as   { Mt. 21 6[a]
{ Lu. 19 32[b]
   Mt. 21 6[b]

---

[1] Omitting 8[a]: "She hath done what she could."
[2] S. John's order continued.   [3] Or, "rode."
[4] So in the Arabic. The dual form is used, "send *ye both* them *both*." Ciasca has taken the alternative rendering, "they *both* sent them *both*," which, however, is contrary to the meaning here.
[5] This verse being a comment of the evangelist, and not a part of the history, is put earlier by Tatian in connection with the prophecy which in a different form S. John puts after the bringing of the ass.
[6] Omitting Mark xi. 4: "and found the colt tied by the door without, in a place where two ways met."

39 27	Jesus had commanded them. And when they had loosed them, the owners thereof	Lu. 19	33
28	said unto them, Why loose ye them? They said unto them, We seek them for our Lord; and they let them go.	„	34
		Mk. 11	6^b
29	And they brought the ass and the colt, and put their garments upon the colt; and	Mt. 21	7
30	Jesus rode thereon. And the most part of the multitude spread their garments before him on the ground; and others cut branches from the trees, and spread them in the way.	„	8
31	And when he drew near his descent of the mount of Olives, all the disciples began to rejoice and praise God with a loud voice for all the mighty works which they had seen;	Lu. 19	37
32	saying, Glory in the highest: glory to the son of David: blessed is he that cometh in the	Mt. 21	9^b
33	name of the Lord: and blessed is the kingdom	Mk. 11	10^a
	which cometh, *even* our father David's: peace in heaven, and glory in the highest.	Lu. 19	38^b
34	And a great multitude that had come to the feast, when they had heard that Jesus	Ju. 12	12
35	was coming to Jerusalem, took the branches of the palm trees, and went forth to meet him, and cried out, saying, Praise: blessed is he that cometh in the name of the Lord,	„	13
36	even the King of Israel. And some of the Pharisees from the multitudes said unto him,	Lu. 19	39
37	Master, rebuke thy disciples. He saith unto them, Verily I say unto you, If these held their peace, the stones would cry out.	„	40
38	And when he drew nigh, and had seen	„	41
39	the city, he wept over it, saying, Would that thou hadst known the things which are for thy peace in this thy day! this now is	„	42
40	hidden from thine eyes. The days shall come unto thee, when thine enemies shall compass thee round, and keep thee in on	„¹	43
41	every side, and shall take possession of thee,	„	44

¹ Cf. note to xli. 30.

		and of thy children that are within thee; and they shall not leave in thee one stone upon another; because thou knewest not the time of thy visitation.		
39	42	And when Jesus had entered into Jerusalem, all the city was stirred, saying, Who	Mt. 21	10
	43	is this? And the multitudes said, This is Jesus, the prophet from Nazareth of Galilee.	„	11
	44	And the multitude that was with him bare witness, that he had called Lazarus out of the tomb, and raised him from the dead.	Jn. 12	17
	45	For this cause many multitudes went out to meet him, for they heard the sign that he had done.	„	18
40	1	And when Jesus had gone into the temple, they brought unto him the blind and the	Mt. 21	14
	2	lame; and he healed them. But when the chief priests and the Pharisees saw the wonderful things that he did, and the children that were crying in the temple, and saying, Praise to the son of David; they	„	15
	3	were annoyed, and said, Hearest thou what these are saying? Jesus said unto them, Yea: did ye never read, Out of the mouth of children and babes thou hast selected my	„	16
	4	praise? The Pharisees therefore said among themselves, Lo, see you not, that we get no advantage? for, lo, the whole world followeth him.	Jn. 12	19
	5	Now there were also among them certain Gentiles, that had come up to worship at	„	20
	6	the feast: these therefore came to Philip, which was of Bethsaida of Galilee, and asked him, saying unto him, Sir, we wish to see	„	21
	7	Jesus. Philip came and told Andrew: and	„	22
	8	Andrew and Philip told Jesus. And Jesus answered, and said unto them, The hour is near in which the Son of man shall be glori-	„	23
	9	fied. Verily, verily, I say unto you, Except a grain of wheat fall and die in the earth,	„	24

THE DIATESSARON.

40 10 it[1] abideth by itself alone; but if it die, it beareth much fruit. He that loveth his life shall lose it; and he that hateth his life in this world shall keep it unto life eternal.   Jn. 12 25

11 If any man serveth me, let him follow me; and where I am, there shall also my servant be: and whosoever serveth me, him will the   „ 26

12 Father honour. Now is my soul troubled; and what shall I say? My Father, save[2] me from this hour. But for this cause came   „ 27

13 I unto this hour. My Father, glorify thy name. And a voice was heard out of heaven, *saying*, I have glorified it, and will glorify   „ 28

14 it. The multitude therefore, that stood by, heard it, and said, This is thunder. Others   „ 29

15 said, An angel speaketh to him. Jesus answered, and said unto them, This voice hath not come for my sake, but for your   „ 30

16 sakes. Now is the judgment of this world: and the prince of this world shall now be   „ 31

17 cast out. And I, when I am lifted up from the earth, will draw all men unto myself.   „ 32

18 This he said to signify by what manner of   „ 33

19 death he was going to die. The multitudes said unto him, We have heard from the law that the Messiah abideth for ever: how then sayest thou, that the Son of man is going to   „ 34

20 be lifted up? who is this Son of man? Jesus said unto them, Yet a little while will the light be with you. Walk while ye have the light, that darkness overtake[3] you not: for he that walketh in the darkness knoweth not   „ 35

21 whither he goeth. While ye have the light, believe on the light, that ye may be sons of light.   „ 36ᵃ

22 And when some of the Pharisees had asked Jesus, When will the kingdom of God come? he answered, and said unto them,   Lu. 17 20

---

[1] The Arabic begins ver. 25 here as the Vulgate does.   [2] Or, "deliver."
[3] The Syriac word implied in the Arabic has also the meaning, "lay hold of;" cf. i. 5.

40 23	The kingdom of God will not come with expectation: neither shall they say, Lo, here it is! and, Lo, there! For the kingdom of God is within you.	Lu. 17	21
24	And by day he was teaching in the temple; but at night he went out, and passed the night on the mount that is called	„ 21	37
25	the mount of Olives. And all the people arrived before him in the temple to hear his word.	„	38
26	Then spake Jesus to the multitudes and	Mt. 23	1
27	to his disciples, saying unto them, The scribes and the Pharisees have sat down on Moses'	„	2
28	seat: all things therefore whatsoever they shall bid you to observe, *these* keep and do: but do not ye according to their works; for	„	3
29	they say, and do not. For they bind heavy burdens,[1] and lay them on men's shoulders; but are unwilling to move one of their	„	4
30	fingers towards them. And all their works	„	5ª
31	they do to be seen of men. And all the multitude heard these things with gladness.	Mk. 17	37ᵇ
32	And in his teaching he said unto them, Beware ye of the scribes, which desire to walk in long robes, and love to be saluted in	„	38
33	the streets, and to sit on chief seats in the	„	39
34	synagogues, and chief couches at feasts: for they make broad their phylacteries, and lengthen the fringes of their garments, and	Mt. 23	5ᵇ
		„	7ᵇ
35	*love* to be called of men, Master. But they devour widows' houses, under the pretence of making their prayers long; these truly	Mk. 12	40
36	shall receive greater condemnation. But be not ye called masters: for one is your	Mt. 23	8
37	master, and all ye are brethren. And call no man father on the earth: for one is your	„	9
38	Father, which is in the heavens. Neither be ye called directors:[2] for one is your	„	10

[1] Omitting "and grievous to be borne;" cf. Revised Version, marginal note.
[2] Or, "arrangers;" the Peschito has "guides."

40 39	director, *even* the Messiah. But he that is greater among you shall be your minister.	Mt. 23	11
40	He[1] that exalteth himself shall be humbled; and he that humbleth himself shall be exalted.	,,	12
41	Woe unto you Pharisees! for ye love the front seats in the synagogues, and the salutation in the streets.	Lu. 11	43
42	Woe[2] unto you, scribes and Pharisees, hypocrites, for ye devour widows' houses by reason of your long prayers: and therefore ye shall receive greater condemnation.	Mt. 23	14
43	Woe unto you, scribes and Pharisees, hypocrites! because ye shut the kingdom of God against men.	,,	13a
44	Woe unto you, lawyers! for ye have hidden the keys of knowledge: ye enter not in yourselves, neither suffer ye them that are entering in to enter.	Lu. 11 Mt. 23	52a 13b
45	Woe unto you, scribes and Pharisees, hypocrites! for ye compass sea and land to draw away one proselyte; and when he is become *so*, ye make him twofold more a son of Gehenna than yourselves.	,,	15
46	Woe unto you, ye blind guides, which say, Whosoever shall swear by the temple, it is nothing; but whosoever shall swear by the gold, that is in the temple, he is	,,	16
47	accountable. Ye blind ignorant ones: for whether is greater, the gold, or the temple	,,	17
48	that sanctifieth the gold? And, Whosoever shall swear by the altar, it is nothing; but whosoever shall swear by the offering that	,,	18
49	is upon it, he is accountable. Ye blind ignorant ones : whether is greater, the offering, or the altar that sanctifieth the offering?	,,	19
50	He therefore that sweareth by the altar,	,,	20

[1] Cf. xxx. 5 and xxxii. 21.

[2] Some of the statements regarding the scribes and Pharisees already made in this chapter are now repeated as "woes." Matt. xxiii. 14 is omitted in the Revised Version.

40	51	sweareth by it, and by all things that are thereon. And he that sweareth by the temple, sweareth by it, and by him that	Mt. 23	21
	52	dwelleth therein. And he that sweareth by the heaven, sweareth by the throne of God, and by him that sitteth thereon.	„	22
	53	Woe unto you, scribes and Pharisees, hypocrites! that tithe mint and rue, anise and cummin, and all herbs, and leave undone the weightier matters of the law, judgment, and mercy, and faith, and the love of God: these ye ought to do, and not to leave those	„	23
	54	undone. Ye blind guides, which strain out the gnat, and adorn[1] the camel.	„	24
	55	Woe unto you, scribes and Pharisees, hypocrites! for ye cleanse the outside of the cup and of the platter, but within they are full of iniquity and unrighteousness.	„	25
	56	Ye blind Pharisees, cleanse first the inside of the cup and of the platter, and the outside of them will be clean.	„	26
	57	Woe unto you, scribes and Pharisees, hypocrites! for ye are like unto whited sepulchres, which outwardly appear beautiful, but within are full of dead men's bones and	„	27
	58	of all uncleanness. Even so ye also outwardly appear unto men as if righteous, but within ye are full of iniquity and hypocrisy.	„	28
	59	One of the scribes, answering, said unto him, Teacher, in this thy speech thou makest	Lu. 11	45
	60	a reproach against us. He said, Woe unto you also, ye scribes! for ye lade men with heavy burdens, and ye yourselves touch not those burdens even with one of your fingers.	„	46
	61	Woe unto you, scribes and Pharisees, hypocrites! in that ye build the sepulchres of the prophets, whom your fathers killed, and adorn the tombs of the righteous,	Mt. 23	29ᵃ
			Lu. 11	47ᵇ
			Mt. 23	29ᵇ

[1] Mr. Rendel Harris attributes this peculiar reading to the transposition of two letters of the Arabic word for "swallow."

40 62	and say, If we had been in the days of our fathers, we should not have been partakers with them in the blood of the	Mt. 23	30
63	prophets. See therefore! ye bear witness against yourselves, that ye are sons of them	,,	31
64	that slew the prophets; and ye are finishing	,,	32
65	the path of your fathers. Ye serpents, ye offspring of vipers, whither shall ye flee	,,	33
41 1	from the judgment of Gehenna? Therefore, behold, I, the wisdom of God, send unto you prophets, and apostles, and wise men, and scribes: and some of them shall ye kill and crucify; and some of them shall ye scourge in your synagogues, and	,,[1]	34
2	cast out from city to city: that upon you may come all the blood of righteous men that hath been shed on the earth, from the blood of Abel the innocent unto the blood of Zacharias son of Barachias, whom ye slew between the sanctuary and the altar.	,,	35
3	Verily I say unto you, All these things shall come upon this generation.	,,	36
4	O Jerusalem, Jerusalem, the slayer of the prophets, and the stoner of them that were sent unto her! how often have I wished to gather thy children together, even as a hen gathereth her chickens under her	,,	37
5	wings, and ye would not! Your house[2]	,,	38
6	shall be left unto you deserted. Verily I say unto you, Ye shall not see me henceforth, till ye say,[3] Blessed *is* he that cometh in the name of the Lord.	,,	39
7	And of the rulers also many believed on him; but because of the Pharisees they did	Jn.[4] 12	42

[1] Or omit "shall" throughout this verse; cf. Luke xi. 49. This remarkable change of reading seems connected with Gnostic ideas.

[2] The Doctrine of Addai has "Behold, your house is left desolate."

[3] It is remarkable that this statement should come after the account of the use of these very words by the multitudes; cf. xxxix. 32.

[4] John xii. 42-50 is here inserted before John xii. 36ᵇ-41; cf. xli. 21-26.

41	8	not confess *it*, lest they should become outside the synagogue: for they loved the glory of men more than to glory of God.	Jn. 12	43
	9	And Jesus cried, and said, He that believeth on me, believeth not on me, but	„	44
	10	on him that sent me. And he that seeth	„	45
	11	me, seeth him that sent me. I am come a light[1] into the world, every man therefore that believeth on me, abideth not in the	„	46
	12	darkness. And whosoever heareth my sayings, and keepeth them not, I judge him not: for I came not to judge the world, but	„	47
	13	to give life to the world. He that rejecteth me, and receiveth not my sayings, there is *one* that judgeth him: the saying that I spake, the same shall judge him in the last	„	48
	14	day. I speak not from myself; but the Father which sent me, he hath given me a commandment, what I should say, and what	„	49
	15	I should speak. And I know that his commandment is life eternal: the things therefore which I speak now, even as the Father hath said unto me, so I speak.	„	50
	16	And when he said these things unto them, the scribes and the Pharisees began to be angry in their malice, and to find fault with his words, and to vex him in many things;	Lu. 11	53
	17	seeking to catch something out of his mouth, that they might be able to accuse him.	„	54
	18	Now when many multitudes were gathering together, so that they almost trode one upon another, Jesus began to say unto his disciples, Beware ye of the leaven of the	„ 12	1
	19	Pharisees, which is hypocrisy. But there is nothing covered up, except that it will be	„	2

Of these verses 42, 43 are a comment of the evangelist, which might be placed at any point in the account of this visit. Ver. 44–50 naturally follow them, and with the verses from S. Luke following them, they explain in a very natural way why Jesus went and hid himself, John xii. 36[b].

[1] Or, "I, a light, am come."

41	20	revealed: nor hidden, except that it will be known. All things that ye have said in the darkness, shall be heard in the light: and that which ye have whispered in the ears in the chambers, shall be proclaimed upon the housetops.	Lu.[1] 12	3
	21	These things spake Jesus, and he departed,	Jn. 12	36[b]
	22	and hid himself from them. And though he had done all these signs before them,	„	37
	23	they believed not on him: that the saying of Isaiah the prophet might be fulfilled, which he spake,	„	38

> Lord, who hath believed, that he may hear us?
> And the arm of the Lord, to whom hath it been revealed?

	24	For this cause they could not believe, for Isaiah said again,	„	39
	25	Blind ye their eyes, and bring darkness to their heart;	„	40

> Lest they should see with their eyes, and understand with their heart,
> And should turn,
> And I should heal them.

	26	These things said Isaiah, when he saw his glory, and spake of him.	„	41
	27	And Jesus went out from the temple; and some of his disciples came to him, and showed him the buildings of the temple, and its	Mt. 24	1
	28	beauty and magnificence, and the strength of the stones used in it, and the elegance of its construction, and how it was adorned with	Mk. 13 Lu. 21	1[b] 5[b]
	29	costly stones and beautiful colours. Jesus answered, and said unto them, See ye these great buildings? Verily I say unto you,	Mt. 24	2[a]
	30[2]	the days will surely come, and there shall not be left here in them one stone upon another, that is not thrown down.	{Lu. 19 { „	43[a] 44[b]

---

[1] See note to xiii. 12[b].

[2] No doubt Tatian meant this for Luke xxi. 6[b]; cf. xxxix. 40, 41.

41	31	And two days before the passover of the unleavened *bread* the chief priests and the scribes sought how they might take him with	Mk.[1] 14 1
	32	subtilty, and kill him: but they said, Not during the feast, lest haply the people make	„ 2
	33	a disturbance. And as Jesus sat on the mount of Olives over against the temple, Simon Cephas and James and John and Andrew came unto him, and said unto him	„ 13 3
	34	between themselves and him, Teacher, tell us, when shall these things be? and what *shall be* the sign of thy coming, and of the	{ Lu.[2] 21 7b { Mt. 24 3b
	35	end of the world? Jesus answered, and said unto them, The days will come, when ye shall desire to see one day of the days of the Son of man, and ye shall not see it.	Mt. 24 4a Lu. 17 22b
	36	Take heed that no man lead you astray.	Mt. 24 4b
	37	Many shall come in my name, saying, I am	„ 5a
	38	the Messiah; and they shall say, The time is at hand; and shall lead many astray:	Lu. 21 8b Mk. 13 6b
	39	go ye not therefore after them. When therefore ye shall hear of wars and rumours of insurrections, see that ye be not troubled: these things must come to pass first; but	{ Lu. 21 8c { Mk. 13 7a Mt. 24 6b Lu. 21 9b
	40	the end hath not yet come. Nation[3] shall rise against nation, and kingdom against	Mt.[4] 24 7a
	41	kingdom: and there shall be great earthquakes in divers places, and famines, and pestilences, and commotions: terrors and	Lu. 21 11

---

[1] No more convenient place could be found for these two verses, in view of the fact that the prolonged discourse which follows immediately is at once followed by a reference made by Jesus to this date; cf. xliv. 1 and 2. The placing Mark xiv. 1, 2 before Mark xiii. 3 does not involve a chronological error, since xliv. 1 shows that the same day is still present.

[2] Besides taking Luke xxi. as the parallel to Matt. xxiv. and Mark xiii., Tatian inserts passages from other parts of S. Luke which deal with the same subject, though their position in the third Gospel implies that they were spoken earlier. In this way he is enabled to present to his readers a more complete account of our Lord's teaching upon this important subject.

[3] Omitting Luke xxi. 10a: "Then said he unto them."

[4] Or Luke xxi. 10b.

	tremblings shall there be, and great signs shall appear from heaven; and great storms		
41	42 shall there be. All these things are the	Mt. 24	8
	43 beginning of troubles. And¹ before all these things, they shall lay hands on you, and shall persecute *you*, and deliver you up to the synagogues and prisons, and shall drag you before kings and governors for my name's	Lu. 21	12
	44 sake. And this shall be unto you for a	„	13
	45 testimony. And my gospel must first be	Mk. 13	10
	46 preached unto all the nations. And when they bring you into the synagogues before the rulers, and the authorities, be not anxious beforehand how to plead, or what ye shall	Lu. 12	11
	47 say: for it is not ye that speak, but the	Mk. 13	11ᵇ
	48 Holy Spirit. Put it therefore in your heart,	Lu. 21	14
	49 not to meditate beforehand what to say: for I will give you understanding and wisdom, which all your adversaries shall not be able to withstand.	„	15
	50 For then shall they deliver you up unto tribulation, and shall kill you: and ye shall be hated of all the nations for my name's	Mt. 24	9
	51 sake. And then shall many be caused to stumble, and shall hate one another, and	„	10
	52 shall deliver up one another to death. And your parents, and brethren, and kinsfolk, and friends shall deliver you up: and *some* of	Lu. 21	16
	53 you shall they put to death. And a lock of the hair of your head shall not perish.	„²	18
	54 In your patience ye shall possess your souls.	„	19
	55 And many false prophets shall arise, and	Mt. 24	11
	56 shall lead many astray. And because of the abundance of iniquity, the love of many	„	12
	57 shall grow weak. But whosoever endureth	„	13
	58 to the end, the same shall be saved. And this gospel of the kingdom shall be preached	„	14

¹ Omitting Mark xiii. 9: "But take heed to yourselves."
² For the substance of ver. 17 see above in xli. 50.

in the whole world for a testimony unto all the nations; and then shall come the end of all.

42 1 But when ye see Jerusalem compassed with armies, then know that her desolation 2 is at hand. At that time let them that are in Judaea flee unto the mountain; and let them that are in the midst of her flee; and let not them that are in the districts enter 3 therein. For these days are the days of vengeance, that all things which are written may be fulfilled. 4 When therefore ye see the abominable[1] desolation, which was spoken of in Daniel the prophet, standing in the holy place (let 5 him that readeth understand), then let them that are in Judaea flee unto the mountain: 6 and let him that is on the housetop not go down, nor enter in, to take anything out of 7 his house: and let him that shall be in the field not return back to take his cloke. 8 Woe unto them that are with child, and to them that give suck in those days! there shall be great distress in the land, and wrath 9 upon this people. And they shall fall on the edge of the sword, and shall be led captive into every country: and Jerusalem shall be trodden down of the Gentiles, until 10[2] the times of the Gentiles be fulfilled. Then if any man shall say unto you, The Messiah is here; or, Lo, he is there; believe *it* not. 11 Then shall arise false Christs, and false prophets, and shall do signs and portents; so as to lead into error, if they could, even 12 the elect. Therefore take ye heed: for I have already told you all things beforehand. 13 If therefore they shall say unto you, Behold, he is in the wilderness; go not forth, that

Reference		
Lu.	21	20
„		21
„		22
Mt.	24	15
„		16
Mk.	13	15
„		16
Lu.	21	23
„		24
Mk.	13	21
Mt.	24	24
Mk.	13	23
Mt.	24	26

[1] Or, "unclean."
[2] Cf. xli. 36, 37. There is a little displacement of internal order here.

		ye may not be seized: and if they shall say unto you, Behold he is in the chamber; be-		
42	14	lieve *it* not. For as the lightning appeareth in the east, and is visible even unto the west; so shall be the coming down of the	Mt. 24	27
	15	Son of man. But first must he suffer many things, and be rejected of this genera-	Lu. 17	25
	16	tion. And pray ye that your flight may not take place in the winter, nor on a sabbath	Mt. 24	20
	17	day: then shall be great tribulation, of which there hath not been the like from the beginning of the world until now, nor shall	„	21
	18	take place. And except the Lord had shortened those days, no flesh would have been saved: but for the elect's sake, whom	Mk. 13	20
	19	he chose, he shortened those days. And there shall be signs in sun and moon and stars; and upon the earth distress of nations, and wringing[1] of hands for the roaring of the noise of the sea and of the earthquake.	Lu. 21	25
	20	Men's souls shall depart for the fear, which	„	26[a]
	21	shall come upon the earth. But in those	Mk. 13	24[a]
		days, immediately after the tribulation of those days, the sun shall be darkened, and the moon shall not give her light, and the stars shall fall from heaven, and the powers of the heavens	Mt. 24	29
	22	shall be shaken: and then shall appear the sign of the Son of man in heaven: and then shall all the tribes of the earth mourn, and they shall look at the Son of man coming on the clouds of heaven with power and	„	30
	23	great majesty. And he shall send forth his angels with a great trumpet, and they shall gather together his elect from the four winds, from the end of heaven even to the end	„	31
	24	thereof. But when these things begin to come to pass, be of good cheer, and lift up your heads; because your deliverance draweth nigh.	Lu. 21	28

[1] This passage is considerably altered from S. Luke.

42 25	From the fig-tree learn the parable: for when its branches are tender, and it putteth forth leaves, ye know that the summer is nigh;	Mt. 24	32
26	even so ye also, when ye see these things begin to take place, know ye that the kingdom	„	33
27	of God hath arrived at the door. Verily I say unto you, This generation shall not pass away, till all these things take place.	„	34
28	Heaven and earth shall pass away, but my words shall not pass away.	„	35
29	Take heed to yourselves, lest haply your hearts be at any time overcharged with iniquity and drunkenness, and cares of the age, and that day come on you suddenly:	Lu. 21	34
30	for just as a blow shall it strike all them that dwell on the face of all the earth.	„	35
31	Watch ye at every season, and pray, that ye may be counted worthy to escape all these things that are going to take place, and to	„	36
32	stand before the Son of man. Of that day and of that hour knoweth no one, not even the angels of heaven, nor the Son, but the	Mk. 13	32
33	Father. Take ye heed, watch and pray: for	„	33
34	ye know not when that time is. Even as a man, who went abroad, and left his house, and gave his authority to his servants, and left each one at his own work, and com-	„	34
35	manded the porter to be watchful. Watch therefore: for ye know not when the lord of the house shall come, whether at even, or at midnight, or at cockcrowing, or in the	„	35
36	morning; lest coming suddenly he find you	„	36
37	sleeping. What I say unto you, I say unto you all, Be watchful.	„	37
38	For even as it happened in the days of Noah, so shall be the coming of the Son of	Mt. 24	37
39	man. Even as before the flood they were eating and drinking, marrying and delivering up to marriage, until the day that Noah	„	38
40	entered into the ark, and they knew not	„	39

	until the flood came, and took them all away; so shall be the coming of the Son of man.		
42 41	And likewise even as it came to pass in the days of Lot; they ate and they drank, they sold and they bought, they planted and they	Lu. 17	28
42	builded; *but* in the same day wherein Lot went out from Sodom, the Lord rained both fire and brimstone from heaven, and destroyed	„	29
43	them all: so shall it be in the day wherein	„	30
44	the Son of man shall appear. And in that day, he which shall be on the housetop, and his garments in the house, let him not go down to take them away: and he which shall be in the field, let him not return	„	31
45) 46)	back. Remember Lot's wife. He that shall wish to save his life shall lose it: but he	{Lu. 17 { „	32 33
47	that shall lose his life shall save it. Verily I say unto you, In that night there shall be two *men* in one bed; the one shall be	Lu. 17	34
48	taken, and the other shall be left. And there shall be two *women* grinding in one mill; the one shall be taken, and the other	„	35
49	shall be left. And there shall be two *men* in the same field; the one shall be taken,	„	36
50	and the other shall be left. They answered, and said unto him, Where, Lord? He[1] said unto them, Wherever the body is, thither will the eagles[2] be gathered together.	„	37
51	Watch therefore; for ye know not in what	Mt. 24	42
52	hour your Lord will come. This know, If the master of the house had known in what watch the thief would come, he would certainly have watched, and his house	„	43
53	could not have been digged through. Therefore be ye also ready: for in an hour that ye think not the Son of man will come.	„	44

[1] In the Arabic ver. 37 begins here, as in the Vulgate, and ver. 36, as marked 37 in the present text.
[2] Or, "vultures."

43 1 Simon Cephas saith unto him, Lord,   Lu.[1] 12 41
speakest thou this parable unto us, or even
2 unto all men? Jesus said unto him,   „   42[a]
Who, think you, is the faithful and wise   Mt. 24 45
overseer[2] of the house, whom his lord hath
set over his household, to give them food in
3 its season? Blessed is that servant, whom   „   46
when his lord is come, he shall find so doing.
4 Verily I say unto you, that he will set him   {Lu.[3] 12 44[a]
                                                {Mt. 24 47[b]
5 over all that he hath. But if that evil   Mt. 24 48
servant shall say in his heart, My lord will
6 delay his coming; and shall begin to beat   Lu. 12 45[b]
his menservants and the maidservants of his
lord, and shall begin to eat and drink with   Mt. 24 49[b]
7 the drunken; the lord of that servant shall   „   50
come in a day wherein he thinketh not, and
8 in an hour which he knoweth not, and shall   „   51[a]
judge him, and appoint his portion with the
hypocrites, and with the unfaithful: there   {Lu. 12 46[b]
                                              {Mt. 24 51[b]
shall be the weeping and gnashing of teeth.
9   Then shall the kingdom of heaven be like   Mt. 25 1
unto ten virgins, which took their lamps,
and went forth to meet the bridegroom and
10 the bride. Five of them were wise, and   „   2
11 five were foolish. Now these foolish *ones*,   „   3
when they took their lamps,[4] took no oil
12 with them: but the wise took oil in vessels   „   4
13 with the lamps. Now while the bridegroom   „   5
14 tarried, they all slumbered and slept. But   „   6
at midnight a cry was made, Behold, the
bridegroom cometh! Go ye forth to meet
15 him. Then all those virgins arose, and   „   7
16 trimmed their lamps. The foolish said unto   „   8
the wise, Give us of your oil; for our lamps

---

[1] The preceding parable is very like that in Luke xii. 39, 40, hence the sequence now; the order is that of S. Matthew.

[2] Cf. Luke xii. 42[b].

[3] Or Matt. xxiv. 47[a].

[4] Lit. "burning-lamps," a different word from that translated "lamps" in ver. 9 and 12, but used in ver. 39.

43 17 are gone¹ out. The wise answered, saying, Mt. 25 9
Peradventure there may not be enough for
us and you: go ye to them that sell, and
18 buy for yourselves. And when they had „ 10
gone to buy, the bridegroom came; and
they that were ready went in with him
to the marriage feast: and the door was
19 shut. But at last came also the other „ 11
20 virgins, saying, Lord, Lord, open to us. He „ 12
answered, and saith unto them, Verily I say
21 unto you, I know you not. Watch there- „ 13
fore; for ye know not that day nor that hour.
22 Even as a man, going abroad, called his „ 14
own servants, and delivered unto them his
23 goods. And unto one he gave five talents, „ 15
and to another two, but to another one; to
each according to his particular ability; and
24 he went on his journey immediately. Now „ 16
he that had received the five talents went
and traded with them, and gained five others.
25 In like manner he also that had received „ 17
26 the two gained two others. But he that „ 18
had received the one went away and digged
into the earth, and hid his lord's money.
27 But after a long time the lord of those „ 19
servants came, and made a reckoning with
28 them. And he that had received the five „ 20
talents came and paid five others, saying,
Lord, thou deliveredst unto me five talents:
lo, I have gained five others beside them.
29 His lord saith unto him, Well done, good „ 21
and faithful servant: thou hast been faithful
over a few things, I will set thee over many
things: enter thou into the joy of thy lord.
30 And he that had received the two talents „ 22
came, and saith, Lord, thou deliveredst unto
me two talents: lo, I have gained two others
31 beside them. His lord saith unto him, Well „ 23

¹ Not "going out," as the Revised Version and the margin of the Authorised Version.

		done, good and faithful servant; thou hast been faithful over a few things, I will set thee over many things: enter thou into the		
43	32	joy of thy lord. And he also that had received the one talent came, and said, Lord, I know that thou art a hard man, thou reapest where thou dost not sow, and gatherest	Mt. 25	24
	33	where thou dost not scatter: and I was afraid, and went away, and hid thy talent in	„	25
	34	the earth: lo, thou hast what is thine. His lord answered, and said unto him, Thou wicked and slothful servant, thou knowest me, that I reap where I did not sow, and	„	26
	35	gather where I did not scatter; thou oughtest to have put my money at the bank,[1] and at my coming I should have exacted it with	„	27
	36	interest. Take ye away therefore the talent from him, and give it unto him that hath	„	28
	37	the ten talents. Unto him that hath shall be given, and he shall have abundance: but from him that hath not, even that which he	„	29
	38	hath shall be taken away from him. And cast ye out the unprofitable servant into the outer darkness: there shall be the weeping and gnashing of teeth.	„	30
	39	Let your loins be girded about, and your	Lu. 12	35
	40	lamps[2] burning; and be ye yourselves like unto men looking for their lord, when he returns from the feast; that, when he cometh and knocketh, they may straightway	„	36
	41	open unto him. Blessed are those servants, whom their lord when he cometh shall find watching: verily I say unto you, that he shall gird his loins, and make them lie down *to meat*, and shall pass by and serve them.	„	37
	42	And if he shall come in the second watch,	„	38

[1] Mr. Rendel Harris thinks the saying, "Be approved money-changers," was in the *Diatessaron* near here.

[2] See note on ver. 11. These verses from Luke xii. serve as a kind of summary of the preceding lessons.

or in the third, and find them so, blessed are those servants.

43 43 But when the Son of man shall come in his glory, and all his holy angels with him, then shall he sit on the throne of his 44 majesty: and before him he shall gather all the nations: and he shall separate them one from another, as the shepherd separateth 45 the rams from the kids: and he shall set the rams on his right, but the kids on the 46 left. Then shall the King say unto them that shall be on his right, Come, ye blessed of my Father, inherit the kingdom prepared for you from the foundation of the world: 47 I was hungry, and ye gave me to eat: I was thirsty, and ye gave me to drink: I was a 48 stranger, and ye took me in: I was naked, and ye clothed me: I was sick, and ye visited me: I was in prison, and ye took 49 care of me. Then shall the righteous say unto him, Lord, when saw we thee hungering, and fed thee? or thirsting, and 50 gave thee a drink? And when saw we thee a stranger, and took thee in? or naked, and 51 clothed thee? And when saw we thee sick, 52 or in prison, and took care of thee? The King shall answer, and say[1] unto them, Verily I say unto you, Whatsoever ye did unto one of the least of these my brethren, 53 ye did unto me. Then shall he say also unto them that shall be on his left, Depart from me, ye cursed, into the eternal fire which is prepared for the devil and his 54 ministers: I was hungry, and ye gave me not to eat: I was thirsty, and ye gave me 55 no drink: I was a stranger, and ye took me not in: I was naked, and ye clothed me not: I was sick, and in prison, and ye visited me 56 not. Then shall they also answer, saying,

Mt. 25 31
„ 32
„ 33
„ 34
„ 35
„ 36
„ 37
„ 38
„ 39
„ 40
„ 41
„ 42
„ 43
„ 44

[1] In the Arabic idiom, "answered and said."

		Lord, when saw we thee hungering, or thirsting, or naked,[1] or a stranger, or sick, or in prison, and did not minister unto thee?			
43	57	Then shall he answer, and say unto them, Verily I say unto you, When ye did it not unto one of these lesser *ones*, ye did it not	Mt.	25	45
	58	even unto me also. And these shall go into eternal punishment: but the righteous into eternal life.	„		46
44	1	And when Jesus had finished all these	„	26	1
	2	sayings, he said unto his disciples, Ye know that after two days[2] the passover will take place, and the Son of man will be delivered	„		2
	3	up to be crucified. Then were gathered together the chief priests and scribes, and the elders of the people, unto the court of	„		3
	4	the high priest, who is called Caiaphas; and they took counsel concerning Jesus that they might take him by subtilty, and kill him.	„		4
	5	But they said, Not during the feast, lest peradventure a tumult arise among the people; for they feared the people.	„		5
			Lu.	22	2[b]
	6	And Satan entered into Judas surnamed Iscariot, who was of the number of the	„		3
	7	twelve. And he went away, and had a conversation in the temple with the chief priests and scribes and rulers, saying unto them, What are ye willing to give me, and	„		4[a]
			Mt.	26	15[b]
	8	I will deliver him unto you? And they, when they heard it, were glad, and they appointed unto him thirty silver drachmas.[3]	Mk.	14	11[a]
			Mt.	26	15[c]
	9	And he promised them: and from that time he sought opportunity to deliver Jesus unto them without the multitudes.	Lu.	22	6
	10	And on the first day of *the feast of* unleavened *bread*, the disciples came to Jesus,	Mk.[4]	14	12

[1] The order of "naked" and "stranger" is here reversed from ver. 47, 50, and 55.

[2] Cf. xli. 31.   [3] Arabic, "dirhems of money."

[4] This verse seems superfluous here; cf. ver. 36.

and said unto him, Where wilt thou that we go and make ready for thee that thou mayest eat the passover?

44 11 Now before the feast of the passover Jesus knew that the hour was come that he should depart out of this world unto his Father, and he loved his own in this world, Jn. 13 1
12 and he loved them unto the end. And at supper[1] time, Satan having put into the heart of Judas, the son of Simon Iscariot, to „ 2
13 betray him, and Jesus, knowing that the Father had delivered all things into his hands, and that he came forth from the Father, and was going unto the Father, „ 3
14 rose from supper, and laid aside his garments; and he took a towel, and girded his loins. „ 4
15 And he poured water into the bason, and began to wash his disciples' feet, and to wipe them with the towel wherewith he had „ 5
16 girded his loins. And when he was come to Simon Cephas, Simon said unto him, „ 6
17 Lord, dost thou wash my feet? Jesus answered, and said unto him, What I do now thou knowest not; but thou shalt know „ 7
18 hereafter. Simon said unto him, Thou shalt never wash my feet. Jesus saith unto him, If I wash thee not, thou shalt have no part „ 8
19 with me. Simon Cephas said unto him, Then, Lord, wash not my feet only, but also „ 9
20 my hands and my head. Jesus said unto him, He that is bathed needeth not save to wash his feet; then he is entirely clean: and „ 10
21 ye are clean, but not all. For Jesus knew who was his betrayer; therefore said he, Ye are not all clean. „ 11
22 So after he had washed their feet, he took „ 12

---

[1] Tatian divides ver. 1-20 of this chapter of S. John from the remainder, and makes the meal here referred to take place before the hiring of the guest-chamber (xliv. 36, etc.), and consequently also before the meal, which preceded the institution of the Lord's Supper (xliv. 41).

	his garments, and, sitting down, he said unto them, Know ye what I have done to you?		
44	23 Ye call me, Master, and, Lord: and ye say	Jn. 13	13
	24 well; so I am. If I then, your Lord and Master, have washed your feet, how much more fit is it, that ye should wash one	„	14
	25 another's feet? For I have given you this example, that ye also may so do, as I have	„	15
	26 done to you. Verily, verily, I say unto you, A servant is not greater than his lord; neither is an apostle greater than he that sent him.	„	16
	27 If ye know these things, happy shall ye be	„	17
	28 if ye do them. This my saying is not for you all: for I know whom I have chosen: but that the scripture may be fulfilled, He that eateth bread with me hath lifted up his	„	18
	29 heel against me. From henceforth I tell you before it come to pass, that when it is come to pass, ye may believe that I am *he*.	„	19
	30 Verily, verily, I say unto you, He that receiveth whomsoever I send receiveth me; and he that receiveth me receiveth him that	„	20
	31 sent me. Which is greater, he that reclineth *at meat*, or he that serveth? is not he that reclineth *at meat*? I am in the midst of you	Lu. 22	27
	32 as he that serveth. But ye are they which	„	28
	33 have continued with me in my sorrows, and I promise unto you, even as my Father promised unto me, a kingdom, that ye may eat and drink upon the table of my kingdom.[1]	„ „	29 30[a]
	34 And the first day of the feast of un- leavened *bread* came, on which the Jews are	„	7
	35 wont to kill the passover. And Jesus sent two of his disciples, Cephas and John, saying unto them, Go and make ready for us the	„	8
	36 passover, that we may eat. And they said unto him, Where[2] wilt thou that we make	„	9
	37 ready for thee? He said unto them, Go,	Lu. 22 10[a] Mk. 14 13[b]	

[1] Omitting "and sit on thrones judging the Twelve Tribes of Israel." But cf. xxix. 7.   [2] Cf. ver. 10.

enter into the city; and as ye are entering in, Lu. 22 10ᵇ
there shall meet you a man bearing a pitcher
of water; follow him; and where he entereth
44 38 in, say to the householder, Our Master saith, { Lu. 22 11ᵃ
  Mt. 26 18ᵇ
My time is come; and I keep the passover
with thee. Where is then the lodging, Lu. 22 11ᵇ
where I may eat *it* with my disciples?
39 And he will show you a large upper room   „   12ᵃ
furnished and prepared: and there make Mk. 14 15ᵇ
40 ready for us. And his two disciples went   „   16
forth, and came into the city, and found
even as he had said unto them: and they
made ready the passover, as he had commanded them.
41¹ And when the evening was come, and it Lu. 22 14
was the hour, Jesus came and lay down *to
meat*, and the twelve apostles with him.
42 And he saith unto them, With desire I have   „   15
desired to eat this passover with you before
43 I suffer: I say unto you, henceforth I will   „   16
not eat it, until it be fulfilled in the kingdom
of God.
44 Saying this, Jesus was troubled in the Jn. 13 21ᵃ
spirit, and testified, and said, Verily, verily,
I say unto you, One of you that eateth with Mk. 14 18ᵇ
45 me, he shall betray me. And they were   „   19
very sorrowful, and began to say unto him
46 one by one, Is it I, Lord? He answereth,   „   20
and saith unto them, One of the twelve, that
dippeth his hand with me in the dish, he
47 shall betray me. And behold, the hand of Lu. 22 21
him that betrayeth me *is* on the table.
48 And the Son of man shall go, even as it is Mk. 14 21
written of him: but woe unto that man
through whom the Son of man shall be
betrayed! better were it for that man if he
49 had not been born. And the disciples Jn. 13 22
observed one another, not knowing whom
50 he signified. And they began to question Lu. 22 23

¹ See note to ver. 12.

among themselves, which of them it was that was going to do this thing.

45 1 Now there was reclining in his bosom one Jn. 13 23
2 of his disciples, whom Jesus loved. Simon „ 24
Cephas beckoned to him, that he should ask
3 him who this was of whom he spake. That „ 25
disciple therefore leaned back on Jesus'
breast, and said unto him, Lord, Who is he?
4 Jesus answered, and saith, He it is to whom „ 26
I shall give the bread *when it is* dipped. And
Jesus dipped the bread, and gave it to Judas,
5 the son of Simon Iscariot. And after the „ 27
bread Satan entered into him. And Jesus
said unto him, What thou wishest to do,
6 make haste to do. Now no one of those „ 28
reclining understood this, for what *intent* he
7 spake unto him. And some thought, because „ 29
Judas had the bag, that he commanded him
to buy what was needed for the feast; or
that he should give something to the poor.
8 Judas the betrayer answered, and said, Is Mt. 26 25
it I, Master? Jesus saith unto him, Thou
9 hast said. And Judas straightway received Jn. 13 30
the bread, and went out: and it was night.
10 And Jesus said, Now[1] shall the Son of „ 31
man be glorified, and God shall be glorified
11 in him; and if God shall be glorified in „ 32
him,[2] God shall also glorify him in himself,
12 and straightway shall he glorify him. And Mk. 14 22[a]
as they were eating, Jesus took bread, and Mt. 26 26[b]
blessed, and brake, and gave *it* to his disciples, and said unto them, Take, and eat;
13 this is my body. And when he had taken Mk. 14 23[a]
a cup, he gave thanks, and blessed it, and
gave *it* to them: and said, Take, and drink Mt. 26 27[b]
14 ye all of this; and they all drank of it. Mk. 14 23[b]

[1] The Doctrine of Addai has "Behold now is the Son of man glorified, and God glorifies Himself in Him by miracles and by wonders, and by honour of being at the right hand."

[2] Retaining the clause omitted in the Revised Version.

45 15 And he said unto them, This is my blood, { Mk. 14 24ᵃ / Mt. 26 28 }
the new testament, shed for many unto
16 remission of sins. I say unto you, I will   Mt. 26 29
not drink henceforth of this juice of the
vine, until the day when I shall drink
it new with you in the kingdom of
God; and so do for my remembrance.[1]   Lu. 22 19ᵇ
17 And Jesus saith unto Simon, Simon, be-   „   31
hold, Satan desires that he may sift you
18 as wheat: but I make supplication for thee,   „   32
that thou lose not thy faith: and do thou
also, when once thou hast turned again,
stablish thy brethren.
19   My children, yet a little while I am with   Jn. 13 33
you; and ye shall seek me: and as I said
unto the Jews, Whither I go, ye cannot
20 come; I say now unto you also. A new   „   34
commandment I give unto you, that ye love
one another; and even as I have loved you,
21 love ye also each other. By this shall all   „   35
men know that ye are my disciples, if ye
22 have love one to another. Simon Cephas   „   36
said unto him, Lord, whither goest thou?
Jesus answered, and said unto him, Whither
I go, thou canst not follow me now; but
thou shalt come afterwards.
23   Then said Jesus unto them, All ye shall   Mt.[2] 26 31
forsake me this night: it is written, I will
smite the shepherd, and the sheep of the
24 flock shall be scattered abroad. But after   „   32
my resurrection I will go before you into
25 Galilee. Simon Cephas answered, and saith   „   33
unto him, Lord, if all forsake thee, I will

---

[1] Aphraates adds here "as often as ye come together," showing clearly that Tatian borrowed from the account in 1 Cor. xi. in compiling the *Diatessaron*. The insertion of the Lord's Supper after the departure of Judas involved a displacement of the subject of Luke xxii. 17–20 from that evangelist's order. The preference was therefore given to other Gospels, only the last clause of Luke xxii. 19 being retained.

[2] S. Matthew and S. Mark put this after the arrival at Gethsemane.

45 26 never withdraw from thee: with¹ thee I Lu. 22 33ᵇ
   am ready for prison and for death, and I Jn. 13 37ᵇ
27 will lay down my life for thee. Jesus said „ 38ᵃ
   unto him, Wilt thou lay down thy life for
   me? Verily, verily, I say unto thee, that Mk.²14 30ᵇ
   thou to-day, *even* this night, before the cock
   crow twice, shalt thrice deny that thou Lu. 22 34ᵇ
28 knowest me. But Cephas kept speaking Mk. 14 31
   further, Even if I come to death with
   thee, I will not deny thee, Lord. And
   in like manner also said all the disciples.
29 Then saith Jesus unto them, Let not your Jn. 14 1
   hearts be troubled: believe in God, and
30 believe in me. In my Father's house are „ 2
   many mansions; if it were not so, I would
   have told you; for I go to prepare³ a place
31 for you. And if I go away to prepare a „ 3
   place for you, I will return again, and
   receive you unto myself; and where I am,
32 there shall ye also be. And the place „ 4
   whither I go, ye know, and the way ye
33 know. Thauma said unto him, Lord, we „ 5
   know not whither thou goest; and how
   shall we have a way to perceive this?
34 Jesus said unto him, I am the way, and „ 6
   the truth, and the life: and no one cometh
35 unto my Father, but by me. And if ye had „ 7
   known me, ye would have known my Father:
   and from henceforth ye have known him,
36 and have seen him. Philip said unto him, „ 8
   Lord, shew us the Father, and it sufficeth
37 us. Jesus said unto him, All this time am „ 9
   I with you, and have ye not yet known me?
   Philip, he that seeth me hath seen the
   Father; how sayest thou then, Shew us the
38 Father? Believest thou not that I am in „ 10

¹ Omitting John xiii. 37: "why cannot I follow Thee now?"
² Cf. xlix. 17.
³ Addai alludes to this, saying, "He is gone to prepare for his worshippers blessed mansions, in which they may dwell."

my Father, and my Father is in me? for the words that I speak I speak not from myself: but my Father, who abideth in me,		
45 39 he doeth these works. Believe that I am in my Father, and my Father is in me:	Jn. 14	11
40 or else believe for the works' sake. Verily, verily, I say unto you, He that believeth on me, the works that I do shall he do also; and greater *works* than these shall he do.	„	12
41 I go unto the Father: and whatsoever ye shall ask in my name, I will do with you, that the Father may be glorified in his Son.	„	13
42 If therefore ye ask in my name, I will do	„	14
43 *it*. If ye love me, keep my commandments.	„	15
44 And I will pray my Father, and he shall send you another Paraclete,[1] that he may be	„	16
45 with you for ever, *even* the Spirit of truth, whom the world cannot receive; for it hath not seen him, neither known him: but ye know him; for he abideth with you, and is	„	17
46 in you. I will not leave you orphans: I	„	18
47 will come unto you. Yet a little while, and the world shall not see me; but ye shall see	„	19
48 me: because I live, ye shall live also. And in that day ye shall know that I am in my	„	20
46 1 Father, and ye in me, and I in you. He that hath my commandments, and keepeth them, he it is that loveth me: and he that loveth me shall be loved of my Father, and I will love him, and will manifest myself	„	21
2 unto him. Judas (not the Iscariot) said unto him, Lord, what is the meaning of thy resolution to manifest thyself unto us, and	„	22
3 not unto the world? Jesus answered, and said unto him, He that loveth me will surely keep my saying: and my Father will love him, and we will come unto him, and make	„	23
4 our abode with him. But he that loveth me not keepeth not my saying: and this	„	24

[1] This Greek form is retained in the Arabic: it is equivalent to "Comforter."

saying which ye hear is not my saying, but the Father's who sent me.

46 5 These things have I spoken unto you, Jn. 14 25
6 while *yet* abiding with you. But the Paraclete, *even* the Holy Spirit, whom my Father will send in my name, he shall teach you all things, and bring to your remembrance „ 26
7 all whatsoever I say unto you. Peace I leave with you; my peace I give unto you: but not as this world giveth, give I unto you. Let not your heart be seized with „ 27
8 forebodings, neither let it be fearful. Ye heard how I said to you, I go away, and I will come unto you. If ye loved me, would ye not surely rejoice, because I go unto my Father? for my Father is greater than I. „ 28
9 And now I tell you before it come to pass, that, when it is come to pass, ye may believe „ 29
10 on me. I will not now speak much with you, the prince of the world shall come, and „ 30
11 shall have nothing in me; but that the world may know that I love my Father, and as my Father gave me commandment, „ 31ᵃ
12 so I do. And he saith unto them, When I sent you forth without purses,¹ and wallets,¹ Lu. 22 35
13 and shoes, lacked ye anything? They said unto him, Nothing. He said unto them, Henceforth he that hath a purse, let him take it, and likewise a wallet also: and he that hath no sword, let him sell his coat, „ 36
14 and buy himself a sword. I say unto you, that this which is written must yet be fulfilled in me, for I shall be reckoned with transgressors: for all things that were said „ 37
15 concerning me are fulfilled in me. His disciples said unto him, Lord, behold, here are two swords. He said unto them, They are enough. Arise, let us go hence. „ 38
   Jn. 14 31ᵇ
16 And they rose up, and when they had Lu. 22 39

¹ Plural; so also in the Doctrine of Addai.

given thanks, they went out, and went, according to their custom, unto the mount of Olives, he and his disciples.

46 17 And he saith unto them, I am the true Jn. 15 1
vine, and my Father is the husbandman.
18 Every branch in me that beareth not fruit, „ 2
he will take it away: and that which beareth
fruit, he will cleanse, that it may bear much
19 fruit. Already ye are clean because of the „ 3
saying which I have spoken unto you.
20 Abide in me, and I in you. For even as „ 4
the branch of the vine cannot bear fruit of
itself, except it abide in the vine; so neither
21 *can* ye, except ye abide in me. I am the „ 5
vine, and ye *are* the branches: He that
abideth in me, and I in him, the same
beareth much fruit: for without me ye can
22 do nothing. But if any man abide not in „ 6
me, he shall be cast forth as a withered
branch, which is gathered, and cast into the
23 fire to burn. If ye abide in me, and my „ 7
word abide in you, whatsoever ye shall wish
24 to ask shall be done unto you. And herein „ 8
shall the Father be glorified, that ye bear
25 much fruit, and be my disciples. And even „ 9
as the Father hath loved me, I also have
26 loved you: abide ye in my love. If ye „ 10
keep my commandments, ye shall abide in
my love; even as I have kept my Father's
27 commandments, and abide in his love. These „ 11
things have I spoken unto you, that my joy
may be in you, and *that* your joy may be
28 fulfilled. This is my commandment, that „ 12
ye love one another, even as I have loved
29 you. And there is no greater love than this, „ 13
30 that a man give his life for his friends. Ye „ 14
are my friends, if ye do all things which I
31 have commanded you. I will not now call „ 15
you servants; for the servant knoweth not
what his lord doeth: but I have called you

46 32 friends; for all things whatsoever I heard from my Father I have made known unto you. Ye did not choose me, but I selected you, and appointed you, that ye also should go and bring fruit, and *that* your fruit should abide: and whatsoever ye shall ask of the Father in my name, he will give it you. Jn. 15 16
33 This I command you, that ye love one „ 17
34 another. And if the world hateth you, „ 18 know that it hath hated me before *it hated*
35 you. For if ye had been of the world, the „ 19 world would love what is its own: but ye are not of the world. I chose you out of the world, therefore the world hateth you.
36 Remember the saying that I spake unto you, „ 20 A servant is not greater than his lord. If therefore they cast me out, they will cast you out also; and if they kept my word,
37 they will keep your words also. But all „ 21 these things will they do unto you for my name's sake, because they know not him
38 that sent me. For if I had not come and „ 22 spoken unto them, they would not have had sin: but now they have no excuse for their
39 sins. He that hateth me hateth my Father „ 23
40 also. And if I had not done before them „ 24 the works which none other did, they would not have had sin: but now have they seen
41 and hated both me and my Father, that the „ 25 saying may be fulfilled that is written in their law, They hated me without a cause.
42 But when the Paraclete is come, whom I „ 26 will send unto you from my Father, *even* the Spirit of truth, which proceedeth from my Father, he shall bear witness of me:
43 and ye shall bear witness, because ye are „ 27 with me from the beginning.
44 These things have I spoken unto you, that „ 16 1
45 ye should not be disquieted. For they shall „ 2 put you out of their synagogues: and the

		hour will come, that every one that shall kill you will think that he presenteth an		
46	46	offering unto God. And these things will they do unto you, because they know not	Jn. 16	3
	47	me, nor my Father. These things have I spoken unto you, that when the hour is come, ye may remember them, how that I	,,	4
	48	told you. And these things I said not unto you before, because I was with you. And now I go unto him that sent me; and none	,,	5
	49	of you asketh me, whither I go. Now I have spoken these things unto you, and sorrow hath come, and seized your hearts.	,,	6
	50	Nevertheless I tell you the truth: It is expedient for you that I go away: for if I go not away, the Paraclete will not come unto you; but if I go, I will send him unto	,,	7
	51	you. And when he cometh, he will convict the world in respect of sin, and of righteous-	,,	8
	52	ness, and of judgment: of sin, because they	,,	9
	53	believed not on me; but of righteousness,	,,	10
	54	because I go to my Father; and of judgment, because the prince of this world is	,,	11
	55	judged. And I have yet many things to say unto you, but ye cannot bear them now.	,,	12
	56	And when the Spirit of truth is come, he shall bring all the truth to your remembrance:[1] he shall not speak anything from himself; but what things soever he shall hear, *these* shall he speak: and he shall teach you those things that are about to	,,	13
	57	come. And he shall glorify me: for he shall take from me, and shall show *it* unto you.	,,	14
	58	All things that my Father hath are mine: therefore said I unto you, that he shall take of mine, and shall show *it* unto you.	,,	15
47	1	A little *while*, and ye shall not see me; and again a little *while*, and ye shall see me,	,,	16
	2	because I go to the Father. His disciples	,,	17

[1] Cf. John xiv. 26.

therefore said one to another, What is this that he said unto us, A little *while*, and ye shall not see me; and again a little *while*, and ye shall see me: and, I go to the
47 3 Father? And they said, What is this little *while* which he said? We know not what 4 he saith. And Jesus perceived that they were desirous to ask him, and said unto them, Do ye inquire of one another, because I said unto you, A little *while*, and ye shall not see me; and again a little *while*, and ye 5 shall see me? Verily, verily, I say unto you, that ye shall lament and be sad, but the world shall rejoice: and ye shall be sorrowful, but your grief shall be turned into joy. 6 For a woman, when the time of bearing draweth near unto her, the coming of the day of her delivery oppresseth her: but when she hath brought forth the child, she remembereth not the anguish, for the joy 7 that a man is born into the world. Even ye therefore are sad now: but I will surely see you, and your heart shall rejoice, and your joy no one shall take away from you. 8 And in that day ye shall ask me nothing. Verily, verily, I say unto you, Whatsoever ye shall ask of my Father in my name, he 9 will give it you. Hitherto have ye asked nothing in my name: ask, and ye shall receive, that your joy may be full.
10   Now have I spoken unto you in proverbs: but an hour and a time shall come, when I shall not speak unto you in proverbs, but shall reveal to you the Father by an open 11 revelation. In that day ye shall ask in my name: and I say not unto you, that I will 12 pray the Father for you; for the Father loveth you, because ye have loved me, and have believed that I came out from my 13 Father. I came out from my Father, and

Jn. 16 18
   „   19
   „   20
   „   21
   „   22
   „   23
   „   24
   „   25
   „   26
   „   27
   „   28

47 14 am come into the world: and I leave the world, and go unto my Father. His disciples said unto him, Lo, now thy words are clear, and thou hast spoken nothing in a Jn. 16 29
15 proverb. Lo, now know we that thou knowest all things, and needest not that any man should ask thee: and by this we believe that thou camest out from God. „ 30
16
17 } Jesus said unto them, Believe that an hour shall come, and is already come, and ye shall be scattered, every man to his own place, and shall leave me alone: and *yet* I am not { Jn. 16 31
„ 32
18 alone, because the Father is with me. These things have I spoken unto you, that in me ye may have peace. For in the world distress shall overtake you: but be of good cheer, for I have overcome the world. Jn. 16 33
19 This spake Jesus; and lifting up his eyes to heaven, he said, My Father, the hour is come; glorify thy Son, that thy Son may „ 17 1
20 glorify thee: even as thou gavest him authority over all flesh, that everything, that thou hast given him, to it he should give „ 2
21 eternal life. And this is life eternal, that they may know that thou art the only true God, and that he, whom thou didst send, *is* „ 3
22 Jesus the Messiah. I have glorified thee on the earth, and I have accomplished the „ 4
23 work which thou gavest me to do. Now therefore, thou Father, glorify me with thine own self with the glory which I had with thee „ 5
24 before the world was. I taught thy name unto the men whom thou gavest me out of the world: thine they were, and thou gavest them to me; and they have kept thy say- „ 6
25 ing. Now they know that all things which „ 7
26 thou hast given me are from thee: and the words which thou gavest me I have presented unto them; and they received *them*, and knew of a truth that I came out from „ 8

47 27 thee, and they believed that thou didst send me. And I pray for them: and my petition is not for the world, but for these whom thou hast given me; for they are   Jn. 17   9

28 thine: and all my things are thine, and all thine are mine: and I am glorified in them.   „   10

29 And now I am not in the world, and these are in the world, and I come to thee. Holy Father, keep them in thy name, whom thou hast given me, that they may be one, even   „   11

30 as we *are*. When I was with them in the world I kept them in thy name. For *those*, whom thou hast given me, have I guarded, and not one of them perished, but the son of perdition;[1] that the scripture might be   „   12

31 fulfilled. Now I turn to thee; and this I speak in the world, that they may have my joy   „   13

32 fulfilled in themselves. I have given them thy saying; and the world hated them, because they are not of the world, even as I   „   14

33 am not of the world. For I seek not this, that thou shouldest take them from the world, but that thou shouldest keep them from   „   15

34 the evil *one*. They are not of the world, even   „   16

35 as I am not of the world. Father, sanctify them in the truth: for thy saying is truth.   „   17

36 And even as thou didst send me into the world, I also send them into the world.   „   18

37 And for their sakes I sanctify myself, that they themselves also may be sanctified in   „   19

38 the truth. And not for them only do I pray, but for them that are about to believe   „   20

39 on me through their word; that they may all be one; even as thou *art* in me, and I in thee, that they also may be one in us: that the world may believe that thou didst send   „   21

40 me. And the glory which thou hast given me I have given unto them; that they may   „   22

41 be one, even as we are one; I in them, and   „   23

---

[1] Lit. "perishing."

		thou in me, that they may be perfected into one; and that the world may know that thou hast sent me, and that I have loved			
47	42	them, even as thou hast loved me. Father, those whom thou hast given me, I will that, where I am, they also may be with me; that they may see my glory, which thou hast given me: for thou lovedst me before the	Jn.	17	24
	43	foundation of the world. O my righteous Father, the world knew thee not, but I know thee; and these knew that thou didst send	,,		25
	44	me; and I made known unto them thy name, and will make it known; that the love wherewith thou lovedst me may be in them, and I may be in them.	,,		26
48	1	This spake Jesus, and went forth with his disciples to the place which is called Gethsemane, over the brook Cedron, to the mountain, the place wherein was a garden, into which he entered, himself and his	,,	18	1
	2	disciples. Now Judas the betrayer knew that place: for Jesus ofttimes resorted	,,		2
	3	thither with his disciples. And when Jesus had arrived at the place, he said unto his disciples, Sit ye here, that I may go and pray.	Lu. Mt.	22 26	40^a 36^b
	4	Pray that ye enter not into temptation.	Lu.	22	40^b
	5	And he took with him Cephas, and at the same time the two sons of Zebedee, James and John, and began to be sorrowful and	Mt.	26	37
	6	anxious. And he saith unto them, My soul is in anguish, even unto death: abide ye	,,		38
	7	here, and watch with me. And he was parted from them a little way, as far as a stone's cast is; and he kneeled down and	Lu.	22	41
	8	fell forward on his face, and prayed that, if it could be done, that hour might pass	Mk.	14	35^b
	9	away from him. And he said, Father, thou canst do all things; if thou be willing, remove this cup from me: nevertheless not	,, Lu.	22	36^a 42^b
	10	my will, but thy will, be done. And he	Mt.	26	40^a

48 11	came unto his disciples, and found them sleeping, and said unto Cephas, Simon, sleepest thou? So, could ye not watch	Mk. 14 37^b
		Mt. 26 40^b
12	with me one hour? Watch and pray, that ye enter not into temptation: the spirit is eager and ready, but the body is weak.	„ 41^a
		Mk.^{1} 14 38^b
13	Again a second time he went away, and prayed, saying, O my Father, if this cup cannot pass away, except I drink it, thy	Mt. 26 42
14	will be done. And again he returned, and found his disciples sleeping, for their eyes were weighed down for sorrow and anxiety; and they knew not what to answer him.	Mk. 14 40
15	And he left them, and went away again, and prayed a third time, saying the same	Mt. 26 44
16	speech. And there appeared unto him an	Lu. 22 43
17	angel from heaven, strengthening him. And while he was afraid² he prayed with uninterrupted prayer: and his sweat became as it were a stream of blood, and fell down	„ 44
18	upon the ground. Then he rose up from the prayer, and came unto his disciples,	„ 45^a
19	and found them sleeping, and said unto them, Sleep on now, and take your rest:	„ 46^a
		Mt. 26 45^b
20	the end is at hand; and the hour is come; and, behold, the Son of man shall be betrayed	Mk. 14 41^b
21	into the hands of sinners. Arise, let us be going: he is at hand that shall betray me.	„ 42^a
		Mt. 26 46^b
22	While he yet spake, came Judas the betrayer, one of the twelve, and with him a great multitude carrying lanterns and torches, and swords and staves, having been sent by the chief priests and scribes and elders of the people: and with him a man of the	„ 47
23	Romans.³ Now Judas the betrayer gave them a sign, saying, He whom I shall kiss,	„ 48

[1] Or continuation of Matt. xxvi. 41.
[2] Cf. Heb. v. 7, "in that he feared."
[3] Probably added to account for the Jews venturing to use armed violence. In Syriac "Romans" is equivalent to "soldiers."

	is he: take him boldly,¹ and lead him away.	Mk.	14	44ᵇ
48 24	And Jesus, knowing all the things that were about to come upon him, went out unto	Jn.	18	4ᵃ
25	them: and straightway the traitor Judas came to Jesus, and said, Hail, Master; and	Mt.	26	49
26	kissed him. And Jesus said unto him,	„		50ᵃ
	Judas, betrayest thou the Son of man	Lu.	22	48ᵇ
	with a kiss? Friend, art thou come for	Mt.	26	50ᵇ
27	this? And Jesus said unto them which	Lu.²	22	52ᵃ
	were come unto him, Whom seek ye?	Jn.	18	4ᵇ
28	They said unto him, Jesus of Nazareth.	„		5
	Jesus said unto them, I am *he*. And Judas also, the betrayer, was standing with them.			
29	And when Jesus said unto them, I am *he*,	„		6
	they went backward, and fell upon the			
30	ground. And again Jesus asked them,	„		7
	Whom seek ye? They answered, Jesus of			
31	Nazareth. Jesus said unto them, I told	„		8
	you that I am *he*: if therefore ye seek me,			
32	let these go their way: that the saying	„		9
	might be fulfilled which he spake, Of those whom thou hast give me I have not lost			
33	one. Then they that were with Judas, came and laid hands on Jesus, and took him.	Mt.	26	50ᶜ
34	And when his disciples saw what happened, they said, Lord, shall we smite them with	Lu.	22	49
35	the swords? Simon Cephas therefore having a sword drew it, and struck the high priest's servant, and cut off his right ear. And that servant's name was Malchus.	Jn.	18	10
36	Jesus said unto Cephas, The cup which my Father hath given me, shall I not drink it?	„		11
37	Put up the sword into its sheath,³ for all they that shall attack with the sword, shall	Mt.	26	52ᵇ
38	perish with the sword. Or thinkest thou	„		53

¹ Perhaps "carefully."

² Tatian has made a convenience of this clause, its true place is at ver. 41 of this chapter.

³ "Put . . . sheath" was omitted from the previous verse.

48 39	that I cannot beseech my Father, and he shall even now furnish unto me more than twelve legions of angels? How then shall the scriptures be fulfilled, which say, that	Mt. 26 54
40	thus it must come to pass? After this he gently touched the ear which he had struck,	Lu. 22 51^b
41	and healed it. And in that hour said Jesus to the multitudes, Are ye come out against me, as an attack is made on a robber, with swords and staves to seize me? I sat daily with you in the temple teaching, and ye	Mt. 26 55
42	took me not: but this is your hour, and the	Lu. 22 53^b
43	power of darkness. And this came to pass, that the scriptures of the prophets might be fulfilled. Then all the disciples left him, and fled.	Mt. 26 56
44	So the band and the captains and the soldiers of the Jews took Jesus, and went	Jn.[1] 18 12
45	their way. And a certain young man was following him, naked, wrapped in a linen	Mk. 14 51
46	cloth; and they laid hold on him; but he let go the linen cloth, and fled away naked.	,, 52
47	Then they seized Jesus, and bound him, and led him to Annas first; for he was father-in-law to Caiaphas, which was high	Jn. 18 12
		,, 13
48	priest that year. Now it was Caiaphas which had given counsel to the Jews, It is expedient that one man should die for the people.	,, 14
49	And Simon Cephas followed Jesus,[2] and *so did* another disciple. Now that disciple was known unto the high priest, and entered in	,, 15
50	with Jesus into the court; but Simon was standing at the door without. And that other disciple, which was known unto the high priest, went out and spake unto the	,, 16

---

[1] See three verses lower.

[2] Omitting "afar off." As the trial of Jesus was going on simultaneously with the denials of S. Peter, evangelists differ in the order in which they relate the various occurrences. Tatian follows S. John's order.

THE DIATESSARON. 237

48 51 portress, and she brought Simon in. And   Jn. 18 17
when the maid, the portress, saw Simon, she
looked at him, and saith unto him, Art not
thou also one of the disciples of this man,
52 that is to say, of Jesus of Nazareth? And   Lu. 22 57
he denied, saying, Woman, I know him not:
nor do I even understand what thou sayest.   Mk. 14 68[b]
53 Now the servants and the soldiers rose up,   Jn. 18 18[a]
and kindled a fire in the midst of the court
54 to warm themselves; for it was cold. And   Lu. 22 55[a]
when they had kindled the fire, they sat
55 down around *it*: and Simon also came, and   Jn. 18 18[b]
sat down with them, to warm himself, that   Mt. 26 58[b]
he might see the end of what would happen.
49 1 The high priest therefore asked Jesus of   Jn. 18 19
2 his disciples, and of his teaching. And   „   20
Jesus said unto him, I was speaking openly
to the people; for I ever taught in the
synagogue, and in the temple, where all the
Jews come together; and in secret spake I
3 nothing. Why askest thou me? ask them   „   21
that have heard, what I was speaking unto
them: for these know all things which I
4 said. And when he had said these *words*,   „   22
one of the soldiers standing by struck the
cheek of Jesus, saying unto him, Answerest
5 thou the high priest so? Jesus answered,   „   23
and saith unto him, If I have spoken evil,
bear witness of the evil: but if well, why
6 smitest thou me? And Annas sent Jesus   „   24
bound unto Caiaphas the high priest.
7 And when Jesus went out, Simon Cephas   „   25[a]
was standing in the outer court, warming
8 himself. And the maid saw him again, and   Mk. 14 69[a]
began to say to them that stood by, This   Mt. 26 71[b]
man also was there with Jesus of Nazareth.
9 And they that stood by came and said to   „   73[a]
Cephas, Of a truth thou art one of his
10 disciples. And again he denied with an   „   72
11 oath, I know not the man. And after a   Lu. 22 58[a]

little while one of the servants of the high | Jn. 18 26ᵃ
priest, a kinsman of him whose ear Simon
49 12 cut off, saw him, and disputing, said, Of a | Lu.[1] 22 59ᵇ
truth this man was with him; he also is a
13 Galilaean, for his speech is similar. And he { Mt. 26 73ᵇ / Jn. 18 26ᵇ
said unto Simon, Did not I see thee in the
14 garden with him? Then Simon began to | Mk. 14 71
curse and to swear, I know not this man,
15 whom ye mention. And immediately, while | Lu. 22 60ᵇ
16 he yet spake, the cock crew twice. And in | „ 61ᵃ
that hour Jesus, who was outside, turned,
and looked upon Cephas. And Simon remembered the word of our Lord, which he
17 had said unto him, Before the cock crow | Mk.[2] 14 30ᵇ
18 twice, thou wilt deny me thrice. And | Lu. 22 62
Simon went out, and wept with a bitter
weeping.
19 And when the morning drew near, there | „ 66ᵃ
came together all the guards of the temple,
the chief priests and scribes, and elders of
the people, and all the multitude, and framed
20 devices; and they took counsel against Jesus | Mt. 27 1ᵇ
21 to put him to death. And they sought | „ 26 59ᵇ
false witnesses, who should bear witness
against Jesus, that they might put him to
22 death; and they found *them* not, and many | „ 60ᵃ
23 false witnesses came; and their witness was | Mk.[3] 14 59
24 not in agreement. But at last came two | Mt. 26 60ᵇ
25 false witnesses, and said, We heard him say, { Mk. 14 57ᵇ / „ 58
I will destroy this temple of God, made
with hands, and after three days I will build
26 another made without hands. And not even | Mk. 14 59
27 so was their witness in agreement. But Jesus | Mt. 26 63ᵃ
held his peace. And the high priest rose | Mk. 14 60ᵃ
up into the midst, and asked Jesus, saying,

---

[1] Tatian omits 59ᵃ, which places this occurrence at "one hour" after the preceding denial, and applies to it the statement of 58ᵃ, "after a little while."

[2] As Mark xiv. 30ᵇ was inserted before at xlv. 27ᵇ, Tatian probably meant this for the rest of Luke xxii. 61, adding the word "twice" from Mark xiv. 72.

[3] A mistake for Mark xiv. 56ᵇ; see ver. 26 below.

49 28 Answerest thou nothing to what these wit-	Mt. 26	62^b
29 ness against thee? But Jesus held his	Mk. 14	61^a
30 peace, and answered him nothing. And	Lu. 22	66^b
they led him up into their temple, saying		
31 unto him, If thou art the Messiah, tell us.	„	67
He^1 said unto them, If I tell you, ye will		
32 not believe me: and if I ask you, ye will	„	68
33 not answer me a word, nor let me go. And	Mt. 26	63^b
the high priest answered, and said unto him,		
I adjure thee by the living God, that thou		
tell us whether thou be the Messiah, the		
34 Son of the living God. Jesus said unto	„	64^a
35 him, Thou hast said *it*, because I am. They	Lu. 22	70
all said unto him, Art thou then the Son of		
God? Jesus saith, Ye say *it*, because I am;		
36 I say unto you, Henceforth ye shall see the	Mt. 26	64^b
Son of man sitting at the right hand of		
power, and coming on the clouds of heaven.		
37 Then the high priest rent his coat, saying,	Mk. 14	63^a
38 He hath spoken blasphemy. And they all	{ Mt. 26	65^b
	Lu. 22	71
said, Why do we still seek for witness? we		
have now heard the blasphemy from his		
39 mouth. What think ye? They all answered,	{ Mk. 14	64^b
	Mt. 26	66^b
40 and said, He is worthy of death. Then	Mk. 14	65^a
some of them came near, and spat into his		
face, and struck him, and mocked him.	Lu. 22	63^b
41 And the soldiers,^{2} smiting his cheeks, said,	Mk. 14	65^b
Prophesy unto us, Messiah, who is he that	Mt. 26	68^b
42 struck thee? And many other things spake	Lu. 22	65
they against him, blaspheming.		
43 And the whole council of them rose up,	Jn. 18	28^a
and took Jesus, and brought him bound		
into the Praetorium;^{3} and delivered him up	Mk. 15	1^b
44 to Pilate the governor: and they themselves	Jn. 18	28^b
entered not into the Praetorium, that they		

^{1} The Arabic and Vulgate begin ver. 67 here.

^{2} Rather the officials attending upon the high priest; cf. the passages here harmonised. The mocking by soldiers is inserted from S. Matthew and S. John at l. 38, etc.

^{3} Arabic, Dîwân.

	might not be found unclean, when they ate		
49 45	the passover. Now Jesus stood before the	Mt. 27	11ª
	governor: and Pilate went out unto them	Jn. 18	29
	outside, and said unto them, What accusa-		
46	tion have ye against this man? They	„	30
	answered, and said unto him, If he had		
	not done evil, we should not have delivered		
47	him up unto thee. We found this man	Lu. 23	2ᵇ
	subverting our people, and forbidding to give		
	tribute to Caesar, and saying that he him-		
48	self is the king, the Messiah. Pilate said	Jn. 18	31
	unto them, Take him yourselves then, and		
	judge him according to your law. The Jews		
	said unto him, We have no authority to put		
49	any man to death: that the word might be	„	32
	fulfilled, which Jesus spake, when he signified		
	by what manner of death he was about to		
	die.		
50	And Pilate entered into the Praetorium,	„	33
	and called Jesus, and said unto him, Art thou		
51	the King of the Jews? Jesus saith unto	„	34
	him, Sayest thou this of thyself, or did		
52	others tell it thee concerning me? Pilate	„	35
	said unto him, Am I a Jew? The sons of		
	thine own nation and the chief priests de-		
	livered thee unto me: what hast thou done?		
53	Jesus said unto him, My kingdom is not of	„	36
	this world: if my kingdom were of this		
	world, my servants would certainly fight,		
	that I should not be delivered to the Jews:		
54	now is my kingdom not from hence. Pilate	„	37
	said unto him, Then thou art a king? Jesus		
	saith unto him, Thou sayest *it*, because I am		
	a king. And for this cause have I been		
	born, and for this am I come into the		
	world, that I should bear witness unto the		
	truth. And every one that is of the truth		
55	heareth my voice. Pilate said unto him,	„	38ª
	And what is truth?		
	And when he had said this, he went out		

50 1 again unto the Jews. And Pilate saith unto   Lu. 23   4
2 the chief priests and the multitudes, I have
found nothing against this man. But they   „   5
cried out, and said, He stirreth up our people
with his teaching in all Judaea, beginning
3 from Galilee even unto this place. But Pilate,   „   6
when he heard the name of Galilee, asked,
4 Is this man a Galilaean? And when he   „   7
knew that he was under Herod's jurisdiction,
he sent him unto Herod, for he was at
Jerusalem in those days.
5   Now Herod, when he saw Jesus, was ex-   „   8
ceeding glad: for he was of a long time
desirous to see him, because he had heard
many things about his deeds; and he ex-
6 pected to see some sign from him. And he   „   9
questioned him in many words; but Jesus
7 answered him nothing. And the scribes and   „   10
the chief priests stood, accusing him violently.
8 And Herod with his attendants set him at   „   11
nought, and after he had mocked him, he
arrayed him in a scarlet robe, and sent him
9 to Pilate. And Pilate and Herod became   „   12
friends on that day: for before there was
enmity between them.
10   And Pilate called together the chief   „   13
11 priests and the rulers of the people, and   „   14
said unto them, Ye brought unto me this
man, as one that perverteth your people:
and I examined him before you, and found
no fault in this man out of all the things
12 whereof ye accuse him: nor did Herod also: „   15
for I sent him unto him; and he hath done
13 nothing whereby he deserveth death. I will   „   16
therefore chastise him, and release him.
14 The whole multitude cried out, saying,   „   18^a
Away with him from us, away with him.
15 And the chief priests and elders accused   Mk. 15   3^a
16 him of many things. And when he was   Mt. 27   12
accused by them, he answered not a word.

50 17 Then saith Pilate unto him, Hearest thou not how many things they witness against	Mt. 27	13
18 thee? And he did not answer him even with one word: and Pilate marvelled thereat.	„	14
19 And when the governor was sitting upon the place of judgment, his wife sent unto him, saying unto him, Take heed that thou hurt not that righteous man: for I have suffered many things this day in my dream because of him.	„[1]	19
20 Now at every feast the governor was wont to release unto the people one prisoner,	„	15
21 whom they would. And there was in their prison a notable prisoner, who was called	„	16
22 Barabbas. When therefore they were gathered together, Pilate said unto them,	„	17[a]
23 Ye have a custom that I should release unto you a prisoner at the passover: will ye that I release unto you the king of the	Jn. 18	39
24 Jews? And they all cried out, and said, Do not release unto us this man, but release unto us Barabbas. Now this Barabbas was	„	40
25 a robber, who for insurrection and murder done in the city had been cast into prison.	Lu. 23	19
26 And all the people cried out, and began to ask *him* to do unto them even as custom	Mk. 15	8
27 allowed. And Pilate answered, and said unto them, Whom will ye that I release unto you? Barabbas, or Jesus, which is called Messiah,	„ Mt. 27	9[a] 17[b]
28 the King[2] of the Jews? For Pilate knew that envy had moved them to deliver him up.	„	18
29 Now the chief priests and the elders besought the multitudes that they should ask for the release of Barabbas, and destroy Jesus.	„	20
30 The governor answered, and saith unto them, Which of the two will ye that I release	„	21

[1] Chronological order is not affected by the displacement of this verse from its setting; whilst greater continuity is given to the combined narrative which follows.

[2] Cf. Mark xv. 9.

50 31 unto you? They said, Barabbas. Pilate　　Mt. 27 22ᵃ
said unto them, What then shall I do concerning Jesus, which is called Messiah?
32 They all cried out, saying, Crucify him.　　Mk. 15 13
33 And Pilate spake unto them again, for he　　Lu. 23 20
34 desired to release Jesus; but they cried out,　　„　21
saying, Crucify, crucify him, and release
35 unto us Barabbas. And Pilate said unto　　„　22
them the third time, What evil hath this
man done? I have found no cause deserving of death in him: I will chastise him
36 and release him. But they were the more　　„　23
urgent with a loud voice, demanding that
he should crucify him. And their voice,
and the voice of the chief priests prevailed.
37 Then Pilate released unto them Barabbas,　　{Mk. 15 15ᵃ
who for insurrection and murder had been　　 Lu. 23 25ᵃ
cast into prison, whom they asked for;
but Jesus he scourged.¹　　Mt. 27 26ᵇ
38　Then the soldiers of the governor took　　„　27
Jesus, and brought him into the Praetorium,
and gathered unto him the whole band.
39 And they stripped him, and clothed him　　„　28
40 in a scarlet cloke, and arrayed him in a　　Jn. 19　2
purple garment; and plaited a crown of
41 thorns, and put it on his head, and a reed　　Mt. 27 29ᵇ
in his right *hand;* and, mocking and deriding him, they kneeled down before him,
and did obeisance, saying, Hail, King of
42 the Jews! And they spat into his face,　　„　30
and took the reed from his hand, and smote
43 his head, and they struck his cheeks. And　　{Jn. 19 3ᵇ
Pilate went out again, and said unto the　　　 „　4
Jews, I bring him out to you, that ye may
know that I find no cause for his condemna-
44 tion. Jesus therefore went out, wearing the　　Jn. 19　5
crown of thorns and the purple garment.
Pilate said unto them, Behold, the man!

¹ The last clause of this verse is omitted, and its equivalent is supplied from S. John at li. 6.

50 45 And when the chief priests and the officers saw him, they cried out, saying, Crucify him, crucify him. Pilate said unto them, Take him yourselves, and crucify him: for I find   Jn. 19 6

46 no cause in him. The Jews said unto him, We have a law, and according to our law he is deserving of death, because he made him-   „   7

47 self the Son of God. And when Pilate heard this saying, he was the more afraid;   „   8

48 and he entered into the judgment-hall[1] again, and said unto Jesus, Whence art thou?   „   9

49 But Jesus answered him not a word. Pilate said unto him, Speakest thou not unto me? knowest thou not that I have power to release thee, and have power to crucify   „   10

50 thee? Jesus saith unto him, Thou wouldest have no power against me, except it were given thee from above: therefore he that delivered me unto thee hath a greater sin   „   11

51 than thy sin. And because of this word Pilate wished to release him: but the Jews cried out, If thou release him, thou art not Caesar's friend: for every one that maketh himself a king opposeth Caesar.   „   12

51 1 And when Pilate had heard this saying, he brought Jesus out, and sat down on the tribunal,[2] at the place called The Pavement,   „   13

2 but in Hebrew it is called Gabbatha. Now that day was the Friday[3] of the passover: and it was about the sixth hour; and he said unto the Jews, Behold your king!   „   14

3 But they cried out, Away with him, away with him, crucify him, crucify him. Pilate said unto them, Shall I crucify your king? The chief priests said unto him, We have   „   15

4 no king but Caesar. And when Pilate saw that he prevailed nothing, but rather that a tumult increased, he took water, and washed   Mt. 27 24

---

[1] Arabic, "riwâk."   [2] Arabic, mimbar.
[3] Or, "assembly."

		his hands before the people, saying, I am innocent of the blood of this righteous man:	
51	5	see ye *to it*. And all the people answered, and said, His blood *be* on us, and on our	Mt. 27 25
	6	children. Then Pilate commanded that consent should be given to their petition, and he delivered Jesus up to be crucified according to their wish.	Jn. 19 16ª
	7	Then Judas the betrayer, when he had seen Jesus condemned,¹ went away, and gave back the thirty pieces of silver to the chief	Mt. 27 3
	8	priests and elders, saying, I have sinned in that I betrayed innocent blood. They said unto him, What is that to us? see thou *to it*.	,, 4
	9	And he cast down the money in the temple, and departed; and he went away, and	,, 5
	10	hanged² himself. And the chief priests took the money, and said, We have no right to put it into the ark of offerings, for it is the	,, 6
	11	price of blood. And they took counsel, and bought with it a potter's field for the burial	,, 7
	12	of strangers. Wherefore that field was called, The field of blood, unto this day.	,, 8
	13	Then was fulfilled that which was spoken through the prophet,³ saying, I took the thirty pieces of silver for the price of the great *one*, which was fixed by the children of	,, 9
	14	Israel; and I paid them for the potter's field, as the Lord commanded me.	,, 10
	15	And the Jews took Jesus, and went away to crucify him: and when he had taken up	{Jn. 19 16ᵇ {Mk. 15 20ᵇ Jn. 19 17ª
	16	his cross and gone out, they took off from	Mt. 27 31ᵇ

¹ Or, "assailed." Judas could scarcely have had this interview with the chief priests before the condemnation by Pilate. Tatian's displacement here would seem therefore to be an improvement.

² As Ephraem refers to the account in Acts i. 18, it has been thought that his copy of the *Diatessaron* contained part of that verse, which was afterwards omitted. At the close of the present verse he adds, "and died." See note to Appendix X.

³ Omitting "Jeremiah," as the Peschito does; "Jeremiah" is a mistake in our Gospel for Zechariah.

him the purple¹ and scarlet garment, with which he was clothed, and clothed him with his own garments.

51 17 And as they were going away with him, they found a man of Cyrene, coming from the country, Simon by name, the father of Alexander and Rufus; him they impressed, 18 that he might bear the cross of Jesus. And they took up the cross, and laid it on him, that he might bear it, and come after Jesus. And Jesus went on with his cross behind him.

19 And there followed him much people, and women who lamented and were excited 20 on account of Jesus. But Jesus turning unto them said, Daughters of Jerusalem, weep not over me, weep over yourselves, and 21 over your children. The days will come, in which they shall say, Blessed are the barren, and the wombs that bare not, and the 22 breasts that gave not suck. Then shall they begin to say to the mountains, Fall on us; 23 and to the hills, Cover us. For if they do thus in the green tree, what shall be done in the dry?

24 And they brought with Jesus two others 25 of the malefactors to be put to death. And when they were come unto the place which is called, The skull, and is called in Hebrew Golgotha: there they crucified him. With him they crucified those two malefactors, one on the right and the other on the left. 26 And the scripture² was fulfilled, which said, 27 He was reckoned with transgressors. And they gave him wine to drink and myrrh, and vinegar mingled with gall; and when

Mt. 27	32ᵃ
Mk. 15	21ᵇ
Mt. 27	32ᵇ
Lu. 23	26ᵇ
„	27
„	28
„	29
„	30
„	31
„	32
„	33ᵃ
Jn. 19	17ᶜ
Lu. 23	33ᵇ
Mk. 15	28
„	23ᵃ
Mt. 27	34ᵇ

---

¹ Cf. Mark xv. 20.

² As a comment of the evangelist himself, Tatian considered himself at liberty to remove this verse, from its position in S. Mark, to a more convenient situation.

		he had tasted it, he would not drink; and he received it not.	Mk. 15	23ᵇ
51	28	And the soldiers, when they had crucified Jesus, took his garments, and divided them into four parts, to each band of soldiers a part. Now his coat was without seam,	Jn. 19	23
	29	woven from the top throughout. They said therefore one to another, Let us not divide it, but cast lots for it, whose it shall be. And the scripture was fulfilled, which saith,	„	24

> They parted my garments among them;
> And for my vesture did they cast lots.

	30	This the soldiers did; and they sat, and	Mt. 27	36
	31	kept guard over him there. And Pilate wrote on a tablet the cause of his death, and put it on the wood of the cross above his head. And there was written thus in it: THIS IS JESUS OF NAZARETH, THE	Jn. 19	19
	32	KING OF THE JEWS. And this board read many of the Jews: for the place where Jesus was crucified was nigh to the city: and it was written in Hebrew, in Greek, and	„	20
	33	in Latin. The chief priests therefore said to Pilate, Write not, The King of the Jews; but, He who said, I am King of the Jews.	„	21
	34	Pilate said unto them, What is written, is	„	22
	35	written. And the people stood beholding. And they that passed by railed on him,	Lu. 23	35ᵃ
			Mt. 27	39
	36	wagging their heads, and saying, Oh! thou that destroyed the temple, and buildest it again in three days! save thyself, if thou art the Son of God, and come down from	{ Mt. 27	40ᵃ
			{ Mk. 15	29ᵇ
			Mt. 27	40ᵇ
	37	the cross. In like manner also the chief priests, and scribes and elders, and the Pharisees mocked him, and laughed to each	„	41
	38	other, saying, The saviour of others cannot	„	42ᵃ
	39	save himself: If he is the Messiah, the chosen of God, and the King of Israel; let him now come down from the cross, that	Lu. 23	35ᵇ
			Mt. 27	42ᵇ
	40	we may see, and believe on him. Having	„	43

	trusted in God, let him deliver him now, if he hath pleasure in him: for he said, I am	
51 41	the Son of God. And the soldiers also mocked him, coming to him, and offering	Lu. 23 36
42	him vinegar, saying unto him, If thou art	„ 37
43	the King of the Jews, save thyself. In like manner the robbers also that were crucified with him reproached him.	Mt. 27 44
44	And one of the two criminals which were crucified with him railed on him, saying, If thou art the Messiah, deliver thyself, and	Lu. 23 39
45	deliver us also. But his companion rebuked him, saying unto him, Dost not even thou fear God, seeing thou art in the same con-	„ 40
46	demnation? We indeed justly, and even as we have deserved, and according as we have done are we rewarded: but this man hath done nothing really deserving of blame.	„ 41
47	And he said unto Jesus, Lord, remember me	„ 42
48	when thou comest into thy kingdom. Jesus said unto him, Verily I say unto thee, To-day shalt thou be with me in Paradise.[1]	„ 43
49	Now there stood by the cross of Jesus his mother, and his mother's sister, Mary, who is named[2] after Cleophas, and Mary Magda-	Jn. 19 25
50	lene. And Jesus saw his mother, and the disciple, whom he loved, standing by, and said unto his mother, Woman, behold, thy	„ 26
51	son! And he saith to the disciple, Behold, thy mother! And from that hour the disciple took her unto himself.	„ 27
52	Now from the sixth hour darkness covered the whole land until the ninth hour; and	Mt. 27 45ᵃ Lu. 23 44ᵇ „ 45ᵃ
53	the sun was darkened. And at the ninth hour Jesus cried with a loud voice, saying, Jâil, Jâili,[3] why hast thou forsaken me? that	Mk. 15 34

[1] Ephraem has, "in the garden of delight." The Curetonian Syriac has, "in the garden of Eden;" and "Eden" means "delight."

[2] Or, "kinswoman of." Cf. lii. 36.

[3] Really Îl Îli, since Ja is Arabic for O.

THE DIATESSARON. 249

51	54	is, My God, my God, why hast thou forsaken me? And some of them that stood there, when they heard it, said, This man calleth Elijah.	Mt.	27	47
52	1	After these things Jesus, knowing that all things were accomplished, and that the scripture might be accomplished, said, I	Jn.	19	28
	2	thirst. Now there was set *there* a vessel full of vinegar: and in that hour one of	,,		29^a
			Mt.	27	48^a
	3	them ran, and took a sponge, and filled it with the vinegar, and fastening it to a reed, held it near his mouth to give him to drink.	Mk.[1]	15	36^b
	4	And when Jesus had received the vinegar,	Jn.	19	30^a
	5	he said, Everything is finished. But the rest said, Let *him* be; let us see whether	Mt.[2]	27	49
	6	Elijah cometh to deliver him. And Jesus said, My[3] Father, forgive them; for they	Lu.	23	34^a
	7	know not what they do. And Jesus, crying again with a loud voice, said, My Father, into thy hands I commend my spirit. This	,,		46^a
		he said; and he bowed his head, and gave up his spirit.	Jn.	19	30^b
	8	And straightway the face of the door of the temple was rent in twain from top to bottom; and the earth did quake; and the	Mt.	27	51
	9	rocks were rent; and the tombs were opened; and the bodies of many saints that slept	,,		52
	10	rose up, and went forth; and after his resurrection they entered into the holy city,	,,		53
	11	and appeared unto many. Now the centurion[4]	,,		54^a

[1] Or Matt. xxvii. 48 continued.

[2] A marginal note opposite this verse, in an eleventh century MS., No. 5647 in the British Museum, says that in the historical Gospel of Diadorus and Tatian there followed the words, "but another took a spear and pierced his side, and there came out water and blood." Cf. John xix. 34. As no such person or Gospel is known, Diadorus may be a mistake for *Diatessaron*. Cf. lii. 17.

[3] Tatian puts this saying later than S. Luke, and connects it less directly with the Roman soldiers, thus making it applicable to all His persecutors, and uttered when He had endured everything. Tatian's object may, in part, have been to group together the sayings from the cross.

[4] Omitting Mark xv. 39: "which stood over against him," and "that he so cried out, and gave up the ghost."

52	12	and they that were with him guarding Jesus, when they saw the earthquake, and the things that were done, feared exceedingly, and glorified God, saying, This man was righteous: and, Truly he was the Son	Lu. Mt.	23 27	47^b 54^b
	13	of God. And all the multitudes that were come together to the sight, when they beheld what had happened, returned smiting their breasts.¹	Lu.	23	48
	14	Now the Jews, because it was the Friday, said, Let not these bodies remain on the wood, for it is the dawn of the sabbath: for that sabbath day was a great day. They asked therefore of Pilate that they might break the legs of them that had been	Jn.	19	31
	15	crucified, and take them away. The soldiers therefore came, and brake the legs of the first, and of the other which was crucified	„		32
	16	with him: but when they came to Jesus, they saw that he was dead already; and	„		33
	17	they brake not his legs: howbeit one of the soldiers with a spear pierced his side, and straightway there came out blood and water.	„		34
	18	And he that hath seen hath borne witness, and his witness is true: and he knoweth that he saith true, that ye also may believe.	„		35
	19	These things came to pass that the scripture might be fulfilled, which saith, A bone shall	„		36
	20	not be broken in him: and also the scripture which saith, They shall look on him whom they pierced.	„		37
	21	And all the acquaintance of Jesus stood afar off, and the women that had come with	Lu.	23	49^a

---

¹ Ephraem here has, "Woe was it, woe was it to us: this was the Son of God!"

The Curetonian Syriac here adds, "and saying, Woe to us, what is this! Woe to us for our sins!" One Latin Codex has a similar reading. A very interesting discussion of the original form of this passage in the *Diatessaron* will be found in Mr. Rendel Harris's Essay, pp. 34, 35. Cf. also Professor Robinson, *The Gospel according to Peter*, pp. 22, 23.

	him from Galilee, who were those who were	Mk. 15 41ᵇ
52 22	following him, and ministering unto him : of	Mt. 27 56ᵃ
	whom one was Mary Magdalene, and Mary	Mk. 15 40ᵇ
	the mother of James the less and of Joses,	
	and the mother of the sons of Zebedee,	Mt. 27 56ᶜ
23	and Salome, and many other women which	{ Mk. 15 40ᶜ
	had come up with him unto Jerusalem;	„ 41ᶜ
	and they saw these things.	Lu. 23 49ᵇ
24	And when the evening of the Friday was	Mk. 15 42
	come, on account of the entrance of the	
25	sabbath, there came a man named Joseph,	Lu. 23 50
	rich *and* a councillor, of Arimathaea, a city	
	of Judaea, who was a good man and upright,	
	and a disciple of Jesus, who concealed him-	Jn. 19 38ᵇ
26	self, being afraid of the Jews; but he had	Lu. 23 51
	not consented to the counsel and deeds of	
	the accusers, and was looking for the kingdom	
27	of God. This man then came, and went in	Mk. 15 43ᵇ
	unto Pilate, and requested of him the body	
28	of Jesus. And Pilate marvelled how he	„ 44
	had already died. And calling unto him the	
	centurion, he asked him about his death	
29	before the *usual* time. And when he had	„ 45ᵃ
	learned it, he commanded him to deliver up	Mt. 27 58ᵇ
30	his body to Joseph. And Joseph bought a	Mk. 15 46ᵃ
	clean linen cloth, and took down the body	
	of Jesus, and wound him in it. They came	Jn. 19 38ᵈ
31	therefore, and took it away. And there	„ 39
	came unto him also Nicodemus, who had	
	before come to Jesus by night, bringing with	
	him a mixture of myrrh and aloe, about a	
32	hundred pounds. So they took the body of	„ 40
	Jesus, and wrapped it in linen cloths and	
	spices, as the custom of the Jews is to bury.	
33	Now in the place where Jesus was crucified	„ 41
	there was a garden; and in the garden a	
	new tomb hewn out in the rock, wherein no	
34	man had ever yet been laid. There then,	„ 42
	because the sabbath had entered in, and	
	because the tomb was nigh at hand, they	

52 35	left Jesus: and they rolled a great stone, and thrust it to the door of the tomb, and	Mt. 27 60ᵇ
36	departed. And Mary Magdalene and Mary named¹ after Joses came after them unto	Mk. 15 47ᵃ
37²	the tomb, and sat down over against the tomb, and saw how they brought in and	Lu. 23 55ᵇ
38	placed the body there. And they returned, and bought spices and ointments, and turned back that they might come and anoint it.	„ 56ᵃ Mk. 16 1ᵇ
39	But on the day which was the day of the sabbath, they left off because of the commandment.	Lu. 23 56ᵇ
40	Now the chief priests and the Pharisees	Mt. 27 62ᵇ
41	came together unto Pilate, and said unto him, Sir, we remember that that misleader said, while he was yet alive, After three	„ 63
42	days I will rise again. And now be beforehand in guarding the sepulchre until three days, lest haply his disciples come and steal him by night, and they will say unto the people, He is risen from the dead: and the last error will be worse than the former.	„ 64
43	He said unto them, Have ye not a guard? go your way, guard it as ye know *how*.	„ 65
44	And they went, and made the sepulchre sure, and sealed the stone, together with the guards.	„ 66
45	Now on the evening of the sabbath which is the dawn of the first *day*, at very early	„ 28 1ᵃ Lu. 24 1ᵇ
46	dawn, behind the rest came Mary Magdalene and the other Mary and the other women to see the sepulchre, carrying with them the	Mt. 28 1ᵇ Lu. 24 1ᶜ
47	spices which they had prepared. And they said among themselves, Who shall remove for us the stone from the door of the tomb?	Mk. 16 3
48	for it was exceeding great. And when they said so, a great earthquake took place; and	{ Mk. 16 4ᵇ { Mt. 28 2ᵃ

¹ Or, "kinswoman of." Cf. li. 49.

² The second leaf missing from the Vatican MS. seems to have extended from this verse to liii. 4 inclusive, this passage being obtained from the Borgian MS. only.

		an angel descended from heaven, and came and rolled away the stone from the door.		
52	49	And they came and found the stone removed from the tomb, and the angel sitting upon	Lu. 24 Mt. 28	2 2^b
	50	the stone. And his appearance was as lightning, and his raiment white as snow:	„	3
	51	and for fear of him the guards were terrified,	„	4
	52	and became as dead men. And when he was gone away, the women entered the tomb,	Lu. 24	3
	53	and found not the body of Jesus: but they saw there a young man sitting on the right side,, arrayed in a white robe; and they	Mk. 16	5^b
	54	were amazed. And the angel answered, and said unto the women, Fear not ye: for I know that ye seek Jesus of Nazareth, which	Mt. 28	5
	55	hath been crucified. He is not here; for he is risen, even as he said. Come and see	„	6
53	[1] 1	the place where our Lord was laid. And while they were perplexed thereabout, behold, two men stood above them in dazzling	Lu. 24	4
	2	apparel; and as they were seized with terror, and bowed down their faces to the earth, they said unto them, Why seek ye the living	„	5
	3	*one* among the dead? He is not here; he is risen: remember what he spake unto you	„	6
	4	when he was yet in Galilee, saying, The Son of man is going to be delivered up into the hands of sinners, and to be crucified, and to	„	7
	5	rise again the third day. But[2] go quickly, and tell his disciples and Cephas, that he is risen from the dead; and lo, he goeth before	Mt. 28	7^a
	6	you into Galilee; and there shall ye see him, where he said unto you; lo, I have	Mk. 16 Mt. 28	7^b 7^c
	7	told you. And they remembered his words;	Lu. 24	8

[1] The marks of division for this new chapter are omitted from the Borgian MS., whilst the passage is absent from the Vatican MS.

[2] In S. Matthew these words are a continuation of lii. 55, and spoken by an "angel," called by S. Mark a "young man;" but here they are spoken by "two men." Cf. liii. 1. Modern harmonisers have felt the same difficulty as Tatian did.

		and they departed quickly from the tomb with joy and great fear, and hastened and	Mt. 28	8
53	8	went their way running; for perplexity and quaking had come upon them: and they said nothing to any one; for they were	Mk. 16	8ᵇ
	9	afraid. But Mary ran, and came to Simon Cephas, and to that other disciple, whom Jesus loved, and said unto them, They have taken away our Lord out of the tomb, and I	Jn. 20	2
	10	know not where they have laid him. Simon therefore went forth and that other disciple,	„	3
	11	and they came to the tomb. And they ran both together: and that disciple hastened and got before Simon, and came first to the	„	4
	12	tomb; and looking[1] in, he saw the linen	„	5
	13	cloths laid; yet entered he not in. After him came Simon, and he entered into the	„	6
	14	tomb; and saw the linen cloths laid, and the napkin, that had been wrapped about his head, was not with the linen cloth, but rolled up and laid on the opposite side in a	„	7
	15	certain place. Then entered in that disciple, which had come first to the tomb, and he	„	8
	16	saw, and believed. For as yet they knew not from the scriptures, that the Messiah was going to rise again from the dead.	„	9
	17	And those two disciples went away unto their own place.	„	10
	18	But Mary was standing near the tomb weeping: so, as she wept, she looked for-	„	11
	19	ward[2] into the tomb; and she saw two angels in white sitting, one on the side of his cushion, and the other on the side of his feet, where the body of Jesus had been laid.	„	12
	20	And they said unto her, Woman, why weepest thou? She said unto them, They have carried away my Lord, and I know not	„	13

[1] Omitting "stooping down;" according to Tatian no stooping was necessary; cf. ver. 18.

[2] No stooping, cf. ver. 12.

53 21 where they have laid him. While saying Jn. 20 14
these *words*, she turned herself back, and
saw Jesus standing, and knew not that it
22 was Jesus. Jesus said unto her, Woman, „ 15
why weepest thou? whom seekest thou?
And she, supposing him to be the gardener,
said, Sir, if thou hast taken him, tell me
where thou hast laid him, that I may go,
23 and take him away. Jesus said unto her, „ 16
Mary. And she turned herself, and said
unto him in Hebrew, Rabboni, which is
24 interpreted The Teacher. Jesus said unto „ 17
her, Touch me not; for I am not yet ascended
to my Father: go unto my brethren, and
say unto them, I ascend unto my Father
and your Father, my God and your God.
25 And on the first day, *the day* whereon he Mk. 16 9
rose, he appeared first to Mary Magdalene,
from whom he had cast out seven devils.
26 And some of the guards[1] came into the Mt. 28 11[b]
city, and told unto the chief priests all the
27 things that had happened. And when they „ 12
were assembled with the elders, and had
taken counsel, they gave no little money
28 unto the guards, saying unto them, Say ye, „ 13
His disciples came by night, and stole him
29 away, while we slept. And if the governor „ 14
hear this, we will answer with him, and
30 make you safe from blame. And when they „ 15
had taken the money, they did as they had
taught them: and this saying was spread
abroad among the Jews, *and continueth* until
this day.
31 And then came Mary Magdalene, and told Jn. 20 18

---

[1] The guards would naturally go to report at the same time as the women. It is therefore, *historically*, a matter of indifference which fact is related first. But it was convenient to Tatian to group the appearance of the Saviour to the women on their way with a series of His other appearances not reported by S. Matthew. To do this he naturally related the proceedings of the guard first.

the disciples, that she had seen our Lord; and that he had said these things unto her.

53 32 And as those women were going on the Mt. 28 8^b
33 way to tell the disciples, Jesus met them, „ 9
saying, All hail! And they came, and took
34 hold of his feet, and worshipped him. Then „ 10
said Jesus unto them, Fear not: but go, tell
my brethren to go into Galilee, and there
35 shall they see me. And those women re- Lu. 24 9
turned, and told all these things to the
eleven, and to the rest of the disciples, and Mk. 16 10^b
to them that had been with him; for they
36 were sad and weeping. And they were Lu. 24 10
Mary Magdalene, and Joanna, and Mary the
mother of James, and the rest of those that
were with them: and these were they that
37 spake unto the apostles. And they, when Mk. 16 11
they had heard them saying that he was
alive, and had appeared unto them, believed
38 not. And these words were in their eyes as Lu. 24 11^a
the words of madness.
39 After these things he was manifested unto Mk. 16 12^a
two of them on that very day, and as they Lu. 24 13^b
were going to a village named Emmaus,
which was at a distance of threescore fur-
40 longs from Jerusalem, and were talking with „ 14
each other of all these things which had
41 happened. For while they communed and „ 15
questioned together, Jesus came, and arrived
even unto them, and walked with them.
42 But their eyes were holden, that they should „ 16
43 not recognise him. And he said unto them, „ 17
What communications are these that ye
address one to another, as ye walk, and
44 are sad? One of them, whose name was „ 18
Cleophas, answered, and said unto him, Art
thou alone a stranger to Jerusalem, since
thou hast not known the things which are
45 come to pass in it in these days? He said „ 19
unto them, What hath happened? They

said unto him, Concerning that Jesus who was from Nazareth, which was a prophet, and mighty in speech and deeds before God		
53 46 and all the people, whom the chief priests and elders delivered up for condemnation to	Lu.	24 20
47 death, and crucified him. But we thought that he was going to deliver Israel. And all these things came to pass three days ago.	„	21
48 Yet certain women also of our company told	„	22
49 us, that they had gone to the tomb; and when they found not his body, they came, and said, that they had seen angels there,	„	23
50 which said of him, that he was alive. And certain also of our company went to the tomb, and found it even so, as the women said, except that they did not see him.	„	24
51 Then said Jesus unto them, O destitute of understanding, and of a heavy heart to	„	25
52 believe! Was[1] it not in all the sayings of the prophets that the Messiah must suffer these things, and enter into his glory?	„	26
53 And beginning from Moses and all the prophets, he interpreted concerning himself	„	27
54 to them out of all the scriptures. And they drew nigh unto the village, whither they were going: and he made them suppose that he was about to go into a more distant	„	28
55 neighbourhood. And they constrained him, saying unto him, Abide with us: for the day hath already declined towards darkness.	„	29
56 And he went in to stay with them. And when he reclined with them *to meat*, he took bread, and blessed it, and brake, and gave to	„	30
57 them. And straightway their eyes were opened, and they recognised him; and he	„	31
58 vanished from them. And they said one to another, Was not our heart heavy within us, while he conversed with us in the way, and	„	32

[1] The change of reading makes it difficult to end the verse at the usual place.

53	59 interpreted to us the scriptures? And they rose up the same hour, and returned to Jerusalem, and found the eleven gathered together, and them that were with them;	Lu.	24 33
	60 and they said, the Lord is really risen, and	,,	34
	61 hath appeared to Simon. But they rehearsed the things that had been done in the way, and how they recognised him, when he brake the bread; neither believed they these things.	,, Mk. 16 13ᵇ	35
54	1 And whilst they were talking, and the evening of that day was come, which was the first day, and the doors were shut where the disciples were, for fear of the Jews, Jesus came and stood in the midst of them, and	{ Lu. 24 36ᵃ { Jn. 20 19	
	2 said unto them, Peace be with you; it is I, be not afraid. And they were disquieted and affrighted, and supposed that they saw	Lu.¹ ,,	24 36ᵇ 37
	3 a spirit. Jesus said unto them, Why are ye troubled? and why do reasonings arise into	,,	38
	4 your hearts? See my hands and my feet, that it is I myself: feel me, and know that a spirit hath not flesh and bones, as ye see	,,	39
	5 me have. And when he had said this, he shewed them his hands and feet and side.²	,,	40
	6 And while they still disbelieved for joy and astonishment, he said, Have ye here anything	,,	41
	7 to eat? And they gave him a piece of a broiled fish and honey. And he took it, and did eat before them.	,, ,,³	42 43
	8 And he said unto them, These are the words which I spake unto you, when I was with you, how that all things must needs be fulfilled, which are written in the law of Moses, and the prophets, and the psalms,	,,	44
	9 concerning me. Then opened he their mind, that they might understand the scriptures;	,,	45

---

[1] The words, "it is I, be not afraid," are a part of this verse in several MSS including the Peschito and the Harclean, but not the Curetonian, Syriac.

[2] Cf. John xx. 20.

[3] This is the whole of our ver. 43; but the Vulgate has more in the verse.

54 10	and he said unto them, Thus it is written,	Lu. 24	46
	and thus it behoved the Messiah to suffer,		
	and to rise again from the dead the third		
11	day; and that repentance unto remission of	„	47
	sins should be preached in his name unto		
	all the nations: but the beginning shall be		
12	from Jerusalem. And ye shall be¹ witnesses	„	48
	of this. And I will send forth the promise	„	49ᵃ
13	of my Father unto you. The disciples, when	Jn. 20	20ᵇ
14	they heard this, were glad. And Jesus said	„²	21
	unto them again, Peace be with you: as the		
	Father hath sent me, I also send you.		
15	When he had said this, he breathed on	„	22
	them, and said unto them, Receive ye the		
16	Holy Spirit: if ye forgive any one's sins,	„	23
	they shall be forgiven him; if ye retain		
	any one's *sins*, they shall be retained.		
17	But Thauma, one of the twelve, who is	„	24
	called Thoma,³ was not there with the		
18	disciples, when Jesus came. The disciples	„	25
	therefore said unto him, We have seen our		
	Lord. He said unto them, Except I see in		
	his hands the prints of the nails, and put		
	my fingers upon them, and thrust my hand		
	into his side, I will not believe.		
19	And after eight days, on the next first *day*,	„	26
	again the disciples were assembled within,		
	and Thauma with them. And Jesus came,		
	the doors being shut, and stood in the midst,		
	and said unto them, Peace be with you.		
20	And he said to Thauma, Reach hither thy	„	27
	finger, and see my hands;⁴ and put forth		
	thy hand, and spread it upon my side: and		

¹ Or, "are." ² Part of this verse is repeated in lv. 5.

³ Cf. xxxvii. 61 n. for the Arabic forms: these have no meaning in Arabic; but they are transliterations of the regular Syriac words for "Thomas" and "Twin," *i.e.* Didymus.

⁴ There is no mention of nails in the *feet* either here or in S. John. Ephraem distinctly implies in his remarks (Moes. p. 248) that the hands only were pierced by nails. And in *The Gospel according to Peter*, in describing the removal of our Lord from the cross, it says, "they drew out the nails from the hands."

54 21	be not faithless, but believing. Thauma answered, and said unto him, My Lord, and	Jn. 20 28
22	my God. Jesus said unto him, Now because thou hast seen me, thou hast believed: blessed *are* they that have not seen, and *yet* have believed.	„ 29
23	And many other signs did Jesus in the sight of his disciples, which are not written	„ 30
24	in this book: but these are both written, that ye may believe on Jesus, the Messiah, the Son of God; and that believing ye may have eternal life in his name.	„ 31
25	And after these things Jesus shewed himself again to his disciples at the sea of Tiberias; and he manifested himself to them	„ 21 1
26	on this wise. There were together Simon Cephas, and Thauma, who is called Thoma, and Nathanael, who was of Cana of Galilee, and the sons of Zebedee, and two others of	„ 2
27	his disciples. Simon Cephas said unto them, I go to catch fishes. They said unto him, We also come with thee. And they went forth, and went up into the boat; and that	„ 3
28	night they caught nothing. But when morning came, Jesus stood on the seashore: but the disciples knew not that it was	„ 4
29	Jesus. Jesus therefore said unto them, Children, have ye anything to eat? They	„ 5
30	said unto him, No. He said unto them, Cast your net on the right side of the ship, and ye shall find. They cast therefore; and they were unable to draw the net for the multitude of fishes, that were come into	„ 6
31	it. And that disciple, whom Jesus loved, said unto Cephas, This is our Lord. And Simon, when he heard that it was our Lord, took up his coat, and girded it up to his loins (for he was naked), and cast himself into the sea, that he might come to Jesus.	„ 7
32	But the other disciples came in the ship	„ 8

			Jn. 21	
54	33	(for they were not far from land, but about two hundred cubits off), dragging the net *full* of fishes. And when they went up unto the land, they saw live coals laid, and		9
	34	a fish laid thereon, and bread. Jesus said unto them, Bring of these fish, which ye	„	10
	35	have now caught. Simon Cephas therefore went up, and drew the net to land, full of great fishes, a hundred and fifty and three: and with so great a weight, the net was not	„	11
	36	rent. Jesus said unto them, Come, *and* sit down. And no one of the disciples dared to ask, who he was, knowing that it was our Lord: yet he did not appear unto them in	„	12
	37	his own form.[1] And Jesus came and took the bread and the fish, and gave unto them.	„	13
	38	This is the third time that Jesus was manifested to his disciples, since he had risen from the dead.	„	14
	39	So when they had broken their fast, Jesus said to Simon Cephas, Simon, son of Jonah, lovest[2] thou me more than these? He said unto him, Yea, Lord; thou knowest that I love thee. Jesus said unto him, Feed	„	15
	40	my lambs for me. He said to him also again, Simon, son of Jonah, lovest thou me? He said unto him, Yea, Lord; thou knowest that I love thee. He said unto him, Feed	„	16
	41	my rams for me. He said unto him also the third time, Simon, son of Jonah, lovest thou me? And Cephas, being grieved because he said three times, Lovest thou me? said unto him, Lord, thou knowest[3] all things; thou knowest that I love thee.	„	17

[1] Tatian seems to have based this addition upon Mark xvi. 12, "in another form." Cf. xxiv. 3.

[2] In the Arabic no distinction is drawn throughout this passage corresponding to the ἀγαπᾶν and φιλεῖν of the Greek.

[3] Or, "recognisest;" a different Arabic word from that rendered "knowest" in other parts of this narrative.

54	42	Jesus said unto him, Feed my sheep for me. Verily, verily, I say unto thee, When thou wast young, thou girdedst thyself, and walkedst whither thou wouldest: but when thou art old, thou shalt stretch forth thy hands, and another shall gird thee, and	Jn. 21	18
	43	bring thee whither thou willest not. This he said unto him to signify by what manner of death he was going to glorify God. And when he had spoken this, he saith unto him,	„	19
	44	Come after me. But Simon Cephas, turning about, saw the disciple whom Jesus loved following him—that one which leaned back on the breast of Jesus at the supper, and said, Lord, who is he that shall betray thee?	„	20
	45	When therefore Cephas had seen him, he said to Jesus, Lord, and this man, what	„	21
	46	shall be concerning him? Jesus said unto him, If I will that he tarry till I come,	„	22
	47	what *is that* to thee? follow thou me. And this saying was spread abroad among the brethren, That disciple will not die: and Jesus said not, that he should not die; but, If I will that he tarry till I come, what *is that* to thee?	„	23
	48	This is that disciple which beareth witness of these things, and wrote them: and we know that his witness is true.	„	24
55	1	But the eleven disciples went into Galilee, unto the mountain where Jesus had appointed	Mt. 28	16
	2	them. And when they saw him, they worshipped *him*: but some of them doubted.	„	17
	3	And as they sat there, he appeared again unto them, and upbraided them with their lack of faith and hardness of heart, because they believed not them, which had seen that	Mk. 16	14
	4	he was risen again. Then saith Jesus unto them, All authority hath been given unto	Mt. 28	18[b]
	5	me in heaven and on earth: for even as my	Jn.[1] 20	21[b]

[1] Repeated from liv. 14.

55	Father sent me, so I also send you. Go ye therefore into all the world, and preach my 6 gospel to every creature; and teach all the nations, and baptize them in the name of the Father and of the Son and of the Holy 7 Spirit: teaching them to observe all things that I commanded you: and lo, I am with you all the days unto the end of the world. 8 For he that believeth and is baptized shall be saved; but he that disbelieveth shall be 9 condemned. And these signs shall follow them that have believed on me: in my name shall they cast out devils; and they 10 shall speak with new tongues; they shall take up serpents; and if they drink a deadly poison, it shall not hurt them; they shall lay hands on the sick, and they shall recover. 11 But tarry ye in the city of Jerusalem, until ye be endued with power from on high. 12 And our Lord Jesus, after he had spoken unto them, led them out unto Bethany: and he lifted up his hands, and blessed them. 13 And while he blessed them, he was separated from them, and ascended into heaven, and 14 sat down at the right hand of God. And they worshipped him, and returned to Jeru- 15 salem with great joy; and they were continually in the temple, praising and blessing God. Amen. 16 And they went forth from thence,[1] and preached everywhere, the Lord helping them, and confirming their sayings with the signs which they did. 17 And there are also many other things which Jesus did, the which if they should be written one by one, according to my opinion even the world itself would not contain the books that must be written.			

Mk. 16 15^b
Mt. 28 19^b
„ 20
Mk. 16 16
„ 17
„ 18
Lu. 24 49^b
Mk. 16 19^a
Lu. 24 50
„ 51
Mk. 16 19^c
Lu. 24 52
„ 53
Mk. 16 20
Jn. 21 25

---

[1] "From thence" is added in connection with "Jerusalem," which was mentioned in ver. 14.

CONCLUDING NOTE IN THE BORGIAN MS.

The Gospel is concluded, which Tatian compiled out of the four Gospels of the four holy apostles the blessed evangelists, on whom be peace, and which he named *Diatessaron*, that is, That which is composed of four. The excellent and learned presbyter, Abû-l-Faraj Abdullah Ibn-aṭ-Ṭayyib, with whom may God be pleased, translated it from Syriac into Arabic, from a copy written by the hand of Gubasi ibn Alî Al-mutayyib, a disciple of Ḥunain ibn Isḥaḵ, on both of whom may God have mercy. Amen.

APPENDICES.

I.

Note.—Brackets in the Column, "Portions of the Gospels," imply that the portions bracketed are not given all in full, but are harmonised together.

Portions of the Diatessaron.	Portions of the Gospels.		Contents of the Diatessaron in order.	Order in the Diatessaron as obtained from other sources.			Order of Modern Harmonists.		
				Zahn's Reconstruction.	Ephraem's Commentary.	Codex Fuldensis.	Greswell.	Stroud.	Tischendorf.
				Section.	Chapter.	Chapter.	Part. Sec.	Page.	Section.
1 1–5	Jn.	1 1–5	Introduction about the Word,	1	1	1	iii. 1	25	1
6–26	Lu.	1 5–25	Zacharias and Elizabeth,	2	1	2	i. 1, 2, 3	3	4
27–39	,,	26–38	The Annunciation,	2	1	3	4	4	5
40–57	,,	39–56	Visit of Mary to Elizabeth,	2	1	3	5, 6	5	6
58–67	,,	57–66	Birth and Circumcision of S. John the Baptist,	2	1	4	7	6	7
68–81	,,	67–80	Song of Zacharias,	2	1	4	7, 9	6	7
2 1–8	Mt.	1 18–25*	Birth of Jesus,	3	2	5	8	8	8
9–15	Lu.	2 1–7	He is laid in a manger,	4	2	5	10	8	9
16–28	,,	8–20	Visit of the Shepherds,	4	2	6	10	9	9
29–46	,,	21–38	Circumcision of Jesus, and Presentation in the Temple,	4	2	7	12	9	9, 10
47	,,	39	Return to Galilee,	Omitted.	—	7	15	10	12
3 1–12	Mt.	2 1–12	Visit of the Wise Men,	5	2	8	13	11	11
13–18	,,	13–18	Flight into Egypt, and murder of the Innocents,	5	2, 3	9, 10	11	11	11
19–23	,,	19–23	Return to Nazareth,	5	3	11	15	12	12
24–36	Lu.	2 40–52	Jesus in the Temple with the Doctors,	7	3	12	16	13	13
37–45	{ Mt. 3 1–3 / Mk. 1 1–4 / Lu. 1–6 }		Commencement of the Ministry of John,	8	3	13	ii. 2	11	14
46–56	Jn.	1 7–17	Testimony of John to Jesus,	6	3	13	1	25	1
4 1–11	,,	18–28	Further testimony of John in reply to Jews,	6	3	13	8	25	18
12–27	{ Mt. 3 4–12 / Mk. 1 5–8 / Lu. 7–18 }		The preaching of John,	9	3	13	2–4	15	14, 15

I. COMPARATIVE TABLE OF CONTENTS.

§	Refs.	Event						
4 28–42	Mt. 3 13–17 Mk. 1 9–11 Lu. 3 21–23* Jn. 1 29–34	Baptism of Jesus,	9	4	11	ii. 6, 9	19, 26	16
43–52	Mt. 4 1–11 Lu. 4 1–13	Temptation of Jesus,	10	4	15	7	20	17
5 1 3	"	Temptation concluded,	10	4	15	7	22	17
4–20	Jn. 1 35–51 Lu. 4 14*	Call of Andrew, Simon, Philip, and Nathanael,	11	4	16, 17	9, 10	26	19, 20
21–32	Jn. 2 1–11	First miracle at Cana of Galilee,	12	5	46	10	27	21
33–41	Lu. 4 14b–22a	Jesus teaches in the synagogue at Nazareth,	32	—	17, 18	17	36	29
42–48	Mt. 4 17–22 Mk. 1 14–20	Call of Andrew, Simon, James, and John,	Omitted.	—	19	19	38	31
49–55	Lu. 5 1–7	Jesus teaches from a boat, miraculous draught of fishes,	14	5	19	24	41	31
6 1–4	"	Effect of miraculous draught on Simon,	14	5	19	24	41	31
5–22	Jn. 3 22–4 3*	Jesus and John baptize in Judaea. John speaks of Jesus,	13	5	21	13–15	30	24
23–24	Lu. 3 19–20	Herod imprisons John on account of Herodias,	Omitted.	—	80	5	18	25
25–35	Jn. 4 46–54	At Cana Jesus heals a king's servant's son,	Omitted.	—	56	16	32	27
36–45	Mt. 4 13–16 Mk. 1 21–28 Lu. 4 31–37	Residence at Capernaum; an unclean spirit cast out in the synagogue,	13	—	22	20	38, 40	32
46–54	Mt. 8 14–17 Mk. 1 29–34 Lu. 4 38–41	Matthew called; Simon's mother-in-law and others cured,	Omitted.	—	20, 49, 51	27, 21	49, 41	37, 33
7 1–10	Mt. 4 35 Mk. 1 35–39 Lu. 4 42–44	Circuit of Galilee; multitudes healed; Levi called,	Omitted.	—	23	ii. 27 iii. 25	43, 49	34
11–24	Mt. 9 2–8 Mk. 2 1–12 Lu. 5 17–26	A paralytic healed at Capernaum; forgiving sins,	14	5	55	ii. 27	46	36
25–36	Mt. 9 9–17 Mk. 2 13–22 Lu. 5 27–39	Levi's feast; fasting; parables of New Cloth and New Wine,	14	5	57	28	49	37

APPENDIX.

Portions of the Diatessaron.	Portions of the Gospels.	Contents of the Diatessaron in order.	Zahn's Reconstruction.	Ephraem's Commentary.	Codex Fuldensis.	Greswell. (Part. Sec.)	Stroud. (Page.)	Tischendorf. (Section.)
7 37-46	Mt. 12 1-8; Mk. 2 23-28; Lu. 6 1-5; Mt. 12 9-21; Mk. 3 1-6; Lu. 6 6-11	In the cornfields,	15	5	69	Part. iii. 2	52	38
47-53		A man with a withered hand healed on the Sabbath,	Omitted.	—	70	3	54	39
8 1-25	Mk. 3 7-19ᵃ; Lu. 6 12-20ᵃ	Near the lake; many healed; the Twelve chosen,	16	6	23	4, 5 {ii. 23, iii. 5}	55, 58	40
26-39	Mt. 5 1-32	Sermon on the Mount:—Beatitudes and Woes,	16	6	23, 24	,,	60	41
40-49	Mk. 4 21-23	Salt; the Light of the World; Jesus came to fulfil the Law,	17	6	25, 26	,,	61	41
50-56	Lu. 6 20ᵇ 16-18	Offences against a brother and reconciliation,	17	6	27, 28	,,	62	41
57-62	,, 12 58-59	Offences of the eye and hand; divorce,	17	6	29, 30	,,	62	41
9 1-5	Mt. 5 33-6 23	Sermon on the Mount contd.:—Swear not,	17	6	31	,,	62	41
6-21	Lu. 6 27-36	Resist not evil; Love your enemies,	17	6	32, 33	,,	63	41
22-41	,, 11 1-4	Almsgiving; Prayer; Fasting,	18	6	34, 35, 36	,,	64	41
42-50	,, 12 34-36 32-34	Treasure in heaven; Light in the body,	18	6	37	,,	65	41
10 1-12	Mt. 6 24-7 27	Sermon on the Mount contd.:—Anxiety for bodily wants,	18	6	38, 39	,,	66	41
13-20	Mk. 4 24-25	Judge not; blind leading blind,	19	6	40	,,	66	41
21-33	Lu. 6 37-49	Good gifts and importunity; the narrow way,	19	6	41	,,	67, 221	41, 39
34-48	,, 11 5-13; ,, 12 22-31	False prophets known by their fruits; building on the rock,	19	6	42, 43, 44	,,	68	41
11 1-16	Mt. 7 28-8 1; ,, 8 5-13; Lu. 7 1-10	Officer's servant healed at Capernaum,	20	6	45	iii. 6	71	42

I. COMPARATIVE TABLE OF CONTENTS.

11 17–23	Ln. 7 11–17	Raising of the widow's son at Nain,	21	6	50	iii. 7	80	43
24–30	Mt. 8 18–22 / Ln. 9 57–62	A scribe and others offer to follow Jesus,	22	6	52	iii. 20 / iv. 25	95, 183	78
31–38	Mt. 8 23–9 1	A storm on the lake going to Galara,	22	6	53	iii. 20	95	51
39–52	Mk. 4 35–5 21 / Ln. 8 22–40	The Gadarene demoniac cured.	22	6	54	20	97	52
12 1–6	Mt. 9 18–26	Return of Jesus across the Lake,	22	6	54	20, 21	101	52
7–32	Mk. 5 22–43 / Ln. 8 41–56	Jairus's daughter; the woman with an issue of blood,	23	7	61	22	102	53
33–37	Mt. 9 27–31	Two blind men healed,	23		62	23	107	90
38–41	Mt. 9 32–33 / „ 10 1–11 1 / „ 35–36	Dumb demoniac cured. Circuit of Galilee,	Omitted.		62	23, 25	107, 109	91, 55
42–55	Mk. 6 7–11 / Ln. 9 1–5 / „ 3–9 / „ 12 51–53	The Twelve disciples instructed for their mission,	21	8	45	26	110	56
13 1–29	Ln. 10 38–42	Further instructions to the Twelve,	24	8	45	26	112	56
30–35	Mk. 6 12–13	Mary chooses the good part,	25	8	64	28	210	88
36–37	Ln. 9 6	The apostles go forth and preach and perform cures,	24		45	iii. 26	113	56
38–47	Mt. 11 2–15 / Ln. 7 18–30	John sends two of his disciples to Jesus,	26	9	65	8, 9	80	44
14 1–9	„ & 16 16–17	John in relation to the Law and the Prophets,	26, 17	9	65	iii. 9 / iv. 43	82, 195	44, 105
10–15	Mt. 11 16–19 / Mk. 3 19ᵇ–20	John and Jesus differed in manners,	26	9	65	iii. 9	82	44
16–31	Ln. 7 31–35 / Mt. 12 24–37 / Mk. 3 22–30	Jesus casts out a demon; the Pharisees say by Beelzebub,	27	10	63	iii. 13 / iv. 30	73	47
32–36	Ln. 11 14–23	A tree known by its fruits; their words betray and condemn them,	27	10	63	iii. 13 / iv. 30	76	47
37–40	Mt. 16 2ᵇ–3 / Ln. 12 54–57	They did not discern the signs of the times,	Omitted		Omitted.	iv. 5, 32	131, 141	95
41–42	Mt. 12 22–23	A dumb and blind demoniac cured,	27	10	Omitted.	iii. 13	73	47

APPENDIX.

Portions of the Diatessaron.	Portions of the Gospels.	Contents of the Diatessaron in order.	Order in the Diatessaron as obtained from other sources.			Order of Modern Harmonists.		
			Zahn's Reconstruction.	Ephraem's Commentary.	Codex Fuldensis.	Greswell.	Stroud.	Tischendorf.
			Section.	Chapter.	Chapter.	Part. Sec.	Page.	Section.
14 43-44 45-48	Mk. 6 30-31 Lu. 9 10-11 ,, 7 36-50	Return of the Twelve, . At a Pharisee's house a woman washes Christ's feet, .	34 28	— 10	67 139	iii. 28 10	117 84	59 45
15 1-11 12-14 15-26	Jn. 2 23-25 Lu. 10 1-12	Her sins are forgiven; parable of two debtors, Many believe; but Jesus does not trust them, Mission of the Seventy, and instructions to them, .	28 Omitted. 29, 24	10 — 10, 8	139 Omitted. 68	10 ii. 12 iv. 26 iii. 9 iv. 26	81 28 183	45 22 85
27-32	Mt. 11 20-24 Lu. 10 13-16	Jesus upbraids Bethsaida and Capernaum, .	Omitted.	—	66	iii. 9 iv. 26	83, 181	85
33-38	Mt. 11 25-27 Lu. 10 17-22	Return of the Seventy, and the address to them, .	29	10	68	iv. 26	184	86
39-50	Mt. 11 28-30 Lu. 14 25-33 Mt. 10 34-39	"Come unto me"—but count the cost first, .	29	10	68	iii. 9 iv. 40	84, 192	86, 103
16 1-6 7-12	,, 12 38-45 Lu. 11 24-32	Sign demanded; Jonah; Queen of the South; Ninevites, . Return of the unclean spirit; blessed is the womb, .	30 30	11 11	58 58, 59	iii. 14 iv. 30 iii. 11 iv. 30	78 76	91 91
13-18	Mt. 12 46-50 Mk. 3 31-35 Lu. 8 19-21	The mother and brethren of Jesus, .	30	11	60	iii. 15, 19	77	48
19-21	Lu. 8 1-3	Circuit of Galilee; women minister unto him,	31	11	Omitted.	11	85	46
22-30	Mt. 13 1-23 Mk. 4 1-20 Lu. 8 4-15	The parable of the Sower, .	31	11	71, 72	16	85	49

I. COMPARATIVE TABLE OF CONTENTS.

16 31-40	"		31	11	75	iii. 17, 18	87	49
41-48	"		31	11	76	18	88	49
49-52	Mk. 4 26-29	Christ's reasons for speaking in parables, Explanation of the parable of the Sower, Parable of the Seed growing secretly,	31	11	77	17	91	50
17 1-18	Mt. 13 24-35, Mk. 4 30-34, Lu. 13 18-21, Mt. 13 36-43	Parables of the Tares, Mustard Seed, and Leaven,	31	11	73-75	17	91	50
19-26		Explanation of the parable of the Tares,	31	11	77	18	93	50
27-36	" 44-53	Parables of the Hid Treasure, Pearl, and Draw-net,	31	11	78	18	93	50
37-53	Mt. 13 54-58, Mk. 6 1-6, Lu. 4 16-30	Jesus visits Nazareth; opinions of him; attempt to throw him down,	32	11	79	{iii. 24, ii. 17}	108, 37	54, 29
18 1-20	Mt. 14 1-12, Mk. 6 14-29, Lu. 9 7-9	Herod hears reports of Jesus; how he put John to death,	33	11	80	iii. 27	114	58, 57
21-43	Mt. 14 13-21, Mk. 6 32-44, Lu. 9 12-17, Jn. 6 1-15	Jesus crosses the Lake, and feeds 5000 men,	34	12	80, 81	28	117	59
44-50	Mt. 14 22-24, Mk. 6 45-47, Jn. 6 16-18	Jesus sends the disciples to Bethsaida; remains to pray; storm,	34	12	81, 82	29	122	60
19 1-13	Mt. 14 25-33, Mk. 6 48-53, Jn. 6 19-21	Jesus walks on the water; and Simon also,	34	12	82	29	123	60
14-15	Mt. 14 34-36, Mk. 6 54-56	The sick brought and healed,	Omitted.	—	83	30	124	61
16-54	Jn. 6 22-60	Those fed cross the Lake; Jesus bids them seek the bread of heaven,	35	12	83	31	125	62
20 1-11	" 61-71	Many desert him; the Twelve remain true,	35	12	83	31	127	70
12-16	Lu. 11 37-41	Jesus breakfasts with unwashen hands,	77	—	81	31	79	92
17-45	Mt. 15 1-20, Mk. 7 1-23	Traditions; Corban; what really defiles,	36	12	85	iv. 1	131	63

272 APPENDIX.

Portions of the Diatessaron.	Portions of the Gospels.	Contents of the Diatessaron in order.	Order in the Diatessaron as obtained from other sources.			Order of Modern Harmonists.		
			Zahn's Reconstruction.	Ephraem's Commentary.	Codex Fuldensis.	Greswell.		Stroud.	Tischendorf.
			Section.	Chapter.	Chapter.	Part.	Sec.	Page.	Section.
20 46-58	Mt. 15 21-28 Mk. 7 24-30	Jesus visits Tyre and Sidon, and heals the Canaanite's daughter,	37	12	86	iv.	2	137	61
21 1-7 8-24 25-42 43-49	Mk. 7 31-37 Jn. 4 4-30 ,, 4 31-38 ,, 4 39-45	Jesus cures a deaf and dumb man, Discourse with a Samaritan woman at Sychar, Christ's food; remarks to his disciples, The woman returns with other Samaritans,	Omitted. 38 38 38	— 12 12 12	87 88 88 88	ii.	3 15 15 15	139 31 31 32	65 26 26 26
22 1-8 9-26 27-55	Mt. 8 2-4 Mk. 1 40-45 Ln. 5 12-10 Jn. 5 1-18 ,, 19-47	Cure of one leper; departure to the desert, Cure of a man thirty-eight years sick on the sabbath, Reply of Jesus to those who complained of his bidding the sick man carry his bed,	39 40 40	12 13 13	47 89 89	25, 26 iii.	1 1	44 33 34	35 29 28
23 1-12 13-25 26-30 31-39 40-44 45-50	Mt. 15 29-39 Mk. 8 1-10 Mt. 16 1,4-12 Mk. 8 11-21 ,, 22-26 Mt. 16 13-23 Mk. 8 27-33 Ln. 9 18-22 ,, Mt. 16 24-28 Mk. 8 34-9 1 Ln. 9 23-27	He heals many in Galilee; feeds 4000; comes to Magheda, He refuses a sign to the Pharisees, etc.; their leaven, Jesus heals a blind man at Bethsaida, Jesus asks his disciples what men say of him; Simon's reply, He announces his coming sufferings, and rebukes Simon, Jesus tells the multitudes that his disciples must suffer and deny themselves,	Omitted. Omitted. 41 42 42 42	— — 13 14 14 14	90 90 Omitted. 91 91 91	iv.	3, 4, 5 5, 6 7 8 9 9	139 141 144 162 161 165	65, 66 67, 68 69 70 70 70

I. COMPARATIVE TABLE OF CONTENTS.

24 1-19	Mt. 17 1-9 / Mk. 9 2-10 / Lu. 9 28-36	The Transfiguration; tell no man,	43	14	92	iv. 10, 11	167	71
20-24	Mt. 17 10-13 / Mk. 9 11-13	Elias is already come,	43	—	92	11	170	71
25-29	Lu. 13 31-33	Herod seeketh to kill thee,	43	14	93	37	190	101
30-47	Mt. 17 14-21 / Mk. 9 14-29 / Lu. 9 37-42	Jesus casts out a demon, which the disciples could not,	44	14	93	11	170	72
48-52	Mt. 17 22-23 / Mk. 9 30-32 / Lu. 9 43-45	Further reference to his sufferings and death,	Omitted.	—	94	12	174	73
25 1-12	Mt. 17 24-18 6 / Mk. 9 33-37 / Lu. 9 46-48	Which disciple is the greater; the stater in the fish's mouth,	50, 45	14	95, 94	13-15	175	75, 74
13-26	Mt. 18 7-11, 14 / Mk. 9 38-50 / Lu. 9 49-50	One casting out a demon; offences; salt,	50	—	96	14, 15	177	75
27-42	Mt. 19 1-12 / Mk. 10 1-12	Adultery; divorce; eunuchs,	46	14	101	46, 50	188	113
43-46	Mt. 19 13-15 / Mk. 10 13-16 / Lu. 18 15-17	Infants brought to Jesus,	46	—	102	51	196	114
26 1-8	Mt. 18 12-13 / Lu. 15 1-7	Eating with Publicans; parable of the Lost Sheep,	47, 50	14	97	41, 15	192, 179	104, 75
9-11	Lu. 15 8-10	Parable of the Lost Drachma,	47	14	97	41	193	104
12-33	,, 16 11-32	Parable of the Prodigal Son,	48	14	98	42	193	104
34-45	,, 16 1-12	Parable of the Unjust Steward,	49	14	100	43	194	105
27 1-13	Mt. 18 23-35	Parable of the Unmerciful Servant,	50	—	100	15	180	76b
14-23	,, 18 15-22 / Lu. 17 3-4	Offences of a brother,	50	14	99	15	179	76a
24-29	Mt. 17 10-11 / Lu. 12 47-50	The servant that knew his lord's will; I have a baptism,	50, 79	14	109	32	131, 179	75
30-39	,, 13 1-9	The Galilaeans; the tower of Siloam; the fig-tree in the vineyard,	51	11	103	33	131	96
40-47	,, 10-17	The woman with a spirit of infirmity,	Omitted.	—	104	34	133	97

Portions of the Diatessaron.	Portions of the Gospels.	Contents of the Diatessaron in order.	Zahn's Recon-struction.	Ephraem's Comment-ary.	Codex Fuldensis.	Greswell.	Stroud.	Tischen-dorf.
			Section.	Chapter.	Chapter.	Part. Sec.	Page.	Section.
28 1–14	Mt. 19 1–2 Jn. 7 2–13	The Feast of Tabernacles; Jesus expected,	52	14	105	iv. 16, 17	145	77, 79
15–32	" 7 14–31	Address of Jesus at the Feast,	52	14	105	18	146	79
33–41	Lu. 12 13–21	Who made me a judge? parable of the Rich Fool,	Omitted.	—	106	32	129	91
42–51	Mt. 19 16–30 Mk. 10 17–31 Lu. 18 18–30	The Rich Young Ruler,	53	15	107	52	197	115
29 1–5 6–11	"	Difficult for a rich man to enter the Kingdom, Disciples, who gave up all, would be rewarded,	53, note Omitted.	15 —	107 107	53 53	199 200	115 115
12–26	" 16 {14–15 {19–31	Parable of the Rich Man and Lazarus,	54	15	108	43	195	105
27–42	Mt. 20 1–16	Parable of the Labourers in the Vineyard,	55	15	110	54	202	115
43–48	Lu. 14 1–6	A dropsical man healed,	Omitted.	—	111	38	191	102
30 1–9	Mt. 22 7–15 Lu. 14 1–14	Go and sit down in the lowest place, Parable of the Marriage Feast and Wedding Garment,	Omitted.	—	111	39	191	102
10–30	" 14 16–24		Omitted.	—	121	39, 69	192, 230	102, 129
31–39	" 17 11–19	The ten lepers healed,	Omitted.	—	112	45	185	110
40–45	Mt. 20 17–19 Mk. 10 32–34	Jesus describes his coming Passion,	Omitted.	—	113	55	202	116
46–52	Mt. 20 20–28 Mk. 10 35–45	The mother of the sons of Zebedee,	56	15	113	56	201	117
31 1–5 6–11	Lu. 13 22–30	Indignation of the Ten, "Are they few that be saved?"	56 Omitted.	15 —	113 111	56 36	205 190	117 100

I. COMPARATIVE TABLE OF CONTENTS.

31 15-24	Lu. 19	1-10	Zacchaeus,	57	15	115		207	119
25-35	Mt. 20 / Mk. 10	29-34 / 46-52	Bartimaeus,	58	15	116	ir. 59	205	118
36-52	Lu. 18 / ,, 19	35-43 / 11-27	Parable of the Minas (Pounds),	80	—	152	57, 58	208	120
							60		
32 1-11	Mt. 21 / Mk. 11 / Lu. 19 / Jn. 2	12-13 / 15-18 / 45-46 / 13-22	Jesus cleanses the Temple; a sign required,	59	15	118	iv. 65 / ii. 11	28, 219	22, 121
12-15	Mt. 12 / Lu. 21	41-44 / 1-4	The Widow's Offering,	Omitted.	—	119	iv. 75	242	135
16-21	Lu. 18	9-14	Parable of the Pharisee and the Publican,	60	15	119	40	187	112
22-26	Mt. 21 / Mk. 11	17-19a / 12-14	Visit to Bethany; a Fig-tree cursed,	61	16	119, 122	65	218	123
27-47	Jn. 3	1-21	Nicodemus,	62	16	120	ii. 12	29	23
33 1-17	Mt. 21 / Mk. 11 / Lu. 17	19b-22 / 19-26 / 5-10	The Fig-tree withered; power of Faith and Prayer,	61	16	122	iv. 66	181, 222	125, 106
18-25	Lu. 18	5-8	Parable of the Unjust Judge,	63	16	123	48	186	112
26-34	Mt. 21 / Mk. 11	23-27 / 27-33	Christ's authority,	61	16	121	67	224	126
35-39	Lu. 20 / Mt. 21	1-8 / 28-32	Parable of the Two Sons,	61	16	124	67	226	127
40-60	Mt. 21 / Mk. 12 / Lu. 20	33-46 / 1-12 / 9-19	Parable of the Vineyard, and the Rejected Stone,	65	16	125	68	226	128
34 1-8	Mt. 22 / Mk. 12 / Lu. 20	15-22 / 13-17 / 20-26	Tribute to Caesar,	66	16	127	70	231	130
9-23	Mt. 22 / Mk. 12	23-33 / 18-27	Marriage in the Resurrection,	66	16	128	71	233	131
24-45	Mt. 22 / Mk. 12 / Lu. 10	34-40 / 28-34 / 25-37	The first Commandment; parable of the Good Samaritan,	67	16	129	27, 72	185, 236	87, 132

APPENDIX.

Portions of the Diatessaron.	Portions of the Gospels.	Contents of the Diatessaron in order.	Zahn's Reconstruction. Section.	Ephraem's Commentary. Chapter.	Codex Fuldensis. Chapter.	Greswell. Part, Sec.	Stroud. Page.	Tischendorf. Section.
34 46–53	Lu. 19 47–48 Jn. 7 31–36	Jesus daily in the Temple; soldiers sent to take him,	68	—	130	iv. 65, 19	146, 220	79
35 1–16	,, 37–52	Last day of the Feast; the soldiers return without him,	68	16	130	19	147	80
17–22	Mt. 22 41–46 Mk. 12 35–37	Whose son is the Messiah?	Omitted.	—	131	73	237	133
23–61	Lu. 20 41–44 Jn. 8 12–50	Jesus teaches in the Treasury,	69	16	132	20	150	82, 83
36 1–9	,, 9 51–59 ,, 9 1–38	"Before Abraham was, I am," Cure of one born blind, and its results,	69 70	16 16	132 133, 131	20 20	152 153	83 84
37 1–24 25–45 46–61	,, 10 39–10 21 ,, 10 22–42 ,, 11 1–16	Are we blind? I am the Good Shepherd, The Feast of the Dedication, Death of Lazarus; decision to go to him,	70, 71 71 72	16 16 17	134 135 136	21, 22 23	155 156 158	84 98, 99 107
38 1–29 30–38 39–47	,, 17–45 ,, 46–54 Lu. 9 55–57 51–56	Raising of Lazarus, Proposal of Caiaphas; retirement to Ephraem, Late for the Feast; rejected by a Samaritan village,	72 72 72	17 17 19	136 136 136, 137	23 21 61, 25	159 161 209, 182	107 108 121, 77
39 1–17	Mt. 26 6–13 Mk. 14 3–9 Mt. 21 1–11 Mk. 11 1–11	Mary anoints Jesus,	73	17	133, 139	62, 63	209	121
18–45	Lu. 19 28–44 Jn. 12 12–19	Triumphal entry into Jerusalem,	74	19	117	64	213	122

I. COMPARATIVE TABLE OF CONTENTS.

40	1–4 5–21 22–25 26–65	Mt. 21 14–16 Jn. 12 20–36ª Lu. 17 20, 21 „ 21 37–38 Mt. 23 1–39 Mk. 12 38–40 Lu. 11 42–52 „ 20 45–47	The blind and lame and children in the Temple, Greeks desire to see Jesus, The kingdom of God; daily teaching, Woe unto the scribes, Pharisees, and lawyers,	74 75 76 77	18 18 18 19	118 140 141 142	iv. 64 64 47, 81 31, 77	218 256 186, 221 229	124 136 111, 124 134, 92
41	1–6 7–26 27–32 33–42 43–58	(Jn. 12″ 42–50 Lu. 11 53–12 3 Jn. 12 36ᵇ–41 Mt. 24 1–14 Mk. 13 1–13 „ 14 1–2 Lu. 21 5–19	Treatment of God's messengers; O, Jerusalem, How the teaching of Jesus was received, The adornments of the temple, The signs of Christ's coming, The sufferings of his disciples,	77 78 79 79 79	18 18 18 18 18	142, 143 144 145 146 146	31, 77 31, 76 78 78 78	241 257, 79, 129 243 243 245	134 92, 137 138 138 138
42	1–24 25–28 29–53	Mt. 24 15–44 Mk. 13 14–37 Lu. 17 23–37 „ 21 20–35	How certain signs should affect the disciples, Parable of the Fig-tree putting forth leaves, Warnings to prepare; Noah; Lot,	79 79 79	18 18 18	146 147 148	78 78 78, 47	247 251 252, 186	139 139 139, 111
43	1–8 9–21 22–38 31–42 43–58	Mt. 24 45–51 {Lu. 12 41–46 Mt. 25 1–13 „ „ 14–30 Lu. 12 35–38 Mt. 25 31–46	Servants left in charge, Parable of the Ten Virgins, Parable of the Talents, Watch with your loins girded, Description of the Last Judgment,	79 80 80 80 80	18 18 18 18 18	148 149 150 151 153	79 79 79 32 79	254 254 254 130 255	95 140 120 95 141
44	1–9 10–33 34–50	{Mt. 26 1–5, 14–16 Lu. 22 1–6 Jn. 13 1–20 Lu. 22 24–30ª {Mt. 26 17–24 Mk. 14 13–21 Lu.22 27–16,21–23 Jn. 13 21–22	The death of Jesus planned, He washes the disciples' feet, A lodging engaged; the Paschal Feast begun,	Omitted. 81 81, 82	— — 19	154 155 156	80 84 82, 83, 86	258 262 260, 265	142, 143 145 144, 146

APPENDIX.

Portions of the Diatessaron.	Portions of the Gospels.	Contents of the Diatessaron in order.	Order in the Diatessaron as obtained from other sources.			Order of Modern Harmonists.		
			Zahn's Reconstruction. Section.	Ephraem's Commentary. Chapter.	Codex Fuldensis. Chapter.	Greswell. Part. Sec.	Stroud. Page.	Tischendorf. Section.
45 1-9	Mt. 26 25 / Jn. 13 23-30	The traitor indicated; he goes out,	82	19	156	iv. 86	267	146
10-16	Mt. 26 26-30 / Mk. 14 22-25 / Lu. 22 17-20 / Jn. 13 31-32	The Lord's Supper,	83	19	157	85, 89	264	147
17-28	Mt. 26 31-35 / Mk. 14 26-31 / Lu. 22 31-34 / Jn. 13 33-38	Jesus foretells Simon's denial, etc.,	84	19	157	87, 88, 92	268, 277	148
29-48	„ 14 1-20	"Let not your heart be troubled,"	85	19	158	90	270	149
46 1-16	„ 15 „ 16 21-31 / Lu. 22 35-39	Further address; and departure to the Mount of Olives. The True Vine; love one another; the Comforter,	85, 86 87, 88	19 19	158, 159 160	90, 88 90	271, 269 271	149 150, 151
17-58	Jn. 15 1-16 15							
47 1-44	„ 16 16-17 26	Further Discourse; and Address to the Father,	88, 89	19	160	90, 91	273	151, 152
48 1-46	Mt. 26 36-56 / Mk. 14 32-50 / Lu. 22 40-53 / Jn. 18 1-11	Gethsemane,	90	19, 20	161, 162	92-94	279	153, 154
47-55	Mt. 26 57-58, 69-70 / Mk. 14 51-54, 66-68 / Lu. 22 54-57 / Jn. 18 12-18	Taken to Annas; the First Denial,	91	20	162, 163	95	288	155

I. COMPARATIVE TABLE OF CONTENTS.

						iv.		
49 1-6	Mt. 26 59-68,							
7-18	Mk. 14 55-65, 71-75	Annas sends Jesus to Caiaphas,	92	20	161	95	290	156
		The Second and Third Denials,	91	20	164	95	290	155
19-42	Lu. 22 69-72, 55-71	Trial before the Sanhedrin,	92	20	165, 166	96	292	156
	Jn. 18 58-71, 19-27							
	Mt. 27 1, 2, 11							
43-55	Mk. 15 1-3	Before Pilate; "What is truth"	93	20	167, 168	97, 98	298	157, 159
	Lu. 23 1-3							
	Jn. 18 28-38ᵃ							
50 1-9	Lu. 23 4-12	Jesus sent to Herod,	Omitted.	—	168	99	301	160
10-36	Mt. 27 12-30	Before Pilate again; Barabbas or Jesus?	93	20	168, 169	99	301	161
37-42	Mk. 15 3-20	Barabbas released; Jesus scourged and mocked;	93	20	170	99	305, 308	162
43-51	Lu. 23 13-25	Jesus brought out by Pilate; "not Caesar's friend,"	93	—	168	98	306	162
	Jn. 18 38ᵇ-19 12							
51 1-6	Mt. 27 24-25	The Pavement,	93	20	168	98, 99	307	162
	Jn. 19 13-16ᵃ							
7-11	Mt. 27 3-10	Judas returns the silver,	94	20	167	97	298	158
15-25	Mk. 15 31-33, 21-22	Journey to Calvary,	95	20	170, 171	100	309	163
	Lu. 23 26-32							
	Jn. 19 16ᵇ-17							
26-54	Mt. 27 34-47	The Crucifixion,	96, 97	20	171	100, 101	311	164 166
	Mk. 15 23-35							
	Lu. 23 33, 35-45ᵃ							
	Jn. 19 18-27							
52 1-12	Mt. 27 48-54	Crucifixion concluded; the Centurion,	97	20, 21	171	101, 102	317	166, 167
	Mk. 15 36-39							
	Lu. 23 34, 45ᵇ-48							
	Jn. 19 28-30							
13-20	Mt. 27 31-37	His bones not broken,	97	21	171	102	320	168
	Mk. 15 55-66							
	Jn. 19 40-47							
21-44	Mt. 27 55-66	Interment of the body; the sepulchre sealed,	97	21	172, 173	102, 103	321	167, 169, 170
	Mk. 15 40-47							
	Lu. 23 49-56							
	Jn. 19 38-42							

280 APPENDIX.

Portions of the Diatessaron.	Portions of the Gospels.		Contents of the Diatessaron in order.	Order in the Diatessaron as obtained from other sources.			Order of Modern Harmonists.			
				Zahn's Reconstruction.	Ephraem's Commentary.	Codex Fuldensis.	Greswell.		Stroud.	Tischendorf.
				Section.	Chapter.	Chapter.	Part.	Sec.	Page.	Section.
52 45–55	Mt. 28 Mk. 16 Lu. 24	1–6 1–6 1–3	The tomb found empty; the angel and earthquake,	97	21	174	v.	1	325	171
53 1–8	Mt. 28 Mk. 16 Lu. 24 Jn. 20	7–8 7–8 4–8 1–2	"Go and tell his disciples,"	98	21	174	1,	3	327	171, 172
9–17	Lu. 24 Jn. 20 Mk. 16	12 3–10 9–11	Two disciples visit the tomb,	98	21	174	4,	5	329	173, 174
18–25	Jn. 20 Mt. 28	11–17 11–15	Jesus appears to Mary Magdalene,	98 98	21 21	174 175	6 2		329 330	175 176
26–30			The guards bribed,							
31–38	" Lu. 24 Jn. 20	9–10 9–11 18	Jesus appears to the other women,	98	21	176	1,	11	330	173
39–61	Mk. 16 Lu. 24	12–13 13–35	The walk to Emmaus,	98	21	177	7,	8	331	177
54 1–16	" Jn. 20	36–49ª 19–23	Jesus appears to the Ten, Thomas being absent,	98	21	178	9,	15	333	178
17–24	"	24–31	Jesus appears to the Eleven,	98	21	179	9,	10	334	179
25–48	" 21	1–24	Second miraculous draught; "Lovest thou me?"	99	21	180, 181	13		336	180
55 1–11	Mt. 28 Mk. 16 Lu. 24 Jn. 21	16–20 14–18 49ᵇ 25	At a mountain in Galilee; "Go ye into all the world,"	100	21	182	12,	16	337	181, 182
12–17	Mk. 16 Lu. 24 Jn. 21	19–20 50–53	Ascension from Bethany; the Apostles begin their work,	100	22	182	16–18		339	182, 183

II.

In this table the entire contents of the four Gospels are taken by sections in the order in which they stand in the Gospels, and distinguished from one another according to three varieties:

1. Those which are found in the *Diatessaron*.

Opposite to each of these sections is placed a reference showing the chapter and verses of the present English version at which that particular section is to be found. Occasionally the portion of the English version so indicated will be found to differ slightly from the section to which it is thus related, generally through the insertion of some words from another Gospel in the process of harmonisation.

2. Those of which the *subject-matter* is found in the *Diatessaron* in the form of extracts from *other* Gospels.

Opposite to each of these sections similar references to the English version are given; but the *verse* numbers are printed in italics in order to indicate that a parallel passage only, and not the actual one in question, is to be found at the place indicated. The passage of the *Diatessaron* thus connected with a particular section of a Gospel will often be found to be practically identical with it, so much so sometimes as to suggest that Tatian may in fact have taken it from that Gospel and not from the Gospel mentioned in the references to the Arabic. In other cases, however, considerable differences will be found between them, the *Diatessaron* following some other Gospel which varied considerably at the point. In such cases if anything of importance is *omitted* from the narrative, attention is generally called to it in the notes.

3. Those which are omitted from the *Diatessaron* altogether.

Opposite to these the word "omitted" has been placed, accompanied in most cases by a note suggesting a possible explanation of the omission. Many of these omissions are due to changes in the opening words which connect a fresh paragraph with the preceding narrative; for when a passage was removed from its context in its own Gospel, and placed after something else, the introductory words sometimes ceased to be applicable in its new situation, and were in consequence omitted. Such cases are indicated in the notes by the word "connective."

APPENDIX.

S. Matthew.	Tatian.	S. Matthew.	Tatian.	S. Matthew.	Tatian.
1 1–17[1]	Omitted.	7 28–29	11 1–2	11 12ᵃ	14 4
18–25ᵃ	2 1–8	8 1	3	12ᵇ–15	5ᵇ–8
25ᵇ	29	2–4	22 1–6	16–19	10–14
2 1ᵃ[2]	Omitted.	5ᵃ	11 4ᵃ	20–24	15 27–31
1ᵇ–23	3 1–23	5ᵇ	4ᵇ–5	25–27	37–38
3 1ᵃ	37–39	5ᶜ–6	6	28–30	39–41
1ᵇ–3ᵃ	40–42	7–8	9–10	12 1–2[1]	7 37–38ᵃ
3ᵇ	43	9–10ᵃ	11–12ᵃ	2ᵇ–4	38ᵇ–40
4–10	4 12–18	10ᵇ–13	12ᵇ–15	5–8	42–45
11–12	25, 26	14–15	6 48, 49	9–10	47–48
13	28	16ᵃ	50	11–12	52–53
14–15	33–34	16ᵇ	51	13	51
16ᵃ, 16ᶜ	35, 37	17	52	14–21	8 1–8
16ᵇ	36	18	11 24	22–23	14 41–42
17	38	19–20	25ᵇ–26	24	17
4 1	43	21–23	27, 28, 32	25–26ᵃ	19 20ᵃ
2ᵃ	44ᵃ	24ᵃ	33ᵃ	26ᵇ	21ᵃ
2ᵇ–7	44ᵇ–49	24ᵇ	33ᵇ–34ᵃ	27–29	22–24
8–9	50–52	25	34ᵇ	30–31	27–28
10	5 1	26–28ᵃ	35–39	32–34	31–33
11ᵃ	2	28ᵇ	42ᵇ	35	34
11ᵇ	3	29ᵇ–33	43–52	36–37	35–36
12	6 25	34	12 1	38–39	16 1–2
13–16	36–39	9 1	2	40	4
17ᵃ	5 42	2–7	7 14–22	41	6
17ᵇ	43	8ᵃ	23ᵃ	42	5
18–22	44 48	8ᵇ	23ᶜ	43–45ᵃ	7–9
23	7 7[3]	9ᵃ	6 46·8	45ᵇ	10
24	10	9ᵇ	46ᵇ⁷	46ᵃ	13ᵃ
25	8 10ᵇ–11	10–12	7 27–29	46ᵇ	13ᵇ
5 1ᵃ	18	13	44	46ᶜ	14ᵃ
1ᵇ	19	14–17	31–35	47–50	15–18
2–10	26ᵇ–34	18ᵃ	12 7–8ᵃ	13 1–4ᵃ	22–25ᵃ
11ᵃ	35ᵃ	18ᵇ–19	8ᵇ–9	4ᵇ	25ᵇ
11ᵇ–12	35ᵇ–36	20–25	10–21	5–6	26–27
13–16	40ᵇ–43	26–33	32–39	7–11	28–32
17–25ᵃ	46–54ᵃ	34	14 17	12–16	33–37
25ᵇ	54ᵇ	35ᵃ	7 7ᵃ⁹	17	39
25ᶜ–32	55–62	35–36	12 40–41	18	41
33–42	1–10ᵃ	37–38	15 16	19–21ᵃ	43–45ᵃ
43–46ᵃ	12–15ᵃ	10 1ᵃ	12 42ᵃ	21ᵇ–22ᵃ	46–47ᵃ
46ᵇ	15ᵇ	1ᵇ	42ᵇ	22ᵇ–23ᵃ	47ᵇ–48ᵃ
47–48	20–21	2–4	8 19–22	23ᵇ	48ᵇ
6 1–8	22–29	5ᵃ	43	24–31ᵃ	17 1–8
9ᵃ	31	5ᵇ–10ᵃ	12 44–49ᵃ	31ᵇ	9–10ᵃ
9ᵇ–18	32–41	10ᵇ	50ᵃ	31ᶜ	10ᵇ
19–23	44–48	10ᶜ–14ᵃ	50ᵇ–54ᵃ	32ᵃ	11
24–27	10 1–4	14ᵇ	54ᵇ	32ᵇ	12ᵃ
28ᵃ	5ᵃ	15	55	32ᶜ	12ᵇ
28ᵇ–31	6–9ᵃ	16–27ᵃ	13 1–12ᵃ	33ᵃ	13
32–34	10–12	27ᵇ–28ᵃ	12ᵇ–13ᵃ	33ᵇ–34ᵃ	15–16ᵃ
7 1	13ᵃ	28ᵇ	13ᵇ	34ᵇ–35	16ᵇ–17
2–5	15, 19, 20	28ᶜ	14ᵇ	36–54ᵃ	19–37
6	21	29–33	15–19	54ᵇ	38–39
7–11	26–30	34–35	20–22	55–57ᵃ	40–41
12–16ᵃ	31–34	36–42ᵃ	23–29ᵃ	57ᵇ–58	43, 44, 48
16ᵇ	35	42ᵇ	29ᵇ	14 1	18 1ᵃ
17–18	36–37	11 1	30	2ᵃ	5ᵃ
19–23	39–43	2ᵃ	39ᵃ	2ᵇ	5ᵇ
24	44, 45	2ᵇ–10	39ᵇ–47	3–4	6–7
25–27	46–48	11	14 1	5	10

[1] Genealogy. [2] Connective; cf. p. 50, note. [3] Cf. Matt. ix. 35.
[4] Cf. 2. [5] Except part of 29. [6] Cf. vii. 25.
[7] Cf. vii. 25–26. [8] Duplicate. [9] Cf. Matt. iv. 23.

II. ANALYSIS OF THE GOSPELS.

S. Matthew.	Tatian.	S. Matthew.	Tatian.	S. Matthew.	Tatian.
14 6-12ª	18 *11-19*ª	17 6-9	24 14-17	21 2ᶜ	39 21ᵈ
12ᵇ	19ᵇ	10ª	*20ᵃ*	3ª	*22ᵃ*
13ª	21ª	10ᵇ	20ᵇ	3ᵇ-5	*22ᵇ-24*
13ᵇ-14	*22,23,26*	11-12ª	*21-22*	6ª	*26ᵃ*
15ª	*27*	12ᵇ-13	*23-24*	6ᵇ	*26ᶜ*
15ᵇ	*28*	14ª	*30ᵃ*	7-8	*29-30*
16-17ª	29-30ª	14ᵇ	30ᵇ	9ª	*31*
17ᵇ	*34*	15ª	*30ᶜ*	9ᵇ	*32*
18	*38*	15ᵇ	31ᵇ	10-11	42-43
19ª	*36,37,39*	15ᶜ	33ª	12ª	32 1ª
19ᵇ-20ª	40	16-17	34-35	12ᵇ	2ª
20ᵇ	*41, 42*	18ª	*41, 42*	12ᶜ-13	2ᶜ-3
21	*43*	18ᵇ	44ª	14-16	40 1-3
22-23	*44, 46*	19	*45*	17	32 22ᵇ
24	*50*	20	*46*	18-19ª	*24-26*
25	19 1	21-23ª	*47-50*	19ᵇ	Omitted.
26-33	3-10	23ᵇ	*52*	20ª	33 *2*
34-36	*11-15*	24ª	25 *2ª*	20ᵇ	3
15 1-2	20 *17-21*	24ᵇ-27	4-7	21ª	*5, 6*
3-4ª	*22-23ª*	18 1	8	21ᵇ-22	7-8
4ᵇ-6	*23ᵇ-28*	2	9	23-24ª	*27-29ª*
7-9	29-31	3	10	24ᵇ-25ª	*29ᵇ-30ª*
10-11	*32-33*	4-5	*11-12*	25ᵇ-26ª	31-32ª
12-14	35-37	6	13	26ᵇ-27	*32ᵇ-34*
15-16ª	38ᵇ-39ª	7-8	17-18	28-33ª	35-40
16ᵇ-17	*39ᵇ-40*	9ª	20	33ᵇ	41
18	41	9ᵇ	*21*	34	42
19-20ª	*42-44*	10-11	27 28-29	35-36	46-47
20ᵇ-21ª	45-46ª	12-13ª	26 *4*	37	*49*
21ᵇ-22ª	*46ᵇ-48*	13ᵇ	*5*	38ª	50
22ᵇ-28ª	49-55	14	*7*	38ᵇ	*51*
28ᵇ	*57*	15-22	27 16-23	39-42ª	52-55ª
29-30ª	23 1-2	23-35	1-13	42ᵇ	*55ᵇ*
30ᵇ-32	3ᵇ-5ª	19 1ª	Omitted.	42ᶜ-46	56-60
33-39	6-12	1ᵇ-2	28 9ᵇ-10	22 1-2	30 10-11ª
16 1ª	13ª	3-4ª	25 *28, 31ª*	3ª	*12ª*
1ᵇ	*13ᵇ*	4ᵇ-9ª	31ᵇ-36	3ᵇ	12ᵇ
2ª	14 *37ª*	9ᵇ-13ª	*39ᵇ-43ª*	4-6	16-18
2ᵇ-3	39-40	13ᵇ-15	*43ᵇ-44,46*	7-8	20-21
4ª	23 *14ª*	16-17ª	28 *42-43*	9ª	*24ª*
4ᵇ	14ᵇ	17ᵇ-18ª	44ᵇ-45	9ᵇ	24ᵇ
5-6	*16-18*	18ᵇ-19ª	*46ª*	10-14	26-30
7-8ª	19-20ª	19ᵇ-20	46ᵇ-47	15	34 1ª
8ᵇ-10	*20ᵇ,22-23*	21ª	*48*	16-17	2-3ª
11-12	24ᵇ-25	21ᵇ-22ª	49-50ª	18ª	*4*
13ª	*31*	22ᵇ-23ª	*50ᵇ-51*	18ᵇ-21	4ᵇ-7
13ᵇ-21ᵇ	*32-40*	23ᵇ-24	29 1-2	22 ³	*8*
14ᵇ ¹	18 3ª	25 27ª	*3-6ª*	23-25ª	9-11ª
21ᵇ	23 *41*	27ᵇ-28	6ᵇ-7	25ᵇ-26	*11ᵇ-13*
22	42ᵇ	29-30	8-11	27-29ª	14-16ª
23ª	*43*	20 1-15	27-42	29ᵇ-30	*16ᵇ-19*
23ᵇ	*44*	17-19	30 *40-44*	31ª	*20ª*
24-26	*45-48*	20-21ª	*46*	31ᵇ-32	*20ᵇ-21ª*
27	*50*	21ᵇ-23	*47-52*	33	*22*
28ª	24 *1ª*	24-27	31 *1-4*	34-35ª	*24-25ª*
28ᵇ	1ᵇ	28	*5*	35ᵇ-37ª	*26, 28ª*
17 1	2	29ª	*25ª*	37ᵇ-38	*28ᵇ-29*
2ª	*3*	29ᵇ	25ᵇ	39	*30*
2ᵇ	4ª	30-33	*26-33*	40	31
3-4ª	*5, 8*	34ª	34ª	41-46	35 17-22
4ᵇ	9ª	34ᵇ	*35*	23 1-5ª	40 26-30
4ᶜ	9ᵇ	21 1ª	39 *18-19*	5ᵇ	34ª
5ª	10	1ᵇ-2ª	20	6-7ª	*32ᵇ-33*
5ᵇ	12	2ᵇ	21ᵇ	7ᵇ	34ᵇ

¹ Duplicate.   ² Connective changed for John vii. 10ª.   ³ Varied.

S. Matthew.	Tatian.	S. Matthew.	Tatian.	S. Matthew.	Tatian.
23 8–12	40 36–40	26 28–29	45 15–16ª	27 26ᵇ	50 37ᶜ
13ª	43	30	46 *16*	26ᶜ	51 *6*
13ᵇ	44ᵇ	31–33	45 23–25	27–28	50 38–39
14	42	34–35	*27, 28*	29ª	*40*
15–28	45–58	36ª	48 *1, 3*ª	29ᵇ–30	41–42ª
29ª	61ª	36ᵇ	3ᵇ	31–32ª	51 16–17ª
29ᵇ–33	61ᶜ–65	37–38	48 5–6	32ᵇ	17ᶜ
34–39	41 1–6	39	7	33–34ª	*25, 27*ª
24 1	27	40ª	10	34ᵇ	27ᵇ
2ª	29	40ᵇ–41ª	11ᵇ–12ª	35	28–29
2ᵇ–3ª	*30, 33*	41ᵇ	*12*ᵇ	36	30
3ᵇ–4ª	34ᵇ–35ª	42	13	37–38	*31, 25*ᶜ
4ᵇ–5ª	36–37	43	*14*	39–40ª	35ᵇ
5ᵇ–6ª	38ᵇ–39ª	44	15	40ᵇ	*36*ª
6ᵇ	39ᵇ	45ª	*18–19*ª	40ᶜ–42ª	36ᵇ–38
6ᶜ	*39*ᶜ	45ᵇ	19ᵇ	42ᵇ	*39*ª
7ª	40	46ª	*21*ª	42ᶜ–43	39ᵇ–40
7ᵇ	*41*	46ᵇ–48	21ᵇ–23ª	44	43
8	42	49–50ª	25–26ª	45ª	*52*ª
9–10	50–51	50ᵇ	26ᶜ	45ᵇ–46	*52*ᵇ, *53*
11–14	55–58	50ᶜ	33	47	*54*
15–16	42 4–5	51–52ª	*35, 36*	48ª	52 *2*ᵇ
17–19	*6–8*	52ᵇ–54	37–39	48ᵇ	*3*
20–21	16–17	55	41	49	*5*
22	*18*	56	43	50	*7*
23	*10*	57–58ª	*47, 49,*	51–54ª	8–11
24	*11*		*50, 55*ª	54ᵇ	*12*ᵇ
25	*12*	58ᵇ	55ᵇ	55	*21*
26–27	13–14	59ª	49 *19, 20*	56ª	*22*ª
28	*50*ᵇ	59ᵇ–60ª ¹	21–22	56ᵇ	*22*ᵇ
29–31	21ᵇ–23	60ᵇ	24ª	56ᶜ	*22*ᶜ
32–35	25–28	61–62ª	*24*ᵇ, *25,*	57–58ª	*24,25,27*
36	*32*		*27*ᵇ	58ᵇ	29ᵇ
37–39	38–40	62ᵇ	28	59–60ª	*30, 33*
40–41	*49, 48*	63ª	27ª	60ᵇ	35
42–44	51 53	63ᵇ–64ª	33–34	61–62ª	*36,37,39*
45–46	43 2ᵇ–3	64ᵇ	36	62ᵇ–66	40–44
47ª	*4*ª	65ª	*37*ª	28 1ª	*45*ª
47ᵇ–48	4ᵇ–5	65ᵇ	37ᵇ	1ᵇ	*46*ª
49ª	*6*ª	66ª	*35*ᵇ	2ª	*48*
49ᵇ–51ª	6ᵇ–8ª	66ᵇ	39	2ᵇ–4	*49*ᵇ–*51*
51ᵇ	*8*ᶜ	67–68ª	*40–41*ª	5–6	*54–55*
25 1–30	9–38	68ᵇ	41ᵇ	7ª	53 *5*
26 31–46	43–58	69–70	48 *51–52*	7ᵇ	*6*ª
26 1–5	44 1–5ª	71ª	49 *8*ª	7ᶜ	*6*ᵇ
6–8	39 *3, 7, 12*	71ᵇ	8ᵇ	8ª	*7*ᵇ
9	*13*ª	72	10	8ᵇ–10	32–34
10ª	*14*ª	73ª	9	11ª ²	Omitted.
10ᵇ–11	*14*ᵇ, *15*	73ᵇ	*12*ᵇ	11ᵇ–15	26–30
12	*16*ª	74–75	*14–18*	16–17	55 1–2
13	*17*	27 1ª	*19*	18	*4*
14–15ª	44 *6, 7*ª	1ᵇ	20	19ª	*5*ᵇ
15ᵇ	*7*ᵇ	2	*43*	19ᵇ–20	6–7
15ᶜ	*8*ᵇ	3–10	51 *7–14*		
16–17	*9, 10*	11ª	49 *45*ª	S. Mark.	
18ª	*37*	11ᵇ	*50, 54*	1 1	Title
18ᵇ	38ª	12–14	50 *16–18*	2–11	⎰ 3 *57–56*
19–24	*40–41,*	15–17ª	20–22		⎨ 4 *1–38*
	44–48	17ᵇ–18	27ᵇ–28		⎩ 13 *47*
25	45 *8*	19	19	12	4 *43*ª
26ª	*12*ª	20–22ª	29–31	13ª	*44*
26ᵇ	*12*ᵇ	22ᵇ–23	*32, 35*	13ᵇ	43ᵇ
27ª	*13*ª	24–25	51 4–5		
27ᵇ	13ᵇ	26	50 *37*ª, ᵇ		

¹ Omitting, "*yet found they none.*"   ² Connective.

II. ANALYSIS OF THE GOSPELS.

S. Mark.	Tatian.	S. Mark.	Tatian.	S. Mark.	Tatian.
1 13ª	5 *3*	4 22-23	8 44-45	6 7	12 *42, 44*
14 [1]	*42*	24-25	10 15-16	8ª	*49ª*
15	*43*	26-29	16 49-52	8ᵇ	49ᵇ
16-20 [2]	*44-46*	30ª	17 *9ª*	9ª	50ª
21-29ª	6 *36,*	30ᵇ	9ᵇ	9ᵇ	*49ᶜ*
	40-46ª	31ª	*10ª*	10	*51*
29ᵇ	47	31ᵇ	11	11ª	*54ª*
30-32	*48-52*	32ª	*12ª*	11ᵇ	54ᵇ
33	53	32ᵇ	12ᵇ	11ᶜ	55
34	*54*	33ª [6]	*16ª*	12-13	13 36-37
35-38	7 1-4	33ᵇ	16ᵇ	14ª	18 *1ª*
39ª	*7ª*	34ª	*16ᶜ*	14ᵇ	1ᶜ
39ᵇ	7ᵇ	34ᵃ	18	14ᶜ	*2, 5ᵇ*
40	22 *1*	35ª	11 31ª	15ª	*2*
41-45ª	2-6	35ᵇ	*31ᵇ*	15ᵇ-16	4-5ª
45ᵇ	*7*	36ª	32ª	17-20	6-9
2 1-2	7 11-12	36ᵇ	*32ᵇ*	21-29	11-19ª
3-7 [3]	*13-17*	36ᵃ	32ᶜ	30-31	14 43-44
8-12ª	18-22ª	37	*33*	32	18 *21*
12ᵇ	*23*	38ª	34ª	33	22ª
12ᶜ	24ᵇ	38ᵇ-39ª	*34ᵇ-35ª*	34ª	*25ª*
13 [4]	Omitted.	39ᵇ-41ª	*35ᵇ-36*	34ᵇ	25ᵇ
14	7 9	41ᵇ	*37*	35	*27*
15-20	*27-33*	5 1-2ª	*38-39ª*	36	28
21-22	34ᵇ-35ª	2ᵇ	39ᵇ	37-39⁹	*29, 34, 36*
23-24ª	*37-38ª*	3ª	*39ᶜ*	40	37
24ᵇ-27	38ᵇ-41	3ᵇ-4ª	40	41	39
28	*45*	4ᵇ-5ª	41ᵇ-42ª	42-44	*40ᵇ, 42-43*
3 1-4ª	*47-50ª*	5ᵇ-7ª	*42ᶜ-44ª*	45	44
4ᵇ-5	50ᵇ-51	7ᵇ	*44ᵇ*	46-47	*46, 48-50*
6 [5]	8 *1*	7ᶜ	44ᶜ	48-51ª	19 *1-9*
7ª	*10ª*	8-13ª	*45-49ª*	51ᵇ-52	12ᵇ-13
7ᵇ-12	10ᵇ-15	13ᵇ	49ᵇ	53 [10]	*11*
13	*18-19*	14-16ª	*50-52ª*	54ª	12ª
14-15	24-25	16ᵇ	52ᵇ	54ᵇ-56	14-15
16-19ª	*20-22*	17-19	12 *1-4*	7 1-5	20 *17-21*
19ᵇ-20	14 15	20-21ª	5-6ª	6-7	*29-31*
21	7 46	21ᵇ-22 [7]	*6ᵇ-7*	8ª	27
22-26ª	14 *17-19,*	23ª	8ª	8ᵇ	*26ᵇ*
	20ª	23ᵇ-24ª	8ᵇ-9	9	28
26ᵇ	20ᵇ	24ᵇ-30	10-16	10ª	*29*
27	*24*	31	17	10ᵇ-13	23ᵇ-26ª,ᶜ
28-30	28-30	32 [8]	Omitted.	14-16	32-34
31ª	16 *13ᵇ*	33ª	12 19ᵇ	17ª	38ª
31ᵇ	14ᶜ	33ᵇ-34ª	*20-21ª*	17ᵇ	*38ᵇ*
32-35	*15-18*	34ᵇ	21ᵇ	18-19	39-40
4 1-7ª	*22-28ª*	35-36	*22-23*	20	*41*
7ᵇ	28ᵇ	37-39	24-26	21-23	42-44
8ª	*29ª*	40ª	*27*	24ª	*46ª*
8ᵇ	29ᵇ	40ᵇ-41	28-29ª	24ᵇ-26ª	46ᵇ-48
9	*30*	42ª	*29ᵇ*	26ᵇ-29ª [11]	*49-55*
10-11	31-32	42ᵇ	30ª	29ᵇ	56
12-13ª	*34, 39*	43	*30ᵇ, 31*	30	58
13ᵇ	40	6 1	17 *36-37*	31-37	21 *1-7*
14	*42*	2	38-39	8 1-3ª	23 *2-5ª*
15-19ª	*43-47ª*	3-4ª	*40-41, 43*	3ᵇ	5ᵇ
19ᵇ	47ᵇ	4ᵇ	44	4-11ª	*6-13ª*
20	*48*	5-6ª	48-49	11ᵇ-12ª	13ᵇ-14ª
21	8 *42*	6ᵇ	53	12ᵇ-15	15-18

[1] Cf. vi. 25.   [2] Except parts of 18 and 19.
[3] Omitting from ver. 3, "which was borne of four."   [4] Connective.
[5] Omitting, "with the Herodians."   [6] Varied.
[7] Omitting, "and he was nigh unto the sea;" cf. 6ª.   [8] Implied at xii. 16.
[9] Varied.   [10] Varied.   [11] Varied.

APPENDIX

S. Mark.	Tatian.	S. Mark.	Tatian.	S. Mark.	Tatian.
8 16–17ᵃ	23 19–20ᵃ	10 19ᵇ	28 46ᵃ	12 25–26ᵃ	34 18–20ᵃ
17ᵇ–21ᵃ	20ᵇ–24ᵃ	20	47	26ᵇ	20ᵇ
21ᵇ	24ᵇ	21ᵃ	48	27ᵃ	21ᵃ
22–27ᵃ	26–31	21ᵇ–22	49–50	27ᵇ	21ᵇ
27ᵇ–31ᵃ	32–40	23	51ᵇ	28ᵃ	24ᵃ
31ᵇ–32ᵃ	41–42ᵃ	24	29 3	28ᵇ	24ᵇ
32ᵇ	42ᵇ	25	2	28ᶜ–30ᵃ	26–28ᵃ
33ᵃ	43	26–27	4–5	30ᵇ	28ᵇ–29
33ᵇ	44	28–29ᵃ	6ᵃ, 7	31	30
34ᵃ	45ᵃ	29ᵇ	8	32–34ᵃ	32–34
34ᵇ	45ᵇ	30ᵃ	9	34ᵇ	45
35	46	30ᵇ–31	10–11	35–37ᵃ	35 17–22
36	47	32	30 40	37ᵇ–39	40 31–33
37ᵃ–38	48–49	33ᵃ	41	40	35
9 1	24 1ᵃ	33ᵇ–34ᵃ	42–43	41–42ᵃ	32 12–13
2–3ᵃ	2, 4ᵇ	34ᵇ	44	42ᵇ?	Omitted.
3ᵇ–4	4ᶜ–5	35–40	47–52	43	14
5–6ᵃ	8–9ᵇ	41–44	31 1–4	44	15
6ᵇ	9ᶜ	45	5	13 1ᵃ	41 27
7–9	10, 13, 17	46ᵃ	25, 26ᵃ	1ᵇ	28ᵃ
10ᵃ	18	46ᵇ	26ᵇ	2	29–30
10ᵇ–11ᵃ	19–20ᵃ	47ᵃ	29ᵃ	3	33
11ᵇ	20ᵇ	47ᵇ–48ᵃ	29ᵇ–30ᵃ	4–6ᵃ	34–38ᵃ
12–13	21–22	48ᵇ–51	30ᵇ–33	6ᵇ	38ᵇ
14–15	25–26	52	34–35	7ᵃ	39
16	Omitted.	11 1–2ᵃ	39 18–20	7ᵇ–9	39ᵇ–44
17	30	2ᵇ	21ᵃ	10	45
18	32	2ᶜ	21ᵇ, ᶜ, ᵈ	11ᵃ	46
19	35	3	22	11ᵇ	47
20–21	36–37	4–6ᵃ ²	26–28ᵃ	12–13	13 6–7
22ᵃ	33ᵃ	6ᵇ	28ᵇ	14	42 4–5
22ᵇ–27ᵃ	38–43	7–9	29–32	15–16	6–7
27ᵇ	Omitted.	10ᵃ	33ᵃ	17	8
28	45	10ᵇ	33	18–19	16–17
29–31ᵃ	47–49ᵃ	11 ³	32 1, 22	20	18
31ᵇ	50	12–15ᵃ	24–27ᵃ	21	10
32	51	15ᵃ ⁴	33 26	22	11
33–34ᵃ	25 2–3	15ᵇ	32 1, 2	23	12
34ᵇ	1	16	5	24ᵃ	21ᵃ
35	40 30 ¹	17	3	24ᵇ–27	21ᵇ–24
36	25 9ᵇ	18 ⁵	Omitted.	28–31	25–28
37ᵃ	11ᵃ	19ᵃ ⁶	22ᵃ	32–37	32–37
37ᵇ	11ᵇ	19–20	33 1–2	14 1–2	41 31–32
38	14	21–23	4–6	3ᵃ	39 3
39	15	24–26	15–17	3ᵇ	7ᵃ
40	16	27–28ᵃ	26–28ᵃ	3ᶜ	7ᵇ
41ᵃ	13 29ᵃ	28ᵇ–29ᵃ	28ᵇ–29ᵃ	4	12
41ᵇ	29ᵇ	29ᵇ–30ᵃ	29ᵇ–30ᵃ	5ᵃ	13ᵃ
42–43	25 13, 18	30ᵇ	30ᵇ	5ᵇ	13ᵇ
44	19	31–32ᵃ	31–32	6ᵃ	14
45–47ᵃ	18–20	32ᵇ–33	33ᵇ–34	6ᵇ	14ᵇ
47ᵇ–50ᵃ	21–24ᵃ	12 1–2	40–42	7ᵃ	15ᵃ
50ᵇ	24ᵇ	3–5ᵃ	43–45	7ᵇ	15ᵇ
50ᶜ	26	5ᵇ	46	8ᵃ	Omitted.
10 1–5ᵃ	27–31ᵃ	6ᵃ	49	8ᵇ–9	16ᵇ–17
5ᵇ–9	31ᵇ–35	6ᵇ–12	48ᵇ, 50–60	10	44 6, 7
10–12	37–39ᵃ	13–14	34 1–3ᵃ	11ᵃ	8ᵃ
13ᵃ	43ᵃ	15ᵃ, ᵇ	3ᵇ–4ᵃ	11ᵇ	8ᵇ–9
13ᵇ–16	43ᵇ–46	15ᶜ–24ᵃ	4ᵇ–16ᵃ	12	10
17–19ᵃ	28 42–44ᵃ	24ᵇ	16ᵇ	13ᵃ	35

¹ Cf. *Diat.* xxxi. 4.
² Omitting ver. 4, "tied by the door without, in a place where two ways met."
³ Partly. ⁴ Duplicate. ⁵ Cf. viii. 1 and xxxviii. 37.
⁶ Duplicate. ⁷ Interpreting clause.

II. ANALYSIS OF THE GOSPELS.

S. Mark.	Tatian.	S. Mark.	Tatian.	S. Luke.	Tatian.
14 13^b	44 37^b	15 14	50 *35–36*	16 19^a	55 *12^a*
13^c–15^a	*37^c–39^a*	15^a	37^a	19^b	*13^a*
15^b–16	39^b–40	15^b–19	*37^b–42*	19^c	13^b
17–18^a	*41, 44^a*	20^a	51 *16*	20	16
18^b–20	44^b–46	20^b	15^b		
21	48	21^a, ^{c}	*17^a, ^{c}*	S. Luke.	
22^a	45 *12^a*	21^b	17^b		
22^b	*12^b*	22	*25^a, ^{b}*	1 1–4 ^{4}	Omitted.
23^a	*13^a*	23^a	*27^a*	5–80	1 6–81
23^b–24^a	14	23^b	27^c	2 1–39	2 9–47
24^b–25	*15, 16^a*	24–27	*28–31, 25^c*	40–52	3 24–36
26	46 *16*	28	26	3 1–3	37–39
27–30^a	45 *23–27^a*	29^a	*35^b, ^{c}*	4^a	*42*
30^b	27^b	29^b	*36^a*	4^b–6	43–45
30^1	49 17	30–32^a	*36^b–39*	7–9	4 *15–18*
31	45 28	32^b	*43*	10–18	19–27
32	48 *1, 3*	33	*52*	19–20	6 23–24
33–35^a	*5–7*	34	53	21^a ^{5}	4 35
35^b–36^a	*8–9^a*	35–36^a {52	*54*	21^b	*36*
36^b–37^a	*9^b–10*		*2^b*	22^a	37
37^b	11^a	36^b	3	22^b	*38*
37^c	*11^b*	36^c	*5*	23^a	29
38^a	*12^a*	37–38	*7–8*	23^b–38 ^{6}	Omitted.
38^b	12^b	39	*11–12*	4 1^a	42
39	*13*	40^a	*21–22*	1^b–2^a, ^{c}	*43–44^a*
40	14	40^b	22^b	2^b	44^b
41^a	*18–19*	40^c	22^d	3–4	*45–46*
41^b–42^a	20–21^a	41^a	*21^a*	5–7	*50–52*
42^b–44^a	*21^b–23^a*	41^b	21^b	8	5 *1*
44^b	23^b	41^c	*23^a*	9–12	4 *47–49*
45	*25*	42	24	13	5 *2*
46–47	*33, 35*	43^a	*25–26*	14^a	*21*
48–50	*41, 43*	43^b–45^a	*27–29^a*	14^b–22^a	*33–41*
51–52	45–46	45^b	*29*	14^b–15 ^{7}	7 8
53–54	*47–55*	46^a	*30^a*	22^b	17 *39, 40*
55–57^a	49 *20–24^a*	46^b	*33, 35*	23–24	*42–43*
57^b–59	*24^b–26*	47^a	36	25–27	*45–47*
59^2	23	47^b	*37*	28–30	*50–52*
60^a	27^b	16 1^a	*45*	31^a	6 *36*
60^b	28	1^b	38^b ^{3}	31^b–38^a	40–46^a
61^a	29	2	*45*	38^b	*47*
61^b–62	*33, 34, 36*	3	*47^a*	38^c–39	*48–49*
63^a	*37^a*	4^a	*49^a*	40^a	*50*
63^b–64^a	*38^a*	4^b	*47^b*	40^b	*51*
64^b	38^b	5^a	*49^b*	41	*54*
64^c	*39*	5^b	53	42^a	7 *1*
65^a	40^a	6	*54–55*	42^b–43	*5–6*
65^b	41^a	7^a	53 *5*	44	6 35
66–68^a	48 *50–52^a*	7^b	6^a	5 1–7	5 49–55
68^b	52^b	8^a	7^b	8–11	6 *1–4*
68^c	49 7	8^b	8	12	22 *1*
69^a	*8^a*	9	*25*	13–15^a	*2–6*
69^b–70	*8^b–12*	10^a	*31*	15^b–16	*7–8*
71	14	10^b	35^b	17^a	7 *12*
72	*15–18*	11	*37*	17^b–21	13–17
15 1^a	*19, 20, 43^a*	12^a	*39^a*	22–25^a	*18–22^a*
1^b	*43^b*	12^b	*39^b*	25^b	22^b
2	*54*	13^a	*61^a*	26^a	*23^b*
3^a	50 *15*	13^b	61^b	26^b	*23^c*
3^b–7	*16–21, 25*	14	55 *3*	26^c	*24*
8–9^a	*26–27^a*	15^a	*4*	27–36^a	*25–31^a*
9^b–12	*27^b–31*	15^b	*5^b*	36^b–38^a	*34^b–35^a*
13	32	16–18	8–10		

[1] Duplicate; cf. Mark xiv. 72.   [2] Duplicate; but cf. Mark xiv. 56^b.   [3] Cf. 46.
[4] Introduction.   [5] Omitting, "and praying."   [6] Genealogy.   [7] Duplicate.

APPENDIX.

S. Luke.	Tatian.	S. Luke.	Tatian.	S. Luke.	Tatian.
5 38^b–39	7 35^b–36^a	8 19^a	16 13^b	9 27–28	24 1, 2
6 1–5	37–45	19^b	14^b	29^a	3
6–9	47–50	20–21	15–18	29^b	4^b
10	51	22^a	11 32^a	30	5
11	8 1	22^b	32^b	31$^{a\,6}$	Omitted.
12–13^a	9–10^a	22^c	31^b	31^b–33^a	6–8
13^b–17	17–23	23$^{a,\,b}$	33^a, 34^a	33^b	9^a
18–19	16–17	23^c	33^b	33^c	9^b
20^a	26^a	24^a	34^b	34^a	10
20^b–21	27, 28, 30	24^b	35^a	34^b	11
22^a	35^a	24^c	35^b	35	12
22^b–23	35^b–36	25^a	36	36^a	13
24–27^a	37–40^a	25^b–27^a	37–39^a	36^b	18^b
27^b–28	9 13	27^b	39^b	37	25
29	7–8	27^c	39^c	38^a	30^a
30^a	10	28^a	43, 44^a	38^b–39^a	30^c–31^a
30^b–31	10^b–11	28^b	44^b	39^b	32
32	15^a	28^c	44^c	39^c	33^b
32^b–36	15^b–19	29^a	45	40–42^a	34–43^a
37^a	10 13^a	29^b	40^b	42^b	43^b
37^b–38	13^b–14	29^c	41^a	43^a	44^b
39–42	17–20	30–33^a	46–49^a	43$^{b\,7}$	49
43	37	33^b	49^b	44^a	49^b
44	35	34–36	50–52^a	44^b	50
45	38	37^a	12 1	45	51
45$^{a\,1}$	14 31	37^b	2	46	25 1
46	10 41–42	38–39^a	3–4	47^a	9^a
47–48^a	44–45	39^b–40^a	5–6^a	47^b	9^b
48^b–49	46–48	40^b–41^a	6^b–7	48^a	11^a
7 1	11 1, 4^a	41^b–45^a	8–16	48^b	11^b
2–3^a	4^b–5	45^b–47^a	17–19^a	48^c	12
3^b–4^a	6	47^b–48	20–21^a	49	14
4^b–5	7–8	49–50	22–23	50^a	15
6–7^2	10	51–52	25–26, 28	50^b	16
8–9^a	11–12^a	53	27	51–56	38 42–47
9^b	12^b	54	29^a	57$^{a\,8}$	Omitted.
10–17	16–23	55^a	29^b	57^b	11 25^a
18	13 38	55^b–56	30^b–31	57^c	25^b
19–27	39^b–47	9 1^a	42^a	58	26
28	14 1	1^b–2	42^b–43	59–62	27–30
29–30	2–3	3^a	40$^{a,\,b}$	10 1–12	15 15–26
31$^{a\,3}$	Omitted.	3^b	40^c	13–15	28–30
31^b–35	10–14	4–5	51, 54	16–22	32–38
36–39	45–48	6	13 36–37	23$^{a\,9}$	16 31–32
40–50	15 1–11	7^a	18 1^a	23^b	38
8 1–3	16 19–21	7^b	1^b	24	39
4–5^a	22–25^a	7^c–8^a	2	25^a	34 25^a
5^b	25^b	8^b	3^b	25^b	26^a
6	26	9	20	26–28$^{a\,10}$	26^b–34
7	28^a	10^4	14 43–44	28^b–37	35–44
8^a	29^a	11^5	32 23	38–42	13 31–35
8^b	29^b	11^b	18 26	11 1$^{a\,11}$	Omitted.
8^c	30	12–13^a	27–34	1^b–2^a	9 30–31
9–10	31–32	13^b	35	2^b–4	32–36
11–13^a	41–45^a	14–17	36–43	5–13	10 22–30
13^b	45^b	18–23^a	23 31 45^a	14	14 16
14	47	23^b	45^b	15	17
15	48^a	24	46	16	18
16–17	8 42, 44	25	47	17–18^a	19–21^a
18	16 33	26	49	18^b	21^b

[1] Duplicate. [2] Varied, omitting part of 7.
[3] A connective, omitted also by Revised Version. [4] Omitting Bethsaida.
[5] Duplicate. [6] *I.e.* "Who appeared in glory." [7] Varied. [8] *I.e.* ἐγένετο.
[9] Varied. [10] Varied. [11] Connective.

II. ANALYSIS OF THE GOSPELS.

S. Luke.	Tatian.	S. Luke.	Tatian.	S. Luke.	Tatian.
11 19-20	14 22-23	13 19ᵃ	17 10ᵃ	19 11ᵇ-27	31 36-52
21-23	25-27	19ᵇ-20ᵃ	10-13	28-29ᵃ	39 18-19
24-26	16 7-9	20ᵇ	14	29ᵇ-30ᵃ	20, 21ᵃ,ᵇ
27-28	11-12	21	15	30ᵇ	21ᶜ
29	1-2	22-30	31 6-14	30ᶜ	21ᵈ
30	3	31-33	24 27-29	31ᵃ	22ᵃ
31	5	34-35	41 4-6	31ᵇ-32ᵃ	22ᵇ, 26ᵃ
32	6	14 1-6	29 43-48	32ᵇ	26ᵇ
33	8 42	7-15	30 1-9	33-34	27-28ᵃ
34	9 47-48	16ᵃ	10-11ᵃ	35-36	29, 30
35-36	49-50	16ᵇ-17	11ᵇ-12¹	37	31
37-41	20 12-16	18-20	13-15	38ᵃ	32-33ᵃ
42	40 53	21ᵃ	19	38ᵇ	33ᵇ
43	41	21ᵇ-23ᵃ	22-24ᵃ	39-44	36-41
44¹	57	23ᵇ-24	24ᶜ-25	43ᵃ ⁶	41 30ᵃ
45-46	59-60	25-33	15 42-50	44ᵇ ᶜ	30ᵇ
47ᵃ	61ᵃ	34ᵃ	25 24ᵃ	45-46	32 1-5
47ᵇ	61ᵇ	34ᵇ-35	24ᵇ-25	47-48	34 46-47
48	63	15 1-4	26 1-4	20 1-2ᵃ	33 27-28ᵃ
49-51	41 1-3	5ᵃ	5	2ᵇ-6ᵃ	28ᵇ-32ᵃ
52ᵃ	40 44ᵃ	5ᵇ-6	6	6ᵇ	32ᵇ
52ᵇ	44ᵇ	7-32	8-33	7-9ᵃ	34, 40
53-54	41 16-17	34-35	9ᵇ	41
12 1-3	18-20	16 1-12	26 1-4	10-12	42-45
3ᵇ-4ᵃ ²	13 12ᵇ-13ᵃ	13	10 1	13	48
4ᵇ	13ᵇ	14-15	29 12-13	14ᵃ	50
5ᵃ	14ᵃ	16	14 5ᵃ	14ᵇ	51
5ᵇ	14ᵇ	17	9	15-17ᵃ ⁷	52-55ᵃ
5ᶜ	14ᶜ	18	25 38-39	17ᵇ	55ᵇ
6-9	15-19	19-31	29 14-26	18-19	58-60
10	14 31	17 1-2 ³	25 13, 17	20ᵃ	34 1ᵃ
11	41 46	3-4	27 14-15	20ᵇ	1ᵇ
12	47	5-10	33 9-14	21-25	2-7
13-21	28 33-41	11ᵃ,ᶜ ⁴	Omitted.	26	8
22-25	10 2-4	11ᵇ-19	30 31ᵇ-39	27-29ᵃ	9-11ᵃ
26	5	20-21	40 22-23	29ᵇ-31	11ᵇ-13
27-29ᵃ	6-9ᵃ	22ᵃ	41 35ᵃ	32-34ᵃ	14-16ᵃ
29ᵇ	9ᵇ	22ᵇ	35ᵇ	34ᵇ-36	17-19
30-31	10-11	23-24	42 13-14	37	20
32-33ᵃ	9 42-43	25	15	38	21ᵃ
33ᵇ-34	44-46	26-27	38-40	39	23
35-38	43 39-42	28-37	41-50	40	45
39-40	42 52-53	18 1-8	33 18-25	41-44	35 17-22
41-42ᵃ	43 1-2ᵃ	9-14	32 16-21	45-47	40 32-45
42ᵇ-43	2ᵇ-3	15-17	25 43-46	21 1-2	42-43
44ᵃ	4ᵃ	18-23ᵃ	28 42-50ᵃ	3	32 14
44ᵇ-45ᵃ	4ᵇ-5	23ᵇ-24ᵃ	50ᵇ-51ᵃ	4	15
45ᵇ	6ᵃ	24ᵇ	51ᵇ	5ᵃ	41 27-28ᵃ
45ᶜ	6ᵇ	25-27	29 2, 4, 5	5ᵇ	28ᵇ
46ᵃ	7-8ᵃ	28	6ᵃ	6-7	29-34
46ᵇ	8ᵇ	29	8	8ᵃ	35-37
47-50	27 24-27	30	9	8ᵇ	38ᵃ
51-53	13 20-22	31ᵃ	30 40	8ᶜ	38ᶜ
54-55	14 37-38	31ᵇ	41	9ᵃ	39ᵃ,ᵇ
56	40ᵇ	32	42-43	9ᵇ	39ᶜ
57	Omitted.	33-34	44-45	10	40
58ᵃ	8 54ᵃ	35ᵃ	31 25ᵃ	11	41
58ᵇ	54ᵇ	35ᵇ	26ᵃ	12-13	43-44
58ᶜ	55	36-37	27-28	14-15	48-49
59	56	38-39ᵃ	29ᵇ-30ᵃ	16	52
13 1-17	27 31-47	39ᵇ-42ᵃ	30ᵇ-34ᵃ	17	13 7 ⁸
18ᵃ	17 8	42ᵇ-43	34ᵇ-35	18-19	41 53-54
18ᵇ	9ᵃ	19 1-10	15-24	20-22	42 1-3
		11ᵃ ⁵	Omitted.		

¹ Varied.   ² Partly duplicate.   ³ Varied.   ⁴ Connective.   ⁵ Connective.
⁶ Duplicate; but cf. Luke xxi. 6.   ⁷ Omitting 16ᵇ, "God forbid."   ⁸ Cf. xli. 50-51.

APPENDIX.

S. Luke.	Tatian.	S. Luke.	Tatian.	S. John.	Tatian.
21 23-24	42 8-9	22 62	49 18	24 11ᵇ	53 37
25-26ᵃ	19-20	63ᵃ	40ᵃ	12	10-17
26ᵇ-27	21-22	63ᵇ	40ᵇ	13ᵃ	39ᵃ
28	24	63ᶜ	41ᵃ	13ᵇ-35	39ᵇ-61ᵃ
29-33	25-28	64	41ᵇ	36ᵃ	54 1ᵃ
34-36	29-31	65	42	36ᵇ	1ᵇ
37-38	40 24-25	66	19	36ᶜ-49ᵃ	2-12
22 1-2ᵃ	41 2-3	66ᵇ-68	30-32	49ᵇ	55 11
2ᵇ-4ᵃ	5ᵇ-7ᵃ	69	36	50-51	12ᵇ-13ᵃ
4ᵇ-5	7ᵇ-8	70	35	52-53	14-15
6	9	71	38ᵃ		
7-10ᵃ	34-37ᵃ	23 1	43		
10ᵇ-11ᵃ	37ᶜ	2ᵃ	45-46	S. John.	
11ᵇ-12ᵃ	38ᵇ-39ᵃ	2ᵇ	47		
12ᵇ-13	39ᵇ-40	3	50, 54	1 1-5	1 1-5
14-16	41-43	4-16	50 1-13	6³	Omitted.
17	45 13	17	20	7-17	3 46-56
18	10ᵃ	18ᵃ	14	18-28	4 1-11
19ᵃ	12ᵇ	18ᵇ	24	29-31	30-32
19ᵇ	16ᵇ	19	25	32-34	39-41
20	13-15	20-23	33-36	35-51	5 4-20
21	44 47	24	51 6	2 1-11	22-32
22	48	25ᵃ	50 37ᵇ	12 ⁴	6 36
23	50	25ᵇ	51 6	13	32 1ᵃ
24-26	31 1-3	26ᵃ	17	14ᵃ	1ᵇ
27-30ᵃ	44 31-33	26ᵇ-33ᵃ	18-25ᵃ	14ᵇ-15	2ᵇ, ᶜ
30ᵇ	29 7	33ᵇ	25ᶜ	16	4
31-32	45 17-18	34ᵃ	52 6	17-22	6-11
33ᵃ	25	34ᵇ	51 28-29	23ᵃ ⁵	Omitted.
33ᵇ	26ᵃ	35ᵃ	35ᵃ	23ᵇ-25	15 12-14
34ᵃ	27ᶜ, ᵇ	35ᵇ	37-38	3 1-21	32 27ᵇ-47
34ᵇ	27ᵈ	35ᶜ	39ᵃ	22-36	6 5-19
35-38	46 12-15ᵃ	36-37	41-42	4 1-3ᵃ	20-22
39	16	38	31-32	3ᵇ	25
40ᵃ	48 3ᵃ	39-43	44-48	4-45ᵃ	21 8-49
40ᵇ	4	44ᵃ	52ᵃ	45ᵇ	23 3ᵃ
41	7	44ᵇ-45ᵃ	52ᵇ	46-54	6 26-34
42ᵃ	9ᵃ	45ᵇ	52 8	5 1-47	22 9-55
42ᵇ	9ᵇ	46ᵃ	7ᵃ	1ᵃ ⁶	30 31ᵃ
43-45	16-18	46ᵇ	7ᵇ	6 1ᵃ	18 21ᵃ
46ᵃ	19ᵃ	47ᵃ	11	1ᵇ	21ᵇ
46ᵇ	12ᵃ, 19ᵇ	47ᵇ	12ᵃ	2ᵃ	22
47	22	48	13	2ᵇ-5ᵃ	22ᵇ-25ᵃ
48ᵃ	20ᵃ	49ᵃ	21ᵃ	5ᵇ-9	30ᵇ-34
48ᵇ	26ᵇ	49ᵇ	23ᵃ	10	36
49	31	50	25ᵃ	11	39
50-51ᵃ ¹	35-36ᵃ	51	26	12-13	41-42
51ᵇ	40	52-55ᵃ	27-36	14-18	45-49
52ᵃ	41	55ᵇ-56ᵃ	37-38ᵃ	19ᵃ	19 2
52ᵇ-53ᵃ	42	56ᵇ	38	19ᵇ-20	3-4
53ᵇ	44, 47	56ᵃ	39	21ᵃ	9-10
54	54	24 1ᵃ	45ᵃ	21ᵇ	11
55ᵃ	55ᵃ, 51	1ᵇ	45ᵇ	22-60	16-54
55ᵇ-56	52ᵃ	1ᶜ	46ᵇ	61-71	20 1-11
57	49 11ᵃ	2	49ᵃ	7 1	27 30
58ᵃ	11ᵇ	3	52	2-10ᵃ	28 1-9ᵃ
58ᵇ-59ᵃ	12ᵃ	4-7	53 1-4	10ᵇ-31	11-32
59ᵇ	14	8	7ᵃ	31-35 ⁷	34 48-53
60ᵃ	15-16	10	36	37-52	35 1-16
60ᵇ-61ᵃ	17	11ᵃ	38	53 ⁸	Omitted
61ᵇ				8 1-11	,,

¹ Omitting ver. 51, "Suffer ye thus far." ² Cf. 41. ³ Implied in *Diat.* i.
⁴ Part omitted. ⁵ A connective. ⁶ Duplicate. ⁷ Duplicate of ver. 31.
⁸ The woman taken in adultery entirely absent. Cf. Revised Version and Introduction, p. 25.

II. ANALYSIS OF THE GOSPELS. 291

S. John.	Tatian.	S. John.	Tatian.	S. John.	Tatian.
8 12-50	35 23-61	13 38ᵇ	45 27ᵇ,ᶜ	19 3ᵃ	50 41
51-59	36 1-9	14 1-20	29-48	3ᵇ-12	42ᵇ-51
9 1-38	10-47	21-31ᵃ	46 1-11	13-15	51 1-3
39-41	37 1-3	31ᵇ	15ᵇ	16ᵃ	6
10 1-42	4-45	15 1-27	17-43	16ᵇ	15ᵃ
11 1-16	46-61	16 1-15	44-58	17ᵃ	15ᶜ
17-57	38 1-41	16-33	47 1-18	17ᵇ	25ᵃ
12 1-2	39 1-2	17 1-26	19-44	17ᵃ	25ᵇ
3ᵃ	7ᵃ	18 1-2	48 1-2	18	25ᵃ
3ᵇ-6	8-11	3	22	19-22	31-34
7ᵃ	14ᵃ,ᵇ	4ᵃ	24	23-24	28-29
7ᵇ-8ᵃ	14ᶜ-15ᵃ	4ᵇ-9	27ᵇ-32	25-27	49-51
8ᵇ	15ᵇ	10-11	35-36	28-29ᵃ	52 1-2ᵃ
9-11	4-6	12ᵃ	44	29ᵇ	2ᵇ-3
12-13	34-35	12ᵇ-17	47-51	30ᵃ	4
14-15	20-24,	18ᵃ	53	30ᵇ	7ᵇ
	26-29	18ᵇ	55ᵃ	31-37	14-20
16	25	19-25ᵃ	49 1-7	38ᵃ	25ᵃ
17-18	44-45	25ᵇ	8-10	38ᵇ	25ᵇ
19-36ᵃ	40 4-21	26ᵃ	11ᵇ	38ᶜ	27-29
36ᵇ-41	41 21-26	26ᵇ	13	38ᵈ-42	30ᵇ-34
42-50	7-15	27	14-15	20 1	45-49
13 1-20	44 11-30	28ᵃ	43ᵃ	2-17	53 9-24
21ᵃ	44ᵃ	28ᵇ ²	44	18	31
21ᵇ	44ᵇ	29-30	45ᵇ-46	19	54 1ᵇ
22	49	31-38ᵃ	48-55	20ᵃ	5
23-29	45 1-7	38ᵇ	50 1	20ᵇ-31	13-24
30-32	9-11	39-40	23-24	21ᵇ ³	55 5ᵃ
33-36¹	19-22	19 1	37	21 1-24	54 25-48
37ᵃ	25, 26ᵃ	2	40	25	55 17
37ᵇ-38ᵃ	26ᵇ-27ᵃ				

¹ Omitting, "why cannot I follow thee now?"
² Omitting, "and it was early."
³ Duplicate.

III.

Various Readings in the Arabic Diatessaron.

Note.—The various readings marked (P) or (C) are supported wholly *or in part* by the Peschito or the Curetonian Syriac respectively. Those marked (P*) or (C*) are not so supported, but seem to have arisen from mistranslation of those versions, either through mis-pointing, or choosing the wrong rendering where a word had more than one meaning, or through misunderstanding an idiom. Those marked (P†) or (C†) are such as are not correct reproductions of those versions, nor yet definite mistranslations of them, but yet seem to have been suggested by something in the Peschito or Curetonian Syriac respectively. Those marked with an asterisk (*) are deserving of special notice, as being probably due to Tatian himself. A large number of various readings have been excluded from this list, because they arose from idiomatic differences in the languages through which the Gospel narrative passed before reaching the present form. It is probable that some of those contained in the present table are due to the same cause, but they have been retained here as their origin was less obvious. Others have been omitted because they appeared to be due to the blending together of parallel passages. A few have been added from Dr. Sellin's Tables, which came to hand after this table had been drawn up. The Authorised Version is used unless otherwise stated.

	Diatessaron.	Gospel.	
1	9	and he entered (P)	it came to pass	Lu. 1 8
	10		when he went	,, 9
	16	while he is yet in his mother's womb (P)	even from his mother's womb	,, 15
	22	were standing waiting (P)	waited	,, 21
	24	. . . . (P)	it came to pass	,, 23
	29	*O thou* blessed among women (P)	blessed art thou among women	,, 28
	35	be done unto me since no man hath known me (P*)	be, seeing I know not a man	,, 34
	36	that which shall be born of thee, shall be holy, and (P)	that holy thing which shall be born of thee	,, 35
	42		it came to pass	,, 41
	43	fruit that is in thy womb (P)	fruit of thy womb	,, 42
	45		for lo,	,, 44
	51	Embraceth them that fear him	is on them that fear him	,, 50
	60		it came to pass	,, 59

III. VARIOUS READINGS.

Lu.	1	78	knowledge of life (P*)	knowledge of salvation	Lu. 1 77
		81	was waiting in the deserts (P)	was in the deserts	,, 80
	2	1	his mother	his mother Mary	Mt. 1 18
		6	Our God is with us (P) (C)	God with us	,, 23
		9		it came to pass	Lu. 2 1
		15	all the people of his dominion (P)	all the world	,, 7
		22	where they were staying (P)	in the inn	,, 14
		23	good hope to men (P)	good will toward men	,, 15
		28		it came to pass	,, 20
		29	seen and heard (P)	heard and seen	,, 21
		35	and this is what he was called	which was so named	,, 27
		39	offer a sacrifice for him, as it is written in (P†)	do for him after the custom of	,, 31
		42	on account of	before the face of	,, 34
			of contradiction (P)	which shall be spoken against	
	3	5	Judah (P) (C)	Judaea	Mt. 2 5
		11	myrrh, and frankincense (P) (C)	frankincense, and myrrh	,, 11
		12	they saw in sleep (P) (C)	being warned of God	,, 12
		18	for the loss of them	because they are not	,, 18
		22	he saw in a dream that he should go (P) (C)	being warned of God in a dream he turned aside	,, 22
		23	and that he should dwell	And he came and dwelt	,, 23
		28	with the children of their company (P)	in the company	Lu. 2 44
		32	were seeking thee with great anxiety (P) (C)	have sought thee sorrowing	,, 48
		43	establish in the plain a way for our God (P) (C)	make his paths straight	,, 3 4
		56	truth and grace (P)	grace and truth	Jn. 1 17
	4	1	only-begotten, God (P)	only-begotten Son	,, 18
		3	acknowledged that he was not	confessed, I am not	,, 20
		10	of whom I said	who	,, 27
		11	Bethany (P)	Bethabara	,, 28
		12		about his loins	Mt. 3 4
		18	shall be taken away	is hewn down	,, 10
		26	who, grasping a fan in his hand to cleanse (P)	whose fan is in his hand, and he will throughly purge	Lu. 3 17

Diatessaron.		Gospel.	
4 27	And other things he taught, and preached (P)	And many other things in his exhortation preached he	Lu. 3 18
37	in the form of a dove's body (P)	in a bodily shape like a dove	,, 22
46	Man liveth not (P) (G)	Man shall not live	Mt. 4 4
51	glory of it .... (P)	glory of them ...	Lu. 4 6
5 *8	that I may give them to whomsoever I will	and to whomsoever I will I give it.	,, ,,
11	the place of his abode . (P)	where he dwelt	Jn. 1 39
14	to be Jesus (P)	which is by interpretation, A stone. Jesus	,, 42
16	This is indeed a son of Israel (P)	Behold an Israelite indeed	,, 45
*25	hath not my hour come ?	mine hour is not yet come.	,, 47
27	for the purification of the Jews (P)	after the manner of the purifying of the Jews	,, 2 4
*29	they did so	they bare it	,, 6
30	knew, because they had drawn the water. (P)	which drew the water knew	,, 8
37	forgiveness to the wicked (P*). Cf. note.	deliverance to the captives	Lu. 4 18
,,	To bring the broken into forgiveness (P*)	to set at liberty them that are bruised	,, ,,
39	and went away and sat down (P)	and sat down	,, 20
6 1	Lord, I beseech thee, that thou depart from me (P)	Depart from me ... O Lord	,, 5 8
8	a disciple of John (P)	some of John's disciples	Jn. 3 25
9	many come (P)	all men come	,, 26
*16	set his seal to this, that he is truly God	set to his seal that God is true.	,, 33
20	had admitted, and that he baptized	made and baptized	,, 4 1
42	thou art come (P†)	art thou come	Lu. 4 34
51	grievous and divers diseases.	divers diseases	,, 40
*53	unto the door of Jesus	at the door	Mk. 1 33
5	until they overtook him (P†)	unto him	Lu. 4 42
6	because for the sake of this Gospel (P†)	for therefore	,, 43
14	there came some with	men brought in	,, 5 18

III. VARIOUS READINGS.

7 25	among the publicans (P*)	at the receipt of custom	Lu. 5 27
29	A physician doth not seek the whole (P*)	They that are whole need not a physician	,, 31
31	the Pharisees	the *disciples* of the Pharisees	Mk. 2 33
34	putteth on a new patch, and seweth it (P)	seweth a piece of new cloth	,, 21
,, 35	. . . a great rent be made (P)	. . . the rent is made worse.	,, 22
37	skins perish, and the wine be poured out (P)	wine is spilled, and the bottles will be marred	Mt. 12 1
		began to pluck	
30	Have ye not heretofore read . . .	Have ye never read . . .	Mk. 2 25
40	the bread of the Lord's table (P)	the shewbread	,, 26
44	that I love	what this meaneth, I will have	Mt. 12 7
48	a way to blame him	an accusation against him.	Lu. 6 7
49	Rise up, and come into the midst of the synagogue (P)	stand forth in the midst	,, 8
50	What is lawful to do on the sabbath day, good or evil ? (P)	Is it lawful on the sabbath days to do good, or to do evil ?	,, 9
8 8	shall he preach good tidings unto the nations. (P*)(C*)	shall the Gentiles trust.	Mt. 12 21
9		it came to pass	Lu. 6 12
12	they should bring unto him a boat (P)	a small ship should wait on him	Mk. 3 9
22	and this is he that betrayed him	which also was the traitor	Lu. 6 16
34	that are cast out	which are persecuted	Mt. 5 10
53	leave thy gift upon the altar, and go thy way first, and be	Leave there thy gift before the altar, and go thy way; first be	,, 24
54	give a ransom (P)	give diligence	Lu. 12 58
60	injureth thee	offend thee	Mt. 5 30
9 *1	but call thou upon God in thy faith	but shall perform unto the Lord thine oaths	,, 33
5	either, Yes, or No	Yea, yea ; Nay, nay	Lu. 6 37
10	do not restrain	ask *them* not again	,, 30
13	receive you harshly, and drive you out (P†)	persecute you	Mt. 5 44
15	what reward shall ye have ?	what reward have ye ?	,, 46
*16, 17	where is your superiority ?	what thank have ye ?	Lu. 6 33, 34
18	cut off no man's hope, that . . . (P)	hoping for nothing again, and . . .	,, 35
29	your petition (P*)(C*)	what things ye have need of	Mt. 6 8

	Diatessaron.	Gospel.	
9 40	wash thy face, and anoint thy head (P) (C)	anoint thine head, and wash thy face	Mt. 6 17
47	unimpaired	single	,, 22
50	as a lamp lightens thee with its bright shining (P)	as when the bright shining of a candle doth give thee light	Lu. 11 36
10 1	he is obliged to hate one of them . . . to honour	either he will hate the one . . . else he will hold to	Mt. 6 24
*4	when he tries, shall be able to add	by taking thought can add	,, 27
6	though they toil not (P†) (C†)	they toil not	,, 28
8	how much rather shall it be done to you (P)	*shall he* not much more *clothe* you	,, 30
9	nor let your mind be troubled because of this (P)	neither be ye of doubtful mind	Lu. 12 29
12	for what is its own (P) (C)	for the things of itself	Mt. 6 34
14	release, and ye shall be released	.	Lu. 6 38
16	even that which he can have	even that which he hath	Mk. 4 25
28, 29	what father . . . do you think [3 times]	of which of you that is a father . . . [R.V.]	Lu. 11 11, 12
30	know good gifts, and give them	know how to give good gifts	Lu. 11 13
33	How narrow is the gate (P) (C)	Because straight is the gate. Cf. R.V. margin.	Mt. 7 14
34	lambs' clothing (P) (C)	sheep's clothing	,, 15
11 1	. . . . (C)	it came to pass	,, 28
5	came unto him with	sent unto him	Lu. 7 3
10	my roof should overshadow thee . . . it is enough	thou shouldest come under my roof . . . only	Mt. 8 8
11	under obedience to authority	set under authority	Lu. 7 8
12	in Israel	no, not in Israel	Mt. 8 10
16	already (P†)	.	Lu. 7 10
18	he saw people that were attending one that was dead (P)	behold, there was a dead man carried out	,, 12
,,	and his mother was a widow (P)	and she was a widow	Mt. 8 20
26	a place, where (C†)	where	
33	by a whirlwind and a wind	.	,, 24

III. VARIOUS READINGS.

11 33	the boat was nigh to be sunk through the abundance of the waves (P) (C)	they were filled *with water*, and were in jeopardy	Lu. 8 23
37	think you	.	
40	as often as he was confined (P)	he had been often bound	Mk. 5 4
45	he was in captivity to it (P)	it had caught him	Lu. 8 29
49	ran to the summit, and fell into the middle of (P)	ran violently down a steep place into	Mk. 5 13
12 14	secretly	.	
29	Maid, arise. (P)	Talitha cumi, which is, being interpreted . . . arise.	,, 28
35	Even as ye have believed (P)	According to your faith	Mt. 9 29
40	And many followed him	.	
45	attend chiefly	.	,, 10 35
47	. . . . (P)	go rather	,, 10 6
13 8	shall cast you out of	raise the dead	,, 8
	complete all the cities of the people of Israel (P)	persecute you in	,, 23
	especially	have gone over the cities of Israel	
,, 14	in a shop (P*)	.	Lu. 12 5
15	. . . .	the very hairs	Mt. 10 29
16	in what relates to you, even the hairs (P)	more than me	,, 10 30
24	with a deeper love than me	also sat	,, 37
32	came and sat (P) (C)	they . . . preached that men	Lu. 10 39
36	the apostles . . . preached unto men, that they	plagues, and of evil spirits	Mk. 6 12
41	plagues of an evil spirit	gorgeously apparelled, and live delicately	Lu. 7 21
45	in a costly robe and luxuries (P)	being baptized	,, 25
14 2	for they had been baptized (P)	prince of the devils	Mt. 12 24
*17	prince of the devils, who is in him	.	
19	in parables	bind	,, 25
24	render himself safe from	his goods	Lu. 11 21
25	those things which he possesseth	He hath an unclean spirit	Mk. 3 30
30	that there was in him an unclean spirit (P)	Either make . . . or else make	Mt. 12 33
32	Either ye make . . . or ye make	they shall give account	,, 36
35	there shall be exacted from them an account	fair weather: for the sky is red	,, 16 2
*39	fair: for the heavens are dull	foul weather . . .: for the sky is red and lowring	,, 3
*40	a storm: for the redness of the heavens is dull		

APPENDIX.

	Diatessaron.	Gospel.	
14 45	After these things came a certain man (P)	And one	Lu. 7 36
15 2	Jesus said unto him (P) (C)	. . .	,, 41
5	See	Seest thou	,, 44
15	Jesus appointed out of his disciples seventy others (P)	the Lord appointed other seventy also	,, 10 1
20	if he be not *there*, your peace (P)	if not, it	,, 6
21	of their substance (P) (C)	such things as they give	,, 7
27	many mighty works (P†) (C)	most of his mighty works.	Mt. 11 20
29	There shall be rest for Tyre and Sidon in the day of judgment, rather than (P*) (C*)	It shall be more tolerable for Tyre and Sidon at the day of judgment, than	,, 22
*30	shalt sink down into the abyss	shalt be brought down to hell	,, 23
*32	and he that heareth me, heareth him that sent me (C)	. . .	Lu. 10 16
35	every kind of enemies	all the power of the enemy	,, 19
36	ye need not to rejoice	in this rejoice not	,, 20
38	And he turned unto his disciples, and said unto them (P)	. . . . . [in some MSS.]	,, 22
43	brethren, and sisters, and wife, and children (P) (C)	wife, and children, and brethren, and sisters	,, 14 26
*49	And if he is not equal to it	Or else	,, 32
*50	let every one of you, that wisheth to be my disciple, consider: for if he renounce not	likewise, whosoever he be of you that forsaketh not	,, 33
16 7	walketh and goeth about . . . to find rest for itself (P) (C)	walketh . . . seeking rest	,, 11 24
8	if it come, and find (P) (C)	when he cometh, he findeth	,, 25
*17	motioning with his hand outstretched	he stretched forth his hand	Mt. 12 49
20	he had cast out (C)	went	Lu. 8 2
*23	and when the press of men around him was great		Mt. 13 2
32	it is not given		Mt. 4 11
35	they shall hear	all these things are done in parables ye shall hear	Mt. 13 14
36	in their ears their hearing hath become dull	their ears are dull of hearing	,, 15
42	The sower, that soweth, soweth (P)	The sower soweth	Mk. 4 14

III. VARIOUS READINGS.

16 45	but his faith in it is for a time (P)	which for a while believe	Lu. 8 13
47	the remaining lusts (P)	the lusts of other things	Mk. 4 19
48	my word . . . (P)	the word . . .	Mt. 13 23
,, 51	either a hundredfold, or . . . (P)	some an hundredfold, some . . .	Mk. 4 28
	the earth bringeth it through into fruit (P)	the earth bringeth forth fruit of herself	
17 11	of all things that are sown	when it is sown	Mt. 13 31
17	by the Lord through the prophet	by the prophet	,, 13 35
31	to pick them out, and they cast (P)	and gathered	,, 13 48
*39	And many envied him, and did not apply their mind to him, but said	.	Mk. 6 2
41	suspicious of him	offended in him	Mt. 13 57
42	knowing their thoughts	.	Lu. 4 23
45, 47	among the children of Israel (P*)	in Israel	,, 25, 27
*47	Nabathaean	Syrian	,, 27
50	when they that were in the synagogue had heard (P)	in the synagogue, when they heard these things	,, 28
53	around Nazareth, and taught in their synagogues	teaching	Mk. 6 6
18 11	there occurred a festival ; for (P)	when a convenient day was come, that	,, 21
*12	in the midst of the assembly	.	,, 22
34	this amount, what is it for all these (P) (C)	what are they among so many that they would come	Jn. 6 9
46	of their intention to come		,, 15
50	many furlongs distant from the land (P) (C)	now in the midst of the sea. Cf. margin R.V.	Mt. 14 24
19 3	thinking that it was an apparition (P)	saying, It is a spirit	,, 26
*9	Jesus had come near, he went up . . . himself and Simon	they were come . . .	,, 32
15	but there were . . . . (P)	or country	Mk. 6 56
17	beforehand (P*) (C*)	Howbeit there came	Jn. 6 23
20 4	and think that ye are clean	from the beginning	,, 64
19	all the Jews and Pharisees (P)	the Pharisees and all the Jews	Lu. 11 39
*20	and that which is bought from the market	And *when they come* from the market	Mk. 7 3
21	without having washed their hands	with unwashen hands	,, 4
24-26	[Several variations ; the text seems corrupt here.]		,, 5
			,, 11-13

Diatessaron		Gospel	
20 31	filled with indignation	for doctrines	Mt. 15 9
35		offended	,, 12
39	Do ye also so comprehend not?	Are ye so without understanding also?	Mk. 7 18
*40	goeth . . .	into the draught, purging all meats	,, 19
,, 45	in purgation, which maketh all meats clean (P)		
	if any one eat without having washed *his* hands he is not defiled. (P) (C)	to eat with unwashen hands defileth not a man	Mt. 15 20
48	a Syrophoenician by nation	Mk. 7 26
49	from Emesa of Syria	of the same coasts	Mt. 15 22
*52	have mercy on me		,, 25
54	and live (P) (C)		,, 27
21 1	towards (P)	through the midst of	Mk. 7 31
2	a deaf and dumb *man*	one that was deaf, and had an impediment in his speech	,, 32
*3	spitting on his own fingers, put them	put his fingers	,, 33
6	and all things, which he forbade them, they published the more (P*)	but the more he charged them, so much the more a great deal they published *it*	,, 36
8	as he was passing through the land of Samaria	he must needs go through Samaria	Jn. 4 4
11	Give me water, that I may drink (P) (C)	Give me to drink	,, 7
14	water of life	living water	,, 10
21	She said unto him (P) (C)	The woman answered, and said	,, 17
29		which is called Christ	,, 25
31	while he was speaking (P) (C) . . . (P) (C)	upon this . . . no man	,, 27
33	Perhaps he is the Messiah? (P†) (C†)	Is not this the Christ?	,, 29
*39	white; for the harvest is come before the time	white already to harvest	,, 35
40	and he that soweth, and he that reapeth, rejoice (P)	that both he that soweth and he that reapeth may rejoice	,, 36
41	There is one that soweth, and there is another that reapeth	One soweth, and another reapeth	,, 37

III. VARIOUS READINGS. 301

21	43	bare witness and said (C)	testified himself	Jn. 4 39
	48			,, 44
22	1	when Jesus was come to a certain village, there came near unto him ... and falling down at his feet, he	it came to pass, when he was in a certain city, behold ... who seeing Jesus fell on his face, and	Lu. 5 12
	2	I will that thou be made clean.	I will, be thou clean	Mk. 1 41
	5	for their testimony (P)	for a testimony unto them.	,, 44
	*6	any of the cities, because his fame was spread abroad exceedingly	the city	,, 45
	10	a place prepared for bathing (P) (C) in Hebrew Baitharrahmat	by the sheep *marked*, a pool in the Hebrew tongue Bethesda	Jn. 5 2
	,, 15	passeth before me, and goeth down	steppeth down before me	,, 7
	21	for Jesus turned aside from that place into another, because of the press of the multitude, which was there. (P) (C)	for Jesus had conveyed himself away, a multitude being in that place.	,, 13
	32	shall pass	is passed	,, 24
	36	at this : namely the arrival of the hour (P*)	at this : for the hour is coming	,, 28
	42, 49	seek	receive	,, 34, 41
	46	his word is not confirmed (P*) (C*)	ye have not his word abiding	,, 38
	47	in which ye boast (P*) (C*)	in them ye think	,, 39
	48	may have eternal life (P)	might have life	,, 40
23	*3	when they were assembled on the feast day	at the feast : for they also went unto the feast.	,, 4 45
	17	even one loaf (P†)	more than one loaf	Mk. 8 14
	23	He said unto them (P)		,, 20
	*25	which he called leaven		Mt. 16 12
	27	What seest thou ? (P†)	if he saw aught	Mk. 8 23
	39	charged ... and warned	charged	Mt. 16 20
	*42	spake clearly	spake that saying openly	Mk. 8 32
24	2	Simon Cephas, as if sympathising with him, said (C)	Peter took him and began to rebuke him, saying, apart by themselves. Cf. Mark ix. 2.	Mt. 17 1
	*3	the three of them apart		Lu. 9 29
	*4	and made into the form of another person	the fashion of his countenance was altered	Mk. 9 3
		so that nothing on earth can become so white	so as no fuller on earth can white them	

APPENDIX.

	Diatessaron.	Gospel.		
24	6	they thought that his decease, etc. (P*) (C*)	and spake of his decease, etc.	Lu. 9 31
	8	when these had begun to depart (P) (C)	it came to pass, as they departed	" 33
	9, 14	because of the fear, which had seized them	for they were sore afraid	{Mk. 9 6 / Mt. 17 6}
	11	when they had seen Moses and Elijah entering into the cloud, they feared again (P) (C')	and they feared as they entered into the cloud	Lu. 9 34
	*12	whom I have chosen. Cf. R.V. Luke ix. 35.	in whom I am well pleased	Mt. 17 5
	*16	saw Jesus even as he was	saw no man, save Jesus only	" 8
	19	What is this word which he said unto us, When I shall have risen . . . (P)	what the rising . . . should mean	Mk. 9 10
	26	they drew near . . . for joy	were greatly amazed	Lu. 13 15
	29	be careful to-day . . . depart the day following (P)	walk to-day . . . the day following	" 33
	31	cometh unexpectedly upon him	taketh him	" 9 39
	37	From youth even until now	Of a child	Mk. 9 21
	41	saw a running together of men, and their assembling together at the cry . . . (P)	saw . . . the people came running together . . .	" 25
	42	Thou deaf spirit, which speakest not (P)	Thou dumb and deaf spirit	" 26
	47	and the child fell as dead	he was as one dead	" 26
	49	fasting and prayer (P).	prayer and fasting Cf. R.V.	" 29
	51	Keep ye these sayings in your ears and hearts (P†)(C†) that they should not understand it (P) (C)	Let these sayings sink down into your ears that they perceived it not	Lu. 9 44 / " 45
25	1	for they said, Who of them was the greater? (P)	which of them should be greatest	" 46
	*6	Simon saith unto him, Yea. Jesus said unto him, Give thou also unto them as if a stranger		Mt. 17 26
	*7	And lest it should distress them	Notwithstanding, lest we should offend them	" 27
	14	followeth thee not with us (P) (C)	followeth not with us	Lu. 9 49
	17		for it must needs be that offences come offend thee	Mt. 18 7
	*20	incite thee to strife		" 9
	21	fall into the fire (P)	be cast into . . . fire	Mk. 9 47

III. VARIOUS READINGS.

25 24	How good is salt!	Salt is good:	Mk. 9 50
25	dung (P)(C)	dunghill	Lu. 14 35
30	gave us permission, that, if any man wished, he might write (P†)	suffered to write	Mk. 10 4
*34	Why did Moses consent	Why did Moses then command	Mt. 19 7
*38	exposeth her to adultery	committeth adultery against her	Mk. 10 11
*40	between a husband and a wife there is such blame (P)(C)	the case of the man be so with his wife	Mt. 19 10
41	do not endure this saying	cannot receive this saying	" 11
42	He that is able to refrain, let him refrain (C†)	He that is able to receive it, let him receive it	" 12
26 *3	Jesus, when he had perceived their murmuring, said	he spake	Lu. 15 3
4	go and seek the straying one (P)	go after that which is lost	" 4
6	shoulders, and bringing it home (P)	shoulders, rejoicing. And when he cometh home	" 5, 6
*7	should perish, whom after erring he calleth to repentance	should perish	Mt. 18 14
*11	more than over ninety and nine righteous persons, which need no repentance	. Cf. Luke xv. 7.	Lu. 15 10
12	again Jesus saith unto them another parable (P)(C)	he said	" 11
18	in my father's house (P)(C)	of my father's	" 17
19	to my father's house	to my father	" 18
26	heard the sound of the singing of many (P)	heard musick and dancing	" 25
27	asked him, What is this? (P)	asked what these things meant	" 26
28	found him well (P†)	received him safe and sound	" 27
29	intreated him to enter	intreated him	" 28
37	I know what I will do (P)	I am resolved what to do	" 16 4
40	sit down (P)	.	" 7
27 *6	treated him with harshness	took him by the throat	Mt. 18 28
18	as a publican and a heathen. (P)	as an heathen man and a publican	" 17
20	to ask anything	as touching anything that they shall ask	" 19
25	much is committed, at his hand much will be sought (P)	men have committed much, of him they will ask the more	Lu. 12 48

APPENDIX

		Diatessaron.	Gospel.	
27	26	I could wish that it were (P)	what will I, if it be	Lu. 12 49
	28	which believe in me (C) [so D b c, etc.	. Cf. Matt. xviii. 6.	Mt. 18 10
	31	came some (P) (C)	were present at that season some	Lu. 13 1
	32	so that this happened unto them? (P)(C)	because they suffered such things?	,, ,, 2
	37	why doth it leave the ground unoccupied?	why cumbereth it the ground?	,, ,, 7
	39	next year cut it down	then after that thou shalt cut it down	,, ,, 9
	47	standing by (P†)(C†)		,, ,, 17
28	4	until this time (C)		Jn. 7 5
	13	in the great multitude, which had come to the feast	among the multitudes [R.V.]	,, ,, 12
,,	28	unrighteousness is not found in his heart (P)	no unrighteousness is in him	,, ,, 27
,,	35	this man is known	we know this man	
		Beware of every evil (P) (C)	Take heed, and beware of covetousness	Lu. 12 15
,,	38	possessions (P) (‡)	the things which he possesseth	,, ,, 18
		the buildings of my barns, and build again, and make greater ones (P) (C)	my barns, and build greater	
	40	shall be taken away from thee	shall be required of thee (Cf. A.V. margin.	,, ,, 20
	*45	Which commandments?	Which?	Mt. 19 18
	*50	At this word the young man frowned	when the young man heard that saying	,, ,, 22
29	2	to press through	to go through	,, ,, 24
	*4	being now afraid, Who, think you	Who then	Mk. 10 26
	9	twice as many (P) [((?) has "a hundredfold"]	manifold more	Lu. 18 30
	13	But Jesus, knowing what was in their hearts, (P)	And he	16 15
		small in the sight	abomination in the sight	
	14	And he began to say, A certain man was rich . . .	There was a certain rich man . . .	,, ,, 19
,,	18	silk and purple, and enjoyed himself surpassingly (P)	purple and fine linen, and fared sumptuously	,, ,, 23
,,	19	while he was tormented in the lower world . . . (P)	in hell . . . being in torments	,, ,, 24
		cried with a loud voice (P)	cried	
,,	20	wet the tip of his finger with water, and moisten (P)	dip the tip of his finger in water, and cool	,, ,, 25
		but now behold, he resteth here, but thou (P*)	but now he is comforted, and thou	

III. VARIOUS READINGS.

29 21	may not be able, nor to cross over from thence to us (P)	cannot, neither can they pass to us, that would come from thence	Lu. 16 26
*23	go, lest they also sin, and come Cf. note.	testify unto them, lest they also come	,, 28
25	one of the dead go to them (P)	one went unto them from the dead	,, 30
26	not even if one of the dead rise again, will they believe him (P)	neither will they be persuaded, though one rose from the dead	,, 31
*28	for each labourer (C)	. . .	Mt. 20 2
*31	and sent them	. . .	,, 5
34	begin indeed from the last, and continue until (P)(C)	beginning from the last unto	,, 8
35	the labourers of the eleventh hour came (P)(C)	when they came that *were hired* about the eleventh hour	,, 9
38	scorching heat of the day and its burden (P†)	burden and heat of the day	,, 12
40	even as I have given unto thee	even as unto thee	,, 14
41	Either . . . will about mine own business? or perchance (P)(C)	. . . will with mine own?	,, 15
43	when Jesus entered (C)	it came to pass, as he went	Lu. 14 1
*,,	to see what he would do (C)	. . .	,, ,,
47	sabbath day . . . draw him up and give him to drink (P)(C)	pull him out on the sabbath day	,, 5
30 1	because he saw them choosing (P)	when he marked how they chose	,, 7
*3	bade you both	bade thee and him	,, 9
,,	be put to shame in the presence of them that stand by, and another place shall receive thee (P*)	begin with shame to take the lowest room	,, ,,
4	all them that are invited	them that sit at meat	,, 10
8	that thy recompense may be made	for thou shalt be recompensed	,, 14
9	were bidden had heard	sat at meat with him heard	,, 15
*13	them, Tell him, I have bought	him, I have bought	,, 18
,,	let me go, for I am excused (P*)	I pray thee have me excused	,, 19
14	look at them . . . let me go, for I am excused (P)(C)	prove them . . . have me excused	,, 21
19	one of the servants came	the servant came	,, 22
*22, 23	And the servants did as the king had commanded them; and they came, and said unto him	And the servant said	

20

Diatessaron.		Gospel.	
30	24 highways and lanes and wider roads	highways and hedges	Lu. 14 23
	32 was making the journey	entered into a certain village	,, 17 12
	37 Were not they that were cleansed ten? (P) and the nine, where are they?	Were there not ten cleansed? but where are the nine?	,, 17
	38 turned aside to come and ... (P*)	returned to ...	,, 18
	*40 one, who is of an alien tribe (P)	stranger	Mk. 10 32
	*44 make known to them, between himself and them	tell them	Lu. 18 33
	52 they shall condemn him		Mk. 10 40
31	6 my Father hath prepared it	it is prepared of my Father Cf. Matt. xx. 23.	Lu. 13 22
	9 He said these things, and went round	And he went through	,, 25
	From the hour when ... shall rise up (P) (C)	When once ... is risen up	
	11 say, I say unto you (P)	say unto you	,, 27
	18 so he was going to pass by (P) (C)	I tell you Cf. note.	
		he was to pass that way	,, 19 4
	*25 when Jesus went out from Jericho	it came to pass, that as he was come nigh unto Jericho	,, 18 35
	*26 and his name was Bartimaeus	blind Bartimaeus	Mk. 10 46
	27 who it was. (P) (C)	what it meant	Lu. 18 36
	30 in front of Jesus (P) (C)	before	,, 39
	*33 My lord and master, that thou mayest open mine eyes, and I may see thee	Lord, that I might receive my sight	Mk. 10 51
	*46 thou exactest that which thou gavest not		Lu. 19 21
	47 servant, negligent and unfaithful (C)	servant	,, 22
32	*10 that when they destroyed it, he would raise it up in three days		Jn. 2 21
	15 all that she possessed	all that she had, *even* all her living	Mk. 12 44
	18 unjust, adulterers, extortioners	extortioners, unjust, adulterers	Lu. 18 11
	21 the Pharisee (P)	the other	,, 14
	23 all the people, because they knew the place, came	the people, when they knew it, followed	,, 9 11

III. VARIOUS READINGS.

32	24	to the city	art a teacher come from God	Mk. 11 12
	28	wast sent from God as a teacher (P)		Jn. 3 2
		except he with whom God is. (P)	except God be with him.	,, ,,
	31	and said unto him (P)		,, 5
	42, 44	only Son (P) (C)	only begotten Son . . . . Cf. xxxii. 22.	,, 16,18
33	1	himself and his disciples		Mk. 11 19
	5	Let the faith of God be in you (P)	Have faith in God.	Mt. 21 22
	7	Remove, and fall (P) (C)	Be thou removed, and be thou cast	,, 21 21
	*8	of God . . . he shall give you.	. . . ye shall receive	,, 22
	11	guiding oxen or feeding sheep (P)	plowing or feeding cattle	Lu. 17 7
	13	Will that servant who . . . receive his thanks. (P*)	Doth he thank that servant because he . . .	,, 9
	18	not be slothful (P) (C)	not to faint, Saying	,, 18 1
	22	that she may not come perpetually, and bring me weariness (P) (C)	lest by her continual coming she weary me	,, 5
	43	This was done by God	caught him, and	Mk. 12 3
	*56	authority of the court	this is the Lord's doing	Mt. 21 42
34	*1	they could not bring it to pass that he should fall in his speech before the people	they could not take hold of his words before the people	Lu. 20 20
	*8			,, 26
	9	and said unto him, The dead have no life. (P) (C)	which say that there is no resurrection	Mt. 22 23
	19	because they have been made (P)	being the	Lu. 20 36
	24	silence in this way . . . against him, to strive with him. (C)	silence	Mt. 22 34
	31	the law (P) (C)	all the law	,, 40
	32	An excellent opinion, Master! with truth thou hast said (P)	Well, Master, thou hast said the truth	Mk. 12 32
	37	robbers fell upon him, which plundered him (P)	fell among thieves, which stripped him of his raiment	Lu. 10 30
	43	seems to thee to have been more a neighbour	thinkest thou, was neighbour	,, 36
	44	He said unto him (C)	And he said	,, 37
	52	Do you think, that he is about to go unto the countries of the Gentiles, and teach the heathen? (P)	will he go unto the dispersed among the Gentiles, and teach the Gentiles?	Jn. 7 35

	Diatessaron.	Gospel.		
35	2	sweet water	living water	Jn. 7 38
	6	of David? (P) (C)	where David was?	,, 42
	9	the priests said (P)	they said	,, 45
	13	who		,, 49
	48	ye are unequal to my word (P)	my word hath no place in you	,, 8 37
	53	came down	came	,, 42
	55	the father of lies	the father of it	,, 44
	56	I, that speak in the truth (P*)	because I tell *you* the truth	,, 45
	57	ye do not believe me.	why do ye not believe me?	,, 46
36	4	He is our God (P)	that he is your God	,, 54
	6	longed (P)	rejoiced	,, 56
	15	rubbed it upon the eyes . . . (P)	anointed the eyes . . . with the clay	,, 9 6
	24	How didst thou receive thy sight? (P)	how he had received his sight.	,, 15
	26	He said unto them, I say, that he is (P)	He said, He is	,, 17
	30	. . . (P)	we know not (1st)	,, 21
	40	he that feareth him (P)	if any man be a worshipper of God	,, 31
	45	that had been made whole (P)		,, 36
37	1	For judging the world am I come (P)	For judgment I am come into this world	,, 39
	6	they go out unto him	leadeth them out	,, 10 3
	*6, 7, 15, 29, 30	}		,, 3, 4, 12, 26,
	11	rams	sheep	,, 27
	*23	came (P)	came before me	,, 8
	,,	and suffereth from epilepsy	and is mad	,, 20
	27	why are ye silent in his presence?	why hear ye him?	,, ,,
	34	wilt thou torment our hearts?	dost thou make us to doubt?	,, 24
	38	nothing can be broken in the scripture	again the scripture cannot be broken	,, 31 35
	39	that he blasphemeth.	Thou blasphemest.	,, 36

III. VARIOUS READINGS.

37	47	whose brother was Lazarus the sick man (P)	whose brother Lazarus was sick	Jn. 11 2
	53	now wish to stone thee (P†)	of late sought to stone thee	,, 8
38	9	though he die, shall live (P)	though he were dead, yet shall he live	,, 25
	*17	And Jesus came, and when he saw . .	When Jesus therefore saw . . .	,, 33
	,,	was distressed in his soul, and sighed	groaned in the Spirit, and was troubled	,, ,,
	19	And the tears of Jesus were shed (P)	Jesus wept	,, 35
	22	at the mouth of it (P)	upon it	,, 38
	31	gathered together (P)	gathered . . . a council	,, 47
	36	at one time the children of God that had been scattered	in one the children of God that were scattered	,, 52
	*38	into a hermitage which is called Ephraem	into a city called Ephraim	,, 54
	,,	and there he was going about (P)	and there continued	,, ,,
	42	when the days of his going up were fulfilled, he prepared himself (P) (C)	it came to pass, when the time was come that he should be received up, he steadfastly set his face	{ Lu. 9 51
39	2	was made	they made	Jn. 12 2
	12	is this ointment wasted	was this waste of the ointment made	Mk. 14 4
	*18	Jesus went forth slowly to proceed	he went before, ascending up	Lu. 19 28
	21	loose it and bring them	loose *them* and bring *them*	Mt. 21 2
	*22	they sent them hither	he will send them	,, 3
	28	We seek them for our Lord (P†)	The Lord hath need of him	Lu. 19 34
	31	drew near his descent (P)	was come nigh, even now at the descent	,, 37
	32	Glory in the highest	.	Mt. 21 9
	*41	take possession of thee, and of thy children that are	even thou, at least	Lu. 19 42
			lay thee even with the ground, and thy children	,, 44
	44	bare witness, that he had called (P)	when he called . . . bare record	Jn. 12 17
	45	the sign that he had done	that he had done this miracle	,, 18
40	5	also among them certain Gentiles, that had come up (P)	certain Greeks among them that came up	,, 20
	8	is near	is come	,, 23
	13	And a voice was heard (P)	Then came there a voice	,, 28
	14	This is thunder	that it thundered	,, 29

APPENDIX.

	Diatessaron.	Gospel.	
40	17	when I am lifted up (P)	if I be lifted up	Jn. 12 32
	22	some of the Pharisees had asked Jesus, When will . . . come? (P)	he was demanded of the Pharisees, when . . . should come,	Lu. 17 20
	29	under the pretence of . . . (P) (C)	and grievous to be borne Cf. R.V. margin.	Mt. 23 4
	35	making their prayers long (P)	and for a pretence make long prayers	Mk. 12 40
	38	called directors: for one is your director (P)	called masters: for one is your Master	Mt. 23 10
	44	ye have hidden the keys (C). [(P) keys.]	ye have taken away the key.	Lu. 11 52
	47, 49	Ye blind ignorant ones	Ye fools and blind	Mt. 23 17, 19
	*54	adorn the camel	swallow a camel	,, 24
41	*1	I, the wisdom of God, send	said the wisdom of God, I will send	,, 34 / Lu. 11 49
	2	blood of righteous men that hath been shed (P)	righteous blood shed	Mt. 23 35
	8	more than to glory	more than the praise [R.V. "glory."]	Jn. 12 43
	16	to be angry in their malice, and to find fault with his words, and to vex him in many things (P)	to urge *him* vehemently, and to provoke him to speak of many things	Lu. 11 53
	23	that he may hear us? (P†)	our report?	Jn. 12 38
	25	Blind ye their eyes, and bring darkness to (P)	He hath blinded their eyes, and hardened	,, 40
	32	the people make a disturbance	there be an uproar of the people	Mk. 14 2
	41	and great storms shall there be (P) (C)		Lu. 21 11
	49	understanding and wisdom.	a mouth and wisdom	,, 15
	52	And your parents . . . shall deliver you up (P) (C)	And ye shall be betrayed both by parents . . .	,, 16
	53	a lock of the hair of your head shall not . . .	there shall not a hair of your head . . .	,, 18
42	4	abominable desolation	abomination of desolation	Mt. 24 15
	*13	that ye may not be seized		,, 26
	14	appeareth in the east, and is visible	cometh out of the east, and shineth	,, 27
	19	and wringing of hands for the roaring of the noise of the sea and of the earthquake. (P) (C)	with perplexity, the sea and the waves roaring	Lu. 21 25

III. VARIOUS READINGS.

42	20	which shall come upon the earth (P) (C)	and for looking after those things which are coming on the earth	Lu. 21 26
	24	be of good cheer (P)	look up	,, 28
	29	iniquity and drunkenness	surfeiting, and drunkenness	,, 34
	*30	just as a blow	as a snare	,, 35
	34	left each one at his own work	to every man his work	Mk. 13 34
	52	his house could not have been digged through	would not have suffered his house to be broken up [R.V. margin, "digged through."]	Mt. 24 43
43	2	overseer of the house	servant	,, 45
	6	beat his menservants and the maidservants of his lord (P)	beat the menservants and the maidservants [R.V.]	Lu. 12 45
	*8	judge him	cut him asunder	Mt. 24 51
	9	and the bride (P)		,, 25 1
	28	five } others beside them (P)	other { five } talents [R.V.]	,, 20
	30	two }	{ two }	,, 22
	*44, 45	rams	sheep	,, 32, 33
	*48, 51	his armies	his angels	,, 36, 39
	53	took care of	communed with	,, 41
44	*7	had a conversation in the temple with		Lu. 22 4
	19	Then, Lord, wash not my feet only (P)	Lord, not my feet only	Jn. 13 9
	24	how much more fit is it, that ye should (P)	ye also ought to	,, 14
	28	This my saying is not for you all	I speak not of you all	,, 18
	32	my sorrows (I*) (C*)	my temptations	Lu. 22 28
	33	promise ... promised (P) (C)	appoint ... appointed	,, 29
	34	the Jews are wont to kill the passover (P)	the passover must be killed	,, 7
	*49	not knowing whom he signified	doubting of whom he spake	Jn. 13 22
	34	That disciple therefore leaned back ... and said (P)	He then lying ... saith	,, 25
	6	What thou wishest to do, make haste to do	That thou doest, do quickly	,, 27
45	3	he commanded him to buy what was needed (P)	Jesus had said unto him, Buy those *things* that we have need of	,, 29
	10	shall ... be ... shall be	is ... is	Mt. 26 31
	16	juice	fruit	,, 29

APPENDIX.

	Diatessaron.	Gospel.	
45 17	Jesus saith unto Simon, Simon . . . (P) (C)	the Lord said, Simon, Simon	Lu. 22 31
*23	forsake me	be offended because of me	Mt. 26 31
24	after my resurrection	after I am risen again	" 32
29	believe in God, and believe in me. (P)	ye believe in God, believe also in me.	Jn. 14 1
33	how shall we have a way to perceive this?	how can we know the way?	" 5
46 *14	for I shall be reckoned with transgressors: for all things that were said concerning me are fulfilled in me	And he was reckoned among the transgressors: for the things concerning me have an end	Lu. 22 37
15	They are enough (P) (C)	It is enough	" 38
20	of the vine		Jn. 15 4
22	shall be cast forth as a withered branch, which is gathered . . . to burn (P)	is cast forth as a branch, and is withered; and men gather them . . . and they are burned	" 6
23	whatsoever ye shall wish to ask shall . . . (P)	ye shall ask what ye will, and it shall . . .	" 7
29	And there is no greater love (P)	Greater love hath no man	" 13
34	know that (P)	ye know that	" 18
44	disquieted	offended	" 16 1
45	presenteth an offering unto God (P)	doeth God service. Cf. R.V.	" 2
48	whither I go	Whither goest thou?	" 5
49	come, and seized your hearts (P)	filled your heart	" 6
53		and ye see me no more	" 10
56	bring all the truth to your remembrance	guide you into all truth	" 13
47 6	when the time of bearing draweth near unto her, the coming of the day of her delivery oppresseth her (P†)	when she is in travail hath sorrow, because her hour is come	" 21
10	an hour and a time shall come . . . reveal to you the Father by an open revelation (I†)	the time cometh . . . shew you plainly of the Father.	" 25
14	thy words are clear, and thou hast spoken nothing in a proverb	speakest thou plainly, and speakest no proverb	" 29
*17	Believe that an hour shall come	Do ye now believe? Behold, the hour cometh	" 31,32

III. VARIOUS READINGS.

47 18	distress shall overtake you	ye shall have tribulation	Jn. 16 33
*21	may know that thou art (P) . . . and that he, whom thou didst send, *is* Jesus the Messiah	may know thee . . . and Jesus Christ whom thou hast sent	,, 17 3
27	and my petition is	I pray [2nd]	,, ,, 9
33	For I seek not this	I pray not	,, ,, 15
41	that I have loved them (P)	hast loved them	,, ,, 23
48 5	at the same time	.	Mt. 26 37
12	eager and ready (P)	ready	Mk. 14 38
*14	were weighed down for sorrow and anxiety	were heavy	,, ,, 40
17	while he was afraid he prayed with uninterrupted prayer (P)	being in an agony he prayed more earnestly	Lu. 22 44
,,	became as it were a stream of blood	was as it were great drops of blood	,, ,, ,,
18	.	for sorrow	,, ,, 45
20	the end is at hand, and (P) . Cf. ver. 14.	it is enough	Mk. 14 41
22	the betrayer (P)	.	Mt. 26 47
*,,	and with them a man of the Romans.	.	,, ,, ,,
23	boldly, and lead him away. (P)	and lead him away safely.	Mk. 14 44
26	art thou come for this?	wherefore art thou come?	Mt. 26 50
34	his disciples saw what happened (P)	they which were about him saw what would follow	Lu. 22 49
37	that shall attack with the sword	that take the sword	Mt. 26 52
40	gently touched the ear which he had struck (P*)	Suffer ye thus far. And he touched his ear	Lu. 22 51
41	against me as an attack is made on a robber	as against a thief	Mt. 26 55
45	naked, wrapped in a linen cloth (P)	having a linen cloth cast about *his* naked *body*	Mk. 14 51
*51	that is to say, of Jesus of Nazareth	.	Jn. 18 17
53	soldiers rose up, and kindled a fire in the midst of the court to warm themselves (P)	officers stood there, who had made a fire of coals . . . and they warmed themselves	,, ,, 18
*55	the end of what would happen	the end	Mt. 26 58
49 2	to the people (P)	to the world	Jn. 18 20
*7	And when Jesus went out	.	,, ,, 25
*,,	in the outer court	.	,, ,, ,,
12	and disputing, said (P)	confidently affirmed, saying,	Lu. 22 59
16	in that hour Jesus, who was outside, turned (P)	the Lord turned	,, ,, 61

	Diatessaron.	Gospel.	
49 *19	all the guards of the temple	what is it, which these witness	Lu. 22 66
28	to what these witness		Mt. 26 62
30	synagogue (P*) (C**)	Council	Lu. 22 66
37	rent his coat (P)	rent his clothes	Mk. 14 63
38	Why do we still seek for ... (P*)	What need we any further ...	Lu. 22 71
43	Pilate the governor (P)	Pilate	Mk. 15 1
44	found unclean, when they ate ... (P)	defiled, but that they might eat ...	Jn. 18 28
52	The sons of thine own nation (P)	Thine own nation	,, 35
50 1, 2	nothing against this man ... cried out and said (P) (C)	no fault in this man ... were the more fierce, saying,	Lu. 23 4, 5
3	the name of Galilee (P)	of Galilee	,, 6
5	about his deeds	of him	,, 8
8	scarlet (P)	gorgeous	,, 11
*14	Away with him from us, away with him.	Away with this man	,, 18
26	even as custom allowed (P)	as he had ever done unto them	Mk. 15 8
28	envy had moved them to deliver him up	for envy they had delivered him	Mt. 27 18
29	ask for the release of Barabbas	ask Barabbas	,, 20
36	he should crucify him. (P†)	he might be crucified	Lu. 23 23
*42	took the reed from his hand	took the reed	Mt. 27 30
43	cause for his condemnation	fault in him	Jn. 19 4
50	hath a greater sin than thy sin (P)	hath the greater sin	,, 11
51 *6	Pilate commanded that consent should be given ...	Cf. Luke xxiii. 24.	Mt. 27 16
7	went away, and gave back (P)	repented himself, and brought again	Mt. 27 3
13	through the prophet (P)	by Jeremy the prophet Cf. note.	,, 9
,, 15	the great one, which was fixed by ... (P) the Jews	him that was valued, whom they ... did value they	Jn. 19 16
*16	the purple and scarlet garment, with which he was clothed	the robe off from him. Cf. Mark xv. 20.	Mt. 27 31
*18	And Jesus went on with his cross behind him		Lu. 23 26

III. VARIOUS READINGS.

61 19	lamented and were excited on account of Jesus (P)(C)	
27	wine . . . and myrrh	Lu. 23 27
	bewailed and lamented him	Mk. 15 23
	wine mingled with myrrh	Jn. 19 23
*28	each band of soldiers	
	every soldier	" 19
	(P)	
*31	on a tablet the cause of his death, and put it on the wood of the cross (P)	
	a title, and put it on the cross	" 21
33	He who said,	
*34	What is written, is written	
	that he said	" 22
	What I have written, I have written	Mt. 27 41
37	and the Pharisees. (P)	
*„	and laughed to each other	
38	The saviour of others cannot save himself	
	deliver thyself, and deliver us also (P) (C)	
	He saved others; himself he cannot save	" 42
	save thyself and us	Lu. 23 39
44	his companion (P) (C)	
45		the other answering	" 40
46	even as we have deserved, and according as we have done are we rewarded . . . (P) (C)	
	for we receive the due reward of our deeds .	" 41
*49	who is named after Cleophas. Cf. note.	
52 3	fastening it to a reed, held it near his mouth to give (P)	
	the *wife* of Cleophas	Jn. 19 25
	put it on a reed, and gave	Mk. 15 36
*4	Everything is finished	
8	straightway the face of the door (P)	
14	said, Let not these bodies remain on the wood, for it is the dawn of . . . (P)	
	It is finished	Jn. 19 30
	behold, the veil	Mt. 27 51
	that the bodies should not remain upon the cross on . . .	Jn. 19 31
„	they might break the legs of them that had been crucified, and take them away. (P)	
	their legs might be broken, and that they might be taken away.	" "
19	shall not be broken in him (P)	
20	also the scripture which saith (P)	
	of him shall not be broken	" 36
	again another scripture saith	" 37
*24	of the Friday (P) . . . on account of the entrance of	
	because it was the preparation, that is, the day before	Mk. 15 42
26	deeds of the lost, and was looking. Arabic corrupt. about his death before the *usual* time. (P)	
28		
34	because the sabbath had entered in (P)	
*36	named after Joses. Cf. note.	
	deed of them . . . who also himself waited	Lu. 23 51
	whether he had been any while dead	Mk. 15 44
	because of the Jews' preparation day	Jn. 19 42
	the *mother* of Joses	Mk. 15 47

APPENDIX.

Diatessaron.		Gospel.	
52 *37	how they brought in and placed the body there	how his body was laid	Lu. 23 55
30	on the day which was the day of the sabbath, they left off because of the commandment.	and rested the sabbath day according to the commandment.	,, 56
42	And now be beforehand in guarding the sepulchre until three days. (P)	Command therefore that the sepulchre be made sure until the third day.	Mt. 27 64
45	which is the dawn of (P)	as it began to dawn toward	,, 28 1
*,,	at very early dawn, behind the rest	very early in the morning	Lu. 24 1
*48	angel	angel of the Lord	Mt. 28 2
*52	when he was gone away	.	Lu. 24 3
53 12	.	stooping down	Jn. 20 5
14	rolled up and laid on the opposite side in a certain place (P)	wrapped together in a place by itself	,, 7
19	one on the side of his cushion ... on the side of his feet (P)	the one at the head, and the other at the feet	,, 12
23	in Hebrew, Rabboni (P)	Rabboni	,, 16
*25	on the first day, *the day* whereon he rose	When *Jesus* was risen early, the first day of the week	Mk. 16 9
29	and make you safe from blame	and secure you	Mt. 28 14
30	as they had taught them (P)	as they were taught	,, 15
38	as the words of madness (P)	as idle tales	Lu. 24 11
41	For (P) (C)	And it came to pass, that	,, 15
45	What hath happened?	What things?	,, 19
48	told us, that they had gone (P†) (C†)	made us astonished, which were early	,, 22
50	also of our company [(P) and (U) "of us"]	of them which were with us	,, 24
51,52	believe! Was it not in all the sayings of the prophets that the Messiah must ... (P) (C)	believe all that the prophets have spoken: Ought not Christ ...	,, 25
54	made them suppose that he was about to go ... (P)	made as though he would have gone ...	,, 28
55	hath already declined towards darkness (P) (C)	is far spent	,, 29
54 2	it is I, be not afraid (P) Cf. note.		,, 36

III. VARIOUS READINGS.

54 11	repentance unto remission	repentance and remission	Lu. 24 47
*,, 13	but the beginning shall be from (P)	beginning at	,, 20 20
18	when they heard this	when they saw the Lord	,, 25
*,, 19	upon them (P)	into the print of the nails	,, 26
20	on the next first *day* (P)	.	,, 27
24	spread it upon my side (P)	thrust it into my side	,, 31
30	eternal life (P)	life	,, 21 6
31	that were come into it (P†)	.	,, 7
,, 35	took up his coat, and girded it up to his loins (P)	girt his fisher's coat *unto him*	,, 11
36	that he might come to Jesus (P)	.	,, 12
*,,	with so great a weight (P)	for all there were so many	
	sit down	dine	
,, 40	yet he did not appear unto them in his own form	.	Cf. Mark xvi 12
41	Feed my rams for me (P)	Feed my sheep	,, 16
45	three times	unto him the third time	,, 17
55 3	this man, what shall be concerning him? (P)	what *shall* this man *do?*	,, 21
13	seen that he was risen again (P)	seen him after he was risen	Mk. 16 14
*,, 16	And while ascended (P)	And it came to pass, while carried up	Lu. 24 51
,,	from thence	.	Mk. 16 20
,,	their sayings with the signs which they did (P) (C)	the word with signs following	,,

IV.

SPECIALLY RECORDED MIRACLES, WITH THEIR POSITION IN THE DIATESSARON.

Diatessaron.	Nature of Miracle.
5 22–32	Water changed into wine at Cana.
,, 49–6 4	First miraculous draught of fishes.
6 41–45	Unclean spirit cast out in the synagogue.
,, 48, 49	Simon's wife's mother cured of a fever.
7 13–24	The paralytic cured at Capernaum.
,, 47–53	A man with a withered hand cured.
11 3–16	An officer's servant healed at Capernaum.
,, 17–23	The widow's son at Nain raised to life.
,, 31–37	The storm on the lake quelled.
,, 38–52	The Gadarene demoniac cured, and the swine destroyed.
12 10–21	The woman with an issue of blood healed.
,, 7–9 ,, 22–32	The daughter of Jaïrus raised to life.
,, 33–37	Two blind men cured.
,, 38, 39	A dumb demoniac cured.
14 16–31	Another dumb demoniac cured.
,, 41, 42	A dumb and blind demoniac cured.
18 25–43	Five thousand fed.
19 1–13	Walking upon the water.
20 46–58	The daughter of a Canaanite cured.
21 1–7	A deaf and dumb man cured.
22 1–6	One leper cured.
,, 10–24	A man cured at Bethesda.
23 5–12	Four thousand fed.
,, 26–30	A blind man cured at Bethsaïda.
24 30–47	A demoniac cured after the disciples had failed.
25 4–7	The stater in the fish's mouth.
27 40–47	A woman cured of an infirmity.
29 43–48	A dropsical man cured in a Pharisee's house.
30 32–39	Ten lepers cured.
31 25–35	Blind Bartimaeus restored to sight.
32 24–26 33 1–8	The fig-tree withered.
36 10–47	A man that was born blind cured.
38 1–30	Lazarus raised to life.
48 27–33	Judas and others prostrated.
,, 34–40	The ear of Malchus healed.
54 28–38	Second miraculous draught of fishes.

V.

THE PARABLES, WITH THEIR POSITION IN THE DIATESSARON.

Diatessaron.	Subject of Parable.
7 34	A new piece of cloth on an old garment.
„ 35	New wine in old wine-skins.
„ 52, 53	A sheep fallen into a well.
10 22–27	Borrowing three loaves from a friend.
„ 28–30	A father giving good gifts.
„ 44–48	Building upon the rock.
14 10–14	Children sitting in the market-place.
„ 24–26	The strong man, armed.
15 1–4	The two debtors.
„ 45–47	Counting the cost of building.
„ 48–50	Counting armies before going to war.
16 7–10	The unclean spirit.
„ 24–48	The sower.
„ 49–52	The seed growing secretly.
17 1–7 } „ 19–26	The tares in the field.
„ 8–12	The mustard seed.
„ 13–15	The leaven.
„ 27	The hid treasure.
„ 28, 29	The pearl of great price.
„ 30–33	The draw-net.
26 1–8	The lost sheep.
„ 9–11	The lost drachma.
„ 12–33	The prodigal son.
„ 34–45	The unjust steward.
27 1–13	The unmerciful servant.
„ 36–39	The fig-tree in the vineyard.
28 36–41	The rich fool.
29 12–26	The rich man and Lazarus.
„ 27–42	The labourers in the vineyard.
30 10–30	The marriage feast and wedding garment.[1]
31 36–52	The minas.
32 16–21	The Pharisee and the publican.
33 11–14	The servant coming home from the field.
„ 18–25	The unjust judge.
„ 35–39	The two sons.
„ 40–58	The vineyard let to husbandmen.
34 37–44	The good Samaritan.
37 4–21	The Good Shepherd.
42 25, 26	The fig-tree putting forth leaves.
„ 32–37	The servants watching for their lord.
„ 51–53	The thief coming at an unknown hour.
43 1–8	The steward left in charge.
„ 9–21	The ten virgins.
„ 22–38	The talents.
„ 39–42	The servants with their loins girded.

[1] The parables of S. Matthew and S. Luke harmonised together.

VI.

Allusions to S. John the Baptist in the Diatessaron.

Tatian.	New Testament.	References to S. John the Baptist.
1 6–26	Lu. 1 5–25	John's birth foretold.
„ 40–81	„ 39–80	John's birth, circumcision, etc.
3 37 to 4 27	Mt. 3 1–12 Mk. 1 2–8 Lu. 3 1–18 Jn. 1 7–28	Preaching and witness of John. „ „ „
4 28–42	Mt. 3 13–17 Mk. 1 9–11 Lu. 3 21, 22 Jn. 1 29–34	Jesus baptized by John. „ „ „
5 4–6	Jn. 1 35–37	John points out Jesus to two disciples.
6 5–21	Jn. 3 22–4 2	John baptizes at Aennon, his witness there.—Jesus baptizes near him.
6 23–25	Mk. 1 14 Lu. 3 19, 20 Mt. 4 12	Imprisonment of John; Jesus withdraws to Galilee in consequence. „
7 31–36	Mt. 9 14–17 Mk. 2 18–22 Lu. 5 33–39	John's disciples fast, whilst those of Jesus do not.
9 30–36	Lu. 11 1–4	Jesus teaches to pray, as John taught his disciples.
13 38 to 14 14	Mt. 11 2–19 Lu. 7 18–35 Lu. 16 16, 17	John sends two of his disciples to Jesus, who afterwards discourses about John.
18 1–20	Mt. 14 1–12 Mk. 6 14–29 Lu. 9 7–9	John's death. „ „
22 39–45	Jn. 5 31–37	John cited by Jesus as a witness for Him.
23 33	Mt. 16 13–20 Mk. 8 27–30 Lu. 9 18–21	Men supposed Jesus to be John. „ „
24 20–24	Mt. 17 10–13 Mk. 9 11–13	Elijah already come in John. „
33 27–39	Mt. 21 23–32 Mk. 11 27–33 Lu. 20 1–8	When questioned as to His authority, Jesus asks a question as to John's authority.—John came in the way of righteousness.
37 43–45	Jn. 10 40–42	Jesus visits the place where John at first baptized.
Omitted	Jn. 1 6	John sent from God.

APPENDIX. 321

VII.

MOVEMENTS OF JESUS DURING HIS PUBLIC MINISTRY, AS GIVEN IN THE DIATESSARON.

Diatessaron.	Gospel.	Nature of Movement.
4 28	Mt. 3 13	From Galilee to Jordan to be baptized.
,, 43	Mk. 1 12	From Jordan to the wilderness.
,, 47	Mt. 4 5	Brought by Satan to the temple.
,, 50	Lu. 4 5	Brought by Satan to a high mountain.
5 4	Jn. 1 35	Has returned to Jordan.
,, 21	Lu. 4 14	From Jordan to Galilee.
,, 22	Jn. 2 1	To Cana.
,, 34	Lu. 4 15	Makes a circuit of Galilee.
,, 35	,, 16	Comes to Nazareth.
6 5	Jn. 3 22	To Judah near Jordan.
,, 22	Jn. 4 3	Leaves Judaea.
,, 25	Mt. 4 12	Arrives in Galilee.
,, 26	Jn. 4 46	Revisits Cana.
,, 35	Lu. 4 44	Makes a circuit of Galilee.
,, 36	Mt. 4 13	Leaves Nazareth and resides in Capernaum.
7 7	Mt. 9 35	Makes a circuit of Galilee.
,, 11	Mk. 2 1	Returns to Capernaum.
8 2	Mt. 12 15	Withdraws from Capernaum.
,, 9	Lu. 6 12	To the mountain to pray.
,, 10	Mk. 3 7	To the Lake of Gennesareth.
,, 18	Mt. 5 1	To the mountain.
11 4	Mt. 8 5	To Capernaum.
,, 17	Lu. 7 11	To Nain.
,, 38	Lu. 8 26	Across the Lake to Gadara. (Cf. 11 32.
12 2	Mt. 9 1	Recrosses to Capernaum.
,, 40	,, 35	Makes a circuit of Galilee.
13 30	Mt. 11 1	Makes a circuit of Galilee.
,, 31	Lu. 10 38	To the house of Martha and Mary.
14 15	Mk. 3 19	At Capernaum.
,, 44	Mk. 6 31	To a desert place temporarily.
16 19	Lu. 8 1	Makes a circuit of Galilee.
17 37	Mt. 13 54	To Nazareth.
,, 53	Mk. 6 6	Makes a circuit round Nazareth.
18 21	Mt. 14 13	To a desert place across the Lake.
,, 23	Jn. 6 3	To the mountain.
19 11	,, 21	To Capernaum. Cf. 18 48.
20 46	Mk. 7 24	To the borders of Tyre and Sidon.
21 1	,, 31	To the Lake near Decapolis.
,, 8	Jn. 4 4	Through Samaria.
,, 9	,, 5	To Sychar.
,, 47	,, 43	To Galilee.
22 1	Lu. 5 12	To a village.
,, 6	Mk. 1 45	To a desert place.
,, 8	Lu. 5 16	To the desert.
,, 9	Jn. 5 1	To Jerusalem.
23 1	Mt. 15 29	To the Lake and the mountain.

VII.—*Continued.*

Diatessaron.	Gospel.	Nature of Movement.
23 12	Mt. 15 39	Across the Lake to Magheda.
,, 16	Mk. 8 13	Recrosses the Lake.
,, 26	,, 22	To Bethsaïda.[1]
,, 31	,, 27	To the villages of Caesarea Philippi.
24 2	Mt. 17 1	To a high mountain.
,, 17	,, 9	Returns from the mountain.
,, 45	Mk. 9 28	To Capernaum.
,, 48	,, 30	Passes through Galilee.
25 2	,, 33	To Capernaum.
,, 27	,, 10 1	To the borders of Judaea beyond Jordan.[2]
27 30	Jn. 7 1	Walks in Galilee.
28 9	Mt. 19 1	To the borders of Judaea beyond Jordan.[2]
,, 11	Jn. 7 10	To Jerusalem for the Feast of Tabernacles.
,, 42	Mk. 10 17	Walks in the way.
30 31	Lu. 17 11	Starts for Jerusalem for the Feast of Unleavened Bread.[3] Cf. 30 40, 41.
31 6	Lu. 13 22	Makes a circuit of cities and villages.
,, 15	Lu. 19 1	Passes through Jericho.
,, 25	Lu. 18 35	Leaves Jericho.
32 1	Mt. 21 12	Enters Jerusalem.
,, 22	,, 17	To Bethany.
,, 27	Mk. 11 15	To Jerusalem.
33 1	,, 19	To Bethany.
,, 26	,, 27[4]	To Jerusalem.
34 46	Lu. 19 47	Visits the Temple daily.
37 25	Jn. 10 22	} Visits the Temple at the Feast of Dedication.
,, 26	,, 23	
,, 43	,, 40	To the other side of Jordan, where John at first baptized.
38 1	Jn. 11 17	To Bethany to raise Lazarus.
,, 38	,, 54	To Ephraem.
,, 42	Lu. 9 51	Starts for Jerusalem.
,, 47	,, 56	Arrives at a village.
39 1	Jn. 12 1	Reaches Bethany.
,, 42	Mt. 21 10	Enters Jerusalem.
40 24	Lu. 21 37	From the Mount of Olives to Jerusalem and back daily until His betrayal.

[1] Apparently Bethsaïda Julias; cf. 23 16.

[2] In the Gospels these refer to the same journey; and Tatian himself has identified the interview with the Pharisees about divorce that took place during it; cf. 25 27-42.

[3] Tatian omits "he passed through the midst of Samaria and Galilee," and substitutes part of Jn. 5 1 already inserted at 22 9.

[4] Called 15 in Ciasca by mistake.

Note.—The visit to Jerusalem mentioned in Jn. 2 13 is identified by Tatian with a late visit recorded in the Synoptic Gospels, because he identifies the two accounts of the Cleansing of the Temple. According to him this visit occurs at 32 1; and the further allusion to it in Jn. 2 23a is omitted from the same cause. The visit to the Mount of Olives, Jn. 8 1, which would occur after 35 16, is omitted along with the account of the woman taken in adultery; cf. R.V. margin.

VII.—*Continued.*

Minor Movements during the Last Visit to Jerusalem.

Diatessaron.	Gospel.	Nature of Movement.
41 21	Jn. 12 36	Leaves the Temple and hides Himself. Cf. 41 27.
,, 33	Mk. 13 3	Sits on the Mount of Olives.
46 16	Lu. 22 39	Goes after supper to the Mount of Olives.
48 1	Jn. 18 1	To Gethsemane.
,, 47	,, 13	To the house of Annas.
49 6	,, 24	To the house of Caiaphas.
,, 30	Lu. 22 66	To the Council.
,, 43	Jn. 18 28	To the Praetorium.
50 4	Lu. 23 7	To Herod.
,, 8	,, 11	To the Praetorium.
51 15	Jn. 19 17	Starts for Calvary.
,, 25	Lu. 23 33	Arrives at Calvary.

VIII.

Principal Allusions to the Diatessaron in Ancient Writings.

1. *The Doctrine of Addai*,[1] an apocryphal work supposed to have been published at Edessa before the middle of the third century, says (cap. xxxv. 15-17): "Moreover, much people day by day assembled and came together for prayer, and for the reading of the Old Testament and the New, the *Diatessaron*."

2. Eusebius (A.D. 325), in his *Ecclesiastical History* (cap. iv. 29), says:

"Tatian, their former leader, composed a sort of connection and compilation, I know not how, of the Gospels, and called it the *Diatessaron*. This work is current with some persons even to the present day."

3. Epiphanius, in his work on Heresies, begun A.D. 374 (cap. xlvi. 1), says:

"The *Diatessaron Gospel* is said to have been composed by him [*i.e.* Tatian], which some call *according to the Hebrews*."

4. In a list of Canons put forth by Rabbula, Bishop of Edessa, A.D. 412-435, he says: "Let the presbyters and deacons have a care that in all the churches there be provided and read a copy of the distinct Gospel."

In the Syriac Gospels discovered by Cureton the MS. of the first bears the title: "Distinct Gospel of Matthew," evidently in contrast to the combined or compiled Gospel of the *Diatessaron*. We may infer therefore that Rabbula wished to exclude the latter from use in the churches of his diocese.

5. Theodoret, who became Bishop of Cyrus or Cyrrhus near the Euphrates about A.D. 420, in a book on Heresies, written A.D. 453, cap. i. 20, says:

"He [*i.e.* Tatian] also composed the Gospel, which is called *Diatessaron*, cutting out the genealogies and whatever other passages show that the Lord was born of the seed of David according to the flesh. And not only did the members of his sect make use of this work, but even those that follow the apostolic doctrine, not perceiving the mischief of the composition, but using the book too simply as an abridgment. And I myself found more than two hundred such books held in respect in the churches of our parts: and I collected and put them all away, and put the Gospels of the four Evangelists in their place."

6. Bar-Ali (A.D. 885), in his *Glossary* (Payne Smith, *Thesaurus Syr.* i. 869), gives:

"*Diastarsun* [or *Diakutrun*], the Gospel which is the *Diatessaron*, made by Titianos, the compiled Gospel. A Gospel made in a general sense on the sense of the four evangelists (God's blessing be upon them!). It contains neither the natural nor the traditional genealogy of our Lord Christ: and he who made it (Titianos) has on that account been anathematised."

7. Bar-Bahlul, in his Syriac Lexicon written in the tenth century (Payne Smith, *Thesaurus Syr.* i. 870), gives:

---

[1] In Cureton's *Ancient Syriac Documents*, and *The Doctrine of Addai*, Dr. Phillips, where see note p. 34. Quotations of the Gospels in the *Doctrine of Addai* are referred to in the notes of the present work.

"*Diatessaron*, that is to say, the compiled Gospel from the four evangelists. This was composed in Alexandria, and was written by Tatian the bishop."

As Bar-Bahlul speaks elsewhere of S. Matthew's as the "distinct Gospel," we may infer that he drew the same distinction between "distinct" and "compiled" as we before attributed to Rabbula. Bar-Ali seems to have done the same. Bar-Bahlul confuses Tatian with Ammonius of Alexandria.

8. Dionysius Bar-Salibi, Bishop of Amida in Mesopotamia, who died A.D. 1207, in his commentary on the Gospels, says in the preface to S. Mark's :

"Tatian, the disciple of Justin the philosopher and martyr, selected from the Gospels and patched together and constructed a Gospel, which he called *Diatessaron*, that is, *Miscellanies*. On this work Mar Ephraem wrote a commentary ; and its commencement was, *In the beginning was the Word*. Elias of Salamia, who is also called Aphthonius, constructed a Gospel on the model of the *Diatessaron* of Ammonius, mentioned by Eusebius in his introduction to the Canons, which he made for the Gospel. Elias sought for that *Diatessaron*, and could not find it ; and so he constructed another after the likeness of it. And this Elias finds fault with several things in the Canons of Eusebius, and points out errors in them, and with good reason. But this work which Elias compiled is not often met with."

9. Gregory Bar-Hebraeus, a Syrian writer of the latter half of the thirteenth century (Assemani, *Bibl. Orient.* i. 57), writes :

"Eusebius of Caesarea, seeing the corruption which Ammonius of Alexandria had introduced into the Gospel of the *Diatessaron*, that is, *Miscellanies*, the commencement of which was, *In the beginning was the Word*, and which Mar Ephraem expounded, kept the four Gospels entire, as they are in the text, but marked the agreement of the words by a common canon."

This writer is evidently quoting from Bar-Salibi, and has misunderstood him, supposing the *Diatessaron* of Tatian to be the same as the Harmony of Ammonius.

10. Ebed-Jesu, a Syrian writer early in the fourteenth century (Assemani, *Bibl. Orient.* iii. 12), makes a similar error, apparently through misunderstanding Bar-Salibi, and perhaps led astray by Bar-Hebraeus, saying :

"A Gospel, which a man of Alexandria compiled, Ammonius, who is also Tatian, and he called it *Diatessaron*."

But the same writer, in the preface to his collection of Canons (Mai, *Script. Vet. Nov. Coll.* x. 23 and 191), avoids this error, saying :

"Tatian, a certain philosopher, when he had comprehended intellectually the meaning of the evangelists in relating, and had fixed in his own mind the object of their divine narration, collected out of the four one admirable Gospel, which he also named *Diatessaron ;* in which, whilst he preserved most carefully the right order of those things which were said and done by the Saviour, he did not add a single saying of his own."

IX.

CONTAINING AN ANALYSIS OF THE PASSAGES IN WHICH ZAHN'S RECONSTRUCTION GAVE A DIFFERENT ORDER FROM THAT OF THE ARABIC DIATESSARON.

IN this Appendix no attempt is made to enter into all the reasons which Dr. Zahn assigns for the conclusions he arrived at as to the order occupied by different passages in Ephraem's copy of the *Diatessaron*. The sole object is to ascertain whether there is in the result of his labours anything calculated to throw discredit upon the order of the Arabic version. Passages which Zahn, before the recovery of the Arabic, placed in the same order as they occupy in the Arabic—even though he so placed them with some degree of doubt or hesitation—are here presumed to throw no serious doubt upon the accuracy of the Arabic order. The question considered here is whether those passages which he placed in a different order from that which has since been found in the Arabic, were *necessarily* in a different order in Ephraem's *Diatessaron*, or whether the new light now obtained may not serve to explain away the discrepancies. Many of the passages were necessarily placed by Zahn in his reconstruction more or less by inference, conjecture, and probability; and if the Borgian and Vatican MSS. serve to modify in a few of these doubtful cases the conclusions at which he arrived, there is nothing in that to cast any reflection upon the excellence of his work, of which no one is more convinced than the writer. In this Appendix *all* the passages in which his order disagrees with the Arabic are considered, and no others.

I. *Diat.* iii. 46–iv. 11; John i. 7–28; Moes. pp. 37–40; Zahn, § 6.

Ephraem has commented upon the mission and testimony of S. John the Baptist before the scene between the child Jesus and the doctors in the temple. This arrangement is historically impossible; and we cannot therefore suppose that it was so arranged in Ephraem's copy of the *Diatessaron*, nor is it in the Arabic or the *Codex Fuldensis*. There can be no doubt that Ephraem's Commentary in its present form departs at this point from the order of the work upon which he was commenting. There are, in fact, signs of confusion in Ephraem's remarks, since he puts the temple scene after the preaching of S. John, and yet before the account of S. John's dress.

II. *Diat.* v. 33–41 ; Luke iv. 14b–22a ; Moes. pp. 128–131 ; Zahn, § 32.

This passage forms in S. Luke a portion only of a longer passage giving an account of what took place at Nazareth on *one* occasion. But in the Arabic this is divided, and represented as taking place on two different occasions, the latter of these coinciding with a visit to Nazareth described at Matt. xiii. 54–58 and Mark vi. 1–6. This mode of dividing the passage enabled the harmonist to escape a serious difficulty ; for in S. Luke the visit to Nazareth is put at the very beginning of our Lord's ministry. Immediately after His temptation He is represented as proceeding to Galilee, where He goes about preaching in the synagogues of towns and villages, arriving at Nazareth in the course of His journey. There He makes a public claim to be fulfilling a prophecy of Isaiah at a time when He has not yet called any of the twelve disciples nor wrought any *recorded* miracle, though it is implied that He had wrought miracles at Capernaum. Yet this reference to Capernaum seems to apply better to a later stage of His ministry ; and the remarks of the Nazarenes and His reply to them bear marks of close resemblance to those recorded in the first two Gospels at the places already mentioned, which are represented there as made at a much later period, and long after the calling of the disciples. In fact, one part of S. Luke's narrative postulates a date at the very beginning of Christ's ministry ; and the other part appears to belong to a much later date ; and yet the evangelist treats the two parts as referring to the same occasion. It would seem as if S. Luke's informant had unconsciously blended together incidents belonging to two different visits of Jesus to Nazareth ; and if we suppose the division found in the Arabic to be due to Tatian, the thought arises, whether he may have been aware of some tradition existing in the time of Justin to the effect that the facts warranted this separation.

As the phrase, "as his custom was," which is given by Moesinger (p. 129) in spaced type, certainly belongs to Luke iv. 16, near the beginning of these verses, and is followed by part of ver. 24, and a little later by ver. 25–27, Zahn had no alternative in the absence of the Arabic but to suppose that the whole block occurred at the later position in Ephraem's *Diatessaron.*

In order to understand the situation, now that we have the Arabic to help us, we must go somewhat into detail. Ephraem opens this subject by quoting Matt. xiii. 54 (*Diat.* xvii. 37). Upon this verse, which speaks of "his own city," he remarks that it was written to convict the Marcionites of falsehood—*i.e.*, as Moesinger rightly suggests, the falsehood that Jesus had no human birth or parentage. Then, according to Codex B, which Moesinger follows at this point, he goes on thus : "After these things, it saith, he entered, as his custom was, into their synagogues on the sabbath day." "After these things" is not found in any Gospel in this connection ; and Professor Robinson prefers the reading of Codex A, which makes this part a remark of Ephraem and not a quotation, the meaning being, "After this it saith, 'He entered,'" etc. If this be the better reading, the words of Ephraem would imply that this citation came next after Matt. xiii. 54 in his copy. Turning now to the Arabic, we find in the corresponding place (*Diat.* xvii. 38) the similar words from S. Mark, "And when the sabbath was come, Jesus began to teach in the synagogue." The probability therefore is that Ephraem's *Diatessaron* contained this verse more in the form of Luke iv. 16 than of Mark vi. 2, and including in particular the clause, "as his custom was."

But how does this affect the following verses, Luke iv. 17-22^a, which describe the actual teaching in the synagogue? The reasoning of Ephraem seems to prove decisively that these were not in his copy at this point. For he is dealing with an argument of the Marcionites, which may be thus stated: It was in the synagogue that Jesus taught the Nazarenes; therefore His teaching was necessarily of a religious character, and had reference to their God—the God of the Old Testament, or Demiurge. *Something* which He said so enraged them that they brought Him out to cast Him down headlong from the precipice. What was that something? Presumably He told them that He came from the superior God of the universe, and in opposition to their God—nothing short of this could have inflamed them so. To this argument Ephraem gives a double reply: (1) that it was the "custom" of Jesus, as shown by this verse, to teach in the synagogue wherever He went; and His teaching did not usually enrage His hearers, as it certainly would have done, if He had been in the habit of preaching such a doctrine as the Marcionites attributed to Him; and (2) that our Lord Himself stated the reason for their rejection of Him, and it was not anything of that kind, nor founded on what He had *said*, but it was the fact of His having been born there that caused Him to receive such different treatment there. Now in Luke iv. 17-21 we have some particulars of what Christ said in the synagogue at Nazareth; and if these verses followed immediately in Ephraem's copy, and were applied to the same occasion, he would not have failed to draw attention to them, and to reply to the Marcionites that, so far from setting up a new God in opposition to the God of the Old Testament, Jesus declared in that synagogue that He was fulfilling the words of Isaiah, the prophet of the Old Testament God. Moreover, in *Marcion's Gospel*, ver. 17-19 of Luke iv. are omitted, and ver. 20, 21 modified so as to contain no allusion to this teaching of Jesus; and Ephraem would not have failed to charge the Marcionites, as other Fathers did, with deliberate excision of the passage to suit their own views. His silence on these points seems to us conclusive evidence that these verses did not occur here in Ephraem's *Diatessaron*. If so, there is no reason to doubt that it was Tatian who divided S. Luke's narrative; and that he placed the two portions where we find them in the Arabic— excepting part of Luke iv. 16, which he may have inserted at both places, for we find other connective verses used more than once. This view is confirmed by the fact that they are similarly divided in the *Codex Fuldensis*, where the two parts of S. Luke's narrative occur at cap. 18 and cap. 79 respectively.

III. *Diat.* v. 49–vi. 4 ; Luke v. 1–11 ; Moes. p. 59 ; Zahn, § 14.

A few lines only are devoted by Ephraem to the miraculous draught of fishes, which accompanied the final calling of S. Peter ; and Zahn, following the order of the Commentary, places this occurrence later than it is found in the Arabic. Here then is a real difference between the two, and it only remains to consider which is more likely to be the true order of Tatian. One fact seems to us decisive in favour of the Arabic order, and that is the relative position of the remarks upon the baptism by the disciples at Aennon. According to S. John, who alone records it, Jesus after His baptism and temptation, and calling some disciples, visited Galilee, and it was not until He had been to Jerusalem for a Passover, and had received the visit of Nicodemus, that His disciples baptized in Jordan. Is it to be supposed that Tatian—who puts the visit of Nicodemus at a later period than S. John does—would put this baptism before the final calling of the chief of the disciples, thus either excluding him from all share in that work, or representing our Lord as delegating the important office of baptism to men who had not yet finally abandoned their worldly calling ? We cannot doubt, therefore, that the Arabic preserves in this case the original order of Tatian ; nor does it seem improbable that this order existed also in Ephraem's copy of it ; for (1) there are evidences in other places that some passages of the Commentary have become displaced from their true position, perhaps by accidental confusion of the leaves ; and (2) though we find Ephraem adhering with remarkable consistency to the order of the Arabic, we cannot be certain that he never once departed from the order of his copy. The *Codex Fuldensis* supports the Arabic order.

IV. *Diat.* vii. 46 ; Mark iii. 21 ; Zahn, § 27.

The attempt of Christ's relations to take Him is not mentioned in the Commentary, and therefore no difference between Ephraem's copy and the Arabic can be traced here. The position of this verse in the Arabic is peculiar. Cf. *Diat.* vii. 46, note.

V. *Diat.* xiii. 36–37 ; Mark vi. 12–13 ; Zahn, § 24.

This passage also is not in Ephraem ; and it is therefore only the inference of Zahn, which differs from the Arabic. He naturally supposed that the subject of these verses followed immediately after that of ver. 11 was concluded, and could not have guessed that the account of our Lord's visit to the home of Martha and Mary came between His address to the Twelve before sending them away, and the account of their doings when they were away.

VI. *Diat.* xiv. 9 ; Luke xvi. 17 ; Moes. p. 65 ; Zahn, § 26.

Part of the preceding verse, "The law and the prophets *were* until John," is quoted by Ephraem, evidently parenthetically (Moes. p. 42), in connection with the baptism of Jesus, and a second time (Moes. p. 104) in a very appropriate place among the comments passed by Jesus upon John the Baptist on the occasion of the visit of two of John's disciples. It is at this point that the whole verse occurs in the Arabic, followed almost immediately, and in a very natural sequence, by the succeeding verse now under consideration, viz.: "It is easier for heaven and earth to pass away than for one jot to perish from the law." But in Ephraem's Commentary this latter is found only at p. 65, between the two citations, "I am not come to destroy the law or the prophets, but to fulfil ;" and, "Whosoever shall break one of the commandments." These passages come from Matt. v. 17 and 19, and between them occurs in S. Matthew a very similar verse to that which we are considering, viz.: "Verily I say unto you, Till heaven and earth pass away, one jot or one tittle shall not pass from the law till all be fulfilled." Now it is, of course, possible that Tatian exchanged these verses; but it seems highly improbable that he entirely separated Luke xvi. 17 from Luke xvi. 16 in order to substitute it for the similar verse of S. Matthew; and we may more reasonably conclude either that Ephraem, trusting to memory, quoted the wrong verse owing to their similarity, or that he intentionally quoted a parallel passage from elsewhere. In any case, there is not sufficient evidence to show decisively that Ephraem's copy differed here from the Arabic versions. Here also the *Codex Fuldensis* agrees with the Arabic.

VII. *Diat.* xiv. 43, 44 ; Mark vi. 30, 31 ; Zahn, § 34.

This account of the return of the twelve disciples is not mentioned in the Commentary ; and there is therefore no evidence here of any difference of order. It is Zahn's inference alone which disagrees with the Arabic.

VIII. *Diat.* xv. 17-26 ; Luke x. 3-12 ; Moes. pp. 90-98 ; Zahn, § 24.

These verses, which contain the instructions of Jesus to the seventy (or seventy-two) disciples before sending them forth on their mission, are placed by Zahn along with the similar instructions to the Twelve, and consequently in a different order from the Arabic. This is due to the fact that Ephraem, who mentions both the sending of the Twelve and the sending of the Seventy apparently just at the places where they occur in the Arabic, says nothing about any instructions to the latter, but proceeds at once to comment on what took place at their return ; whereas he discusses at great length the instructions to the former, and in citing them he introduces several readings peculiar to the verses we are considering, thus suggesting that he found these blended with the very similar verses of Matt. x. Of course it might have been the case that Ephraem was quoting from memory, and owing to his familiarity with S. Luke's Gospel, inadvertently adopted his phraseology in quoting verses so much like his;

or it might have been that Ephraem, in arranging the order of his Commentary, found it more convenient to consider the two sets of instructions at one time because of their similarity, and therefore deliberately discussed these verses out of the order of his *Diatessaron*. But we are satisfied that the true explanation is, that Tatian, whilst preserving a separate mention of the mission of the Seventy, did not preserve a separate account of the directions they received from our Lord, but harmonised the two sets of directions into one more complete set, and placed this in connection with the earlier mission—the sending of the Twelve. The chief evidence of this is to be found in the *Codex Fuldensis*, in which the instructions to the Twelve (cap. 45) contain several clauses borrowed from Luke x., thus showing evident signs of harmonisation. But where we should have expected (cap. 68) to find the injunctions to the Seventy, we find instead that the narrative passes at once from Luke x. 2^a to Luke x. 16, skipping the verses now in question, and also three others denouncing Chorazin and other cities; and Ranke informs us that the MS. of the Codex shows no signs of discontinuity at the place. This independent testimony renders it practically certain that in the version represented by the Arabic these verses have been removed from participating in the earlier passage where Tatian harmonised them, and have been restored in full to their true place in relation to the mission of the Seventy, by persons who found the statement that the Seventy were sent forth, and naturally missed the directions for their journey. With them they probably moved also the denunciation of the cities. In making this restoration, however, they did not altogether obliterate the traces of harmonisation from the earlier passage, the expressions "two and two" (*Diat.* xii. 43) and "lambs" (*Diat.* xiii. 1) being apparently derived from Luke x. 1 and 3.

According to the *Codex Fuldensis*, it would appear that, while Tatian removed the instructions given to the Seventy, he left as applying to them the comforting assurance which follows at ver. 16, "He that heareth you heareth me; and he that rejecteth you rejecteth me: but he that rejecteth me rejecteth Him that sent me." This might very naturally be the case; but Ephraem quotes part of this (Moes. p. 94) when commenting on the charge given to the Twelve. The question therefore arises, whether this also stood at the earlier place in his copy. On the whole, the evidence seems against this view. Had it been there, it could not well have stood in the exact order in which it is quoted; and the drift of the passage in which it stands, seems rather to point to it as an illustration taken from a distance.

IX. *Diat.* xx. 12–16; Luke xi. 37–41; Zahn, § 77.

These verses are not mentioned by Ephraem; and we have therefore no evidence that they occupied in his harmony a different position from that which they have in the Arabic. Zahn very naturally assumed that they were placed in connection with the discourse which follows them in their Gospel; but in reality Tatian removed them from their setting in St. Luke to combine them with other remarks of our Lord upon clean and unclean things.

X. *Diat.* xxv.-xxvii.; Matt. xviii.; Moes. pp. 162-165;
Zahn, §§ 45-50.

This chapter of S. Matthew is very curiously subdivided and arranged in the Arabic; and if Ephraem's copy followed the same order, it was impossible for Zahn to discover that order from the brief fragments which Ephraem has cited. He has therefore constructed a different arrangement; but now that we have access to the Arabic, we find that Ephraem's citations occupy exactly the same relative order in his Commentary as they do in the Arabic. There is thus no evidence here of disagreement between the respective copies; but their agreement, as far as they go together, in so singular a sequence, furnishes a strong ground for supposing that they agreed throughout in the treatment of this chapter.

XI. *Diat.* xxvii. 24-25; Luke xii. 47-48; Zahn, § 79.

There is no allusion to these verses in the Commentary, and therefore no apparent difference from the Arabic. Zahn naturally assumed that they went with the preceding verses, but the Arabic shows that they did not.

XII. *Diat.* xxviii. 33-41; Luke xii. 13-21; Zahn, § 54.

The parable of the Rich Fool. This also is not in the Commentary. Zahn was very nearly right in his inference; but he put it after instead of before the incident of the Rich Young Ruler.

XIII. *Diat.* xxxi. 36-52; Luke xix. 11-27; Zahn, § 80.

The parable of the Minas (Pounds) is not alluded to in the Commentary. Zahn supposed it to have been harmonised with the parable of the Talents, and placed it accordingly. His reasons for the supposition were not derived from anything Ephraem said, but from Aphraates. This passage therefore furnishes no ascertainable difference of order between Ephraem's copy and the Arabic.

XIV. *Diat.* xxxiii. 1-17; Mark xi. 19-26; Moes. pp. 182-189;
Zahn, § 61.

The visit of Nicodemus is placed between the Cursing of the Fig-tree and the discovery by the disciples, on the following day, that it had withered. Ephraem comments upon both the cursing and the withering before he speaks of Nicodemus. There is in this nothing to suggest that his order differed from the Arabic; for any one commenting on the Gospel narrative in the order of the Arabic, and consequently beginning to refer to the Fig-tree before he spoke of Nicodemus, would naturally prefer to close the incident of the Fig-tree before proceeding further. See Introduction, p. 19.

X.

THE EPHRAEM FRAGMENTS, OR THE PORTIONS OF THE DIATESSARON CITED BY S. EPHRAEM THE SYRIAN IN THE COURSE OF A COMMENTARY WHICH HE WROTE UPON IT.

THESE fragments are here presented throughout in the order in which they occur in the Arabic *Diatessaron*; cf. Introduction, pp. 12–16. References to the corresponding passages of the English version of the Arabic are given in the margin to the left; and in the margin to the right are placed the numbers of the pages of Dr. Moesinger's Latin version of Ephraem's Commentary at which the fragments are to be found. By observing the sequence of these numbers, the reader can see for himself where Ephraem quotes in a different order from the Arabic. In a few instances this may be due to the existence of a different order in his copy of the *Diatessaron*; but in general it arises from his having quoted a passage from a distant part of the *Diatessaron* by way of illustrating a point or giving force to an argument. Thus at xii. 52 we find 63 in the midst of a series steadily increasing from 88 to 94; and, on referring to Moes. p. 63, we find that this fragment, containing the words, " Peace be to the house," is quoted to illustrate the beatitude, " Blessed are the peacemakers," etc., and does not intimate that the Instructions to the Twelve occurred in the middle of the beatitudes. In this case the fragment is quoted again in its true order at p. 92.

By turning to the corresponding passage in the body of the present work, as shown by the marginal references at the left, the reader can find the Gospel reference corresponding to each fragment as it is given in the Arabic. In some instances the fragment, as quoted by Ephraem, agrees more closely with the parallel passage of another Gospel. Of this the reader, who is interested in such points, can judge for himself by looking out the passage suggested by the Arabic in his reference Bible, and examining the parallel passages there referred to.

As stated in the Introduction (p. 15), the entire text of these fragments has been revised by Professor Robinson, who has examined both the Armenian MSS., and has expressed his willingness to be responsible for the renderings given to them in this Appendix, as well as for such portions of the notes as deal with the Armenian text. A brief explanation of the reasons for a particular reading is sometimes offered in the notes; but in a few cases, where the reasons were of a complex nature, or involved points of controversy too lengthy for a note, it has been thought better to say nothing.

Brackets are used in this Appendix as follows: < > enclose words not in the Armenian, but almost certain to have been in Tatian; [ ] words in the Armenian, but idiomatic and not implying a various reading; ( ) words in the Armenian, but probably a paraphrase and not an actual quotation. Words not in the Armenian, but necessary in English to complete the sentence, are printed in italics. In very obvious cases, however, these indications are omitted.

In the notes Codex A signifies the MS. from which the Armenian text was printed in A.D. 1836, and Codex B the MS. written by Nerses. Simple page references thus, p. 13, refer to Dr. Moesinger's work; simple references to chapter and verses thus, vi. 14, refer to the left hand margin of this Appendix; similar references with the prefix "*Diat.*" apply to the English text of the Arabic *Diatessaron*; Arm. Vulg. means the Armenian Vulgate.

Diatessaron. Moesinger.

1 1 In the beginning was the Word, <and>   3, 4, 5, 168
      [itself] the Word was with God, and the Word
   2 was God. The same was in the beginning 5
   3 with God. All things were made by him;
      and without him was not anything made.
   4 And that which was made, by him was life,
   5 and the life was the light of men. And   5, 6
      [itself] the light was shining in darkness; and
      darkness overcame it not.
   6 But¹ there was in the days of Herod, king 6, 7
      of Judaea, a certain priest, and his name was
   7 Zacharias, and his wife Elizabeth. . . . They 7
      were blameless in all their habitation . . .
14,15 thy prayer is heard before God. . . . And 8, 12, 14: 7
      there shall be joy and gladness unto thee.
   16 . . . and wine and strong drink he shall not 7
   18 drink . . . to turn the hearts of *the* fathers 14
      to *the* children . . . he shall make ready
   19 for the Lord a perfected people. . . . How 8, 9, 13
   25 should this be? . . . Elizabeth hid herself 14, 15
   27 five months . . . in the sixth month . . . 15
   29²Health *be* with thee, thou blessed among 49
   33 women. . . . the Lord God shall give unto 15, 16

¹ Codex B omits, "But;" the Arm. Vulg. has, "And;" there is no corresponding Greek.

² At p. 16 Ephraem cites as a quotation concerning Joseph and Mary: "they were both of the house of David." Moesinger thinks he is referring to *Diat.* i. 28; but Zahn thinks it more likely that he has in view *Diat.* ii. 12, 13, with a slightly different reading from our own. In his Commentary on 2 Tim. ii. 8, Ephraem again cites the same words.

| Diatessaron. | Moesinger. |

1 36 him the throne of David his father. . . . The   255–6
  Spirit shall come, and the power of the
  Highest shall overshadow thee: because that
  which shall be born of thee, shall surely be
37 called *the* Son of God. And Elizabeth thy   15, 16
  sister hath conceived in her old age; <and>   18
39 this is the sixth month with her. . . . Mary   15
  saith, Behold, I am the handmaid of the
  Lord: be it unto me according to thy word.
40 . . . Mary arose and went (to Elizabeth) . . .   17
42,43 <the babe> leaped for joy. . . . Blessed art   19 : 19, 49
  thou among women, and blessed is the fruit
44 of thy womb. <And> whence is this to   17
  me, that the mother of my Lord should come
46 to me? . . . Blessed is she, which believed,   17, 18
  that there should be a fulfilment of all the
  words, which were with her from the Lord.
47,49 . . . (Bless the Lord, O my soul.) . . . from   18 : 17, 18
  henceforth all generations shall call me
57 blessed. . . . (after three months) she re-   18
64 turned to her own house. . . . (The fingers   12
  wrote on the tablet,) His name *is* John.
77 . . . And thou, child, shalt be called the   7
  prophet of the Highest: thou shalt go before
  the face of the Lord to prepare his ways,
78 to give perfect knowledge of salvation. . . .
79 whereby the sun[1] from on high shall appear   20, 30
80 unto us, <to give light to them>, which
  sat in darkness and in the shadow of death,
  <and> to guide our feet into the way of
  peace.
2 1 The generation of Jesus Christ was on this
  wise: When his mother Mary was espoused
  to Joseph, and before she was given to a
  husband,[2] she was found with child of the

---

[1] "Sun;" so in the Arm. Vulg. here. At p. 30 Ephraem quotes it thus: "The sunrise from on high shall give light." Cod. B reads, "hath appeared." After "unto us" Cod. A adds, "to lighten our darkness."

[2] "She . . . husband" differs from the Arm. Vulg.

Diatessaron.		Moesinger.
2	2 Holy Ghost. Joseph, because he was a just	22
	man, was not[1] willing to make Mary a public	
	example, and was minded to put her away	
	3 quietly. . . . (the) angel appeared unto him,	22–3
	and saith, Fear not to take Mary. . . .	
	5, 6 (Isaiah the prophet, that he saith,) Behold,	22
	7 the virgin shall conceive . . . he took her.	25
	8 . . . He dwelt with her in purity,[2] until	23, 25–6
	11 she brought forth the first-born. . . . They	26
	were written,[3] each in his own city. . . .	
	19 Unto you is born this day a Saviour, who is	27
	22 the Anointed of[4] the Lord. . . . Glory to	27, 63
	God in the highest, and peace on earth, good	
	31 hope[5] to the sons of men. . . . Every first-	25
	born, that openeth the womb, shall be called	
	34 holy to the Lord. . . . And it was revealed[6]	226
	unto him by the Holy Ghost, that he should	
	not taste[7] death, until he should see the	
	36 Lord Christ. . . . He took up (our Lord)	
	37 into his arms . . . and said, Lord, now	28, 226
	lettest thou thy servant depart in peace	
	38 according to thy word. . . . Behold, mine	28
	39 eyes have seen thy mercy, which thou hast	
	42 prepared before all Gentiles.[8] . . . Behold,	28, 119
	this *child* standeth for falling and for rising	
	43 again, <and> for a sign of contradiction even	28–9, 269
	in thine own soul: thou shalt cause a sword	
	to pass away.[9]	

[1] Cod. B has, "and was not." "Quietly," as in the Curetonian Syriac.

[2] So in the Curetonian Syriac; the Arm. Vulg. has, "He knew her not."

[3] For "were written" the Arm. Vulg. has, "entered into the census." For ver. 12, 13, see note at i. 29.

[4] This reading is found in the Jerusalem Syriac.

[5] This is supported by Aphraates and the Arabic. Cf. *Diat.* ii. 22. Cod. A has words which may mean, "hope of good things to the sons of men," or, "hope to the good sons of men."

[6] Lit. "he received warning;" but the same as the Arm. Vulg.

[7] Cod. B has, "see."

[8] Arm. Vulg. has, "peoples." Eusebius, *On the Psalms*, p. 223, has, "Gentiles."

[9] So Cod. B; the text in Cod. A is corrupt. The reading as here given,

X. THE EPHRAEM FRAGMENTS. 337

Diatessaron.		Moesinger.

3 3, 8[1]   ... Jerusalem was moved ... I also   208 : 30, 31
   11 will come *and* worship him. ... and they   31
       opened their treasures, and presented unto
       him an offering,[2] gold, and myrrh, and frank-
   12 incense. And they were warned in a vision,   30
       that they should not return to (him). ...
   15 Then was fulfilled the true word, which was   32, 36
       spoken by the prophet, *who* saith, Out of
   16 Egypt will I call my son. And when   32, 34
       Herod saw that he was mocked of the wise
       men, he was exceeding wroth, and sent *and*
   17 slew every infant child. ... The word was   32
       fulfilled, which was spoken by Jeremiah the
   18 prophet. In Rama a voice was cried[3];   32-4
       Rachel was weeping for her sons, because
   23 they were not. ... He shall be called a   36
   32 Nazarene. ... Behold,[4] I and thy father,   24, 40
       sorrowing *and* grieving, were going about and
   33 seeking thee. ... I must be in my Father's   40
   35 house. ... (she) kept everything in her   52
   50 heart. ... He came unto his own, and his   5
   53 own received him not. ... And the Word   6, 37
   56 was made flesh, and dwelt in us. ... For   7, 36, 55
       the law was given by Moses; grace and
       truth[5] came by Jesus.
4 1   No man hath been able to see God at any   3

which is supported by Ephraem's comments, is apparently the result of some confusion in the Syriac. Ephraem adds, as from "the Greek," "thoughts from many hearts shall be revealed." At p. 269 the passage is quoted quite differently, "and through thine own soul altogether shall a sword pass."

[1] At p. 162 there is a reference to iii. 5, but not a quotation. Ephraem there speaks of the scribes as saying, "out of the town of Bethlehem shall he arise."

[2] So in the Curetonian Syriac. In the Arm. Vulg. "offerings;" so here in Cod. B.

[3] In the Arm. Vulg. "lamented."

[4] Ephraem, by a curious displacement, comments on this section immediately before *Diat.* iv. 12.

[5] In one passage (p. 36) Ephraem, instead of "grace and truth," has, "and the truth of it," *i.e.* of the law; Cod. B, however, has, "and the truth of them,' *i.e.* of the signs already mentioned in his remarks.

Diatessaron.   **Moesinger.**

4	time; but the Only-begotten, which is in[1] the bosom of the Father, he declared to us 2 concerning him. The Jews sent unto John,	37
	3 and say unto him, Who art thou? He confessed *and* saith, I am not the Christ.	
	4 They say unto him, Art thou Elijah? He	37–8
	10 saith, No. . . . and the latchet of his shoes	41, 192
	12 I am not worthy to bear. . . . And John	40, 101
	17 was clad in raiment of hair. . . . God is able of these stones to raise up children unto	40
	18 Abraham. . . . Behold, the axe is come to	39
	25 the root of the trees. . . . I am not worthy	99
	29 to unloose the latchet of his shoes. . . . And Jesus himself was about thirty years of age at the time when he came[2] to be baptized of	41
	30 John. . . . Behold, this is the Lamb of God; this is he that cometh[3] to take away the sin	{ 41, 43, 99, 101, 103, 208, 238 }
	31 of the world. . . . After me shall come a	192
	33 man, who [indeed] is before *me*. . . . I have	99, 104
	34 need to be baptized of thee. . . . Suffer it now, that we may fulfil all righteousness.[4]	41–2
38, 39	. . . This is my beloved Son.[5] . . . (John bears record,) I saw the Spirit in the likeness of the body of a dove, that it descended, and	99 : 128
	40 rested upon him. < And > I knew him not:	155
	but he that sent me . . . the same said unto	151
	43 me. . . . Immediately the Holy[6] Spirit took	42–3

---

[1] "In:" so the Arm. Vulg.; but immediately below Ephraem gives, as a quotation, "He was begotten from the bosom of his Father."

[2] "When he came" implies a variant ἐρχόμενος for ἀρχόμενος. Cf. Clem. Alex. p. 407, and Iren. p. 148, as quoted by Tischendorf.

[3] So at p. 41, but the form of the quotation varies elsewhere.

[4] The word is in the plural, as in the Arm. Vulg.

[5] Ephraem's comment (p. 43), "By the shining of the light which was upon the waters, and by the voice which came from heaven," etc., shows that he was acquainted with the story of the fire on the Jordan, which is found in two Old Latin MSS., but leaves it uncertain whether he learnt it from the *Diatessaron* or from other sources. It is not in the Arabic.

[6] So Cod. D at Mark i. 12; cf. Peschito and the Curetonian Syriac at Matt. iv. 1.

X. THE EPHRAEM FRAGMENTS. 339

Diatessaron.   Moesinger.

       and led him out into a desert, to be tempted
4 44 by Satan. . . . And after forty days,[1] that he   44
   45 fasted, he hungered. . . . If thou be the Son   44–7
      of God, command these stones, that they be
   46 made bread. . . . Man shall not live by bread   46
      alone, but by every word that proceedeth out
   47 of the mouth of God. . . . He brought *him*   44
      and took *him and* set him on a corner of
   48 the temple, <and> saith unto him, Cast thy-   44, 47
      self down,[2] for it is written, They shall keep
      thee, lest at any time thy foot be dashed
   50 against a stone. . . . Again the devil brought   45
      him *and* took *him* into an exceeding high
   51 mountain . . . and saith unto him, The king-   45, 47
      doms and the glory of them will I give thee.[3]
      All these kingdoms are mine; to me it hath   45
      been given: I have authority over all this.
   52 Thou shalt fall upon thy face, and humbly
      worship me.
5 1, 2   . . . Get thee behind *me*, Satan, . . . he   49
   3 departed from him for a time. . . . Angels
   5 came and ministered unto him. . . . Behold,   197
  10 the Lamb of God.[4] . . . We have found   50
  15 Christ. . . . Can it be, that any good thing
  16 should come out of Nazareth? . . . Behold,
      indeed a scribe, an Israelite, in whom is no
  19 guile. . . . If thou shalt believe, thou shalt   185
  22 see greater things than these.[5] . . . there   52

---

[1] Omitting, "and forty nights;" see note to *Diat.* iv. 44.

[2] Lit. "from above down."

[3] Ephraem cites these passages in a different order from the Arabic, thus: (p. 45) "Mine are all these kingdoms. . . . To me it hath been given. . . . I have authority over all this. . . . Thou shalt fall upon thy face and humbly worship me." . . . (p. 47) "The kingdoms and the glory of them will I give thee."

[4] Ephraem alludes to this event as follows (p. 99): "When, it says, his other disciples heard that he was speaking concerning our Lord, and they saw Him, they left John without sorrow and followed him."

[5] See note to *Diat.* v. 20.

Diatessaron.   Moesinger.

was a marriage-feast[1] in Cana of Galilee.
5 24 . . . his mother saith unto him, Son,[2] they
25 have no wine here. Jesus saith unto her,
Woman, what have I to do with thee? my
26 time has not come on. She saith unto the
servants, Whatsoever my son saith unto you,
31 do. . . . Every man setteth on first the good   55
wine, and then that which is worse.[3] . . .
32 (For a beginning of his signs he made wine).   132
35 . . . he[4] entered, as his custom was, into   129
their synagogues on the sabbath day.[5] . . .
43, 53 The times are fulfilled. . . . we have toiled   57 : 59
55 all the night.[6] . . . they beckoned unto their   59
partners.
6 5 . . . His disciples were baptizing. . . .   58
13 He *must* increase, but I *must* decrease.[7] . . .   30, 105
17 And not by measure gave he to his Son.[8]   105
38 The land of Zabulon and Nephthali, the   6
way of the sea, and the passage of the
39 river Jordan, Galilee of the Gentiles. A   6, 51
people which sat[9] in darkness, saw a great
42 light. . . . Thou art the Holy One of God.   113
50 . . . the sun did set. . . .   122
7 16 . . . Our Lord saw their faith, *and* saith   59, 60
28 unto him, Thy sins be forgiven thee. . . . The   61
Pharisees and scribes murmur and say, Why
do ye eat and drink with publicans and
29 sinners? . . . They that are whole have no
need of a physician, but they that are sick.
30 . . . And I came not to call the righteous, but
32 sinners. . . . The companions of the bride-

---

[1] As in the Arm. Vulg.: Ephraem (p. 53) says: "The Greek writes, He sat down and the wine failed."

[2] "Son" is found in the Old Latin versions *e* and *l*, and in Amb.

[3] Lit. "the bad;" but the same is in the Arm. Vulg.

[4] Cod. B has, "after these things he entered," etc. Cf. Appendix IX.

[5] This clause is quoted by Ephraem immediately after xvii. 37.

[6] Ephraem also mentions the "two ships."

[7] Lit. "To him to increase, and to me to decrease."

[8] Cod. B has, "sons."   [9] At p. 51 Ephraem has, "walked."

| Diatessaron. | Moesinger. |

groom cannot fast, while the bride-	
7 37 groom is with them. . . . began to pluck the ears,	
38 to rub and to eat. . . . Behold, thy disciples do on the sabbath day that which is not	
39 lawful to do. . . . Have ye never read what	148
40 David did, how he ate the shewbread, which it was not lawful for him to eat, neither for	
41 them that were with him. . . . The sabbath	62
42 was made for man . . . their priests in the temple break the sabbath, and are blame-	
45 less. . . . Therefore the Son of man is lord of the sabbath.	148
8, 14, 17 Thou art[1] the Son of God . . . much[2]	235 : 83
power was going forth from him, and was	
26 healing all. . . . Jesus lifted up his eyes on	62
27 them, and began to say, Blessed are the	62, 64
28 poor in their spirits. . . . Blessed are they that weep; for they shall laugh.[3] . . .	63
29, 30 Blessed are the meek.[4] . . . Blessed are they that hunger and thirst after righteousness.	62 : 63
32 . . . Blessed are they that are pure in *their*	63
33 hearts; for they shall see God. Blessed are the peacemakers; for they shall be called	
34 sons of God. Blessed are they that are persecuted for righteousness' sake. . . .	
36 Rejoice ye, and be exceeding glad; for great is your reward in heaven, and in that day	64
37 rejoice. . . . Woe unto you, *that are* rich:	
40, 41 . . . Ye are the salt of the earth. . . . Ye	
43 are the light of the world.[5] . . . Let your light shine before men, that they may see your good works, and glorify your Father,	219

[1] Cod. B has, "the Christ, the Son of God."

[2] So in the Arm. Vulg. Ephraem prefaces this with, "But the evangelist writes."

[3] So in the Arm. Vulg. Cf. Matt. v. 4 and Luke vi. 21.

[4] Ephraem quotes this beatitude before the preceding one, as if his *Diatessaron* had it in the order of the Curetonian Syriac and Aphraates.

[5] Ephraem puts this clause just before "Ye are the salt of the earth;" but he has probably altered the order to suit his previous remarks.

Diatessaron.		Moesinger.
8	46 which is in heaven. . . . I am not come to destroy the law or the prophets, but to 48 fulfil.[1] . . . And whosoever shall break one	64, 170
		65
	49 of the commandments.[2] . . . Except your righteousness be found more than that of the scribes and Pharisees, ye cannot enter into 50 the kingdom of heaven. This ye have heard, that it was said: Do not kill; for he 51 that killeth is in danger of judgment. But I say unto you: He that calleth his brother 52 senseless.[3] . . . When thou hast offered thy gift upon the altar, leave thy gift and go, 57 be reconciled.[4] . . . Ye have heard that it 58 was said: Do not commit adultery. But I say unto you: Whosoever looketh and lusteth, hath committed adultery.[5] . . .	65, 66
		66
		66, 68
		65
		66
9	6 Ye have heard that it was said: An eye 7 for an eye.[6] . . . But I say unto you: Resist not evil[7] at all; <but> he that smiteth thy cheek, offer to him the other side also.	9, 69
		69
		{65, 69, 70, (133, 223
	32 . . . Our Father, which art in heaven. . . .	271
	40 But thou, when thou fastest, wash thy face, 41 and anoint thine head,[8] <that> thou appear not unto men to fast . . . thy Father, which seeth in secret, shall reward thee openly.	71
	42, 46 Fear not, little flock. . . . Where your	127 : 72, 170

[1] Ephraem shortly after quotes Luke xvi. 17 as if it followed at this point; but as the Arabic has at viii. 47 the similar passage Matt. v. 18, and places the former at xiv. 9, near where Ephraem places Luke xvi. 16, that was probably the order in Ephraem's *Diatessaron*.

[2] Ephraem adds, "of the New Testament," as if these words formed part of the *Diatessaron*.

[3] At p. 68 Ephraem has, "that saith to his brother, Vile or senseless one." The word here rendered "senseless" is that used for "Raca" in the Arm. Vulg.

[4] Cod. B, "first be reconciled."

[5] Ephraem here adds, "If thy hand or thy foot offend thee;" but cf. note at xxv. 18.

[6] Ephraem (p. 65) quotes twice, "a blow for a blow," as if it formed part of the text before him. Cf. *Ep. Polyc.* 2, χρόνου ἀντὶ χρόνου.

[7] Lit. "the evil," as in the Arm. Vulg.

[8] The same transposition of these clauses is found in the Arabic.

Diatessaron.   Moesinger.

		treasure is, there will your hearts be also.	
9	48	... If the light that is in thee be darkness.	72
10	13	... Judge not, that ye be not judged;[1] forgive, and it shall be forgiven you. Con-	
	16	demn[2] not. ... He that hath, to him shall be given: and he that hath not, from him shall they take even that which he thinketh[3]	72–3
	18	he hath. ... There is no disciple better[4]	223
	21	than his master. ... Give not that which	73
	31	is holy[5] to *the* dogs. ... Whatsoever ye would that the sons of men should do unto	224
	33	you, even so also do ye. ... Strait is the	263
	34	gate, ... who come to you in lambs' clothing, and inwardly they are ravening wolves. ...	94
	43	I know you not. ...	97, 216
11	5,6	He came with the elders of the people, and besought him (that he would not dis-	74
	9	dain to come and save his servant. And	
	10	when he undertook to go,) he saith unto him, Lord, trouble not thyself, but say *it* by	
	12	a word,[6] and he shall be healed. ... And, when he heard this, he marvelled. ... I have not found so great faith even in any one	
	14	in Israel. ... They shall go forth into outer	
	25	darkness.[7] ... I also[8] will follow thee. ...	
	26	Foxes have their resting-places;[9] and the Son of man hath no place where to lay his	

[1] A different word is used in the second place, which may also mean "condemned;" but it is not the same as in "Condemn not."

[2] The same word as in the Arm. Vulg. (Luke vi. 37).

[3] Cf. Luke viii. 18, margin, and the Revised Version. See also xliii. 37.

[4] So in the Arm. Vulg. at Luke vi. 40. Cod. B has, "greater than the master."

[5] Lit. "holiness;" but the same as in the Arm. Vulg.

[6] Or, "speak with a word."

[7] This is followed by, "The virgin's son met the son of the widow," showing that the raising of the widow's son at Nain followed here in Ephraem's copy, as it does in the Arabic.

[8] So in the Arm. Vulg. at Matt. viii. 19. Cod. B omits, "also."

[9] Or, "dens"—not the same word as in the Arm. Vulg.

Diatessaron.		Moesinger.
11	35 head . . . he rebuked the wind, and it	75
	47 ceased. . . . And the devils began to beseech him, that he would not drive them out of that place, and would not send them	
	49 into Gehenna before the time . . . and, when they had entered into the swine, immediately they choked them.	
12	3 . . . he sent (the man) away, saying,	76
	4, 13 Go *and* preach . . . fearing and trembling	90
	behind him, she touched the fringe of his	
	15 garment . . . and she knew in herself, that	84
	16 she was healed of her plague. . . . Who	78, 81
	17 touched my clothes ? . . . multitudes surround thee and press thee, and sayest thou,	77, 80, 86, 89
	18 Who touched me ? . . . I know that some one hath touched me, <for> I know that much[1] power hath gone forth from me. . . .	81, 83, 88
	19 But when she saw that this also was not	80
	21 hid from him . . . Go in peace: thy faith	
	23 hath made thee whole . . . believe, and thy	88, 89
	30 daughter shall live[2] . . . and he commanded to give her food to eat. . . . He sent them forth two *and* two after his own	90
	44 likeness.[3] . . . Go not into the way of the	91
	45 Gentiles[4] . . . to the lost sheep of the	
	47 house of Israel . . . freely ye have received,	
	48, 49 freely also[5] give. Possess[6] no gold <nor>	
	50 silver . . . a staff . . . no shoes, no stick,[7]	
	52 but sandals. . . . Into whatsoever house ye	63, 92
	54 enter, first say, Peace[8] to the house . . . shake	93

[1] "Much power" differs from the Arm. Vulg. here; but cf. viii. 17 and note.

[2] This clause must have occurred earlier in Ephraem's *Diatessaron*, as he distinctly implies (p. 88) that the woman heard it before her cure.

[3] Cf. xv. 15.

[4] The mention of Samaritans also is implied at p. 95.

[5] So in the Arm. Vulg.   [6] So in the Arm. Vulg. of Matt. x. 9.

[7] Cf. note to *Diat.* xii. 49.

[8] At p. 92 Cod. B has, "give peace," or "salutation" (the Armenian does not distinguish between these two words here).

X. THE EPHRAEM FRAGMENTS. 345

Diatessaron.   Moesinger.

12 55 off the dust of your feet. . . . It shall be   94
       more tolerable for the land of Sodom.¹ . . .
13 1 Now, behold, I send you forth as lambs²   91
       in the midst of wolves; be ye then innocent   94
    2 as doves, and wise as serpents.³ Beware of
       men: . . . they will deliver you up. . . .
    8 Into whatsoever city ye enter, and they re-
       ceive you not, remove⁴ from thence into
       another city; and, if from that they per-   94, 95
       secute you, flee into another city. If from   94
       this land they shall persecute you, go ye
       into another. Verily I say unto you, ye   95
       shall not be able to finish⁵ all the cities, until
   12 I come to you. . . . What I say unto you in   96
       darkness, that say ye in light; <and> what
       ye hear in the ear, that preach ye upon the
   13 housetops. . . . Be not afraid of them   95–6, 230–1
       which kill the body, but are not able to kill
   15 the soul. . . . Two sparrows are sold for a   97
       farthing; and one of them doth⁶ not fall on
   18 the ground without your Father . . . him
   19 will I confess⁷ before *my* Father. . . . He   97, 228
       that denieth me, him will I deny. . . .
   20 Think not that I am come to send peace   97
   22 on earth . . . a sword. I am come to set
       a man at variance against *his* father. . . .
   26 He that will find his life,⁸ shall lose it: 98
       <and> he that loseth his life⁸ for my sake

---

¹ Lit. "of the Sodomites," as in the Arm. Vulg.

² So in the Arabic, and in the address to the Seventy, Luke x. 3; Cod. B has, "sheep."

³ Note the change of order here.

⁴ The Armenian word here is the same as in Luke x. 7, "go not from house to house;" but it may be a mistake for "flee," as the Armenian words are nearly alike. In the second clause Cod. B has again "remove" for "flee."

⁵ Lit. "exhaust," as in the Arm. Vulg.

⁶ Cod. B, "shall."

⁷ Lit. "I will give thanks concerning him." The Arm. Vulg. has, "confess."

⁸ Or, "soul."

Diatessaron.		Moesinger.
	shall find it. He[1] that loveth me not	
13 27	more than his own life.[2] . . . He that re-	91
32	ceiveth you receiveth me.[3] . . . Mary came[4]	98
33	and sat at Jesus' feet . . . carest thou not	
	for me? speak to my sister, that she help	
35	me. . . . hath chosen the good part . . . not	
39	be taken away from her. . . . Art thou	99, 101
	he that should come, or look we for another?	
42	. . . Go *and* tell John what ye have seen.[5]	100
	Behold, the blind see, and the lame walk,	
	and the lepers are cleansed, and the deaf	
43	hear, and the dead[6] are raised. . . . Blessed	
	is he, whosoever shall not be offended in	
44	me. But when the apostles[7] of John were	
	departed, he began to say unto the people	
	concerning John, What went ye out to see	101
	in the wilderness? a reed shaken with the	
45	wind? or a man adorned in soft[8] raiment?	
	Such are found[9] in the chambers of kings.	
46, 47	. . . he is more than the prophets. . . . Be-	101 : 102
	hold, I send my messenger[10] before thee. . . .	
14 1	Verily I say unto you, that there hath	7, 103, 104, 107
	not arisen among them that are born of	
	women a greater than John . . . but he	103
	that is less in the kingdom of heaven is	
5	greater than he. . . . The law and the	42, 104
	prophets *were* until John : henceforth the	57
9	kingdom of heaven[11] is preached. . . . It	65
	is easier[12] for heaven and earth to pass	

[1] This clause does not occur in our Gospels exactly in this form; but it is found in Aphraates; cf. Luke xiv. 26.

[2] Or, "soul."   [3] Cf. note at xv. 32.

[4] Cf. *Diat.* xiii. 32, note.

[5] Ephraem says expressly, "not what ye have heard."

[6] This clause is not in the Arabic. Ephraem, however, speaks of it as closing the list like a seal; and he omits, "to the poor the gospel is preached."

[7] Different from the Arm. Vulg., which has "messengers."

[8] Lit. "garments of delicacy," as in the Arm. Vulg.

[9] Lit. "go about."   [10] Or, "angel."

[11] Cod. B, "of God."   [12] See note at viii. 46.

Diatessaron.		Moesinger.
	away, than for one tittle to fall from the	
14 17	law. . . . He through Beelzebul, the prince	160
24	of the devils, casteth out devils.[1] . . . No	44
	man can enter into a strong man's house,	
	and spoil his treasures, except he first bind	
	the strong man, and then he may spoil his	
29	treasures. . . . shall be guilty of the eter-	111
30	nal sin.[2] . . . An unclean spirit is in him.	113
31	. . . Whosoever shall speak a word against[3]	112
	the Son of man, it shall be forgiven him:	
	but whosoever shall speak against[3] the	
	Holy Ghost, it shall not be forgiven him,	111, 112
	neither[4] in this world, nor in that. . . .	
41	They brought unto him a certain man pos-	113
	sessed with a devil, deaf and dumb and	
	blind; <and> he healed him, and caused	
	him to hear,[5] to speak, and to see. . . .	
48	This man, if he were a prophet, how knew	
	he not of what manner of works this woman	
15 2	is, that is,[6] that she is a sinner? . . . A	114
	certain man, that was a creditor, had two	
	debtors: the one owed five hundred pence,	
5	and the other fifty. . . . he said unto Simon	
	the Pharisee: I entered into thine house;	
	and thou gavest me no water for my feet.	
6	. . . A kiss of greeting thou gavest me not;	
	and she, behold, since the time she came in,	
8	hath not ceased to kiss my feet. . . . And	
	therefore her sins, *which are* many, shall be	
	forgiven her; for she loved much;[7] for he,	

---

[1] So in Cod. A, as in the Arm. Vulg. But Cod. B and the margin of Cod. A have, "This is Beelzebul, the prince of the devils: he casteth out the devils." At p. 75, where there is a brief allusion to this passage, the MSS. are again at variance.

[2] Cf. the Revised Version at Mark iii. 29.

[3] Lit. "concerning," as in the Arm. Vulg.

[4] In two out of three places it is literally, "neither here nor there."

[5] Cf. the Curetonian Syriac.

[6] Cod. B omits, "that is."

[7] Cod. B omits, "for she loved much."

Diatessaron.   Moesinger.

to whom little is forgiven, loveth[1] little . . .

15 15 (He chose seventy and two[2] and sent them   160
     forth from himself.) he sent them two and   115
  20 two after his own likeness. . . . \<And\> if   105
     a son of peace is there, it shall rest upon
     him;[3] but if not, your peace shall return to
  30 you. . . . If the mighty works had been   230
     done in Sodom, which have been done in
     thee, it would have remained[4] until now.
  32 . . . he that rejecteth you, rejecteth me.[5]   94
  34 . . . I beheld Satan, that he fell as lightning   116
  35 from heaven. Behold, I gave unto you
     power to tread on serpents and scorpions
  36 and all the power of the enemy . . . rejoice   206
     not, that the spirits are subject unto you;
     but rejoice, that your names are written in
  37 heaven among the angels. . . . In that time   216
     and in that hour Jesus rejoiced in his spirit.
     . . . I thank thee, heavenly Father,[6] that   116 : 117
     thou hast hid these things from the wise
     and from the prudent, and hast revealed
  38 them unto babes . . . no man knoweth the   117, 216
     Father, but the Son, and[7] no man knoweth
  39 the Son, but the Father. . . . Come unto   117, 127
     me, all ye that labour and toil, and that
     have heavy burdens, and I *will* refresh[8] you.

[1] Cod. B has, "will love."

[2] Ephraem elsewhere (p. 59) says: "the mystery of the seventy-two," showing that his *Diatessaron* had that number instead of seventy. Cf. *Diat.* xv. 15, note.

[3] Cod. A omits, "it shall rest upon him." This passage may have occurred at xii. 52 in Ephraem's copy.

[4] Lit. "been an inhabited place."

[5] This clause is quoted by Ephraem in connection with the Mission of the Twelve. It may have occurred so in his *Diatessaron*, perhaps as a continuation of xiii. 27.

[6] Ephraem adds, "The Greek says, I thank thee, O God the Father, Lord of heaven and earth." Marcion's Gospel had simply, "I thank thee, Lord of the heaven," leaving out the allusion to earth, as Tatian seems to have done.

[7] Shortened at p. 117, "neither the Son, but the Father."

[8] Or, "give you rest."

X. THE EPHRAEM FRAGMENTS.

Diatessaron.   Moesinger.

15 40 ... learn of me, for I am meek and lowly   63
       in heart [1]; and ye shall find rest unto your
   43 souls. ... He that hateth not his own life   118
   45 cannot be my disciple. ... Who is there
       of you, who willeth to build a tower, and
       doth not first sit down, and count the cost
       thereof? ...

16 1 ... we would see signs from thee. ...
    2 This generation is an evil and adulterous
       generation; it seeketh after a sign, and   118, 119
       there shall no sign be given to it, but the
    4 sign of Jonah the prophet. ... For, as   118, 230
       Jonah was three days and three nights in
       the belly of the fish,[2] so shall[3] the Son of   119
       man be three days and three nights in the
    5 heart of the earth. The queen of the south   120
    6 shall condemn it. ... The men of Nineveh   119
    7 ... But the unclean spirit, when it goeth   120
       out of a man, (went) about through dry   121
       places, to seek rest, (but found) none. ...
       I will return to my former house. ...   122
    9 The unclean spirit goeth *and* taketh seven   120, 121
       others, his companions, who are more wicked
       than himself, and they come *and* dwell in
       him; and the last *state* of that man becometh
   10 worse than the first. So shall it be also   120, 122
   11 unto this generation. ... Blessed is the   122-3
   12 womb that bare thee,[4] ... blessed are they   123
       that hear the word of God and keep it. ...
   15 Behold, thy mother and thy brethren seek   122
   20 thee. ... (the) women (who went) with   120
       him, who had been healed of diseases and
       unclean spirits; Mary Magdalene, out of
   21 whom he had cast seven devils, and Joanna,

---

[1] Cod. A omits, "in heart."   [2] Not the word used in the Arm. Vulg.

[3] Cited as, "must enter into," in the first instance (p. 118), but three times afterwards as, "shall be in."

[4] Cod. B adds at p. 122, "and the paps which gave thee suck," as in the Arm. Vulg.

Diatessaron. Moesinger.

	the wife of Chuza, Herod's steward, and	
16	24 Susanna. . . . Behold, a sower went forth	124
	25 to sow *his* seed; and in his sowing some fell	
	26 by the wayside . . . And some fell on rocky	
	28 ground . . . And some fell among thorns	
	29 . . . And other fell on fertile[1] and good	
	30 ground . . . He that hath ears to hear, let	72, 123
	36 him hear. . . . The heart of this people is	113
	waxed gross: they have made heavy their ears; and they have shut their eyes, that they should not see with their eyes, and should not hear with their ears . . .	
	39 prophets and righteous men and kings[2] have	155
	43 desired . . . That, which fell by the way-	124
	44 side . . . And that, which was upon rocky	125
	48 ground. . . . But the good and fertile land . . . thirtyfold and sixtyfold and a hundred-	126
50, 51	fold . . . he knoweth not. For[3] the earth of itself bringeth forth fruit.	
17	4 . . . Sir, didst not thou sow seeds of holiness[4] of corn in thy field? from whence	
	5 then came[5] tares? He saith unto them,	127
	10 That is the work of an enemy. . . . Again the kingdom is like a grain <of mustard	
	11 seed> . . . for it is less than all seeds . . .	
	12 And when it groweth, it increaseth *and* becometh a tree, and becometh greater than all herbs; and the birds of heaven come and	
13–15	dwell in its branches. . . . (Again he compared it to leaven, which was mixed with	128
	20 meal.) . . . He that sowed the seeds of corn	174
	21 of holiness,[6] he is the Son of man . . . and	

[1] Lit. "fat;" the Arm. Vulg. has, "good and fat." Cf. ver. 48 and the Curetonian Syriac.
[2] Cod. B, "prophets and kings and righteous men."
[3] Cod. B, "he knoweth not that," etc., as in the Arm. Vulg.
[4] A Syriac expression for "holy seeds of corn." Cf. ver. 20.
[5] Cod. B has, "hath it."
[6] Cf. note at ver. 4. Cod. B, "the seeds of holiness of corn."

X. THE EPHRAEM FRAGMENTS.   351

Diatessaron.   Moesinger.

		the seed of good *things are* the children of	
17	24	the kingdom . . . he will cleanse the house	211
		of his kingdom from everything that offends.[1]	
	30	. . . Again, it is likened unto a net, that is	128
		cast into the sea, and gathereth into itself of	
	31	every kind . . . (they draw near to) choose[2]	
	37	the best,[3] and cast the bad away. . . . On	
		account of this he came into his own city,	
		and taught them[4] in their synagogues. . . .	
42,	43	Physician,[5] heal thyself. . . . A prophet	129, 130
		is not acceptable in his own city.[6] . . .	
	45	There were many widows in the house of[7]	130
	46	Israel . . . and to one of them <Elijah>	
	47	was not sent . . . lepers in the house of[7]	
	48	Israel. . . . He could not do <there> any	
	50	mighty work. . . . They were filled with	
	51	anger . . . they took him out . . . and	129
		brought him to the side of the mountain	
		. . . *and* cast him down. . . .	130–1, 212
18	12	. . . (at the dancing of the daughter of	132
	14	Herodias). . . . Cause to be brought the	131
	41	head of John the Baptist. . . . Gather up	134
		the fragments of the tables, that nothing at	
	45	all be lost therefrom. . . . This is of a truth	
		the prophet, of whom it was said that he	
	46	should come into the world. And our Lord	
		. . . went up into the mountain to pray	
	47	[8]alone. And when the day was toward	

[1] Lit. "every stumbling-block."   [2] Cod. B, "gather."
[3] Lit. "the good good," as in the Arm. Vulg. and in the Curetonian Syriac. Codex Bezae and many Old Latin MSS. read, "the best."
[4] Cod. B omits, "them." Immediately after this clause Ephraem quotes Luke iv. 16 ; cf. v. 35 and Appendix IX.
[5] Just before this clause Ephraem has, "He entered *into Bethsaida*," implying that this took place there. The idea that he may have quoted this from the Marcionite Gospel is not supported by anything that we know of that document ; cf. *Marcion's Gospel*, Parker, London. Probably there is some error in the Armenian text at this point.   [6] So in the Arm. Vulg.
[7] A literal translation of the idiomatic Syriac rendering of "in Israel."
[8] Ephraem cites ver. 47 of the Arabic before ver. 46, as if his *Dia-*

Diatessaron.   Moesinger.

18 48 evening, his disciples arose and went up into a ship, *and* went to go unto Capernaum.
19 4,8 ... It is I, be not afraid ... of little   135 : 136
     9 faith. ... When our Lord came and went   136
       up into the ship with Simon, and the winds
   10 rested and ceased. And they ... came
       and drew near before our Lord, and began
       to worship him and say, Of a truth thou art
   24 the Son of God. ... What signs[1] doest
       thou,[2] that we may see and believe on thee?
   25 ... Our fathers did eat manna in the
       desert, as also it is written, He gave them
   32 bread of[3] heaven to eat. ... I came not   234
       to do mine own will, but the will of him
   33 that sent me. And this is his will, that,
       whatsoever he hath given me, I should lose
   38 none of it. ... No man can come to me,   137
       except my Father, which hath sent me, draw
   44 him unto himself.[4] ... This is the bread,
       which cometh down from heaven, that a man
   45 should eat of it and die.[5] ... every one
       that eateth of this bread shall live for ever:
       (for the bread of God came down from
       heaven, and is given to all the world.) ...
   47 Except ye eat his flesh,[6] and drink his blood,   58, 245
   49 there is no life unto you. ... My flesh is   37
   54 meat. ... This word is hard, who can hear   125
       it? ...
20 7 ... (He) saith unto the twelve, Will ye   58

tessaron here followed the order of Matt. xiv. 22, 23, instead of S. John's order.

    [1] Cod. B has, "sign."   [2] Cod. B adds, "for us."
    [3] So in the Arm. Vulg., but perhaps only equivalent to "from" in our Authorised Version.
    [4] Cod. B. has, "unto me."
    [5] Cod. A omits, "not," as the Curetonian Syriac; but Cod. B has, "not." Ephraem seems to understand this clause of the manna given by Moses in the wilderness, after which all who ate it died.
    [6] Paraphrased at p. 245, "if any man taketh not my flesh, he receiveth not life."

X. THE EPHRAEM FRAGMENTS.

Diatessaron.   Moesinger.

20   8 also go[1] from me? Simon ... saith unto
       9 him, ... We have believed and known
   10, 23 ... one of you is a devil. ... God said,   206 : 138
         Honour thy father and mother. He that   137
         speaketh evil[2] of his father or his mother,
         let him die the death: and he that blas-
    24 phemeth God, let him be crucified. And ye   138
         say, every one[3] to your father and mother,
         Behold,[4] it is a gift,[5] whatsoever thou mayest
    25 be profited from me. ... (he) careth not
         henceforth to honour his father and mother.
    36 ... Every plant, which is not planted by
         my heavenly Father, shall be rooted out.
    42 ... In the heart arise[6] all thoughts of   63
    49 wickedness. ... The woman was crying   138
         out and following him, and saying, Have
    50 mercy on me. ... And he answered her
    53 not at all. ... It is not good to take the   139
         children's bread, and to cast it to dogs. ...
    54 Yea, Lord, even dogs eat[7] of the crumbs of 139, 59, 138
    55 their master's[8] table. ... On this account[9]   139
         I say unto thee, O woman, great[10] is thy
         faith.
21 7, 11 ... He did all things well. ... Give   186 : 140
    13 me water[11] to drink. ... The woman saith   140
    14 unto him, Behold, thou art a Jew. ... He
         saith unto her, If thou knewest him that   141
         said unto to thee, Give me water therefrom[12]

---

[1] Lit. "Is it that ye also wish to go?"
[2] As in the Revised Version.   [3] Cf. the Curetonian Syriac.
[4] More lit. "Come on, thou."   [5] Or, "offering."
[6] Lit. "come to be." Cod. B has, "from the heart," as the Arm. Vulg.
[7] At p. 59 we have simply, "even the dogs are fed."
[8] So in the Arm. Vulg. at Matt. xv. 27. Cod. B has, "the children's," as in the Arm. Vulg. at Mark vii. 28.
[9] Cf. Mark vii. 29; but it is also possible to regard these words as part of Ephraem's comment.
[10] Lit. "something great."
[11] Cod. B omits "water" in one place, and transposes it in another.
[12] Cod. B has, "Give me of this water."

Diatessaron.	Moesinger.

        to drink, thou wouldest have asked of him.
21 15 . . . The woman saith unto him, Thou,
        because¹ thou hast no bucket, and the well
  17 is deep. . . . He saith unto her, My waters
  18 come down from heaven. . . . He that
        drinketh of this water, that I shall give
  19 him, shall never thirst. . . . The woman
        saith unto him, Sir, give me of that water,
        that I thirst not, nor come any more to this
  20 well² to draw water from it. He saith unto
        her, Go, call thy husband unto me,³ . . .
  22 Thou hast had in turn⁴ five husbands, and   141, 142
        he whom thou now hast is not thy husband.
  23 . . . The woman saith unto him, Sir, thus   141
        thou seemest to me,⁵ that thou art a prophet.
  24 Our fathers worshipped in this mountain,   141–143
        <and> ye say that in Jerusalem only is the
  25 place of worship. He saith unto her, Verily
        I say unto thee, Neither in this mountain
        nor in Jerusalem shall they worship. . . .
  27 but true worshippers shall worship⁶ in spirit   141, 143
  29 and in truth. . . . Behold, Christ cometh;   141
        and, when he shall come, he will give us all
  30 things. He saith unto her, I that speak
  31 unto thee am he. . . . they marvelled, that   140
        he was [standing and] speaking with the
  46 woman. . . . They said unto the woman,   142
        Henceforth we believe on him not because
        of thy words, but because we have heard
        (his teaching, and seen his works, that he is
        God;) and we have known that this is

---

¹ So also in the Arm. Vulg.

² Cod. B omits, "any more to this well," and reads "hither" instead.

³ Cod. B omits, "unto me."

⁴ Lit. "hast changed," as in the Arm. Vulg.

⁵ Cod. B, "thus it seemeth to me;" the Arm. Vulg. has, "it seemeth to me."

⁶ At p. 141 Cod. B inserts, "the Father." At p. 143 Cod. A has, "shall worship the Father by the Holy Spirit in truth;" Cod. B omits this passage by homoeoteleuton.

X. THE EPHRAEM FRAGMENTS. 355

Diatessaron.		Moesinger.

21 49 indeed the true Christ. . . . the Galilaeans 130
reccived him.
22 1 . . . Lord, if thou wilt, thou canst heal[1] 143–145
2 me. . . . and he stretched forth *his* hand 145
5 <and> touched him. . . . (Tell) no man, 143–145
<but> go, shew thyself to the priests, and
offer a gift,[2] as Moses commanded,[3] for a testi-
13 mony unto them. . . . A certain man was there, 145
which had been thirty and eight years in his
14 infirmity . . . Our Lord saith unto him,
15 Wilt thou be made whole? The sick man
saith unto him, I have no guardian, that,
when the waters are troubled, he may take
and bring me down; but while I delay to be 146
moved[4] another goeth down before me.[5]
16 (He) saith unto him, Arise, take up thy bed 146, 148
19 and walk.[6] . . . He that made me whole, 147
he said unto me, Arise,[7] take up thy bed
20 and walk. They say unto him, Who said[8] 146,147,199
21 unto thee, Take up thy bed? He saith, I 147
know not: for Jesus, when he beheld the
multitude of the people, withdrew himself[9]
22 from that place. And after a while he saw
him, and saith unto him, Thou art made
whole, behold, sin no more,[10] lest thou have

---

[1] Quoted several times, sometimes as "cleanse."

[2] Or, "sacrifice."

[3] In one place for "commanded" Ephraem has, "taught thee;" probably his own paraphrase.

[4] Cod. A has, "while I delay to be set in order;" the Arm. Vulg. has simply, "while I delay."

[5] Ephraem says in his comment, "If they believed that the angel by means of the waters of Siloam healed the sick folk."

[6] So the passage is first quoted; Ephraem subsequently twice gives, "Stand on thy feet," and once adds, "to thine house."

[7] Cod. B omits, "Arise."

[8] It seems a paraphrase where Ephraem says, "Who bade thee take up thy bed upon thee on the sabbath day?" In narrating the passage in its context he says simply, "They say unto him, But who is he?"

[9] Lit. "slipped away," or "escaped;" so in the Arm. Vulg.

[10] Lit. "henceforth sin not;" quoted also at p. 146.

Diatessaron.   Moesinger.

22 23 need of some one else. And then the man departed and told the Jews, It was Jesus
25 which made me whole. . . . (He) saith unto 147–149
them, My Father worketh a work unto this
26 day; on account of this I also work. But 147–148
the Jews on this account persecuted (the Saviour), not only because he healed on the sabbath day, but also because he called God his Father, and made himself equal with God.
30 . . . The Father judgeth no man, but hath 151, 213
given all judgments into the hands of his
34 Son. . . . As the Father hath life in him- 149
self, so also hath he given to the Son . . . 149, 150
35 <and> hath given him authority, that the 150
Son of man should execute[1] judgment. . . .
42 Not that[2] I receive witness from men . . . 151
43, 44 He is the lamp, that burned. . . . For I have witness, which is greater than that of
John . . . the very works, that I do, bear 152
51 witness of me. . . . if another shall come 210
in his own name, him ye will believe. . . .
53, 54 Moses himself is your accuser . . . Moses 151, 152
wrote of me.

23 29, 32 . . . he saw all things clearly. . . . Who 153 : 153, 156
do men say [concerning me,] that the Son of
33 man is?[3] They said unto him, Some say[4] that he is Elijah; and some say[4] that he is Jeremiah; and some say[4] that he is a pro- 156
34 phet from among the prophets. . . . But 153
who say ye [concerning me,] that I am?
35 Simon saith Thou art Christ,[5] the Son of
36 the living God. Blessed art thou, Simon.
37 . . . Thou art a rock . . . and the gates of hell 154 : 153
39 shall not prevail against thee. . . . Tell no 154

---

[1] Lit. "judge judgments."   [2] So in the Arm. Vulg.

[3] Nearly identical with the Arm. Vulg. of Matt. xvi. 13. At p. 156 Ephraem has, "that I am."

[4] Lit. "a certain saith."

[5] Cod. A has, "the Son Christ, the Son," etc.

Diatessaron.		Moesinger.
	man concerning me, that I am Christ. . . .	
23 40	Behold, we go up to Jerusalem; and all	65, 154
	things are fulfilled, that have been written	
	concerning me; for the Son of man must be	230
41, 42	crucified, and die, and rise again. . . . This	154–6, 229
43	be far from thee, Lord[1] . . . he saith unto	154–5, 229
44	him, Get thee behind me,[2] Satan, thou art a	
	stumbling-block unto me; for thou thinkest	
	not the things that be of God, but those that	
	be of men.	
24 1	There are some that now stand here with	155, 222
	me, *which* shall not taste of death, till they	
2	shall see the kingdom of God. . . . After	159
	six days he took them and brought *them*	
3	up into the mountain. . . . The fashion of	156
9	his countenance was altered. . . . Lord, if	
	thou wilt, let us make here three taber-	
	nacles . . . he knew not, what he spake	
12	. . . (the voice came from heaven,) This is	157 : 156, 157
	my beloved Son: hear him, and live ye. . . .	157
17	And as they came down from the mountain,	154, 157–8
	he gave them a command, and said, Take	
	heed, that ye tell no man that vision, which	
	ye have seen, until the Son of man be risen	
29	from the dead. . . . It is not meet, that a	159, 212
34	prophet perish out of Jerusalem. . . . they	160
35	could not heal him. . . . O evil generation,	
	perverse and faithless, how long shall I be	203
39	with you, and suffer you? . . . He saith unto	160
	the man,[3] He that believeth, all things are	
41	possible to him. . . . I say unto thee,[4] un-	
	clean spirit, deaf and dumb, go out *and*	161
	depart from him, and enter no more into	

[1] Lit. "Propitiation be to thee, Lord, from this." So the Arm. Vulg.
[2] Ephraem sometimes omits "me," and once has, "Go away, Satan."
[3] At p. 70 Ephraem quotes apart from their context the words, "If thou believest."
[4] In connection with this miracle Ephraem adds: "At that time, it saith, his disciples were not as yet established in him."

Diatessaron.　　　　　　　　　　　　　　　　　　　　　　　　Moesinger.

24 45 him. . . . Why could not we heal him?　160
　　46 And he saith unto them, Because of your
　　　little faith. . . . If[1] ye had faith as a grain　204
　　　of mustard seed, ye should say to this moun-
　　　tain, Be removed; and it should be removed
　　50 from before you[2] . . . on the third day[3] I
　　　rise again. . . .

25　4　(Thy master perchance, they say, does not　161
　　5 give). . . . he prevented Simon, and saith
　　　unto him, Of whom do the kings of the
　　　earth[4] take tribute? of sons[5] or of
　　6 strangers? . . . Go *and* give thou also as
　　7 one of the strangers.[6] Lest thou offend
　　　them, go thou to the sea, and cast a net
　　8 there.[7] . . . Who is the greatest[8] in the　107
　　18 kingdom? . . . If[9] thy hand or thy foot　66
　　28 offend thee, . . . They came *and* drew near　162
　　　to ask him, Is it lawful for a man to put
　　29 away his wife? He answered them, and
　　30 saith, It is not lawful. They say unto him,
　　　Moses gave us permission: why is it not
　　35 lawful?[10] Moses, he saith, because of the
　　　hardness of your heart, gave you permission;
　　　but from the beginning of the creation it
　　　was not so.

[1] It is not certain that Ephraem cites this from this chapter, he may be only quoting in a varied form xxxiii. 6, 7.

[2] Lit. "from your face;" this occurs only at p. 204. Cf. pp. 184, 185, 189.

[3] Cod. B has, "after three days."

[4] Cod. B has, "of the nations of the earth."

[5] Cod. B has, "of their sons."　　　　　[6] So in the Arabic.

[7] In his remarks Ephraem says, "when he had drawn out the fish, which had a stater in its mouth."

[8] Lit. "Who [indeed] is great."

[9] Ephraem quotes this clause in connection with the Sermon on the Mount, Matt. v. 30, *Diat.* viii. 60, where, however, the hand only is referred to. Whether Tatian inserted the allusion to the foot in the Sermon, or Ephraem made the addition intentionally or inaccurately, is not certain.

[10] This clause combines into one ver. 30 and 34 of the Arabic, and so proceeds naturally to ver. 35 omitting ver. 31-33. Cod. B omits the clause probably by homoeoteleuton.

Diatessaron.   Moesinger.

26 8 . . . (joy[1] over sinners, that they repent, 163
more than over just persons, that they
14–15 sinned not.) . . . (And when the younger
33 son had wasted his goods) . . . It was meet
to be glad; for this thy brother was dead,
42 and became alive.[2] . . . Make to yourselves 156
friends, that they may receive you into their
eternal dwellings.[3]

27 21   Where one is, there I also am;[4] and 165
where two are, there will I also be. . . .
22 How oft, if my brother sin against me, shall[5] 163
I forgive him? until seven times <in a
23 day,[6]> is it enough?[7] He saith unto him, 163–4
Until seventy times seven seven times.[8]
27 . . . I have a baptism to be baptized with. 229
28 . . . In heaven their angels behold the 165
31 face of my Father. . . . And it came to
pass, when they came[9] *and* told him of the
Galilaeans, whose blood Pilate mingled with
36 their sacrifices. . . . A certain man had a 166, 184
37 fig-tree planted in his vineyard. And he 166, 213
saith unto the husbandman, Behold, *there*
are these three years, that I come seeking
fruit from this fig-tree, and find none: cut
38 it down. The husbandman answered, and 166
saith unto him, Let it alone this year
also. . . .

---

[1] Cod. B adds, "of the angels." A few lines before these words Ephraem has, "Ten drachmas and a hundred sheep."

[2] Cod. A has, "and lived and became alive."

[3] The same word as in the Arm. Vulg., but not the same as "tabernacles" at xxiv. 9. Lit. "dwellings which *are* for ever." Cod. A omits, "which *are*."

[4] Cod. B has, "will be." Ephraem introduces this clause with, "He comforted them in his saying," as though he read it in his *Diatessaron*.

[5] Cod. B has, "How oft shall my brother . . . and," as in the Arm. Vulg.

[6] Ephraem's comment makes it probable that these words followed.

[7] Or, "It is enough," or, "It is much;" perhaps Ephraem's comment.

[8] This is cited twice: in the first case Cod. B omits the second "seven": in the second place we have, "until seventy times seven seven," in both MSS.

[9] "Came," as in the Arm. Vulg.; probably a better translation of our Greek than "were present." The Arabic has the same.

Diatessaron.   Moesinger.

28 3 ... They say unto him, There is no man,   167
       4 that doeth anything in secret. ... For his
       7 brethren did not believe on him. ... I go
    20 not up in[1] this feast. ... Why do ye seek 167, 168, 196
    21 to kill me?[2] ... Who seeketh to kill   196
    27 thee? ... Do our elders know, that this   210
    28 is indeed Christ?[3] ... behold, Christ,
         when he shall come, no man knoweth
    29 whence he is. ... I am not come of   173
    42 myself. ... Good Master, what shall I do,   168, 172
    43 that I may live? ... Why callest thou me   { 123, 168 / 173, 174
         good? There is none good but one only,
         God, the Father, which is in heaven.   168–174
    44 Knowest thou the commandments? if thou   171 : 168
         wilt enter into eternal life keep the
    47 commandments.[4] ... All these things have   125
         I done from my youth up. What lack I   169
    48 yet? ... (He) looked on him with love.   171–3
    49 ... One thing thou lackest : if thou wilt   125, 170–1
         be perfect, go *and* sell all thy possessions,
         that thou hast. ...
29 3   How hard is it *for them* that trust[5] in   170, 172
       6 riches ! ... Behold, we have left all ; what   67, 178
       9 shall we have therefore? ... shall receive   88
    14 sevenfold in this *present* time ... a rich   173
    17 man ... clothed in purple ... the angels
         carried him into Abraham's bosom. ...
    19[6],20 My father, Abraham ... My son, remem-   173 : 175
         ber, that thou in thy lifetime receivedst thy

---

[1] The Arm. Vulg. has, "to."

[2] Ephraem continues, "a man, that speaketh the truth," thus blending John vii. 20 with John viii. 40. These verses he blends again, when discussing the latter (p. 196, cf. *Diat.* xxxv. 51). He may be there citing John viii. 40 as, "Why do ye seek to kill me?"

[3] The words which follow, "*more* true than all," appear to be Ephraem's comment.

[4] Ephraem (p. 171) quotes, "This do, and thou shalt live," as if these words followed here in his *Diatessaron*. Cf. xxxiv. 35.

[5] Lit. "have hoped ;" the same verb as in the Arm. Vulg. of Mark x. 24.

[6] Or, 25.

X. THE EPHRAEM FRAGMENTS.

Diatessaron.		Moesinger.
	good things, and Lazarus his evil things.[1]	
29 24	... They have[2] Moses and the prophets.	173
26	... If they hear not Moses and the prophets.	175
32	... Why stand ye all[3] the day idle?	176
33	... No man came *and* hired us ...	176, 177
36	the first supposed, that they would receive	175
37, 41	more ... they murmured. ... Or have I not power in mine own house to do what I will? If I am good,[4] why is thine eye	176 : 177 174, 176–7
42	evil? \<So\> the last shall be first. ...	108
30 41	... Behold, we go up to Jerusalem ...	178
44, 47	and they take and crucify him. ... We would that thou shouldest do for us, whatso-	
48	ever we may ask. ... He saith unto them,	
49	I will do *it* for you.[5] ... Give us authority	177–8
50	to sit, one on thy right hand and one on the left hand. ... Are ye able to drink of the cup, that I shall drink of? ...	108, 179, 229
31 3	... he, that will be your head, shall be	109
19	your servant. ... Zacchaeus make haste *and* come down (from the fig-tree, for I am	180
22	to be with thee.). ... Behold, Lord, the half of all my goods I will[6] give to the poor; and all things, that I have ever taken from any man wrongfully, I will restore	
23	them fourfold. ... This day is salvation[7] come to this house, forasmuch as he also is	180, 205 180
26	a son of Abraham ... a certain blind man	181

---

[1] Lit. "sufferings;" the word used in the Arm. Vulg. Cod. B has, "evil *things*."

[2] Lit. "There are."

[3] Lit. "the day till evening," as in the Arm. Vulg. The discussion of this parable is commenced by the words, "Concerning the hired labourers, whom the lord of the vineyard hired at the third, sixth, and ninth *hours*."

[4] Lit. "generous;" the same word is used here in the Arm. Vulg.

[5] This represents the second half of the clause, "What will ye *that* I shall do for you?" Ephraem's *Diatessaron* must, like Cod. Bezae, have omitted the first part, and read the second as a promise.

[6] So in the Arm. Vulg.

[7] In the second place Ephraem has, "life."

Diatessaron.   Moesinger.

	sat by the wayside, and his name was	
31	27 Bartimaeus, the son of Timaeus¹ ... (when)	
	28 he asked, Who might² this be? (They say,)	
	29 Jesus of Nazareth. ... He began to cry	180–1
	out, and saith, Jesus, son of David, have	
	30 mercy on me. ... They rebuked, (and	181
	hindered this blind man, that he should not	
	come to Jesus; therefore) he cried out the	
	more, Son of David, have mercy on me.	
	32 ... And he cast away his garment, and	
	34 came *unto him*. ... Receive thy sight:	
	thy faith hath made thee whole.	
32	1 ... (Within the temple they were selling	
	8 sheep and oxen) ... Destroy this temple,	182, 229
	and on the third day I will raise it up. ...	
	9 In forty and six years was this temple built,³	182
	and wilt thou raise it up on the third day?	
	21 ... This man went down justified more	
	than (he) ... every one that humbleth him-	41, 108
24,25	self, shall be exalted. ... He hungered, and	183, 186
	hasted *and* came to that fig-tree ... he	183
	26 found nothing thereon. ... (He cursed the	182–3
	30 fig-tree, and it withered away.)⁴ ... And	189
	is it possible for a man, *when he is* old, to	
	enter again the second time⁵ into his mother's	
	womb, and again⁶ be born out *of it*. ...	
	31 Except a man be born of water and of the	
	Spirit, he cannot enter into the kingdom of	
	32 God. That which is born of the flesh is	
	flesh, and that which is born of the Spirit	
	34 is spirit. ... ye know not the spirit, whence	
	36 it cometh, or whither it goeth. ... Thou	188
	art a master of Israel,⁷ and knowest thou not	

¹ Cod. B, "Timaeus, the son of Bartimaeus."   ² Or, "Who is this?"
³ This clause agrees with the Arm. Vulg.
⁴ Ephraem proceeds at once to discuss the finding the fig-tree withered, and the lesson of faith founded on it. Cf. Introduction, p. 19.
⁵ So in the Arm. Vulg.   ⁶ Cod. B has, "thence."
⁷ So in the Arm. Vulg.

Diatessaron.		Moesinger.
32	38 these things. . . . But now,¹ if I have told you earthly things, and ye have not believed, how shall ye believe, if I tell you heavenly	187–8
	39 things? And there is none that hath ascended up to heaven, but he that came down from heaven, *even* the Son of man.	168, 187–9
	40 . . . And as Moses lifted up the serpent in the wilderness, even so must² the Son of	189, 230
	42 man be lifted up. . . . God so loved the world, even as³ his only-begotten Son. . . .	258
33	3 . . . His disciples marvelled how it had withered away so suddenly. . . . When they	186 184, 186
	4 returned, they say unto him, Behold, the fig-tree, which thou cursedst, how is it withered	184
	6 away suddenly? He saith unto them, Ye also, if ye have faith and doubt not in your	184, 185, 189
	7 heart,⁴ shall say to this mountain,⁵ Go, be cast into the sea; and it shall be removed.	
	8 And whatsoever in your prayers ye shall ask of God with faith,⁶ it shall be given you.	189
9, 27	. . . Increase our faith⁷ . . . while he was teaching the people, and preaching the gospel	189 : 191
	28 to them, (they) came, and say unto him, By what authority doest thou these things? . . .	191, 38
	30 The baptism of John, whence was it? was it	191
	31 from heaven or from men? . . . They began to reason in their minds and to say, If we say that it is from heaven, he will say⁸ unto	
	32 us, Why then did ye not believe him? And	

¹ So in the Arm. Vulg.

² At p. 230 "is" appears instead of "must be;" but that may be a paraphrase.

³ Cod. B has, "that he gave;" but the reading of the text agrees with that of the first hand of ℵ, which omits, "he gave."

⁴ Cod. B has, "mind."

⁵ Cf. also *Diat*. xxiv. 46 and ver. 10 of this chapter in the Arabic.

⁶ "Of God" may be due to Tatian, the rest of the clause is like the Arm. Vulg.

⁷ Later on (p. 190) Ephraem comments on the conduct of the Unjust Judge, which follows here in the Arabic; but he does not quote the words.

⁸ Lit. "saith."

Diatessaron.   Moesinger.

            if we say, From men, we fear the people.
33 35 ... What think ye? A certain man had
37, 38 two sons ... Yea, sir, I go ... Which of
            of them did the will of his father? (They
            say,) The second.[1] ... Therefore the publicans
            and harlots shall go into the kingdom of
    39 heaven before you. John came unto you in 192
    40 the way of righteousness ... A certain
            householder planted for himself a vineyard,
            and hedged it round about, and prepared a
            winepress in it, and built a tower in it. ...
    42 and he sent his servants to bring him *the*
    49 fruit ... Afterwards he sent his son ...
    50 But when they saw the son, that he came,
            they say, This is the heir[2] of the vineyard;
    51 come, let us kill him; and hereafter the in-
            heritance of the vineyard becometh ours.
    53 ... (What do these husbandmen deserve?)
    54 ... He shall miserably destroy those miser-
    55 able men. ... Have ye never read: The 193
            stone, which the builders rejected, the same
            was made the head of the corner? ...
    58 Whosoever stumbleth on it shall be broken to
            pieces, and on whomsoever it shall fall, it
            shall crush and grind him to powder.
34 2   ... They sent unto him their disciples with
     3 the Herodians ... (whether they should give
     7 tribute.) ... Give unto Caesar that which
            is Caesar's, but that which is God's, render *to*
     9 *him*.[3] ... The Sadducees came, and say
            unto him, There is no resurrection of the
    10 dead. ... Moses thus[4] commanded us: If

---

[1] The Arabic has, "first;" but Ephraem remarks, "And they justly discriminating say, The second." The Armenian MSS. of the Gospels vary here in their readings.

[2] Cf. Moes. p. 265.

[3] Lit. "But that which is God's, that which we owe, render." In Cod. B, however, the first clause of this is shorter, "But to God."

[4] Cod. A has, "Moses the patriarch."

Diatessaron.   Moesinger

       a man die having no children, his brother
34 11 shall take his wife. . . . Now a certain 194
    13 woman became *the wife* of seven husbands.
    15 . . . In the resurrection of the dead there-
       fore whose *wife* of them shall she be ? . . .
  16,17 Ye do greatly err . . . For the sons of the
    18 times of this world marry wives . . . but
       they that become worthy of that world . . .
  19,26 they are as the angels . . . What command-
    27 ment is first and great in the law ? He
       saith unto him,[1] Hear, O Israel, the Lord 152, 169
    28 thy God is one Lord. <and> Love the 110, 194
    29 Lord thy God. . . . That is *the* great com- 110
    30 mandment. . . . Love thy neighbour as thy- 194
    35 self. . . . this do, and thou shalt live [2] . . . 171
  36,37 Who is my neighbour ? . . . from Jerusalem 195
    43 to Jericho . . . Which of them, thinkest
       thou, was neighbour to the wounded *man ?*
    44 He saith unto him, He that showed the
       mercy. He saith unto him, Do thou also
       likewise.
35 1 . . . Our Lord cried [3] and said, If any 196
       man of you thirst, let him come unto me
    6 and drink. . . . from the town of Bethlehem 210
    24 the Messiah is to be born. . . . Thou comest 86
       and bearest witness of thyself: thy witness
    44 is not true. . . . We are Abraham's children, 197
    50 . . . If ye were Abraham's children, ye 196, 197
    51 would do the works of Abraham. Why [4] do 168, 196
       ye seek to kill me, a man that speaketh the
    55 truth ? this did not Abraham. . . . Ye are 196
       the children of Satan, who is a murderer from

---

[1] The actual passage (p. 194) is: "He saith unto him, Thou shalt love the Lord thy God, and thy neighbour as thyself." The other clauses are found at the references given, and are placed here in the order of the Arabic.

[2] Cf. note at xxviii. 44.

[3] Cod. B has, "stood *and* cried," as in the Arm. Vulg.

[4] Cf. note at xxviii. 20.

Diatessaron.		Moesinger.
35	57 the beginning. . . . Which of you convinceth	152, 242
	59 me of sin? . . . Thou art a Samaritan.	197
36	6 Abraham desired[1] to see my day; he saw	155, 197, 207
	7 it and was glad. . . . Thou art not fifty	197
	years old; and hast thou seen Abraham?	
	8 He saith unto them, Before Abraham was, I	
	10 was. . . . He caused himself to meet with	197, 203
	a blind man, who was blind from his mother's	
	11 womb. And the disciples asked him, Whose	197
	12 sin[2] is it? . . . He saith unto them, Neither	197, 200
	this man's nor his kinsfolk's, but that the	
	works of God should be made manifest in	
	13 him. And I must work the works of my	
	Father, that sent me, while it is day: the	
	15 night cometh. . . . And when he had thus	198
	spoken, he spat on the ground, and made	
	clay of his spittle, <and> anointed his eyes	
	16 with the clay. . . . Go, wash thy face. . . .	199
	23,31[3](He made clay on the sabbath.) . . . They	199 : 202
	gave commandment to put him out.	
37	1 . . . They which see shall be made blind.	199
	4 . . . (when he entereth in by the door into	210
	10 his sheepfold) . . . <I am> the door of the	137
	11 sheep. All that came before me were thieves	200, 210
	14 and robbers. . . . the good shepherd giveth	174
	21 his life for his sheep. . . . I have power over	242
	my life to lay it down and to take it *again*.	
	35[4] . . . for which of my works do ye stone me?	
	40 . . . If I do[5] not the works, believe me	210
	41 not. . . . if ye believe not me, at least	121, 191
	46 believe the works. . . . And there was there	200
	a certain sick man: Lazarus was his name.	

[1] So in the Arm. Vulg.

[2] The Arm. Vulg. has, "whose fault is it, this man's, or his father's or mother's."

[3] Cf. Moesinger's note, p. 202. This fragment does not agree exactly with any passage in the Gospels or the Arabic. See the latter at xxxvi. 31 and 43.

[4] Cf. note at xlv. 39 for a fragment, which may come before this.

[5] Lit. "work."

Diatessaron.		Moesinger
37	48 ... And his sisters sent unto our Lord, and say, Lord, behold, he, whom thou lovest, is 49 fallen sick.[1] ... This sickness is not unto death, but for the glory of God, that the Son of God may be glorified thereby.[2] ...	
	51,52 he abode in that place two days. He saith unto his disciples, Come,[3] let us go into 53 Judaea. They say unto him, The Jews seek[4] to kill thee, and goest thou thither again?	203 : 200
	54 ... Are there not twelve hours in the day? If any man walk in the light, he stumbleth not, because he seeth the light.	200, 201
	59,60 ... Lazarus, our friend,[5] is dead; and I am 61 glad for your sakes. ... Come, let us go, that we also may die with him.	201
38	5[6] Lord, if thou hadst been here, our brother 9 had not died. ... I am the resurrection and the life; whosoever believeth in me, though 10 he were dead, he is alive. He that is alive, 17 and believeth in me, never dieth ... he 18 was troubled. ... Where have ye laid him?	202, 205 202 203 201, 203
	19,21 ... And[7] our Lord wept. ... He[8] that opened the eyes of the blind, could he not have caused that[9] even this man should not 23 have died?[10] ... Draw near and take away the stone ... by this time he stinketh; <for he hath been> dead four days. ...	203 : 249 204 202 204
	25 I thank thee, that thou hast heard me.	234
	26 And thou hearest me; but because of the people ... I say[11] this, that they may	99, 234

[1] Lit. "sick and fallen." [2] Or, "in him."
[3] So in the Arabic, the Arm. Vulg. and the Peschito.
[4] Cod. B has, "sought." [5] So Cod. Bezae. [6] Or, 16.
[7] So in the Arm. Vulg., ℵ, D, and the Arabic.
[8] Ephraem also has (p. 202), "Did not this *man* open," etc.
[9] Lit. "can he not so do anything that."
[10] Or, "should not die."
[11] So at p. 99 in Cod. A; but in Cod. B, "I do *it*," as in the Arm. Vulg. Both give this latter at p. 234; but the comments at both places show that Ephraem must have had "say."

Diatessaron.		Moesinger.
38	28 believe, that thou hast sent me. . . . Loose	204
	29 him. . . . Many believed on him there. . . .	200
	32 And if we suffer it, all men believe[1] on him; and the Romans will presently come, and take away our nation, the law, and this	204, 205
	42 place[2] . . . when the days were being fulfilled (of his work in Judaea) he turned his face to go to Jerusalem, and he sent (those	224
	45 two wrathful ones) before him. . . . Wilt thou, that we command fire to come down[3] and consume them?	95
39	1, 3 (He came to Bethany.[4]) . . . Simon the	204 : 205
	5 leper. . . . And the chief priests[5] took counsel, that they might put Lazarus also	205
	10[6] to death. . . . This ointment might have been sold for three hundred pence, and given	
	14 to the poor . . . that to the day of my	40
	21 winding-sheet she may keep it.[7] . . . loose the colt, and bring *him* unto me. . . .	207
	24 Rejoice, O daughter of Sion, for behold, a[8]	210
	31 king cometh unto thee. . . . The children	207
	32 were crying and saying, Blessing[9] to the Son of David. . . . Blessing in the highest. . . .	27
	33 Peace in heaven and glory on earth. . . .	
	36[10] The chief priests and scribes were sore displeased, and say, Hearest thou not what these say? . . . Rebuke the children[11] that	207 / 208
	37 they hold their peace. He saith unto them, If these shall hold their peace, yet the stones	
	38 will cry out. When he came to Jerusalem,	207

---

[1] The Arm. Vulg., ℵ* and ff[2] have the present tense.

[2] Cod. B has, "and the law and the kingdom and this place."

[3] Lit. "that we say, and fire should come down:" Cod. B adds, "from heaven."

[4] On the order of these fragments see note to *Diat.* xxxix. 1.

[5] Cod. B, "the priests."   [6] Cf. *Diat.* xxxix. 13.

[7] The whole clause as in the Arm. Vulg.   [8] Cod. B has, "thy."

[9] So in the Arm. Vulg. for "Hosanna."   [10] Cf. *Diat.* xl. 2, 3.

[11] Cod. A has, "the men;" but the comments support the reading, "the children." The "disciples" on the road to Jerusalem are evidently meant.

X. THE EPHRAEM FRAGMENTS.

Diatessaron.   Moesinger.

he beheld it, and began to weep[1] over it;
39 39 and he saith unto it, If thou hadst known   184, 207
at least this day of thy peace[2]! but peace is
hid from thine eyes.[3]
40 16 . . . Now is the judgment of the[4] world: 208
now also[5] the prince of this world is cast
19 out. . . . We have heard out of the law,   209
that the Christ abideth[6] for ever: and thou
sayest, The Son of man must be lifted up.
22 . . . The kingdom of God is[7] not by days
23 of observing . . . behold, the kingdom of   209–211
44 God is within your heart. . . . Woe unto   211
you, lawyers, for ye hide[8] the key.
41 2 . . . there shall come all the blood of
righteous men from the blood of Abel the
righteous unto the blood of Zacharias . . .
4 between the temple and the altar . . . how   213
12 often would I have gathered you. . . . If
any man hear my words, and keep them not,
I judge[9] him not: *for* I came not into the
world to judge the world, but to save the
13 world. . . . He that receiveth not my words,
the word that I have spoken, it judgeth him
14 . . . he, which sent me, he gave me a com-   173
mandment, what I should speak, and what I
30 should say. . . . The days will come, when[10]   44, 183
there shall not remain in it one stone upon

---

[1] At p. 184 Ephraem says, "It is written, The Lord saw it, and wept over it."
[2] At p. 184 in Cod. A it is, "this thy day;" and in Cod. B, "this day." At p. 207 in Cod. A it is, "this day of thy peace;" and in Cod. B, "to-day this day of thy peace."
[3] Lit. "face," as in the Arm. Vulg.
[4] So Cod. Bezae and many Latin MSS. Cod. B has, "this."
[5] For "now also," Cod. B has, "and."
[6] Lit. "liveth," one of the readings of the Arm. Vulg.
[7] Or, "cometh."
[8] The present tense, as in the Arm. Vulg. and in Old Latin MSS. *b e q*.
[9] Cod. A, "know."
[10] At p. 183, "when it shall be destroyed, and Jerusalem shall be overthrown."

Diatessaron.		Moesinger.

41 43 another¹ . . . they shall persecute you and 63
deliver you up.
42 4 When ye shall see the sign of the terror 213
of its desolation, which was spoken of by
 6 Daniel the prophet . . . he that standeth 214
 8 upon the housetops . . . Woe to them that
are with child . . . there shall be anguish²
10 unto this people. . . . If they shall say unto 211
13 you, Lo, he is here, believe *it* not . . . go
14 not forth. . . . As the lightning, which
16 lighteneth. . . . Pray ye and ask, that your 214–5
flight be not in the winter, neither on the
18 sabbath day. . . . And except God³ had 215
shortened those days, no living thing⁴ would
have been saved; <but> for the elect's
25 sake . . . From the fig-tree learn the 186
parable: for⁵ when the branches become
tender, and the leaf springs forth and buds, 187
31 ye know that summer is nigh. . . . pray that 215
ye may be *accounted* worthy to escape all
these things that shall come to pass. . . .
32 That day⁶ <and> that hour⁶ knoweth no 109, 179, 215–6
man, neither the angels, nor the Son . . .
33 watch and pray; for ye know not the time. 216
47, 49 . . . in one bed.⁷ . . . Two *men* shall be in 217
50 a field . . . the body . . . eagles. . . .   218
43 2 . . . Who is⁸ *the* overseer, *the* faithful
 8 servant, good and wise?⁹ . . . He will cut
him asunder, and will separate him, and
appoint him his portion with the hypocrites

---

¹ Lit. "a stone upon a stone."
² Cod. B has, "great anguish."
³ So in the Arm. Vulg. and some other versions. Cod. B omits, "God."
⁴ Cod. A has "flesh" in the text, but not in the margin.
⁵ Cod. B omits, "for."
⁶ Ephraem three times has, "that day," and once (p. 216), "that hour," but not both together. They are together in the Arabic as well as in the Greek.
⁷ These words come immediately after the next clause in Ephraem, but not in the Arabic.
⁸ Cod. B adds, "indeed."   ⁹ Cod. B has, "and wise and good."

Diatessaron.	Moesinger.

43 and[1] with the unbelievers; and there shall
be for him[2] weeping of eyes and gnashing
10 of teeth.... Five of them were foolish
26 and five wise.... his talent... the earth
28 ... he hid it.... He that had received five
32 talents.... He that had received the one   219
36 talent.... Take ye away the talent from   218
37 him.... He that hath,[3] to him shall be   192
given, and he shall have abundance; and he
that hath not, even that which he hath
seized shall they take away from him....
39 Let your loins be girded about and your   218–9
46 lamps burning.... Then shall the King   88
say unto them, that are on the right hand,
53 Come, ye blessed of my Father.... Depart   97: 75, 216
from me, ye cursed of my Father, into the
everlasting fire,[4] which is kept[5] for Satan
and his angels.

44 42   With desire I have desired to eat this   230
44 [6]passover with you, before I suffer.... One   159, 219
of you, he that eateth bread with me, he it
47 is that shall betray me. And behold, the   219
hand of my betrayer *is* with me at the table,
48 dipping.[6] And the Son of man goeth, as also   219, 230
it is written of him; <but> woe to that   224
man!... it were better for him, if he had   220
not been born....

45 12   ... (Our Lord) blessed and brake....   222
16 I will not drink henceforth of this offspring
of the vine until the kingdom of my Father.
17 ... Behold, Satan hath obtained[7] permission
18 to sift you as wheat, and I have prayed the

---

[1] Cod. B omits, "with the hypocrites and."
[2] Cod. B omits, "for him."
[3] Cf. a similar passage at x. 16. The wording here is different, and seems to allude to the taking away of the talent.
[4] At p. 216 there is added, "for I know you not;" cf. x. 43.
[5] Cod. B. has, "prepared."   [6] Cf. also *Diat.* xliv. 46.
[7] Lit. "hath gained his cause," *i.e.* "asked and obtained permission," etc. Our Greek implies this, but the Arm. Vulg. has simply, "asked."

Diatessaron.　　　　　　　　　　　　　　　　　Moesinger.

  Father[1] for thee, that thy faith fail not. . . .
45 20 A new commandment I give unto you: Love   224, 225
  34 one another, as I have loved you. . . . I am   137
  36 the way. . . . Shew us thy Father, and it   222
  37 sufficeth us . . . have ye not known me?
  38 . . . my Father, that is in me, he doeth   173
  39 these works. . . . I *am* in the Father, and   271
   the Father in me; and we are one.[2] . . .
  40 He that believeth on me, the works that   223
   I do shall he also do; and greater *works*
  44 shall he do. . . . Another Advocate I send   225
   unto you.
46 10 . . . and findeth nothing that is his in   223, 263
  13 me . . . he that hath not his[3] sword, let   223
  15 him buy himself a sword. . . . Two are   224
  19 enough. . . . Ye *are* clean through my   58
   word, which I have spoken unto you. . . .
  28,29 This is my commandment. . . . Greater   224: 225
   love than this can none other have, that he
  34 lay down his life for his friends . . . know   106
   that they hated me also, before *they hated*
  35 you. . . . I chose you, before[4] the world   50
  36 was. . . . If they have persecuted me, they   95
  41 will persecute you also . . . as also it is   209
   written in their law: They hated me with-
  42 out a cause. . . . Behold, I send unto you   225
  50 the Advocate.[5] . . . It is expedient for you,
   that I go away; for, if I go not away, the
   Advocate cometh not unto you (and all
   truth is not made known unto you.[6]). . . .
  54 and of judgment because the prince of this   227

---

 [1] A remarkable addition, which Zohrab says was in one MS. of the Arm. Vulg. Cod. A has, "my Father."

 [2] This clause may be a paraphrase of xxxvii. 33, and not belong to this verse, though quoted with it.

 [3] Or, "a sword for himself."

 [4] This clause occurs in a different connection at *Diat.* xlvii. ver. 23 and 42, with the latter of which it agrees closely.

 [5] Cod. A has, "this friend," or, "the friends."

 [6] Cod. A has, "knoweth you not."

Diatessaron.		Moesinger
46 58	world is judged.[1] . . . Whatsoever my Father hath is mine.	179
47 13	. . . And I came from the Father. . . .	3
17	I am not alone, because my[2] Father is with	271
18	me. . . . I have overcome the world. . . .	223
19	The hour is come: glorify thy Son; and thy	228
23	Son will glorify thee . . . give[3] me glory from thyself, of that which thou gavest me	227
28	before the world was . . . (and that which	179
29	I have, is my Father's.[4]) . . . and I come	271
30	to thee, my Father . . . and none of them perished but the son of perdition.[5]	137
48 6,9	. . . My soul is sorrowful. . . . Father, if it be possible, let this cup pass from me;	228: 229, 231
	but not my will,[6] but thine be done. . . .	233, 234
12	And he said unto his disciples, Watch and pray, that ye enter not into temptation. The spirit is willing and ready; but the	231
13	flesh is weak . . . thy will be done . . .	232
17	and his sweat became as *it were* drops of	235
19	blood. . . . Sleep on now, and take your	
26	rest. . . . Judas, comest thou to betray the Son of man with a kiss? Now wherefore	
27	art thou come, friend? . . . Whom seek	236
28	ye? . . . They say unto him, Jesus of Nazareth. Jesus said unto them, I am he.	
29	While Judas was standing with them, they went backward, and fell[7] to the ground.	154, 236

[1] The same word as in the Arm. Vulg.; it might also be rendered "condemned."

[2] Cod. B has, "the."

[3] Ephraem says below: "For also the reading hath, and plainly saith, Glorify me with that glory before thee, before the world was." After "also" Cod. B adds, "in the Greek."

[4] Ephraem adds this to ver. 58, above.

[5] For part of ver. 42 to follow this, cf. xlvi. 35, and note there.

[6] Ephraem, at p. 233, has, "Nay, Father, but thy will be done;" so Cod. A. Cod. B has "O" for "Nay." At p. 234 he has, "Not as my will is, but as thine."

[7] The same as in the Arm. Vulg.

Diatessaron.   Moesinger.

48 37[1] . . . Put up again thy sword into his 186,232,236
    40 place. . . . (He healed the ear) . . . 232
    47 they bound him, and led him away.[2] . . .   237
49 36   Hereafter shall ye see the Son of man
       coming with bright clouds with the angels
    37 of heaven. Then the high priest laid hold
       of his garments, and rent his robe. . . .
    43 And they took *and* led him out, and gave 238
    44 him into the hands of Pilate. And they
       entered not into the judgment hall, lest
       they should be defiled, that they might
    47 first eat the lamb in holiness[3] . . . he 239
       forbiddeth to give tribute to Caesar. . . .
50 14   Away with this man from us, away with 238
    40 *him* from us . . . they put on him a purple 239
    41 robe . . . a crown of thorns . . . (they put
    42 a reed in his hand.) . . . And they spat in
       his face.
51 3   . . . Shall I[4] crucify your king? . . .
    7 When Judas saw, that our Lord was con-
      demned, he repented, and went *and* brought
      back the thirty pieces of silver to the
    8 priests,[5] and saith, I have sinned, in that I
      have betrayed righteous[6] blood. They say
      unto him, We have no care; thou knowest.[7]
    9 And he cast the silver into the temple, and 240
      departed, and went *and* hanged himself, and
   10 died.[8] . . . It is not lawful to receive this
   11 silver into the treasury. . . . (they bought 241

---

[1] On ver. 35, 36 Ephraem comments thus at p. 236: "Simon cut off the ear of one of them; but the kind Lord in his goodness took it, and fastened it on again" . . .

[2] Here follow remarks on the denial of Simon, contrasting it with his confession of Christ afterwards.

[3] After this Ephraem comments on the silence of Jesus before Pilate.

[4] Lit. "Do I."   [5] Col. B has, "chief priests."

[6] So in the Arm. Vulg. and some versions.

[7] "We . . . knowest" is so in the Arm. Vulg.

[8] Ephraem refers to the other account of the death of Judas, Acts i. 18, and says, "his belly was poured forth," and, "he fell and burst asunder in the

| Diatessaron. | Moesinger. |

51 15 with it the place of burial.) . . . And when
he had taken up for himself[1] his cross, and
17 gone forth, . . . they found *and* took a
18 certain man, a Cyrenian, . . . and they
20 laid on him the cross . . . weep for your-   207
21 selves. For the days will come, in the
which they shall say to the mountains,
23 Cover us. . . . If they do this in the green   242
25 tree . . . the dry. . . . When they had
crucified him, they crucified with him two
26 others, malefactors . . . that that might be
accomplished, that it saith: He was reckoned
27 with the transgressors. And they gave[2]   245
28 him to drink vinegar and gall. . . . (his
raiment which was divided into four parts
31 . . . his coat was not rent.) . . . This is   243
38 the Christ, the King of the Jews. . . . He   249, 250
saved others: himself he cannot save. . . .
39 Come down from the cross, that we may see,   116
44 and believe on thee. . . . Art not thou the   242–3
Christ? save thyself and us with thee. . . .
47 Lord, remember me in thy kingdom[3] . . .   243–4
48 to-day,[4] Thou shalt be with me in the garden   244–5
50 of delight.[5] . . . Woman, behold, thy son.   54, 270
51 . . . Thou young man, behold, thy mother.   54
52, 53 . . . The sun was darkened. . . . God, my   245, 257 : 247
God,[6] why hast thou forsaken me?
52 5 . . . Let us see, whether Elijah cometh   247

midst." There can be little doubt that Tatian made use of Acts i. 18 and
1 Cor. xi. 23–25. Cf. *Diat.* xlv. 16, note.

[1] Or, "by himself." So also in the Arm. Vulg.

[2] Ephraem puts this after the conversation with the penitent thief. Cf.
Diat. lii. 2.

[3] So given in the Acts of Pilate.

[4] In his citations Ephraem does not join "to-day" with "Thou shalt be."
He merely refers to it in his comment. Probably his *Diatessaron* had it joined
to, "I say unto thee," as in the Acts of Pilate. It may be so taken in the
Curetonian Syriac, but not in the Peschito.

[5] *I.e.* "of Eden."

[6] Ephraem cites it below as "Eli, Eli" in Cod. A, as "El, El" in Cod. B.

Diatessaron.   Moesinger.

52 6 to take him down. . . . Father, forgive them, 117, 256, 265
    7 for they know not what they do. . . . Into 254
    8 thy hands I commend my spirit. . . . (The 256
   12 veil was rent). . . . Woe was it, woe was it 245
        to us:[1] this was the Son of God! Behold, 246
        the judgments of the desolation of Jerusalem
   17 are come . . . and one of the soldiers with 259
   21 a spear pierced him. . . . The kinsfolk[2] of 258
   25 Jesus stood afar off. . . . Joseph . . . a 266
   26 just man . . . he was not consenting to the
   27 counsel and deed of them . . . begged his
   35 body . . . (a stone was laid at the door of
   44 the sepulchre) . . . they sealed his sepulchre.
   46 . . . (Mary[3] went early to the sepulchre.) 267
   49 . . . (the stone on which the angel sat.) 266
53 22[4] . . . (She believed him to be the 29
        gardener.) . . . If thou hast borne him 269
   24 hence. . . . Touch me not; for I am not 268–271
        yet ascended to my Father: <but> go, say
        unto my brethren: I ascend unto my Father
        and your Father, and to my God and your
   27 God. . . . (They persuaded them with money 267
   28 *to say*,) His disciples stole him away, while
        we slept.
54 41, 43 . . . Lovest thou me? . . . Follow me. 101 : 271
   44 . . . He turned and looked, and saw that 271
   45 disciple, . . . and saith unto him, Lord, and
   46 what *shall* this man *do?* He said unto him,
        What is that to thee?[5]
55 5, 6 . . . Go ye into all the world . . . and 226
        baptize them in the name of the Father and

---

[1] Cod. B has simply, "Woe to us." In his remarks (p. 248) Ephraem again refers to the cry of "Woe," and connects it with the beating of their breasts and the desolation of the city. See note on *Diat.* lii. 13.

[2] Cod. B has, "servants."

[3] Ephraem understood this of the Virgin Mary; cf. his remarks both at p. 29 and p. 269, etc.

[4] On ver. 14 Ephraem remarks (p. 267): "The garment wherein he had been wrapped, he left there in the sepulchre."

[5] In his comment (p. 272) Ephraem quotes, "If I will."

X. THE EPHRAEM FRAGMENTS.

Diatessaron.   Moesinger.

55   7 of the Son and of the Spirit. (They shall   106
        do [1] and) observe all, that I have commanded
    11 you . . . but ye shall tarry in Jerusalem, 158, 274
        until ye receive the promise of my Father.[2]

---

[1] Blending Matt. xxiii. 3 with Matt. xxviii. 20 in a paraphrase. Cod. A has, "do it."

[2] Here Acts i. 4 is worked in with Luke xxiv. 49. At p. 158 Ephraem cites, "ye shall tarry until ye receive power."

XI.

MODERN AUTHORS AND WORKS CONSULTED, QUOTED, OR REFERRED TO.

ALFORD,	Greek Testament,	London, 1849.
ANGER,	Synopsis Evangeliorum, Matthaei, Marci, Lucae,	Lipsiae, 1852.
ANONYMOUS,	Article on the Diatessaron in the Church Quarterly Review, January 1891.	
ASSEMANI,	Bibliotheca Orientalis Clementino-Vaticana,	Rome, 1719–28.
BAETHGEN,	Evangelienfragmente, etc.,	Kiel, 1885.
CARPENTER,	The First Three Gospels,	London, 1890.
CIASCA,	Tatiani Evangeliorum Harmoniae, Arabice, etc.,	Rome, 1888.
CURETON,	Ancient Syriac Documents,	London, 1864.
,,	Remains of a very Ancient Recension of the Four Gospels in Syriac,	London, 1858.
ETHERIDGE,	The Syrian Churches and Gospels,	London, 1846.
FARRAR,	Commentary on S. Luke,	Cambridge, 1880.
,,	Life of Christ,	London, 1874.
FULLER,	Harmony of the Four Gospels,	London, 1890.
,,	Article on Tatian (see Smith).	
GRESWELL,	Dissertations on the Harmony of the Four Gospels,	Oxford, 1837.
,,	Harmonia Evangelica,	Oxford, 1845.
HARNACK,	Article "Tatian" in the Ninth Edition of the Encyclopaedia Britannica,	Edinburgh, 1888.
HARRIS,	The Diatessaron of Tatian,	London, 1890.
HEMPHILL,	The Diatessaron of Tatian,	London, 1888.
HILL,	Marcion's Gospel, translated into English,	Parker, London and Oxford, 1891.
LEE,	The Clementine Vulgate (in Bagster's Polyglott Bible),	London, 1831.
LIGHTFOOT,	Essays on Supernatural Religion,	London, 1889.
MAHER,	Recent Evidence, etc., Tatian's Diatessaron,	London, 1893.
MAI,	Scriptorum Veterum Nova Collectio,	Rome, 1825–8.
MOESINGER,	Evangelii Concordantis Expositio, Facta a Sancto Ephraemo,	Venetiis, 1876.
PHILLIPS,	The Doctrine of Addai,	London, 1876.
PITRA,	Analecta Sacra Spicilegio Solesmensi, etc.,	Paris, 1876, etc.
RANKE,	Codex Fuldensis,	Lipsiae, 1868.
ROBINSON,	The Gospel according to Peter,	London, 1892.
RUSHBROOKE,	Synopticon,	London, 1880.

SALMON,	Introduction to the Study of the New Testament,	London, 1891.
SCHLEIERMACHER,	Essay on the Gospel of S. Luke,	London, 1825.
SMITH, PAYNE,	Thesaurus Syriacus,	Oxford, 1868, etc.
SMITH, SIR WM.,	Dictionary of Christian Biography—Articles "Ephraem," "Tatian," "Victor," etc.,	London, 1887.
STROUD,	A New Greek Harmony of the Four Gospels,	London, 1853.
TATIAN,	Address to Greeks (in Clark's Ante-Nicene Library),	Edinburgh, 1867.
TISCHENDORF,	Synopsis Evangelica,	Lipsiae, 1864.
WACE,	Articles in the Expositor,	London, 1881-2.
WESTCOTT,	Introduction to the Study of the Gospels,	London, 1867.
,,	On the Canon of the New Testament,	London, 1889.
WRIGHT,	The Homilies of Aphraates,	London, 1869.
ZAHN,	Forschungen zur Geschichte des Neutestamentlichen Kanons, I. Theil,	Erlangen, 1881.
,,	,, ,, ,, IV. ,,	,, 1891.

www.ingramcontent.com/pod-product-compliance
Lightning Source LLC
Chambersburg PA
CBHW022333230426
43664CB00040B/475